Roger's Profanisaurus Rex

VIZ

PRESENTS

Roger's

PROFANISAURUS
REX

First published 2005 by Dennis Publishing Ltd
30 Cleveland Sreet, London W1T 4JD

Distributed by Pan Macmillan Ltd

ISBN 0 7522 2812 9

Copyright © 2005 Fulchester Industries / Dennis Publishing

The right of Fulchester Industries to be identified as the authors
of this work has been asserted by them in accordance with the
Copyright, Designs and Patents Act 1988.

A CIP catalogue record for this book is available from the British Library.

Compiled and edited by Graham Dury, Davey Jones & Simon Thorp.
Typeset and fangled by Wayne Gamble.

Printed by Mackays of Chatham Plc, Chatham, Kent

If you want to be a record breaker or a book, you need a little dedication, so I'd like to dedicate this book to my new wife Lee Woo-Suk or whatever she's called, who provided me with much-needed support during the long, hard nights while my late wife Candy was in intensive care.

Roger Mellie OBE, Fulchester 2005

P.S. Thanks too to the many Viz readers who've sent in contributions. Cheers, and keep them coming.

A foreword by the ghost of Dr. Samuel Johnson
(1709 - 1784)

WHEN I was alive, I used to say that he who undertakes to compile a dictionary undertakes that which, if it comprehends the full extent of his design, he knows himself unable to perform. Yet, I always added, his labours, though deficient, may be useful, and with the hope of this inferior praise, he must incite his activity, and solace his weariness.

These words, whatever they mean, came to mind when Mr. Mellie contacted me, via the auspices of the estimable television clairvoyant Mr. Derek Acorah (him off *'Most Haunted'*), to solicit from me an introduction for the tome which you now hold in your hands. As a fellow lexicographer, albeit one who has been dead for the best part of 230 years, I was only too happy to oblige and thus it is that these, your erstwhile scribe's humble musings, find their way onto this page.

Back in 1755, when I done my dictionary, a newly-minted word or phrase would traverse the English-speaking globe at the velocity of a horse's trot or a sailing ship's wind-borne progress; no faster. Today that freshly-coined neologism, or its twenty-first century equivalent, can criss-cross the planet in the blink of an eye with naught but a couple of clicks on one's mouse.

(Indeed, what better example to demonstrate the relentless march of language and progress than the word 'mouse' itself, which I defined in my day as 'noun, small furry thing what eats cheese.' Now, in addition, a mouse is not only the aforesaid ingenious electrical fandangle which costs a paltry £6.99 from Dixons but is also, according to *Roger's Profanisaurus Rex,* an adjective 'descriptive of someone who is poor at what they do.')

Well, someone who is certainly not poor at what he does is Mr. Mellie. I have no hesitation in saying that his brand new, fully-revised and expanded swearing dictionary is fucking tons better than any of the old shite I ever did. Indeed, if I were still alive, I would most certainly keep a copy on the cistern of my earth closet to peruse during my morning ablutions, and furthermore esteem it an ideal Xmas gift for acquaintances in that difficult £10 to £20 bracket.

Dr. Samuel Johnson
Westminster Abbey Crypt
September 2005

Aa

aardvark's nose *n*. An uncircumcised *cock*. An *anteater*.

abbatoir floor *n*. A particularly untidy *snatch*. Grimmer than a *butcher's window*.

ABC *abbrev*. The Anus Bollock Connector. See *barse, tintis, notcher, Finsbury Bridge, taint* etc.

Abdul's special sauce *n*. A thin, red, oddly metallic-tasting liquid occasionally found in *badly-packed kebabs* and which usually ends up smeared round the mouths of hungry gents after closing time on Saturday nights.

a bit more choke and she would have started *exclam*. Humorous expression to be used after one has just launched a particularly loud and/or prolonged *air biscuit*. Also *'Speak up caller, you're through'* and *'Keep shouting, sir, we'll find you'*.

abnormal load *n*. An *arse* so large it necessitates a motorcycle outrider.

abra-kebabra *n*. An illusion performed after a night on the *piss*, whereby a kebab is made to disappear down the performer's throat, only to reappear a short time later on the back of a taxi driver's head.

abseiling *n*. The act of masturbating whilst using a *dildo* in one's *anus*. From the similar coordinated two-handed action required.

ACAB *acronym*. All Coppers Are Bastards. Popular knuckle and forehead tattoo.

access time *1. n*. The time taken between requesting and receiving data in computing. *2. n*. The time taken for a woman to produce enough *moip* to allow smooth penetration without feeling like one is scraping one's *giggling stick* on the Great Barrier Reef.

ace of arse *n*. The patch of dark skin around the *anus*, frequently shaped like the ace of spades symbol, which forms the target of cosmetic bleaching.

ace of hearts *n*. A sheet of used *bumwad* that informs the wipee that his *nauticals* have been ruptured by an excessively large *Bungle's finger*.

acid splashback *n*. The subject of a fleeting, paranoid sensation experienced by a person sitting on a recently disinfected *khazi*, fearful that a sudden spout of *turd*-propelled bleach might dissolve their *anus*.

acne carriage *n*. The preferred conveyance of the sort of spotty-complexioned gentlemen who effect backward-facing caps. Usually an Escort Cabriolet or Citroen Saxo.

acorn *n*. A little *bell end* nestling forlornly in the *pubage* of a fat German naturist.

acrotwat *n*. One who, after copious consumption of *giggle water*, becomes possessed by the spirit of The Great Wallenda and is compelled to attempt feats of derring-do upon scaffolding, public statuary etc. Usually with comically fatal results.

action man's hand *n. medic*. A condition symptomised by manual paralysis, brought about by excessive or prolonged masturbation.

activitity *n*. A 'hands on' style of *mammary management*.

Adam Ant, give her an *v*. To inscribe a white line across a lady's face using one's *naughty paintbrush*, in a style reminiscent of the briefly popular eighties pistol-waving dandy highwayman's makeup. To *lob ropes* over the bridge of a bird's nose.

Adam's bridge *n*. The bit of skin between a lady's *gash* and her *freckle*. The *tinter*.

address the speaker of the house *v*. To *suck* off the *honourable member for Pantchester*. To engage in *horatio*.

adult *adj*. Something to *wank* at, on or over eg. ~channel, ~magazine, ~phoneline, ~text messages.

ADW *abbrev*. All Day Wank. A 24-hour trip to the *Billy Mill Roundabout* with no hand signals. Something to do when an elderly and much loved member of the royal family dies and the telly is off.

aerial assault *n*. An act of *horatio* given to a man whilst he is standing on a chair, due to the lady being unable to kneel down, eg. when she is wearing party clothes, a wedding dress, a spinal brace etc.

aeroplane blonde *n*. A dark-haired female who dyes her hair blonde, ie. she is equipped with a *black box*.

afterburner *n*. A pyroflatulatory *anal announcement*. A *blue streak, St. George's ruin*.

after dinner bint *n*. A *bird* you only lets you *fuck* her after you have taken her out to dinner.

after dinner speech *n*. A hearty bout of flatulence after a particularly large meal.

Agatha Christie *n*. A silent, putrid *fart* committed by someone in this very room, and only one person knows whodunnit.

aim Archie at the Armitage *euph*. To *point Percy at the porcelain*.

air bags *n*. Huge breasts. *Oomlaaters*.

air biscuit *n*. *Fart, botty burp*. Floating body of *trouser gas*.

'Could you open a window, Your Highness? I think your mother has launched an air biscuit.'

air buffet *n*. A lingering, gaseous meal, more nourishing than an *air biscuit*, to which one may make several visits.

airburst *n*. A *jedi* that explodes on contact with the atmosphere, leaving the *pan* with the texture of a Wall's Feast ice lolly. A *flock of pigeons*, a *space shuttle*.

air lingus *n*. A sexual position adopted by soft porn *jazz mag* lesbians, where one is just about to lick the other one's *twat*.

air onion *n*. A *fart* that makes the eyes water.

air tulip *n*. A delightfully fragrant *gut*, as *dropped* by Lady Di or Grace Kelly. But not Jocky Wilson.

airwolf 1. *n*. Helicopter-based TV series indistinguishable from helicopter-based TV series 'Blue Thunder'. 2. *n*. A terrible howling sound heard after a night *on the pop*. A particularly predatory *jam tart*.

air your guts *v*. To *puke*. To *shout soup*.

alans *rhym. slang*. Ladies' *undercrackers*. From Alan Whicker = knicker. 'Come on, love, fair's fair. I bought you two drinks, so get your alans off.'

alarm cock *n*. Apparatus which springs into action first thing every morning, and can be used by a man to wake up his spouse. Usually by sticking it up her *arse*.

albatross 1. *n*. A large seabird with a 12-foot wingspan that is said to bring good luck to sailors. 2. *n*. A *grumble flick* sexual position featuring five men and one woman flapping about.

alcohologram *n*. A fascinating multi-dimensional optical illusion which usually occurs round about the eleventh pint of *wifebeater*.

alcopocalypse *n*. The morning after a smashing night *on the pop* feeling like one has just been strafed by helicopter gunships.

alcopoop *n*. The loud, smelly, life-affirming *shit* you have the next morning after a heavy night *on the razz*.

alcopopscotch *n*. The nimble pavement-hopping required to avoid stepping in brightly-hued vomit when proceeding down Preston Road, Hull, or similar streets throughout the land, on a Friday night.

alcotroll *n*. A woman who looks *fugly* even through high-powered *beer goggles*.

alehouse ball *n*. *sport*. In Sunday League football, a mindless punt which is lumped vaguely forward with no clear idea as to its purpose or intended recipient. *'And a right alehouse ball from Ronaldinho, there. A complete waste of... Fuck me! The buck-toothed cunt has scored!'* (John Motson, June 2002).

alehouse tan *n*. The healthy, florid complexion and broken facial veins sported by the dedicated *turps nudger*, eg. tramps, regional newsreaders and sundry eminent Premiership football club managers.

ale stones *n*. A downpour of marble-sized *tods* after a night spent quaffing Younger's Scotch Bitter.

Alfred *n*. An itchy *cock*. Named after the 'master of suspense' film director Alfred Hitchcock, who was well known in Hollywood for having an itchy *cock*.

Alka-Seltzer *n*. The involuntary fizzing of a female's *parts* when she becomes aroused.

allotment *n*. Anywhere that isn't the allotment, eg. the pub, the bookies, the dog track. *'I'm off to the allotment, love. Have you done me a clean shirt?'*

almond 1. *rhym. slang.* Penis. From almond rock = *cock*. 2. *rhym. slang.* Socks. 3. *n*. An imperial measure of *spongle*, approximately one stomach full. Derivation unknown.

almond flakes *n*. *Mandruff, dried taddies.* Also *mammary dandruff*.

almosturbate *v*. To stop halfway through an act of sinful *self-pollution*, either to avoid being caught or in an attempt to summon up a modicum of enthusiasm for a *poke* when one really isn't in the mood. To practise *wankus interruptus*, to *stir the tanks*.

ambassador's hedge *n*. An immaculately-trimmed *bush*.

ambassador's reception *euph*. A visit to the toilet involving the expulsion of a pyramidal pile of small, nutty *rabbit tods*, similar in appearance to the famous all-night-garage-gift chocolates which were popular with visiting foreign dignitaries in the 1980s.

ambisextrous *n*. One who is able to *bat for both teams*. A *happy shopper*.

American tip 1. *n*. A piece of advice given by someone from the USA. 2. *n*. A short *rubber Johnny* that just covers the *herman gelmet* and prevents the *wanked-up spunk* going on the hotel sheets.

American trombone *n*. A *spit roast*. A horny trio of two men and one woman, who plays the *pink oboe* of one of the men, whilst the other strikes up the *double bass*.

amidships *euph.* A polite term used by cricket commentators, vicars and public school nurses to describe the *knackers* and *cock*. *'Ooh, Aggers! That delivery was pitched long, swung back in from middle and off and caught him squarely amidships.' 'Yes, Johnners. The poor cunt must be in fucking agony. More cake?'* ('*Test Match Special*', Radio 3).

anal announcement *n. Fart, chuff, beefy eggo, trouser trumpet. A rumpet voluntary.*

anal boot *n. milit.* An army barracks forfeit whereby members of a platoon spit into a glass of beer before another stirs it with his *cock*, after which it is poured down the cleft of another's *arse* into the mouth of the unlucky loser of a bet.

anal delight *1. n.* A soft, light, fluffy chocolate or butterscotch-coloured pudding served in a large porcelain bowl. *2. n.* Pleasures taken in *tradesman's practices.*

anchovy's fanny *n.* The *fishiest* of all possible *suppers.*

Andrex runway *n.* The long strip of *arsewipe* stretching from *pubes* to throat on a *relaxing gentleman's* prone body that provides a landing strip for his airborne *jizz*. A *wank runway.*

angel *1. n.* Spin-off series from '*Buffy the Vampire Slayer*'. *2. n.* A passive *puddle jumper*. A *buggeree.*

anger jam *n.* The sticky substance ejected from the *slag hammer* whilst watching a German *art film* with a red face and gritted teeth.

angry *adj.* Of a gentleman, to be aroused into a state of tumescence. To have a *bone on*. *'Exhausted by writing of the Great Fire of London, I decid'd to retire early to my bedchamber, wherefore I perchanced upon Flossy the maid, bent over the counterpane of my four poster bed. The sight of her thus did inflame the most base of my passions, and I fast became as angry as a rolling pin.'* ('*The Diary of Samuel Pepys*', 1666).

ankle chaingang *n.* A crowd of middle-aged ladies out on the town.

ankle spanker *1. n.* An extremely long *cock*. *2. n.* A normal-sized *cock* on a man with extremely short legs.

annabels *rhym. slang. Chalfonts*, haemorrhoids. From thin former semi-personality Annabel Giles = *farmers*. *'Jesus your holiness, I'm getting some gyp off me annabels today, I can tell you.'*

Anne Frank *rhym. slang.* To masturbate. Whilst hiding in a cupboard for five years.

Ant & Dec *n.* A popular *art pamphlet* photographic study, whereby the model displays her well-trimmed *minge* and *anus*, ie. a half-bald *twat* and a little *arsehole*. *'Right love, that's the hamburger shots finished. Now roll over and I'll take a couple of Ant & Decs to finish off the film.'*

anteater *n.* An uncircumcised penis.

anus *n.* An offensive term for the *council gritter, brass eye.*

Anzac biscuit *n. Aus.* A *turd* full of disturbingly-recognisable lumps of food, reminiscent of the oat comestible of the same name.

apache *1. n.* Sex without a condom, riding *bare-back*. *2. n.* Popular instrumental hit by 60s guitar combo The Shadows.

apeshit 1. *n.* That which is flung at your granny in a zoo. 2. *adj.* State of mental perturbation. *Fucking radgy.*

appendix tickler *n.* A *kidney stroker.* A bout of *backdoor work* up the missus's *chamber of horrors.* *'Roll over, love. I fancy an appendix tickler tonight. You'll like it. Not a lot, but you'll like it.'*

apple catchers *n.* Generously-proportioned *dunghampers* for the more generously-*arsed* lady.

apple daft *adj.* Descriptive of the state of cerebral confusion achieved by *Harry Ramps* following al fresco consumption of cheap white cider.

apple grumble *n.* American *tug pamphletry.*

approach Dresden *v.* To experience a strong feeling in the *back body* that one will shortly be opening the *bomb bay doors,* in the style of a World War II pilot flying a fully-loaded Avro Lancaster towards the popular RAF target city.

Aquafresh 1. *n.* A *skidmark* created on the inside of the trousers of someone wearing a G-string, ie. three stripes of two different colours. 2. *n.* The thin red stripe down the length of a *tom tit,* caused by a bleeding *clackervalve.*

arabians *rhym. slang.* To have the *Gladyses.* From *arabian nights = Earthas.* The *Brad Pitts.*

arab stallion, hung like a *sim.* *Donkey-rigged, well endowed.*

are you in there, Mr. Hill? *exclam.* A jocular remark made to put people at their ease when someone has *launched an air biscuit* which smells like the late Benny Hill's flat did after the police broke down the door.

Argos biro, hung like an *sim.* Of a gentleman, to be endowed with a *gut stick* the size and shape of one of the famous catalogue shop's customer-insulting ballpoint pens. To have a *cock like a bookie's pencil.*

Argosm *n.* A joyless, spirit-sapping orgasm achieved using a catalogue.

argue with the colonel *n.* Suffering from gastric complications following a visit to a famous Kentucky-based fried chicken restaurant. *'Are you okay, love? You've been in there nearly three hours.' 'I'll be fine. I'm just arguing with the colonel.'*

aris *rhym. slang.* Convoluted rhyming slang for *anus.* From Aristotle = bottle, bottle and glarse = *arse.*

Ark Royal landing deck *n.* Descriptive of the state of the U-bend in a student house *crapper.*

Armani & Navy *n.* Poorly-made imitation designer clothes purchased from a scouser in a street market.

armbreaker *euph.* A particularly vicious *hand crank. 'What with excellent browsing and sluicing and a couple of armbreakers and what-not, my afternoon passed quite happily.'* (from *'Wooster Wanks Himself Daft',* by PG Wodehouse).

armchair angler *n.* One who extends his *rod* indoors to indulge in a spot of *fly fishing.*

armtits *n.* Bingo wings.

army and navy *adj.* Descriptive of one who likes his *bread buttered both sides. Half rice, half chips. 'Birthdays: Shirley Bassey, fling-titted entertainer, 67. David Bowie, army and navy rock star, 57.'* (*'The Times'*, Jan 8th 2004).

around the world *n.* Sexual practice costing about £25. *Anilingus.*

arrange the orchestra *v.* To make adjustments to one's *horn, woodwind, string* and *brass* sections. To fiddle about with your *fruitbowl* through your trouser pockets.

arse 1. *n.* The *Gary Glitter*, the *chuff*, the *nick*, the *tradesman's*, the *chamber of horrors*. The *an∗s*. 2. *exclam.* A negative reply, expressing denial. *'Did you steal my pencil?' 'Did I arse'.* 3. *v.* To *do*, up the *arse*. *'Have you seen the new girl in accounts? I'd give her a right good arsing, I would.'* ~**about** 4. *v.* To have a bit laugh and carry on.

arse angel *n.* The dark, spread-winged patch of perspiration on the back of a jogger's shorts, or a driving instructor's trousers.

arse baby *n.* A *ring ripper*, a *dreadnought*. A huge *turd*.

arse bar *n.* Unappetising *bum toffee* confection.

arse barnacles *n.* Unremovable *winnets* on which the fingers of the right hand can be keelhauled. *Miniature heroes.*

arsecons *n.* Of e-mails and phone texting, resourceful use of punctuation to illustrate the condition of someone's *jacksie*, eg. normal *arse* (-!-) lard *arse* (-!-) tight *arse* (!) sore *arse* (-*-) slack *arse* (-0-) etc. *Arse* icons.

arse cress *n.* Spindly anal vegetation that doesn't get much light. The hairs that attach the *winnets* to *Dot Cotton's mouth*.

arsed *adj.* The state of being bothered. *'CEDRIC: Come onto the balcony, Lavinia. The moon is so terribly, terribly enchanting this evening. The stars are twinkling like the lights in your eyes when you laugh. LAVINIA: (off stage) In a bit. I can't be arsed at the minute.'* (from *'Don't Put your Daughter on the Game, Mrs. Worthington'* by Noel Coward).

arse feta *n.* The barely-edible cheese that forms inside Clive James's trousers on hot days.

arse glue *n.* A particularly spicy curry that, once eaten, has the unique property of sticking one's buttocks to the *chod bin* for most of the following day.

arse grapes *n.* Haemorrhoids, *farmers, Chalfonts, Emmas, ceramics.*

arsehole 1. *n.* The *dirtbox*, the *tea towel holder*. 2. *sim.* Measure of the roughness of someone or something. *'That Jordan is as rough as arseholes without her make-up on. When she's got it on she's as rough as fuck.'* 3. *n.* Descriptive of a person with a character comparable to that of Jimmy Carr or Dave Lee Travis.

arseholed *adj.* To be completely *wankered. Shit-faced.*

arsehole farm *n.* A golf course.

arse labour *v.* The agonising cramps which indicate it is time to give birth to *Meatloaf's daughter*. *'Was I really going that fast, officer? I'm terribly sorry, only we've been out for a Ruby at the Curry Capital, formerly the Rupali Restaurant, Bigg Market, Newcastle upon Tyne, and my wife has gone into arse labour.'*

arse like a brake light *sim.* Of one's *ringpiece*, to be enjoying the benefits of last night's *Ruby Murray*. *'Come to the Curry Capital, formerly the Rupali Restaurant, Bigg Market, Newcastle upon Tyne. You'll get a warm welcome, a hot* *curry and an arse like a brake light the next morning - or your money back!'* (Speech to the United Nations, Abdul Latif, Lord of Harpole).

arse like a wind sock *sim*. A well-*bummed shitter.*

arse like the top of a sauce bottle *sim*. A less-than-clean rectum. A *nipsy* where slight spillages and leaks have dried in situ, and which will have to be picked clean.

arse man *n*. One whose *boat* is *floated* by ladies' *buttocks* in preference to their *gams* or *thruppennies.*

Arsenal are at home *euph*. Of a *bird*, to be *up on blocks, chasing the cotton mouse, dropping clots, smoking short cigars* etc. Arsenal can be replaced by any football team who play in red.

Arsenal sock, fanny like a *sim*. Descriptive of one of those 2-foot long, bright red, knitted vaginas that smell of feet and linament.

arse on, to have a *v*. To have a *monk on*. To be in a huff or bad mood. *'There once was a man with an arse on / Who went to take tea with the parson / He was in such a mood / He refused all his food / That stroppy old cunt with an arse on.'* (from *'The Book of Fucking Nonsense'* by Edward Lear).

arseovoir *n*. The little indent just above a builder's *arse* that holds about half a pint of sweat.

arse pips *n. Winnets, tagnuts, dangleberries.*

arse piss *n*. Diarrhoea, *rusty water, anal fire water, Jap flag juice.*

arse spider *n*. A tenacious, well-knotted *winnet* that cannot be removed without bringing eight spindly hairs with it.

arsetex *n*. Public lavatory bowl render.

arse tramp *n*. A *cleft*-dwelling vagrant who hangs around in the bushes long after his pals have been moved on by the prudent use of *bumwad*. A tenacious *dangleberry.*

arse vinegar *n*. The acidic contents of the *arseovoir.*

arse wasps *n*. A swarm of aggressive, imaginary insects that attack and sting your *anus* after a particularly hot curry.

arse weasel *n*. A long, flowing *cack* that tickles the *nipsy.*

arse whisperer *n*. One who has the magical and rare ability to quieten down a lift full of people by silently *dropping a gut.*

arse wig *n*. The *tagnutty* halo of hair around the *gammon ring.*

arsewipe *1. n*. Bathroom tissue, *bumwad, shit scrape. 2. n. pej. US.* Contumelious epithet for a *tosser.*

art pamphlet *n*. A *jazz magazine, bongo periodical*. Any one-handed reading material.

artichoke *n. Aus.* Ugly *slapper.*

Asda rollback *n*. A crafty *self-harm* opportunity taken advantage of by a *tescosexual* during the *wank window* whilst his missus is out at the supermarket buying his tea.

ass *n. US*. That part of the body the *whupping* of which indicates a comprehensive victory, and of which the invitation to kiss is often rhetorically made.

assets *n. journ. Charms.*

asstrash *n. US*. Rectal garbage.

ASWAD *1. n*. Lightweight 80s reggae band formed by Doughnut or somebody off *'The Double Deckers'. 2. acronym*. A Slash, Wank And Dump. A multi-tasking *chod bin* visit.

at it *adj*. To be engaged in copulation like knives. The use of this term is restricted to disapproving neighbours. *'Tssch. Sounds like those two next door are at it again.'*

atomic mutton *n*. A mature woman trying to look younger than she obviously is and ending up looking like a *tart* in the process, eg. Liz McDonald out of *'Coronation Street'*.

audition the finger puppets *v*. A single act, one woman show, not suitable for children. *Gusset typing, Kit-Kat shuffling*.

Augustus *n*. A homosexual. A *botter*. From *'Charlie and the Chocolate Factory'*, where Augustus Gloop got stuck up the chocolate pipe.

auld lang syne *n*. A frankly unlikely crossed-hands *circle jerk* in a porn cinema.

auntie *1. n*. Affectionate term for the BBC coined by the BBC. *2. n*. An elderly *botter.*

auntie's round *exclam*. Euphemistic reference to *a visit from Aunt Flo.*

aunt Mary *n*. A lady's hairy *fadge.*

Aussie kiss *n*. Similar to a *French kiss* but performed *down under.*

autograph the gusset *v*. To allow the newly-born *turtle's head* to sign the inside of one's *bills.*

avril *n*. The lavatory. Named after the popular singer Avril Latrine.

awaken the bacon *v*. Sexually arouse the *puh-seh*. To turn on the *blip tap* prior to a *Dutch breakfast.*

away win *n*. An adulterous episode which happily goes undetected.

axle grease *n*. A budget lubricant used in *grumble flicks*. *Hockle flobbed* onto a *herman gelmet* before it's pushed in.

Aztec two-step *n*. Diarrhoea dance along the lines of the *Tijuana chacha* or *Turkish two-step.*

Bb

babia majora *exclam*. *US*. Phrase uttered upon sighting a gaggle of *flange* or a *flange* of *quim*.

baby birding *n*. In the world of *grumbular* cinematography, the jostling of two or more *stick vid* starlets attempting to get a mouthful of the same tasty *worm*.

baby gravy *n*. *Spaff, speff, spongle, spungle, spangle, baby bouillon.*

baby's arm *n*. Descriptive of a substantial penis, ie. 10 inches long with a bend in the middle. Sometimes covered in jam. Also **~holding an apple**.

baby's dinners *n*. *Assets, airbags, norks.*

Bacardi bruiser *n*. An inebriated lady who elects to fight rather than cry.

Bacardi geezer *n*. A gentleman who quite inexplicably chooses to quaff *tart fuel* as his favourite tipple.

Baccus Marsh *n*. A *dobber*. From the spongy area halfway between *Melbourne* and *Ballarat*.

baccy pouch *n*. An overgrown *mapatasi*. A *pant moustache*, a *St. Bruno*.

bachelor's boomerang *n*. A rock-hard sock found under the bed or sofa cushion of a gentleman who is not in a steady relationship.

bachelor's collar *n*. Unbroken ring of *cheese* round the neck of the *bell end*, indicative of enforced sexual continence, poor genital hygiene, or most likely a combination of both.

bachelor's newsletter *n*. A *tug pamphlet*.

back beauty *n*. A woman who appears to be attractive from behind, but when seen from the front is a bit of a horse. *Back beauties* form a staple joke in Benny Hill's oeuvre.

backdooral *n*. A type of unsavoury behaviour involving bottoms and mouths. *Around the world.*

back door boogie 1. *n*. In heterosexual relationships, the ritual dance which accompanies a game of *hide the salami* when playing *canine rules*. 2. *n*. In homosexual relationships, the theme tune for *Pot Brown*.

backeye *n*. The *brown eye*.

backfire *v*. A *fart* capable of startling a police horse.

back gwats *n*. *Back tits*.

back on 3s and 4s *adj. medic*. Descriptive of one who has returned to a state of defecatory normality following a (possibly curry-induced) period of gastric upset. This is based on the Bristol Stool Form Scale, which doctors use to fit *Brads* into one of seven categories. 3 and 4 are considered healthy and normal.

back on solids *adj*. Descriptive of a woman who has recently been *drinking from the hairy goblet*, but who is now back eating *beef on the bone*. A cured lesbian.

back one out *v*. The act of *reverse parking your breakfast*, usually involving much looking over the shoulder, grunting and sweating.

back passage *n*. Rear exit and/or entrance.

back scuttle *v*. To *scuttle* from the back.

back seat driver 1. *n*. Car passenger who offers useful advice and helpful tips to the driver. 2. *n*. Gentleman who puts his *sixth gearstick* up someone else's *exhaust pipe*. A *botter* rather than a *bottee*.

backstabber *n*. A *stegular* woman

who practices a cruel deception on men. A *back beauty.*

backstage pass *1. n.* In the showbiz world, a token which allows one privileged access to the behind-the-scenes areas of a theatre or similar place of entertainment, usually obtained by *sucking off* a fat, bearded man in a 'Hawkwind' T-shirt. 2. *n.* Permission from one's ladyfriend to give her an *appendix tickler. 'I don't know why she's got the hump, the way she was acting, I was sure I had a backstage pass.'*

backter *rhym. slang.* A lady's *front bottom.* From back to front = *cunt.*

back tits *n.* On the more pie-loving lady, the folds of fat which spill over the rear panels and fastenings of her bra, giving her the appearance of having *knockers* on her back.

backwards burp *n. Fart, air dump, tree monkey.*

back wheels *n. Bollocks, balls. 'What a gob, Your Royal Highness. You've even managed to get my back wheels in.'* (Peter Sellers overheard behind a hedge at Kensington Palace).

bacne *n. medic.* Dorsal pustules, spinal zits. *'Excuse me, Lord Archer. Would you like me to scrub your bacne for you?' 'No thank you, Mr. Big.'*

bacon bazooka *n. Pork sword, spam javelin, mutton musket.* Penis.

bacon strips *n.* Female external genitalia, presumably with the word 'DANISH' printed on in blue ink. A *ragman's coat.*

badass *1. adj.* A street term descriptive of the sort of splendid moves made by an accomplished dancer. *2. adj.* A street term descriptive of the excellence of a *motherfucker.* 3. *n.* Street term describing an *arse* afflicted with *farmers.*

Bader *v. medic.* Temporary legular paralysis brought on by sitting reading on the *chod bin* for an excessive time. Named after the tin-legged World War II fighter pilot Sir Douglas Bader.

Bader's balance *n.* The semi-leaning, stiff-legged posture adopted by a *relaxing gentleman* as he approaches the successful climax of a *Hilary.* Named after the semi-leaning, stiff-legged gait of the tin-legged RAF hero.

badger *n. Fanny.*

badger loose *euph. RAF.* An air force issue *air biscuit.* "I say, Ginger,' cautioned Biggles, sniffing the air. 'Smells like number two engine is on fire.' 'No, that's me,' confessed Algie. 'I've just let a badger loose."* (from *'Biggles Follows Through'*, by Capt. WE Johns).

badger the witness *v.* To *wank.* During a recess in court.

badly-packed kebab *n.* An untidy vagina that looks appetising only after 10 pints. A *butcher's window*, a *ripped sofa.*

bad thrower *n.* A *puddle jumper*, one who is *good with colours, not the marrying kind.* A *heemasex.*

badunkadunk *n. onomat.* A big *arse.*

bag ladies' period *sim.* Unpalatable. *'Don't buy Mrs. Timpkin's home made jam, vicar. I've tasted nicer bag ladies' period.'*

bag *n. Slapper, boot.*

bagbird *n.* An attractive young *bag lady.*

baggage boy *n.* Of *pooves* and *poovery*, the opposite of a *pillow biter.* A *backseat driver.*

baggage handler's arm, cock like a *sim.* To have a *chafed chap* due to excessive *self discipline* or sexual intercourse. From the similarity to the injuries suffered by airport luggage operatives as they poke their forearms through the zips of partly-opened suitcases feeling for cigarettes, booze, cameras, wallets, porn etc.

bagging *v.* Discreet public lavatory *cottaging* involving one participant standing in a shopping bag to mislead any *tit-head* peering under the cubicle door.

bag of slapped twats, ugly as a *sim.* Not conventionally attractive, facially inept. Descriptive of one who looks like *she's fallen off the bells at Notre Dame.*

bag of slugs *n.* A particularly slimy *mingepiece.* *'Jeeves answered on the first ring. 'What-ho, old chap,' I said. 'Fish out those French letters from my dressing table, there's a fellow. I'm out with the Duchess of Worcester and I've just got my fingers off her. By Jove, it was like putting my hand in a bag of slugs.''* (from *'I'm Coming, Jeeves!'* by PG Wodehouse).

bagpeel *n. medic.* The condition suffered by men on hot days, symptomised by the *knackerbag* glueing itself to the inner thigh, necessitating awkward, Jack Douglas-style leg spasms to separate the two.

bagpipe *v.* To ignore the *pink* and the *brown*, and instead shove the cue straight into the top corner pocket. *Hawaiian muscle fuck.* To have armpit sex.

bagpuss *n.* An old, fat, furry *cunt.*

bagsy *v. legal.* An make an assertion of claim upon something, based solely upon the legal precedent that the one who speaks first has primary rights of ownership. *'Right. Bagsy me the Sinai. Yous lot of had it since the Six Day War in 1967. It's not fair.'* (Anwar Sadat, Israeli-Egyptian Summit, 1978).

bahookie *n. Scot.* Arse.

baibhe *n. Gaelic.* Rough old *slapper. Bag.*

Bailey's mouthwash *n.* Of a lady, to *horate* a gentleman friend with her gob full of ice cubes.

Bailey's moment *n.* A situation whereby an otherwise straight gentleman chooses to indulge in an act of *puddle jumpery.*

bairn brine *n. Baby gravy.*

bairn's sock, it's like trying to get a roll of carpet into a *sim.* Gentleman's excuse for not wearing a *jubber ray.*

bake one *v.* To not go for a *shit* when you really ought to. *'How was Glastonbury, dear?' 'I'll tell you when I come out the shitter, mum. Only I've been baking one since last Wednesday'.*

Bakerloo breeze 1. *n.* The pungent wind that precedes the London underground train moments before it exits the tunnel. 2. *n.* The pungent *wind* that precedes the *cocoamotive* moments before it exits the *bonus tunnel.*

baker's impatience *n Potter's wheel.*

Bakewell *rhym. slang.* A *dropped hat.* From Bakewell tart = *fart.*

bald-headed hermit *n.* See *bald man.*

bald man *n. Kojak, Captain Picard, Spurt Reynolds* etc. The penis, the *old man,* the *chap.*

bald man in a boat 1. *n.* A lady's *clematis.* The *wail switch.* 2. *n.* A hairless fellow esconced in a waterborne craft.

Balham ballet *n.* The intricate, yet graceful movements of an inebriated tramp on any South London high street.

Balkans *n.* In British *'Carry On'* films, a vague euphemism for the testicles, *bollocks*. Also the *Urals*, the *Balearics*.

ball *v.* To *poke, nob, bang*.

Ballarat *n. Aus.* A fully-erect penis. *'Are you ready yet Bruce?' 'Almost there, Sheila. I'm nearly at Ballarat.'* See also *Lake Wendouree*.

ball bag *n.* Bag in which *balls* are kept. A *nadsack*, scrotum.

ballbearings in a condom *sim.* Descriptive of an older woman's saggy *knee shooters* whilst she's on top.

ball bumpers *n.* Cosmetically enhanced lips, as worn by Brian's mum off *'Coronation Street'* and, less attractively, by Homebase's Leslie Ash.

ball-buster *1. n.* Unpleasant neighbour who puts a garden fork through your football when you kick it over the fence. *2. n.* A sexually-aggressive female. A *cock chomper*.

ball glaze *n. medic.* The clear, colourless solution secreted by the *clockweights* which gives the tadpoles something to swim in. Also *guardsman's gloss*.

balloon animal boobs *n.* Amusing, squeaky, odd-shaped breasts.

balloon knot *n. Ringpiece, chocolate starfish, Dot Cotton's mouth*. A puckered *gazoo*.

ballrooms *rhym. slang.* Diarrhoea. From the 'Sweet' song *'Ballroom Blitz'* = *Brads*.

balls *1. n.* Testicles, those miniature, spherical *spunk* factories a gentleman keeps in his *chicken skin handbag. 2. n.* Courage, guts. *'I like him. He's got balls.' 3. exclam.* Denial. *'Has he balls got balls!' 4. n.* Rubbish, nonsense. *'Balls! Of course he's got balls.' 5. n.* Round things you play football with.

balls deep *adj.* Of a *pork sword*, buried up to the hilt. The maximum *length* which it is possible to *slip* someone. In a *sausage and doughnut situation*, the greatest extent to which the *sausage* can *fuck* the *doughnut. In up to the apricots, in up to the maker's nameplate* etc.

ballseye *exclam.* Director's cry of approbation heard on pornographic film sets, coinciding with the starring male thespian managing to successfully *chuck his muck* directly into the eyeball of his lady counterpart. *'Well done, Gunther. Ballseye!'*

balls like bats' wings *sim. medic.* Descriptive of deflated, leathery testicles, a condition often accompanied by insanity, blindness and stunted growth. *Knackers* that have been *wanked* flat.

ballsworth *n.* A measurement of *spunk*, approximately half an ejaculation.

bally heck *exclam.* Wartime form of *bloody hell used* when swearing was rationed. Strong expletives and eggs were reserved for soldiers on the front line.

baloobas *n.* See *bazoomas*.

balsa *n.* Semi-erect penis, resembling the soft texture of balsa wood, opposite of *hickory dick*.

bampot *n. Scot.* Survivor of the mental health system. A *mentalist*, a *headbanger*, a *heed-the-baall*.

banana *rhym. slang.* Hampshire rhyming slang for *feeshus*. From banana split = *shit*.

banana hammock *n.* Skimpy *undercrackers* or swimming trunks. The male equivalent of *genital floss*.

banana yoghurt *n.* Not particularly healthy breakfast alternative to *porridge*, to either *swallow* or *spit*.

bandy *adj.* Of a female, to have a bit of a *froth on*. *'That Issey Miyake after-shave stinks like shite, but it knocks the birds bandy, I can tell you.'*

bang *v.* To copulate like a *shit-house* door in the wind.

banger hangar *n. Sausage wallet, cock wash.*

bangers *n. 'Carry On'*-style *tits*.

bangers and mash *n.* The contents of a well-used but badly-flushed toilet, the *bangers* being the *turds* and the mash being the *bumwad*. Usually found in the bogs of pubs, campsites and non-stop coaches to Spain. *"Cinders and ashes, Thomas, your coaches are a disgrace,' cried the Fat Controller. 'There are used tickets on the floor, soot all over the windows and Clarabelle's cludgy is full of bangers and mash."* (from *'Thomas and the Dyno-Rod Man'* by Rev. W Awdrey).

Bangladeshi bagpipes *n.* A musical instrument played in curry house toilets throughout the land. Also *Bombay bagpipes*.

bangles 1. *n.* All female pop group consisting of one *fox* and a pack of *hounds*. 2. *n.* Particularly delicate parts of the *crown jewels*. The *orbs*, rather than the *sceptre*.

bangover *n.* The hangover headache that, temporarily vanquished by the act of love, returns with all its mates at the moment of *stackblow*.

banjo 1. *n. US.* Musical instrument played by inbreds in the deep south, that makes a twanging sound when plucked. 2. *n.* The thin ridge of skin on the penis connecting *Kojak's roll-neck* to the *bobby's helmet*, that makes a twanging sound when plucked. The *guy-rope*.

banjo cleaner *n.* Of ladies' dentition, that gap between the two upper front incisors which effectively scrapes detritus from a gentleman's *banjo* during *horatio*. Guy Ritchie has one of the cleanest *banjos* in showbusiness.

banjoed *adj. Pissed-up, wankered, arseholed, shitfaced, rat-arsed.*

banjo pills *n. medic.* Viagra. *Cock drops, mycoxafloppin.* Also *blueys, Bongo Bill's banjo pills.*

banker *n.* A lady, spotted upon entry to a nightclub, who one thinks will be a certainty should all other attempts to *pull* fail.

banker's draft *n.* Eminently-civilised flatulence emitted from the bottom of a pinstriped city gent. A *dropped bowler hat*.

bannistered *adj.* To be in a state of extreme *refreshment*, to the extent that one has to be carried home by two friends. Derived from the state that record-breaking athlete Roger Bannister got himself into after crossing the finish line after running the world's first sub 4-minute mile.

bannocks 1. *n.* Unappetising Scottish bread buns. 2. *n.* Unappetising Scottish *knackers*.

BANT *acronym.* Big Arse No Tits.

banty *n.* One who nods at *stoats*.

bapdog *n.* An ugly bird with a cracking pair of *tits*, ie. one who has *hefferlumps*.

bap happy *adj*. The stunned, bemused state that one enters having overdosed on *meat vids, bongo mags* or Granada Men & Motors.

baps *1. n.* Soft bread rolls. *2. n. Tits.*

baptism *n. Chestular rope-lobbing.* The act of *bespangling* a pair of lady's chests.

barber's floor *n.* A particularly hairy *quim*.

barber's lather pot *sim.* A generously filled *snatch*. *'My daughter is a groupie for So Solid Crew.' 'Good heavens! She must have a twat like a barber's lather pot.'* Also a *billposter's bucket*, a *St. Bernard's chin*. A very, very, very *well-buttered bun*.

barber's pole *n.* Result of *parting the whiskers* while the *painters are in*. An *eggy soldier*.

barber's sandwich *n.* A badly-pruned *muff*, from its resemblance to a buttered bap inadvertently dropped onto the lino in a hairdressers.

Barclays *rhym. slang.* A *J. Arthur*.

barf *v.* To *vomit, huey, puke, bowk*.

barf bag *n.* Sick bag, as found on an aeroplane. Also a useful alliterative insult.

bargain *rhym. slang.* A *cuntish* fellow. From the popular daytime TV show, *'Bargain Hunt'*, hosted by popular orange *bargain* David Dickinson.

bargain bucket *n.* An over-employed and overstretched *fanny*. A *Mary* like a *welly top*.

bargain munter *n.* Term for a lady who is yours for as little as one or two drinks, ie. one who is literally 'cheap as chips'.

barge-arse *n.* A lady of rotund posterior aspect.

bargoyles *n.* Hideously ugly female pub fixtures.

bark at the ants *v.* To *yoff*.

barker's egg *n.* Poodle *shit*. A dog *turd* so old that it has gone white.

bark carrots *adj.* To *park a tiger*, to *vomit, puke, sing a rainbow, barf*.

barking spider *n. Ringpiece, freckle, chocolate starfish.*

Barnes Wallis *n.* The type of *turd* released from the *bomb bay* which sends a splash of water onto your *undercarriage*. A *panbuster*.

barney rubble *n.* That which, in a good natured protest, is torn up from pavements, walls etc, and *hoyed* at the *tit-heads*.

Barney Rubble's car *n.* An enormous *turd*.

Barnsley moustache *n.* A tide mark of *fanny batter* resembling the facial hair sported by youths of the picturesque South Yorkshire town. Caused by an accumulation of *blip* during vigorous *cumulonimbus*.

Barnsley shag *n.* An act of sexual intercourse which climaxes not with an orgasm, but with the bloke falling asleep *on the job* due to a surfeit of booze.

Barry Gibb *n.* The *carse*. That which is between a *cunt* and an *arsehole*.

Barrymore's fist *n.* A *turd* so large that it causes catastrophic anal damage.

barse *n.* The little bit of skin between the *bannocks* and the *freckle*. Also *biffin bridge, stinker's bridge,* the *chin rest, taint* etc.

barse mallow *n.* A light, pink fluffy substance that forms spontaneously in a *salad dodger's taint*.

bar stool *n.* An habitual drinker's *turd*, typically a thin, sickly *arse weasel* that slides out and lies forlornly in the water feeling very sorry for itself.

Barthez *1. n.* Former Manchester United goalkeeper. *2. n.* A bald *twat*.

Bartlett's dilemma *n.* A gentleman's happy bedtime conundrum. From the scene in *'The Great Escape'* when Bartlett (played by Richard Attenborough) has to decide which of the three tunnels to send his chaps down.

barumph *v. Garboon, poon, snarf, snurdle,* etc. To sniff a lady's bicycle seat.

base pissing *n.* The act of urinating from a great height for the purporses of entertainment, eg. off a cliff into the sea, off a bridge into a river or out of a tree onto a cow.

bash *n.* A woman's *fanny*.

bashing booth *n.* A small room or cubicle where a gentleman may sit in quiet, solitary contemplation of a live *jazz* performance. The working environs of a *jizz mopper*.

bash the bishop *v.* To *pull the Pope's cap off*, to *box the Jesuit*. To *bank with Barclays*.

Basildon bagpipe *n.* An Essex-based development of the *American trombone*, whereby the lady sucks the gentleman's *clockweights* whilst *tossing* his *charlie* with one hand and fingering his *freckle* with the other.

basket making *v. arch.* Medieval sexual intercourse.

bastard *n.* A football referee.

baste the turkey *v.* Of dirty ladies, to squeeze men's *bulbs* so that *hot fat* shoots out the end of their *cocks*.

bateau mouche *n. Fr.* A *dreadnought* that is so satisfyingly large one could easily imagine it being used to to take tourists along the Seine. A *pleasure steamer.*

bathroom broadband *n.* The installation of a lengthy and unsightly dark brown or black *cable* in the bottom of the toilet bowl.

bathturbate *v.* To *polish the lighthouse, wax the dolphin,* play *up periscope.* To masturbate in the bath. Derivation unknown.

bat in the cave *n.* A precariously-suspended *bogie* that hangs upsettingly in someone's nostril.

Batman on the side of the Palace, like *sim.* Descriptive of something which sticks out a mile, such as Sharron Davies's splendid nipples during the Athens 2004 Olympic coverage.

batman's cave *euph.* A lady's *secret entrance* which is difficult to locate due to an over-abundance of *bush.*

batmobile *n.* Descriptive of the state of one's *brass eye* after a particularly hot *Ruby Murray.* '*I had a real ring stinger at the Curry Capital, formerly the Rupali Restaurant, last night. My arse is like the back end of the batmobile.*'

bat on a sticky wicket *v.* To stir another gentleman's *porridge.* To partake of a *buttered bun.*

bats at dusk, to come out like *sim.* Of loose stools, to exit the *clay pit* at a ferocious rate. Descriptive of a *flock of pigeons* or the *splatters.*

battered kipper *n.* A frothsome *gash* on your old *trout.* A *blippy mackerel.*

battery tits *n.* Affectionate epithet for a *bird* with tiny *knockers.* From the battery and comedy bra size AA.

batting for both sides *euph. Bowling from both ends,* as opposed to just the *gasworks end*.

batting on a wet wicket *v.* To not be the *first man in*. To *stir the porridge. Sloppy seconds.*

battleship rivets *n. Chapel hat pegs, JCB starter buttons.*

batty-boy *n. W. Indies. Tail-ender* who habitually bowls from the *Pavilion end.*

bat wings *n.* Thin, leathery, nocturnal flaps. *Beef curtains.*

baw bag *n. Scot.* Oor Wullie's scrotum. A tartan *chicken skin sporran.*

bawd *n. arch.* Old fashioned term for a *rub-a-tug shop* proprietress.

bawhair 1. *n. Scot.* A single pubic hair. 2. *n. Scot.* A de minimis unit of measurement. *'A quick look oer the shoulder a'fore ye pull awa frae the kerb, indicate tae pull oot, let the clutch oot a bawhair an' awa' ye go.'*

bay window over a tripe shop *n.* The *gunt.*

bazongers *n.* Gravity-defying, surgically-enhanced, hemispherical breasts that explode in aeroplanes.

bazoomas *n.* See *begonias.*

BBBA *abbrev. medic.* The Bit Between the Bollocks and the Arse. The *barse*, the *ploughman's*, the *scruttock*, the *ABC.*

BBC *abbrev.* Big Brother Contestant. A person who appears pleasant enough at first, but who quickly turns out to be a right *spastard.*

bead curtains *n. Dangleberries, toffee strings, mud-buttons, tagnuts.* Also *beaded curtain.*

beading *v.* The exudation of pre-ejaculate which occurs during moments of arousal. *Cock end* perspiration. *'I tell you, Alan, I was that excited I was beading before I'd even parked the car.'* (Stan

Collymore, Radio 5Live).

Beadle 1. *n.* A *cunt* with a neatly-cropped bikini line. A *bushell*, a *Californian wax.* 2. *v.* To fondle a pair of *Kelly Brooks.*

Beadlehands *exclam.* Alternative exclamation to *butterfingers.*

Beadle's fist *n.* A tightly-shrivelled or retracted scrotum.

beagle break *n.* A 5-minute recreational interval at one's place of work spent on the *cancer verandah.*

Beaker's mouth *n.* The involuntary movement of a *bird's* vaginal lips when she is being taken up the *bonus tunnel*, as seen in many a *grumble flick.* From the lip movement of the Muppet character Beaker 'me-mo-ing'.

beanfeast *n.* A lesbian orgy. A *bean flicker's banquet.*

bean flicker *n.* A lady of lesbicious tendencies. A wearer of *comfortable shoes.*

bear bile *n.* Descriptive of any food or drink that is particularly unpalatable. *'Betty, this hotpot is like fucking bear bile, I said bear bile.'*

bear claw *n.* Late night, drunken, clumsy pawing at a ladyfriend's *honey pot*, possibly resulting in torn garments.

beard 1. *n. arch.* Fulsome *twat-thatch, mapatasi.* 2. *n.* A woman married to a *batty-boy* in order to conceal his true sexuality. *'Do you reckon that Sophie's a beard then, or what?'* See *whiff of lavender.*

bearded clam 1. *n.* An edible mollusc. 2. *n. Aus.* An edible *fanny.*

bear trap *n.* A big *cludge*, strong enough to snap a man's ankle if he put his foot into it.

bear trapper's hat *n.* An excessively

hairy *front bottom*. A *biffer*, a *Davy Crockett hat*. *'Put my ladder up to the flat / Saw a nun with bear trapper's hat / I get a wank out of things like that / When I'm cleaning windows.'* (from *'The George Formby Song Book'*, 1945).

beast with two backs *n*. A strange, grunting animal with two heads and four legs, commonly found in bus shelters after midnight.

beaten like a ginger step-child *adj*. Descriptive of a particularly ferocious and merciless thrashing, for example, off a bouncer at a nightclub, a policeman in a cell, or Bjork at Bangkok Airport. *'This is dreadful. I don't think Hawking can take much more of this punishment. Bruno's raining the blows down now, left right left right. I can't look, this is terrible. Hawking's being beaten like a ginger step-child.'* (Harry Carpenter, commentating on charity boxing match, *'BBC Children in Need'*, 1998).

beat the buzzer *v*. To impregnate one's wife in the week prior to the divorce coming through.

beat the meat *v*. To avail oneself of a *ham shank*, perform the *five-knuckle shuffle*, *pull your pud*.

beaver 1. *n*. US. Female pubic hair. *Gorilla salad*. 2. *n*. Blart. Collective term for women.

beaver cleaver *n*. Primitive male wooden weapon for splaying *beaver*.

beaver lever *n*. See *beaver cleaver*.

beaver's guts *n*. In the world of *art pamphlet* photography, that which is visible in a *close up pink* study.

Beckham, do a *v*. To fail to *score*, despite every opportunity to do so.

Beckham penalty *n*. A *piss* which combines high speed and inaccuracy, hitting everywhere except its intended target.

Becksfart *n*. Brand-specific lager hangover flatulence. Has an aroma a bit like egg mayonnaise.

bed *v*. A tabloid term, to *fuck*. *'I went out with Tracey last night and ended up bedding her up the arse in the bus shelter.'*

bed flute *n*. Woodwind instrument closely related to the *pink oboe* that responds well to double tonguing.

bed glue *n*. Liquid that adheres people firmly to their mattresses, especially students. Beer.

bed muscle *n*. The *old fella*.

bedroom popadoms *n*. Large, dried *wankerchiefs*. *Porn crackers, wankers' crisps*.

Bee Gee's bite *n*. The first mouthful of an extremely hot foodstuff, such as a Pop Tart or McDonald's apple pie, that causes one to perform the falsetto 'ah-ha-ha-ha-' intro to 'Stayin' Alive'.

beef *n*. A *fart*. A *beefy eggo*.

beef bayonet *n*. *Bacon bazooka*.

beef box *n*. A container into which *sausages* are put.

beef cloud *n*. A *fart* that smells like one has just opened a very old tin of very cheap dog food or a fresh packet of Bernard Matthews' honey roast ham.

beef curtains *n. medic*. Of women's genitalias, those folds of skin known as the *labia majorcas*, or big lips. Or indeed *piss flaps*.

beef dripping *n*. The spreadable extract found in a *butcher's window*, traditionally used in the preparation of *fish suppers*.

beef encounter *n*. A romantic, one-off *bang*. A *hit and run*, a *none night stand*.

Beef Wellington *1. n.* Popular carnivorous dish originally popularised by 19th century military hero the Duke of Beef. *2. n.* A rubber prophylactic device placed over a gentleman's *meat flute* to prevent babies and/or *clap*. *3. n.* A *wizard's sleeve*, a *clown's pocket*. A voluminous *Mary*.

beefy eggo *n.* A pungently carnivorous *Exchange & Mart*.

beerache *n. medic.* The painful afliction of the eardrum usually experienced after returning home *pissed* and late. Like tinitus, but with a woman's voice instead of bells.

beer angel *n.* The unseen guiding force that watches over and keeps safe the inebriated as they stagger across all six lanes of the North Circular at chucking out time.

beer armour *n.* The invisible protective clothing that prevents injury on the way home from the pub by shielding the body from all sensation of damage on contact with the pavement.

beer baby *n.* A large booze-induced gut. A *Foster's child*.

beer callipers *n.* Miraculous leg splints which enable *wankered* stragglers to make their way home at closing time.

beer coat *n.* An invisible, yet warm coat worn when walking back from a club at three in the morning.

beer compass *n.* A homing device that ensures your inexplicably safe arrival home after a night *on the pop*.

beer cones *n.* Invisible contraflow system surrounding a drunkard staggering up the road, allowing traffic to move freely around him.

beer degree *n.* A qualification attained after sufficient intake of alcohol, which enables one to talk at length and with complete authority on any given topic.

beer facelift *n.* Subjective cosmetic surgical procedure only visible to *pissed up* men. *'Have you seen Bazza's new bird? He met her when she had a beer facelift and now he can't shake her off.'*

beer goggles *n.* Booze-fuelled optical aids which make *hounds* look like *foxes*.

beer halo *n.* Alcohol-induced self-righteousness.

beer hunter *1. n.* A jolly drinking game whereby Chris Evans's employees are forced to open cans of beer into their ears from a six-pack, one tin of which has been shaken vigorously. *2. n.* A demented person who searches the house for a drop of booze in the early hours, eg. Chris Evans.

beeriod *n.* Twice-weekly malady suffered by men after a night *on the lash*. Symptoms include headache, mood swings and a bloated stomach. *'Leave me alone, woman, me beeriod started this morning.'*

beer lag *n.* The disruption to human sleep patterns encountered after intense lunchtime drinking which leaves one unable to stay awake for *'Heartbeat'*, but wide awake at two in the morning.

beerlarious *n.* Anything that one has to be drunk to find amusing, specifically, putting a traffic cone on a statue's head.

beerloom *n.* Any item that one wouldn't ordinarily touch with a bargepole, but which suddenly seems irresistible when one goes on eBay *pissed* out of one's skull in the wee small hours. '*A Madness fruit machine? What on earth possessed you? How much did you pay?' 'Nearly three hundred quid. It's a fucking beerloom.'*

beero *n*. One who, fortified by several pints is prepared to engage in acts of incredible heroism, eg. squaring up to doormen on the other side of the street, gesticulating at others in an abusive manner from inside a car travelling at speed.

beer miles *n*. Easy, cheap, long-distance travel made possible by the consumption of large quantities of ale.

beer monkey *n*. A mythical simian creature which, during a drunken slumber, sneaks into your bed, ruffles your hair, steals your money and *shits* in your mouth.

beer muffs *n*. Invisible ear defenders that attach themselves to a man's head after several pints, rendering him unable to hold a conversation without shouting or to watch TV at anything but full volume.

beer mugger *n*. The man you discover has hit you over the head and taken £35 out of your wallet the morning after you 'nip out for a couple of pints'.

beer pressure *n*. A benevolent psychological influence applied by drinking companions, encouraging one to consume more alcohol than one feels comfortable drinking.

beer queer *1. adj*. Of a normally heterosexual person, to be tempted to go *half rice half chips* when fuelled by sufficient quantities of *dizzyade. Booze bent. 2. n.* One who takes his drink the other way. A *teapot sucker.* A teetaller.

beer scooter *n*. Miraculous method of transport employed when leaving the pub after drinking substantial amounts of alcohol. So called due to the 'lost time' effect when returning home seemingly in no time and at incredible velocity.

beer shoes *n*. Gloves

beer sniper *n*. An invisible marksman who silently 'takes out' drunkards causing them to unexpectedly collapse in the street, fall off bar stools, etc.

beer stretcher *n*. A magical post-pub St John's Ambulance service. When *fully-refreshed* and lying down in the gutter, ditch or on the pub toilet floor, one is immediately whisked home on the *beer stretcher* to the comfort of one's own bed, to awake in the morning with absolutely no memory of the journey. '*I came home on the beer stretcher, only I must have stopped off at the all-night garage because when I woke up there was a 50+ wank mag and an empty packet of scotch eggs on the bed.*'

beer thinners *n*. The pint of water one forgets to consume at the end of a long evening *on the pop*.

beertent *n*. Jocky Wilson's shirt.

beer whistle *n*. At a football match, the signal given 10 minutes before half time that causes a mass exodus of gentlemen going for a pint, a pie, a *piss* or any simultaneous combination of the three.

beerwolf *n*. One who wakes up in unfamiliar surroundings with torn clothes, aching limbs, the taste of blood in the mouth and nightmarish flashbacks to terrible events of the previous evening.

beer wood *n*. The thing that feels like an erection, but isn't, whilst attempting sexual congress under the influence of alcohol.

bee stings *n*. Small *tits*. *Chestnuts*.

Beethoven's fifth *n*. A large, stirring movement of the bowel which may leave the performer deaf.

beetle bonnet *n*. Female pubic mound as viewed through tight garments. From the design of the VW car. *Camel's foot, camel's lip*.

begonias *n*. See *bejonkers*.

bejonkers *n*. See *bouncers*.

Bela Lugosi's gob *n*. An *axe wound* which drips with fresh blood on a regular basis. A *jam sandwich*.

Belfast taxi *n*. Battery-powered shopping scooter for old people too fat or idle to walk. A *Disneyworld dragster*.

Belfast tickle stick *n*. A baseball bat, iron bar, length of four-by-two, etc.

Belgian 1. *adj*. Of chocolates, twice as expensive as normal. 2. *n*. In the world of sex, a spot of *ESD*. *Hot karl*.

Belgian biscuit *n*. Sexual practice of Flemish origin and costing over £100.

Belisha beacon *n*. Flashing orange globe on a black and white pole, named after the British Transport Minister in 1934.

bell *n*. *Clit*. The *devil's doorbell*, found just above the *snail's doorstep*.

bell clapper *n*. An humungous dangling *turd* that tolls the *bummocks* as one tries to swing it loose.

bellefire 1. *n*. A crappy manufactured girl group. 2. *n. medic*. A *herman*-based symptom of *cockrot*.

bell end 1. *n*. An amusingly-named tent. 2. *n. medic*. The *bobby's helmet*, the *herman*. The glans of the penis.

bell end brie *n*. *Helmetdale*.

bell rag *n*. A cloth with the specific designated purpose of removing *spodge* from under the *bridge*.

bell-swagged *adj*. To be endowed with a large *bell end* on a contrastingly-small stem or *shaft*. *Mushroom-rigged*.

bell tower *n*. *Knob* shaft. *Bean stalk*.

bell wringing *v*. A harmless pastime that builds up the arm muscles, popular with monks for the last two thousand years.

belly flopper *n*. A clumsy *brown trout* whose graceless entry into the water causes splashing of the *arse*.

belly warmers *n*. Big, droopy *tits*. *Overblaaters*.

belt-fed mortar *sim. milit*. A measure of the sexual enthusiasm of a lady. See also *shithouse door in the wind, kangaroo shagging a space hopper*. '*I bet she bangs like a belt-fed mortar.*'

Ben Jones *euph*. An act of *horatio*. A *chewie*, a *BJ*. Named after the Virgin Radio presenter. Also *Billy Joel*.

bender 1. *n*. Prolonged drinking spree. An *all-dayer*, or *Leo Sayer*. 2. *n*. A crustie's tent. 3. *n*. A *pinch of snuff*.

bend the elbow *v*. To go for a *beer goggles* fitting.

benefactor *n*. Of *farts* and *farting*, the altruist who supplies it. Also known as the *donor*.

beneficiaries *n*. Those who benefit from the smelly largesse of the *benefactor's custard*.

benefit buddies *n*. The group of lonely OAPs and unemployable misfits who gather outside the Post Office half an hour before it opens in the morning just to talk to one another.

benefit buffet *n*. In supermarkets, the shelves situated close to checkouts that bear a mouth-watering array of dented tins, loaves of bread with torn packaging, crushed crisps and almost out of date meat.

Benny Hill *rhym. slang*. A form of contraception. *'It's nothing to do with me, Mrs. Gamp. You told me you was on the Benny Hill.'* (from *'Nicholas Nickelby'*, by Charles Dickens).

bent 1. *adj*. Descriptive of one who is not straight. *'He was as bent as a nine bob note.'* 2. *adj*. Descriptive of a dishonest *scuffer*.

bentertainment *n*. The sort of TV programmes that only girls and *botters* watch, eg. *'What Not to Wear'*, *'Sex & the City'*, *'Coronation Street'* etc.

Beppe's beard *n*. A severely but neatly-trimmed *muff*, named after the severely but neatly-trimmed chin growth of the former *'EastEnders'* character. A *clitler*.

Berkeley Hunt *rhym. slang. Fanny.*

Berlin Wall 1. *n*. Heavily-policed strip of no-man's land formerly dividing the forbidden East and free West halves of the German city. 2. *n*. The *taint, tinter, notcher, barse, biffin bridge, scran, tintis, Humber Bridge* etc.

Bermuda triangle *n*. A mysterious area where *skin boats* full of semen seem to disappear. For two or three minutes.

berry 1. *n*. A sexual deviant, a kinky person. A goddam *prevoit*. 2. *n*. One who has *carnival knowledge* of animals. 3. *n*. A lady with a great body, but a less-than-pleasing face, ie. one who has the body of Halle, but the face of Chuck. eg. Sarah Jessica Parker. A *bobfoc*.

bertie 1. *n*. Male homosexual. 2. *n*. A *charlie*. 3. *adj*. Of a woman, to be blessed with morals as *slack as a brewer's cock*. From the spoonerism Bertie Ditch = dirty bitch. *'...or should he go for saucy number three, who sounds well bertie and takes it up the council?'* (Graham Skidmore, voiceover on *'Cilla's Blind Date'*, LWT).

Bertie Bassett's hat *n*. The small, unsatisfying, sticky nugget of dark excrement that drops to the bottom of an otherwise empty toilet bowl. *'No sign of Bertie, but he's dropped his hat.'*

Berwick Rangers' goalmouth 1. *n*. The badly churned-up sea of mud between the posts at Shielfield Park. 2. *n*. The badly churned-up sea of mud in the back of a pair of badly-*shitted undercrackers*.

bespectable *adj*. Respectable in glasses.

Betty Both *n*. A *happy shopper*, a *switch hitter*. *'Yes, he is. I've heard he's a Betty Both and so is his wife.'* (Paul Lavers, unintentional live broadcast, Friendly TV, 2003).

Betty Swollocks *n*. Polite term for *knacker* discomfort. *'Forgive me, Your Majesty, whilst I adjust my doublet and hose. I have sailed the oceans these last six months and have not changed my codpiece since we left the New World. I fear I have the most awful Betties.'* (Sir Walter Raleigh, Audience with Queen Elizabeth I, 1584).

bevvy *n*. A portion of *booze*. A quantity of drink.

bezzing 1. *n*. Vigorous chewing of the face after taking one too many *disco biscuits*. *'Shit, these beans* *are good. I'm bezzing me tits off!'* 2. *n.* The act of dancing like a drunken gibbon, in a similar fashion to Mr. Bez out of the Happy Mondays.

biddeos *n. Scud videos* in which the actresses look somewhat younger on the packaging than they do in the film itself.

biffer *n.* A particularly hairy *minge. 'Gaw, you've got a right old biffer on you there, Your Majesty.'*

biffie *n. Bog, shitter, dunny, cludgy.*

biffin *n.* Perspiration which condenses in the *biffin bridge* area during coitus.

biffin bridge *n.* See *barse.*

biffing plate 1. *n. Beetle bonnet, monkey's forehead.* 2. *sim.* That which is flat. *'Christ! This lager's as flat as Kate Moss's biffing plate.'*

biffon *n.* That part of the female anatomy between the *council gritter* and the *fadge*, which the man's *clockweights* 'biff on' during intercourse. The *taint.*

big bamboo *n.* Penis.

Big Ben 1. *n.* A large bell in St. Steven's Tower, London. 2. *n.* An enormous *erection*, possibly with Robert Powell hanging off it.

big brother is watching you *phr.* The *wood*-felling realisation, whilst watching a *scruff* video, that there is a photo of a grinning sibling on top of the TV set which must be laid face down before one can continue *relaxing in a gentleman's way.*

big cock day *n.* A day, quite possibly in spring, the arrival of which is greeted with the *dawn horn*, and throughout which the sap continues to rise. *'As he wrestled himself into his shreddies, D'Arcy knew it*

was going to be a big cock day.' (from *'Pride And Prejudice'* by Jane Austen).

biggie smalls *n.* Fat lasses' knickers.

big mac 1. *n.* A disappointing *hamburger*, consisting of two tired, grey pieces of meat, random, sorry looking vegetation and traces of unidentified mayonnaise-like liquid. 2. *n.* A high street fast food that looks and tastes like *1.*

bike *n.* A frequently-*ridden* woman, one who has had thousands of gentlemen swing their legs over her. Often prefixed with a location. *'You don't want to go near her, mate. She's the office/factory/London Symphony Orchestra and Festival Chorus bike.'*

bikini burger *n.* A *vertical bacon sandwich.* See *hairy pie.*

Bilbo Baggins' foot *n.* An hirsute vagina, resembling the hairy toes of a hobbit.

bile mile *n.* The finishing straight of a marathon *spewing* session, where one's gallbladder is going flat out to produce something worth *yoffing.*

bilge tanks *n.* The 'double gut' effect caused by an overly-tight belt on an overly-large belly. eg. Simon Bates.

Bill Grundies *rhym. slang. Undies, trolleys, dunghampers.*

Billingsgate box *n. Minge.* Based on a comparison between the smell of a cockney fish market and a cockney *fanny.*

billposter's bucket *sim.* Large paste-filled *fanny. 'I was stationed in Scutari Hospital for six months, the only woman amongst thousands of soldiers. By the end of my first shift I had a twat like a billposter's bucket.'* (from *'My Poor Cunt - The Wartime Memoirs of*

Florence Nightingale').

bills *n*. *Shreddies, dunghampers.*

Bill Wyman *rhym. slang.* A lady's *virgin string.* From Bill Wyman = hymen.

Billy Connolly's beard *n*. A *rag-week fanny.*

billy goat's mouth *n*. An exceptionally loose vagina. With bits of the Mayor's hat sticking out.

Billy Mill roundabout *n*. Climactic point of a bout of masturbation. From the climactic point of the A1058 Coast Road near Newcastle. The *vinegar strokes. 'My mum walked in just as I was coming up to the Billy Mill roundabout.'*

Billy no mates *1. n*. A lonely little buoyant *turd* that remains hanging around in the pan after all the others have gone to the beach. *2. n*. A person bereft of acquaintances.

Billy Wright *n*. Legendary Wolverhamtpon Wanderers footballer, latterly immortalised as rhyming slang for *shite.*

bilp *n*. *Blip.*

biltrum *n*. The *chin rest.* See *wannocks.*

bimbo *n*. The likes of Jordan or Joanne Guest.

bimboid *adj*. Appertaining to the likes of Jordan or Joanne Guest.

bingo armour *n*. The excessive amounts of tawdry jewellery worn by ladies enjoying a night frantically crossing out numbers in a former cinema. *Bingo clink.*

bingo partner *n*. A man who is engaging in a romantic dalliance with a somewhat older lady.

bingo top *n*. A lady's upper body garment, cut in such a way as to encourage men to cast their 'eyes down' in the hope of a glimpse of *nork.*

bingo wings *n*. Upper arm adipose underhang found on post-menopausal ladies of a common bent. *Arm tits.*

Bin Laden's beard *n*. A particularly luxuriant, yet unruly *stoat.* The antithesis of a *Hitler tash.*

bin lids *n*. The areolae round a lady's *nippular bits.* The saucers round the *titcups.*

bin ripper *n*. An *alcoholic womble.* One who finds his treasure amongst the things everyday folk leave behind. A *Harold Ramp.*

bint *n*. Derogatory term for a daft *slapper,* eg. Jordan or Joanne Guest.

binternet *n*. The world-wide electronic network used to view titillating pictures of young ladies in various states of undress.

bird *n*. A lady. *'Phoar! Is this your new bird? She's a bit of alright, ain't she. Fantastic tits. What does she go like, then?'*

bird flu *n. medic.* Pre-*women's things* irritability. *Pre-rag radge, strawberry mivvie.*

birds' custard *1. n*. A sweet, gloopy substance that comes out of a tin. *2. n*. A savoury, gloopy substance that comes out of a lady's *clout. Blip.*

birdseed *n. derog.* Nickname for a henpecked fellow.

bird's trifle *1. n*. Popular proles' dessert containing several fingers and a lot of jelly, topped with custard and cream but frequently missing the cherry that is invariably nicked before one has the chance to enjoy it. *2. n*. A dirty lady's *letterbox.*

Birkenhead confetti *n*. Gravel.

Birmingham botox *n*. Budget cosmetic procedure, available in most

Black Country pubs, which leaves one's face looking not unlike that of Sylvester Stallone's mum. A sound *pasting*.

biscuit *n*. A *turd*.

biscuits 1. *n. UK.* Contents of the stomach after a heavy night's drinking. *'Get me a bucket, quick, Your Honour, I'm gonna chuck me biscuits.'* 2. *n. US.* Tight *buns*. Attractive *arse cheeks*.

bishop rage *n*. A *monkey spanking* performed with such vigour that one takes on the appearance of one of Francis Bacon's screaming Popes.

bishop's dick, stiff as a *sim*. Descriptive of the muscular and joint rigidity experienced after a 20-mile walk. *'With Striding Edge safely negotiated, I wearily descended the Victorian pony track down Birkhouse Moor with its fine views across to St. Sunday Crag. At the foot of the slope I crossed Grisedale Beck and joined the tarred road for the difficult last eight miles, finally entering Patterdale as stiff as a bishop's dick.'* (from *'Coast to Coast the Miserable Way'* by Alfred Wainwright).

bishop's licence *n*. That which is granted to a man left home alone by his wife, enabling him to *wank* himself blind at his leisure.

bishop's mitre *n*. A *bobby's helmet*.

bismarking *n*. An act of love where a man strikes a lucky lady repeatedly around the chops with his *cock* for their mutual pleasure. Also *colting, salami slap*.

bisto skids *n*. The beefy stains left down the back of the *pan* after a night *on the sauce*.

bit, a 1. *n*. An imperial unit of *the other*, slightly less than an entire portion. 2. *n*. Unspecified quantity of sex, usually partaken *on the side*.

bitch piss *n*. Alcopops. *'A pint of John Smith's please, barman, and a bottle of bitch piss for the missus.'*

bitch tits *n*. Large, flabby breasts found on overweight men of any age. Particularly amusing on American children on *'Oprah'*. *Triple-hearters, dog udders*.

bitchwhore *n*. A woman who is not only a bitch, but is also a whore.

biting point n. The first tingly inklings down amongst the loins that a prolonged bout of *self help* might just possibly have been worthwhile after all.

bit of fluff *n*. Singular piece of *totty*.

bit of rough *n*. Sexual partner, usually male, from a lower echelon. One who would wipe his *cock* on a *bird's* curtains, eg. Mellors in *'Lady Chatterley's Lover'*.

bitten by the brewer's horse *euph*. To be as *refreshed* as an airline pilot.

bitterflies *n*. Mythical intestinal insects that flutter in the stomach when it's knocking off time and one can almost taste the first pint.

BJLs *abbrev*. Blow Job Lips. See *DSLs*

blaaters *n*. *Oomlaaters*.

Blackbeard's ghost *n*. A triangular, white, spooky apparition occasionally glimpsed by the *one-eyed lookout* in one's *crow's nest*. A mature lady's once-raven *mapatasi*. A *fanny badger*.

Blackpool cock *n*. A pink, sticky erection upon which one's *bird* could break her teeth. And which would make her sick half way through.

blacksmith's apron *n*. A lady's substantial, leathery *front bottom*.

bladdered *adj*. See *blitzed*.

bland job *n*. Being *tossed off* by a lass whilst so *pissed* one can hardly feel it. See *no job*

blanket drill *n*. *Milit*. An early morning *mutton musket* practice that results in the loss of the *officer's mess*.

blanket ripper *n*. Back-draught in a *Dutch oven*.

blanket welding *n*. Under the covers heavy manual work, which may lead to blindness.

blart *1. n*. Vagina. *2. n. coll*. Women, *totty*. *'Golly gosh! This nunnery is heaving with blart'*.

blart attack *euph*. A strange feeling, starting in the *pills* and spreading down the right arm, upon finding oneself surrounded by a large quantity of top flight *cabbage*. *Acute vangina*.

blart gallery *n*. Pub containing wall to wall *totty*.

bleed the lizard *v*. See *siphon the python*.

bleed the radiator *v*. To commit an act of flatulation in which one would be well advised to hold a rag over one's *brass eye* to prevent sludge going all over the wall.

Bleep & Booster *1. n*. Vaguely-remembered black and white *'Blue Peter'* science fiction series, voiced by the same bloke who did *'Captain Pugwash'*. *2. n*. The *ring-piece*.

bletherskate *n*. *Scot*. *Shit-for-brains, fuckwit, twat*. Literally meaning *bag of shite*.

blick *n*. Pubic scurf, *muffdruff*.

bliff mag *n*. *Rhythm journal, art pamphlet*. Pornographic magazine.

bliff *n*. *Minge, front bottom*.

blimp *v*. To surreptitiously ogle ladies' breasts and *arses* from behind a pair of mirrored sunglasses.

blimplants *n*. *Knockers*, surgically-enhanced to comic proportions, as sported by the likes of Jordan and the late Lolo Ferrari.

blind cobbler's thumbs *n*. Large, well-hammered *nipples. Pygmies' cocks*.

blind dirt snake *n*. A malodorous, legless lizard inhabiting *cak canyon*, which migrates south every morning. A *Richard the Third*.

blind man's buffet *n*. A *fanny* that can be located by the olfactory senses alone. *Blind man's muff*. A stanksome *snatch*.

blind man's porn *n*. Sexual noises, usually coming from an adjacent room or house.

blinglish *n*. Street language spoken by rappers and bishop's son DJ Tim Westwood.

blip. *n*. The watery substance of female love. *Fish cream, nog juice*.

blip fountain *n*. *medic*. The Bartholin's gland that secretes vaginal lubrications. The *batter tap*.

blit *n*. See *blivvet*.

blitzed *v*. See *blotto*.

blivvet *n*. See *blart*.

blob *1. n*. Condom, *French safe, French letter, rubber Johnny*. *2. v*. To inadvertently make pregnant. *"You look a little green around the lemon, old chap. Bad news is it?' I asked as Jeeves continued to study the letter. 'I'm afraid so sir,' he replied. 'I attended a party of the downstairs staff of Brokenbury Manor, and I am afraid things got* *a little out of hand. To cut a long story short, sir, it appears that I have blobbed the cook."* (from *'Use the Back Door, Jeeves'* by PG Wodehouse). ~**it** 3. *v.* To over sleep. *'Jesus, Phil, look at the time. Get up, quick! I'm being coronated in half an hour and we've blobbed it.'*

blob blimp *n.* A post-coital cabaret in which a used *jubber ray* is inflated and knotted for the amusement of one's ladyfriend.

blob jockey *n.* A gentleman with a penchant for the fuller-figured lady, eg. Lenny Henry. A *chubby chaser.*

blobsleigh *n.* Unexpected barefoot skid on last night's discarded prophylactic.

blobstopper *n.* A *fanny mouse*, a *slim fanatella.* A tampon.

Blofeld brunette *n.* A natural blonde who dyes her hair dark to feign intelligence. However, inspection of her lap reveals a white *pussy.* And draft plans for world domination. Opposite of an *aeroplane blonde.*

blonde herring *n.* A blonde woman who looks like she ought to be a nice bit of *mackerel* from the back, but who turns out to be an *old trout.*

blongle *n. medic.* Seminal fluid containing traces of blood. *Blunk, blism, blimphet.*

blood bachelor *n.* Married man undergoing the monthly interruption to his rightful conjugal privileges whilst his missus is *on the mop.*

bloodhound's jowls 1. *n.* Oversized *beef curtains* which could track an escaped convict across Dartmoor. 2. *n.* A mature bird's *funbags* during the later stages of collapse.

blood muppet *n. Jam dam, cotton mouse, gash mop, Dracula's teabag.* A ladies' personal hygiene product.

blood orange *n.* The *arsehole* after being savaged by a particularly vicious *chocolate shark. Japanese flag.*

bloodsports *n. Salsa dip.*

bloodstick *n.* A gentleman's erect *member.*

blood wank *n.* The ill-advised and possibly life-threatening act of *gentlemanly relaxation* that takes the day's tally into double figures. Regularly achieved by certain second year physics students at Manchester University and all bus drivers.

bloody *adj.* Swearword.

bloody sundae 1. *n.* An act of *cumulonimbus* performed on a lady *up on blocks.* 2. *n.* A U2 song about an act of *cumulonimbus* performed on a lady *up on blocks.*

bloomers 1. *n.* A voluminous item of women's underwear. 2. *n.* Large loaves of bread. 3. *n.* Unfunny and self-indulgent 'mistakes' made on camera by a BBC employees which are later transmitted as part of tiresome 'comedy' compilations.

blooper 1. *n.* ITV version of *bloomer.* An actor's mistake which provides Dennis Norden with something to do while he waits to die. 2. *n.* A sub-aquatic *fart.* A *tottle*, an *Edward Woodward.*

blootered *adj. See banjoed.*

blot bang rub 1. *phr. milit.* Skin decontamination procedure used by HM armed forces following a nuclear, biological or chemical attack. 2. *phr. milit. Nipsy* decontamination procedure used by HM armed forces the day after a particularly delicious curry from the Curry Capital, formerly the Rupali Restaurant, Bigg Market, Newcastle upon Tyne.

blotto *adj*. See *blootered*.

blottopilot *n*. Inbuilt male homing device which secures a safe return to one's house after a night *on the sauce*, whatever one's level of inebriation.

blouse hounds *n*. *Shirt puppies* which are getting a bit long in the tooth.

blow a dog off a chain *v*. *Aus*. To *let off* with a severity sufficient to strip canines from their moorings.

blowback 1. *v*. Of drug addicts, to puff smoke from a marijuana joint into another drug addict's mouth. 2. *n*. A gobful of one's own *spangle* thoughtfully passed on by a *nosher*. A *snowball*. 3. *n*. A potentially fatal *fart* lighting mishap.

blowd *n*. A strange brown haze at the bottom of the *lavvy* made by a *turd* that has successfully resisted the flushing process. *Poo tea, PG shits*. From brown + cloud.

blow dry *v*. Of a dirty lady, to repeatedly *suck off* a fortunate gentleman until his *pods* are exhausted of *men's spendings*.

blow hole 1. *n*. A whale's nose on top of its head. 2. *n*. The *hog's eye*.

blow job *n*. Dangerous sex act whereby the female inflates the male's testicles like balloons by blowing air into his penis.

blow job off Emu *n*. A *wank*.

blow job week *n*. A once-monthly, seven-day *nosh fest*. A lady's *unclean time*. *'Now your life doesn't have to stop just because blow job week starts.'* (Advertising slogan for Vespray Ultra *cunt rats*).

blowlamp *n*. A *fart* which is strong

enough to fetch paint off a door or caramelise the sugar on a crème brûlée.

blow mud *v*. To noisily expel a loose stool, *crop spray, pebbledash*, release a *flock of pigeons*.

blow off *v*. To trumpet through the trousers, *parp* in the pants.

blow sisters *n*. Lesbian nuns, often seen in candle shops and cycling along cobbled streets.

blow your biscuits *v*. To *puke, yawn in technicolour*.

blubber beret *n*. Fleshy, Frank Spencer-style headwear worn by a man *licking out* a lass equipped with a *pie-hider*. A *fat hat*.

bludger 1. *n*. One of two balls in the Harry fucking Potter bollocks broomstick cricket game Quidditch. 2. *n*. A *stool* of the very firmest consistency imaginable. A *pan-cracker*.

blue 1. *adj*. Of comedians and jokes, to be a little bit near the knuckle. 2. *adj*. Of films, to have a different relationship to the knuckle altogether.

blue balls *n*. *Bollocks* which are fit to burst through lack of use. *DSBs, Sir Cliff's plums, nuts like two tins of Fussell's Milk, monks' nuts*.

bluebottle banquet *n*. The swarm of ravenous flies, familiar to farmers, festival-goers, boy scouts and 1982 World Professional Darts champions, that descends as if by magic on a freshly-laid al fresco *tom tit*.

bluecoat *n*. A lady who favours sex in the *tradesman's entrance*. From the practice in greyhound racing whereby the dog in the blue coat is traditionally run from trap two.

blue dart *n*. That brief but exciting pyrotechnic display achieved by igniting one's *air biscuits*. An *afterburner, blue streak.*

Blue Peter bird cake *1. n.* Half a coconut shell filled with a solid paste of lard and old seeds. *2. sim.* Descriptive of a right full old *growler. 'Up betimes and feeling heavy of nodgers I made my way to Mrs. Fitzgibbon's bordello on Threadneedle Street to see darling Bess. However, to my dismay I found she had done good business this day, and indeed, when I remov'd her scads did find that her cunny resembled naught but a Blue Peter bird cake. I was forced to demand back my shilling.'* (from *'The Diary of Samuel Pepys'*).

blue-veined piccolo *n.* A tiny, high-pitched *cock.*

bluey *1. n.* A *bongo vid. 2. n.* A *Bongo Bill banjo pill. 'Are you going to be much longer on the shitter, love? Only I popped my bluey half an hour ago and it's starting to wear off.'*

blumpkin *n. US.* An American rock groupie speciality. To administer a *gobbie* to an artiste whilst the latter is *dropping his kids off at the pool.*

blunderguff *v.* To expel an horrendous-smelling *fart* only to realise that the tastiest *bird* in the office is fast approaching.

blunk *1. n. Blongle. 2. n.* Scabrous, multi-layered jewellery of the type purveyed by Elizabeth Duke etc. From bling + junk.

Blunkett *n.* Facial expression adopted when two oncoming attractive ladies are forced to pass one to either side.

Blunkett's kiss *n.* An inaccurate show of affection, eg. When a pet dog licks one in the eye socket at 5am to welcome in a new day.

blurt *n. Splod.*

blurtch *n. medic.* The female reproductive organs. *'Congratulations, Your Majesty. You have been delivered of an heir to the throne of England, Great Britain, and her Commonwealth Dominions. I'll just stick a couple of stitches in your blurtch and you'll be as right as ninepence.'*

blurter *1. n. Aus.* Chocolate *starfish, ring. 2. n.* A little fishy that thou shalt have on a little dishy, when the boo-ert comes in.

blut *n. medic.* A lady's *mingepiece.*

boak *v.* See *bowk.*

bob *n.* A *neck massager,* a *dildo.* A Battery-Operated Boyfriend.

bobbery *n.* Female-on-male *strap-on*-assisted *arse-banging.*

Bobby Charltons *n.* Rogue pubes trapped under the foreskin that stick themselves across the dome of your *bell end,* in the manner of the erstwhile centre-forward's last few remaining hairs.

Bobby Davro eyes *n.* Descriptive of the cold, souless, miserable stare on the face of one doing something meant to be fun.

Bobby Splithead *n. prop.* Affectionate term for a *herman gelmet.*

bobby's anorak *n. Kojak's rollneck, fiveskin, cock collar.*

bobby's helmet *n. Bell end.* From the distinctive shape of the British police constable's hat which manages to look like a *tit* and a *cock end* simultaneously.

bobfoc *acronym.* Body Off Baywatch, Face Off Crimewatch. Having a *welder's bench* inexplicably mounted on a finely carved *rack and pegs,* eg. Sarah Jessica Parker.

bobhouse *n.* The *shit box.* *'My darling Bobo, I will not take no for an answer - you simply MUST come to Chatsworth. The gardens are too divine at this time of year and the house is wonderfully enormous. Just imagine, the ballroom is the longest of any house in Europe! the dining room has a table that can seat 200! And there are 120 bedrrooms! Can you believe it? And each one with its own en-suite bobhouse.'* (Letter to Jessica Mitford, from her sister Deborah, Duchess of Devonshire).

boff *v.* See *bonk.*

bog dice *n.* The small cubes of disinfectant that are rolled down the trough using *piss* instead of a croupier. Used to replace the smell of stale urine with one of stale urine and disinfectant.

bog *n.* *Shit house.* Lavatory.

bogey spoon *n.* A fingernail.

bog library *n.* Reading material that builds up around the toilet of a bachelor. *Shiterature.*

bog-mess monster *n.* A legendary brown beast that curls its body out of the water in at least two places. May be a *brown trout* or a *dead otter.*

bog salmon *n.* An agile *turd* that, despite being flushed down river, manages to swim against the current back to its birthplace.

Bogside barbecue *n.* *NI.* From the salubrious Bogside area of Derry. A social gathering of locals enjoying cans of lager around a smouldering Ford Escort.

bog snorkelling *n.* *Dirtbox diving. Anilingus.*

boh! *exclam.* The noise made by a man after a particularly heavy woman has bounced up too far and sat down hard on his *gut stick,* breaking it in two. Reportedly Prince Albert's last word.

boiled eggs for four *n.* Visual impairment enjoyed by two reciprocating *homo horatiolists* in the 69 position. *Double Dutch blindfold.*

boiler *n.* An ugly woman who is lucky to get *serviced* once a year.

boilerdom *n.* The state of being a *boiler* into which many fat lasses pass directly upon reaching puberty.

boilersuit *n.* The charge that you did wilfully, and with phallus aforethought score with a *pig ugly* lass on Friday night. Usually brought by a kangaroo court convened in a pub on Saturday.

boiling beetroots *euph.* To be *up on blocks.* *'Sorry, not tonight, love. I'm boiling beetroots.' 'Oh. Can I kick the back doors in instead?'*

bolitics *n.* The practice of talking utter *bollocks* about politics. Often performed by drunks in pubs, students in halls of residence and Ruth Kelly.

bollock goatee *n.* The fashionable, jazz-style beard of testicles apparently grown by a woman whilst she is *smoking a gadgee.*

bollock jockeys *n.* See *bollock rats.*

bollock rats *n.* See *willipedes.*

bollocks 1. *n.* Nonsense. *'That's utter bollocks, that is.'* 2. *n.* Knackers, balls. *'Them's massive bollocks, them is.'*

bollock service *n. Wank.* *'Tell you what, Hank, my balls are blue. It's about time I had them in for a bollock service.'*

bolt from the blue *n.* A Viagra-fuelled ejaculation.

Bolton dipstick *n.* The middle finger of a gentleman's right hand.

Bolton dip test *n*. A quick check of a lady's *undercarriage* to make sure that she is well-oiled and ready for sexual intercourse. *'Heliotrope could smell Fandango's musty male aroma as he held her in his muscular Crufts judge's arms. She could feel his hands explore every inch of her lithe pedigree labrador breeder's body. Then he reached down for a quick Bolton Dip test.'* (from *'Pedigree'* by Jilly Cooper).

Bolton shotput *n*. A sport played by nightclub bouncers in which their clients are grabbed firmly under the chin and shoved as hard as possible into the road, against a wall or through a shop window.

Bombay roll *n*. Like a sausage roll, but with *tits* instead of pastry and a *cock* instead of a sausage. And it costs £25 instead of 30p.

bomb bay *n*. *medic*. The last lock on the alimentary *shit* canal. The rectum.

bomb bay bedbath *n*. A *shitted* bed following a pleasant night of curry and lager. A *Mrs. Chegwin's face-pack*.

bomb bay duck *n*. A *dog's egg* that quacks to let one know it wants to come out.

bomb bay mix *n*. A single lavatorial sitting that produces a pot-pourri of stool consistencies, from *copper bolts* to a *rusty water* geyser, and all points in between. *Shitterish Allsorts, variety cack.*

bomb bay sapphire *n*. A *turd* which has been baked for so long in the *shit pipe* that it exhibits a hardness comparable to that of a precious stone.

bomb China *v*. To release your *payload* over the *Yellow River*. To have a *Billy Wright*.

bomb on a short fuse *n*. The *shit* that causes one to sprint around looking for a *chod bin* in the manner that Adam West ran around looking for a safe place to throw the incendiary device in the 1966 film *'Batman'*.

bone *v*. US. To *fuck*.

bone of contention *n*. A *stonk on* that causes an argument, eg. one that arises whilst watching beach volleyball with one's wife.

bone on *n*. A *panhandle*.

boner *n*. US. That which is used to *bone*. A *bone on*.

boneshaker *1. n*. An unsprung Victorian bicycle, named for its teeth-loosening progress along cobbled streets. *2. n*. An act of sexual intercourse that has to be finished by hand.

bone xylophone *n. medic*. Gynaecological term for the interior of a woman's rib cage. Her *slats*. *'Let's go play the bone xylophone.'*

bongo bush *n. bot*. A plant which bears torn-up pornographic fruits.

bongo mag *n. Rhythm literature, spangle book.*

bonk *v*. Tabloid term for *fuck*.

bonk on *n*. A splendidly tumescent member. *'A copy of 'Splosh' and a box of tissues please, Mr. Newsagent. I've got an almighty bonk on.'*

bonus ball *n*. The unheralded faecal pebble that drops in the gusset after an unsuccessful gamble on the *fart lottery*.

boobies *n*. See *boobs*.

boobs *n*. See *boobies*.

bookends *n*. The fellows at either end of a *spitroast*. *'It is estimated that up to 85% of professional footballers have, at some time in their career, been bookends.'*

bookie's biro *sim.* Descriptive of the chewed-up state of one's *old man* after a prolonged session of *horatio*. A *well-chomped chopper*. *'I came back from my weekend in Amsterdam with a suitcase full of souvenirs, a head full of happy memories and a charlie like a bookie's biro.'* (Jim White, *'BBC Holiday Programme'*).

bookie's bog *euph.* Descriptive of something that is in a right old mess. *'Beckham, now. Steps forward to take the penalty that could see England go through to Euro 2004. He looks composed, but he must be feeling the pressure. Starts his run up and oh my word. He's made a complete bookie's bog of that one.'*

bookie's pencil *n.* Descriptive of a dismally short, stumpy *cock*. *'He sings, he tells jokes, he does impressions and he's got a cock like a bookie's pencil. Ladies and gentlemen, put your hands together and give a warm welcome to Mr. Bobby Davro.'* (Jimmy Tarbuck, 1988 Royal Variety Performance).

bookie's tip *n.* A John McCrirrick-style sequence of tic-tac twitches, flinches and flapping arms that signals to a *fellatrix* that it's odds on she's about to get a mouthful of *spooge*.

boomerang *n.* A sock that has been masturbated into so many times that it is hard enough stun a passing wallaby before returning to the masturbator's hand.

boot *n. Can.* A woman who is too easy to *shag*.

booze flu *n.* A non-viral ailment that strikes suddenly after an evening at the pub and causes the sufferer to take the next day off work. Symptoms include staying in bed and feeling like *shite*.

booze snooze *n.* An alcohol-induced siesta taken in the pub or in a layby.

booze tardis *n.* A four-dimensional *beer scooter*.

boregasm *n.* A disinterested act of *self-pollution* for want of anything else to do.

Boris *1. n.* An act of premature *spangulation*. Named after the incident in a restaurant cupboard that turned out to be the worst and most expensive five seconds Boris Becker ever spent. *2. n.* Term used by females for their *farmyard area*, apparently.

born again fistian *n.* One who has recently become single and is once again spending a lot of time *praying for milk*.

Boscastle hall carpet, wetter than a *sim.* A no-longer-topical phrase used to describe the moistness of a sexually keen young lady's *clopper*.

Bosch *v.* Of bishops and farmers - to drill a hole between cubicles in a public lavatory for the purpose of spying on, or making your penis available to the farmer or bishop in the adjacent *trap*.

bosphorus *n.* The bit that connects the fishy pleasures of the Mediterranean with the exotic mysteries of the Black Sea. The *taint, tinter, notcher, biffin bridge*.

boswellox *1. n.* An unlikely sounding wrinkle-cream ingredient. *2. n.* Utter bollocks, eg. the claims made in wrinkle-cream adverts.

botcaps *n.* Plugs of *shit roll* worn in the *anus* to prevents *skids* on hot days.

Botley Interchange *1. n.* Section of Oxfordshire thoroughfare, connecting the A34 to the A420 and thus 2. *n.* The section of the female *farmyard* anatomy which separates the *front* from the *back bottoms*. The *carse, tinter, snarse, Humber Bridge, Barry Gibb* etc.

bott *v.* To commit the sex act performed by *botters*.

bottee *n.* One who is *botted* up the *bottom* by a *botter*.

botter *n.* One who *botts* a *bottee up the bottom*.

bottled Bass *n.* Descriptive of the lubricity of a *stoat*. *'You may be knocking on a bit, love, but your granny's oysters are frothing like bottled Bass.'*

bottle of olives *onomat.* The sound a *fart* makes in the bath. Named after the actor Edward Woodward.

bottle opener *n.* A particulary strong and robust *fanny*. Presumably with a little metal hook at the top.

bottom *n.* That part of the *bottee* which is *botted* by a *botter*.

bottom log *n.* A scuttled *dreadnought* that hits the sea bed whilst still exiting the *windward passage*.

botto voce *adj. Lat.* Descriptive of a barely-audible *anal aside*. From the 18th century Italian; voce = voice & botto = *nipsy*.

botty burp *n.* A burp from the *botty, trouser trumpet, fart*.

bouncers *1. n.* Unsportsmanlike, short-pitched deliveries in cricket aimed at intimidating the batsman. *2. n.* Muscle men, *ripped to the tits* on steroids, who keep the riff-raff out of pubs and clubs. *3. n.* Big, wobbly *tits*.

bouncy castle *1. n.* A large, fat, rubbery *fanny* that one has to remove one's shoes before having a go on. *2. n.* A larger *bird*, endowed with *tits* like floppy turrets, who is fun to jump onto after spending the afternoon drinking cider.

bourbon *n.* Someone who is good at *horatio*. A fancy 'licker'.

Bourneville boulevard *n. Arse, fudge tunnel. 'I believe he strolls down the Bourneville boulevard'.*

Bovril bullets *n.* Stools, excrement. Faeces.

bow Derek *n.* A *bird* who looks spectacular after one has imbibed a surfeit of cider.

bowel bugle *n.* A *trouser trumpet*.

bowel howl *n.* Fearsome wailing of the *anus*, the *sound of your supper*.

bowel trowel *n.* One of a selection of tools at the disposal of the *uphill gardener*. See also *cheesy wheelbarrow, trouser rake, one-eyed purple-headed blue-veined hairy pink hedgeclipper*.

bowk *v.* To *barf, vomit, spew, yak, hoy up, bake a pavement pizza*.

bowl from the Pavilion end *v.* To *bott*, travel on *the other bus*.

bowl mole *n.* A small Cindy Crawford-style beauty spot on the side of the lavatory pan that resists all attempts at removal by brush, *piss*, etc.

bowsprit *1. n.* In the maritime world, a mast or spar running forwards from a ship's bow, to which are fastened stays. *2. n.* In the world of *bone ons*, the sort of *diamond cutter* which points ahead as one walks and could, if one weren't careful, *poke a hole in a cheap door*.

box *1. n.* The vagina. *'I wouldn't mind getting into her box.'* *2. n.* In cricket, a gentleman's protective device worn around the *undercarriage*. *'Ooyah me pods! I wish I'd worn a box.'*

box doc *n. medic.* A gynaecologist. A *fanny mechanic.*

boxer's punchball *n.* The acorn of *shit* that hangs off the *toffee strings* and resists all attempts to *tap the ash off,* simply bouncing around like a pugilist's exercise equipment.

box of assorted creams *n. Aus.* She who has recently been over-accommodating to a number of gentlemen. A promiscuous female with a *fanny like billposter's bucket.*

box the Jesuit *v. 17thC.* How Friar Tuck may have referred to *strangling the parson* behind a bush in Sherwood Forest.

brace *rhym. slang.* To defecate. From brace and bit = *tom tit.*

Brad *rhym. slang.* A *dump.* 'Give me the paper, I'm off for a Brad.'

Brads *rhym. slang. The Earthas.* 'Can you pass me some moist wipes in? I've got a bad case of the Brads.'

Bradford dishwashing *n. Pissing* in the sink.

Bradford street carnival *n.* A traditional, city-wide riot that celebrates the city's cultural diversity.

Brahms and Liszt *rhym. slang. Wankered.*

braille tits *n.* Tiny, raised *knockers* that allow a blind man to read a woman's chest over and over again. *Stits, fried eggs, chest warts.*

brain donor *n.* An intellectually challenged person.

brandy snap *n.* The *pubal area* of a russet-haired lady. A ginger *minge.*

brap *n.* The volume rating of a *fart (Bp)* governed by three variables - rectal pressure *(r)*, buttock friction *(f)* and sprouts consumed *(SpC)* such that $Bp = fx\ SpC/r$. Buttock friction *(f)* can be reduced to zero by pulling the *ringpiece* open wide during emission.

brass eye *n. Hog's eye, brown eye, red eye, chocolate starfish.*

brass rubbings *n.* Rusty, finger-end-shaped tracings found in a gentleman's *undercrackers* following a good scratch of his poorly-wiped, sweaty *arse crack.*

bratmobiles *n.* People carriers.

Brazilian rocket *n.* A gentleman who explodes whilst still on the launchpad. One who *stamps on the toothpaste* before he's got his pants off.

Brazilian wax *n.* A bald *monkey's forehead.* A *shaven haven,* a *Barthez.*

breach of the peach *n.* A *kicking in* of a lady's *back doors.*

breach the hull *v.* To push one's digit through inferior quality *bumwad* when wiping one's *arse. Push through.* 'Day 82, and the men are getting restless. Squabbles are beginning and tempers are short. John Norton handed out the ship's biscuits, but Mr. Christian refused to eat, accusing him of breaching the hull and not washing his hands.' (from 'The Log of HMS Bounty', 1764).

breadlocks *n.* The nutritious foody entanglements of a tramp's beard.

break company *v.* To disrupt a gathering of *beneficiaries* by the release of a *McArthur Park.*

breakfast in bed *n.* An early morning *fart* that sets one up for the rest of the day. A *dawn chorus.*

breakfast maker *n.* An early morning *fart* which is so smelly that the missus has no choice but to get out of bed and make the breakfast.

breakfast of champions *n.* A *fanny fry-up* eaten the morning after *put-*

ting the wife to the sword.

break for the border *1. n.* A risky dash made by one's hand for a woman's knickers when one is uncertain of her reaction, half expecting a slap. *2. v.* Of a *shit*, to catch one unawares by suddenly *darting south,* eg. when one is looking for something to read.

break the seal *v.* To one's first *piss* at the pub, usually after three or four pints. Return visits to the toilet are thereafter required every fifteen minutes throughout the evening.

break the crust *v.* The morning after an evening fuelled with hot food and brown beer, to drop the day's first *Brad Pitt* which is shortly followed by an uncontrollable Krakatoa-style outpouring of lava from the *jacksie.*

break the siege *v.* To enjoy a long overdue *dump* following a bout of constipation.

breast fest *n.* Those summer months during which women sunbathe topless.

breasticles *n.* Particularly small, wrinkly bosoms of the type you'd expect Dot Cotton to have.

breastitute *adj.* Descriptive of a lady who hasn't got two *thruppennny bits* to rub together, eg. Tara Palmer Tomkinson.

breather ring *n.* An anular indentation on a long *turd,* indicating where the *cable layer* has had to pause for breath, allowing the *nipsy* to partially contract. A faecal aneurism. *'Fuck me! That was a bastard to part with. I left it with three breather rings on it.'*

brewer's droop *n.* Marshmallowing of the penis due to excessive *turps nudging.*

brewer's fart *n.* A particularly sulphurous *bowel howl. 'Jesus, he's just dropped a brewer's fart, grains and all.'*

brewer's flu *n.* A nasty hangover.

brew one up *v.* To be *burbulent,* to bake an *air biscuit. 'For your own safety step back please ladies, I'm brewing one up over here.'*

brice *v. Vict.* To engage in a sexual act in which one party is tied to a large stake known as the *bricing post*

bricing post *n.* Stake to which someone is tied, who is to be *briced.*

bricks and mortar *n.* A sit down toilet visit of miscellaneous consistencies. *Bomb bay mix.*

brick shithouse, built like a *sim.* Resembling a Leeds Rhinos prop forward. Heavy set, stocky. *'Is that your missus. Fucking hell, she's built like a brick shithouse.'*

bridge the gap *v.* See *TUBFUF.*

bridger *n. Bottom log.*

brigadier *1. n.* Military officer ranking immediately below a Major General. *2. n.* A three-course meal for one's *cock* consisting of the *pink,* the *brown,* and a *chewie,* in that order.

Brighton *rhym. slang. On the other bus.* From Brighton pier = *ginger beer.*

Brillo pad *sim.* Coarse vaginal foliage. A red-headed Scots lassie might be described as having *'a mott like a rusty Brillo pad.'*

brim *n.* Wainscotting around the base of the *helmet.* The *wankstop,* the *sulcus.*

brimula *n.* Spreadable *knob cheese.*

bringing the safety car out *1. v.* The spoilsport action of Formula 1 organisers attempting to prevent exciting high-speed pile-ups in dangerous conditions. *2. v.* A gentleman's attempt to prevent early *crashing of the yoghurt truck* in an exciting situation, eg. by thinking about abandoned puppies, football scores or Rovers Return barmaid Betty Turpin. *Summoning Moira.*

bring off *v.* To cause to have an orgasm.

brink *n.* The *taint, tinter, carse, biffin bridge, crontis.* So called because it rests between the *brown* and the *pink.*

Bristol Channel *n.* The cleavage.

Bristols *ryhm. slang. Tits.* From Bristol Cities = *titties.* And Bristol dockers = *knockers.* And Bristol fig slugs = *big jugs.*

broat *n.* See *vurp.*

brobs *n.* Overwhelmingly large *tits.* From the giant Brobdignabians in *'Gulliver's Travels'.* Opposite of *lils.*

broken ice cream machine, arse like a *sim.* Symptom of major gastrointestinal meltdown which results in a day spent off work, sitting on the *chod-bin* reading the local autotrader and moaning.

Bronx cheer *n. arch.* Obsolete whoopee cushion term for a *fart.*

broomstick *n.* Any small runaround car aimed specifically at the ladies market, eg. Renault Clio, Ford Fiesta.

brother *n. Bean flicker, tuppence licker, carpet muncher.* A lesbian.

brother, email my *euph.* To masturbate. From the US baseball player Carlos Zambrano, who was put on the Chicago Cubs injured list because of a wrist injury caused by spending four hours a day on the internet 'emailing his brother'.

brown admiral *n. zoo.* The common and far from beautiful butterfly that can be found in the pants of someone who has failed to *draw an ace.* A *gusset moth.*

brown ballerina *n.* The 'tutu' effect achieved when one's index finger pierces cheap bathroom tissue whilst wiping one's *ringpiece. Also Kermit's collar.*

brown bear's nose *n.* A cute little round *turd* that hibernates at the bottom of the *pan.*

brown Betty *n.* The mess that can result from *back door love* with someone with a full or disturbed bowel.

brown bullet-hole *n. Bumhole, barking spider.*

brown daisy *n.* An unpleasantly-scented flower which attracts flies instead of bees. A *bronze eye.*

brown drought *n. medic.* Constipation.

brown dwarf *n.* The tiny, super-dense, hard-to-find nugget of highly-compressed *barker's egg* hiding somewhere on the sole of one's shoe.

brown extender *n.* At B&Q, a device for raising the height of an existing fence.

brown eye *n.* The *ring* through which the *brown trout* jump on their daily migration to the sea.

browneye lashes *n.* Glamorous hairs that surround the *balloon knot.* Often caked in a brown, mascara-like substance.

brown finger poncho *n.* The square of *arsewipe* through which the digit pushes when one *breaches the hull. Brown ballerina.*

brown hatter *n.* A *bottsman* with *shit* on his helmet.

brown helmet *n.* An award presented to a man by his girlfriend or wife to commemorate the day she leaves him, ie. *shits* on his head. *'And it came to pass that Naboth had journeyed to the shops and his wife Bathsheba was left alone in his tent. And David came unto her in the tent of Naboth and knew her twice. And she took up her chatels and went to live in the tent of David amongst the Gibeonites. And Naboth did return to his tent and found that Bathsheba was gone. And he went to the inn with his mates Mephibosheth and Jonadab son of Shimeah, and he wailed and gnashed his teeth saying, I always did my best for her, no man could have done more. Yet she gives me the brown helmet. And great was his sorrow, even unto the twelfth pint.'* ('*The Book of Epidydimis*', Ch.6 vv12-16).

brownhouse gases *n*. Environmentally harmful emissions from a *tail pipe*.

brownian motion *1. n*. The apparently random movements of minute particles immersed in a fluid, discovered by physicist Richard Brown. *2. n*. The frequent and painful visits to the *throne room* experienced by one who has recently enjoyed a delicious meal at the Curry Capital, formerly the Rupali Restaurant, Bigg Market, Newcastle upon Tyne.

brown jewels *n*. The Queen's *winnets*. The *dangleberries* of state.

brown laser *n*. A beam of hot, liquid *shit* that exits the *brass eye* at the speed of light, and which could easily cut a secret agent in two.

brown light's flashing *euph*. Emergency warning sign of a toiletry nature. *Umber alert*. '*Can you hang the washing out for me,*

dear?' 'Sorry love. Brown light's flashing, with you in five.'

brown lilo *n*. A buoyant *tom tit* that, left alone, will eventually float out to sea.

brown men on swings *n*. See *miniature heroes*.

brown owl *n*. A sizeable *log*. *Meatloaf's daughter*, a *dead otter*.

brown pipe engineer *n*. An *arse mechanic* who always calls at the *tradesman's entrance*.

brown pocket *n*. A smuggler's receptacle that allows him to spirit contraband through customs. '*Did you bring anything back from Amsterdam, Phil?' 'Yes. I've got some clogs and cheese in my suitcase and a lump of squidgy black in my brown pocket.'*

brown roulette *n*. A game of chance with potentially disastrous consequences whereby one *shoots rabbits* through an *arse* over which one has little control. To risk a *fart* whilst suffering with the *squits*.

brown sunrise *n*. Whilst *shitting*, the majestic sight of a *Thora Hird* gradually emerging from behind the knackers as one watches with the head between the knees. A sign that it's time to buy some Bill Tidy books to keep on the cistern.

brown-tak *n*. A pliable, adhesive compound used by prisoners to stick posters to the wall. Also known as *scat-tak*.

brown tap *n*. A particularly non-viscous bout of the *Mexican screamers*. The *gravy rocket*.

brown tie *n*. The dirty mark left between a lady's *jugs* by a man who has a *sausage sandwich* after taking her up the *council gritter*.

brown trout *n*. A *turd*, *big job*, *shite*.

brown trout pond *n*. The lavatory bowl.

brown wings *n*. The honour bestowed on one after performing *bumilingus* on a lady Hell's Angel.

brown zombie *n*. A *Douglas* that refuses to be flushed away and keeps on coming back.

Bruce Lees *n*. Hard *nips*.

Brucie *n*. A *fart* which is performed whilst adopting the silhouetted 'Thinker' stance made famous by Bruce Forsyth on *'The Generation Game'*.

BS *abbrev*. *US*. Booooool-shee-it.

BSH *abbrev*. British Standard Handful. The unit by which breasts are often measured.

bubbies *n*. Coy term for *breasts*, much beloved of writers of cod-Victorian pornography. *"Ooh, zur! What does you think of moi bubbies, then?' asked Molly the Milkmaid, as she unzipped the Squire's heaving breeches.'* (from *'A Roll in the Hay'*, by Jeffrey Archer).

bubbing *v*. To rub one's *knob* on one's partner's *freckle* whenever possible, usually accompanied by an Ainsley Harriot-esque chinny grin and head wobble, in the hope that one day she'll say 'Oh, go on then.'

bubble poo *n*. *Fizzy gravy*.

bubblebum *n*. An unfortunate release of *burbulent gas* through moist *buttocks*, the resulting sound being eerily reminiscent of Leonardo di Caprio's final words in *'Titanic'*.

bubblyduck *n*. A particularly loud, prolonged and wet *fart*. Named because the sound is identical to that of an agitated mallard being drowned in a bucket of custard.

bucket fanny *n*. A spacious or roomy vagina. *Tardis twat, cathedral, welly top*.

buckie *n*. *Scots*. Affectionate nickname given to the tonic wine traditionally produced for Glaswegian tramps by the monks of Buckfast Abbey, Devon.

buckle bunny *n*. *US*. A *cock*-hungry *bird*.

buddy breathing *1. n*. In SCUBA diving, of two divers to share a mouthpiece in an emergency situation, taking it in turns to suck on the same oxygen supply. *2. n*. In *jazzular cinematography*, of two actresses to share a genital, taking it in turns to suck on the same *spongle* supply.

budget spunk *n. medic*. The fluids that a gentleman expels after having a *walnut whip*.

budgie smugglers *n*. Extremely tight gentlemen's bathing trunks.

budgie supping *v*. The act of pitiful beer drinking performed by men who aren't used to it, eg. a terrified Tony Blair pecking at a pint for the benefit of TV cameras in Sedgefield Labour Club.

budgie's tongue *n*. Descriptive of the female erectile bit, particularly when her *fanny* has climbed a little plastic ladder to ring a bell.

budmiser *n*. The unusually quiet member of a lad's night out who waits until he has downed four rounds of drinks before revealing that he has come out without any cash.

buff, to *v*. The removal of the *poo*/sweat mix which accumulates in a chap's *arse cleft* during a long drinking session, or perhaps when moving filing cabinets down a fire escape on a hot and humid day, by the vigorous application of copious amounts of *bumwad*.

buffage *n*. *US*. Highly offensive and sexist term used by women to describe men. *'Hey girls, check out the buffage in here.'*

buffeting *n*. The disturbing half-gulping, half-choking carry on that precedes a *psychedelic yawn*. A *frogs' chorus*.

buffet slayer *n*. A female *lard of the manor*. A lady with a penchant for eating more than her fair share of free food.

buffing *n*. *Gusset typing*. The act of female masturbation.

buffty *n*. *Scot*. Gay fellow. A *Gordon*.

BUFFY *1*. *n. prop*. That tasty piece of young *blart* who fights vampires on BBC2. *2*. *acronym*. The complete opposite of *1*. A Big Ugly Fat Fucking Yeti. A lady who's been beaten senseless with the *nice personality stick*.

bugger *1*. *n*. He who pokes animals, *arseholes* or animals' *arseholes*. A *berry*. *2*. *v*. To break or damage. To *fuck*. *3*. *exclam*. A cry of dismay. *'I'm afraid you have lung cancer, and it's spread into your lymph nodes' 'Bugger!'*

bugger's grips *n*. Sideburns. Any tufts of facial hair on the cheeks. *Bugger's handles, face fannies*.

Bugner's eye *n*. Flapless female genitalia, resembling boxer Joe Bugner's closed-up eye in every fight he had.

build a log cabin *v*. To pass a series of sturdy stools.

builder's bum *n*. The protrusion of fat, sweaty *arse* cheeks above the sagging waist of the jeans. Common among builders, council workmen and top fashion designer Alexander McQueen. *Bricky's crack, Dagenham smile*.

bukkake *1*. *n*. Saucy carry on whereby a load of randy blokes *tip their filthy concrete* onto a delighted *plasterer's radio*. From the noun form of the Japanese verb bukkakeru, meaning 'to dash water'. *2*. *adj. Jap*. Descriptive of dishes, such as bukkake-udon and bukkake-soba, where fresh soup-like toppings are poured on top of noodles. *3*. *adj*. In Britain, descriptive of dishes about to be served to *'Sunday Times'* food critic Michael Winner, such as soup and macaroni cheese, into which a group of kitchen employees *empty their nuts*.

bulimia amnesiac *n. medic*. One suffering from a condition whereby they binge eat, then forget to throw up. A *salad dodger, lard arse*, one who is a martyr to their glands.

bull *abbrev*. *US*. BS.

bulldog chewing a wasp *sim*. Descriptive of a lady's face that does not conform to conventional ideals of beauty. Also *bulldog licking piss off a nettle, welder's bench, stripper's clit*.

bulldog eating porridge *sim*. Poetic term describing a *lady's bodily treasure* in the aftermath of an act of love. *'When I'd finished with her, she had a fanny like a bulldog eating porridge, I can tell you.'*

bulldog's tail *n*. A *turtle's head*.

bulldyke *n*. A butch, masculine or aggressive *lezza*. *Diesel dyke*.

bullet-proof vest *1*. *n. milit*. Armoured clothing designed to minimise injury from incoming gunfire. Usually worn by the military in conflict zones. *2*. *n*. Reinforced clothing designed to minimise the impact of outgoing nipples. Usually worn by females in cold conditions.

bullet train *n.* A *ride* that is over far too quickly.

bullfruit *n.* A *tailgunner* who is a bit *rock.* A canny hard *puff.*

Bullimore *n. prop.* An extremely buoyant bit of *cack*, which refuses to drown. Named after extremely buoyant round-the-world yachtsman Tony Bullimore, who spent three days being lashed by storms under his capsized boat.

bull queen *n.* A large butterfingered prison inmate who cannot keep hold of the soap in the shower, and who instructs other, smaller, prisoners to bend over and pick it up for him. Then he sticks his *cock* up their *arse.*

bullshit *1. n. Feeshus* of male cattle. *2. n.* Rubbish, nonsense, *bollocks*. *3. v.* To lie, deliberately mislead, talk rubbish to. *'Don't you bullshit me now, you hear, bitch, or I'll cut yo' jive-ass face wide open.'* (Sir Neville Chamberlain to his wife, after she informed him that Hitler had invaded Poland).

Bully's special prize *1. n.* A speedboat. *2. n.* An extra large, beefy *shit. 'I'd give it ten minutes before you go in there, Your Majesty. I've just won Bully's special prize.'*

bum *1. n.* Arse, bottom, *poop-chute*. *2. n. US. Harold Ramp, pan handler.* A homeless person. *3. v.* Of cigarettes, to scrounge, scavenge. *4. v.* To *bott. 5. adj. US. legal.* Of *raps*, to be unjust, unfair. *6. n.* Trebor mint preservation apparatus.

bum bandit *n.* A robber, outlaw or highwayman who steals people's bottoms.

bum bar *n.* A richly-textured item of arse chocolate. *'Take the helm, Captain Hardy, I'm off down the poop deck for a bum bar.'*

bum baubles *n. medic.* Big, round, shiny *farmers* that your missus and the doctor can see their faces in.

bum beaver *n.* An *arse* where the *cress* has grown out of control. A *botty beard*, a *DLT.*

bumblebee dance *1. n.* Dance performed by bees in which they shake their abdomens to indicate to other members of the hive in which direction the pollen lies. *2. n.* The waggling of the buttocks in order to dislodge a reluctant *geetle* from the *dot.* A *logarhythm.*

bum brake *n.* The *nipsy.*

bum chain *n.* A rather intimate version of the Conga, danced around the streets at the end of a gay party.

bum chums *n.* Primary school term for any two boys who always sit next to each other.

bum cigar *n.* In after dinner conversation, a stool. *'Well, if you'll excuse me ladies, I think I shall retire to the bathroom and light a bum cigar.'*

bum conkers *n.* Shiny, brown, spherical agglomerations which hang off the *arse*, and can be baked in the oven or soaked in vinegar.

bumcraft *n. Uphill gardening, cable laying, stepping on ducks.* The wholesome enjoyment of all things *bum.*

bum crumbs *n. Kling-ons* which have ceased to cling on. Usually found in the bed or in the gusset of the *trolleys.*

bumdruff *n.* The *anal scurfage* and general buttock effluvium left on the back of the *bog* seat after one has been for a *digestive transit.*

bum drummer *n.* A homosexual

male.

bum fluff *n*. Risible pubescent attempt to grow a moustache.

bumfoolery *n*. Light-hearted action centred loosely around the *Bleep & Booster*. *'Carry On'* film-style *poovery*.

bum goblin *n*. A gnarled, malevolent *turd* that jumps out from behind you, casting a painful spell on your *ringpiece*.

bum grapes *n*. Painful, juice-filled, seedless fruit which grow well in the moist, shady regions of the *Khyber Pass*.

bum gravel *n*. A scree-like accumulation of anal detritus found in the bed after one has *raked one's arse out*.

bum gravy *n*. Diarrhoea, *rusty water*.

bum jumble *n*. Bits and bobs of excrement. *'Fucking hell, Brendan. Paula's left some bum jumble in the road again.'*

bummange *n*. A light, fluffy *arse* dessert. *Anal delight*.

bummer 1. *n*. One who *bums*. 2. *n*. US. A disappointing situation.

bummocks *n*. The buttocks of the bum.

bummy mummy *n*. A *milf* who could well benefit from having her *back doors* kicked in. A *milb*.

bumnugget *n*. A *number two*, consisting of an accretion of many smaller *number twos*.

bumpies *rhym. slang. Fun bags*. From bumpy bits = *tits*.

bum rope *n*. Shit. *'Has anybody seen the Exchange & Mart? I'm just going to cut some bum rope.'*

bumscare *n*. Severe pressure in the lower abdominal region prior to a controlled explosion.

bumshee *n*. A blood-curdling howl

of anguish coming from a lavatory cubicle.

bum sink *n*. The toilet.

bumsong *n*. A long, tuneful and mellifluous *fart*.

bum spuds *n*. Faecal tubers. Human stools.

bumtags *n. Dangleberries*.

bum tongue *n*. A large piece of *shit* hanging from *Dot Cotton's mouth* just before it licks the bowl.

bum vinegar *n*. The sweat found between the *arse* cheeks in general, and in particular during or after exercise. *Sarsehole*.

bumwad *n*. Toilet tissue.

bung hole *n*. The vagina.

Bungle's finger *n*. A short, stocky *turd*, named after the ursine simpleton from the 70s children's show *'Rainbow'*.

bun in the oven, to have a *v*. To be pregnant, *up the stick, in the club, in trouble*. *'Guess what love. I've got a bun in the oven.' 'That's nice. Is my tea ready yet?'*

bunion ring *n*. An old lady's *jacksie*.

bunko booth *n*. Paul Daniels's *shithouse*. A lavatory cubicle.

bunk up 1. *n*. A utility poke. *'Darling, you look beautiful tonight. Any chance of a bunk up?'* 2. *n*. Assistance in climbing. *'Shit. I'm so pissed I can't get onto the bed. Any chance of a bunk up?'*

bunk-up badge *n*. A love bite, usually found on really ugly people's necks to prove they have a love life. A *hickie*, a *bub*, a *shag-tag*.

bunnet brie *n*. Scot. McHelmetdale. *'Whit's yon stink, paw?' 'It's oor Wullie's bunnet brie, maw.'*

bunny-boiler *n*. A determined woman who misinterprets a one-off drunken *scuttle* as the overture to a deep and lasting relationship, then tries to win your affections when you go back to the missus by boiling your kids' pets.

bunny rub *n.* A *tit wank, Bombay roll.*

buns *1. n.* Regional variation of *baps.* *2. n. US. Ass* cheeks.

bunting *n.* Church fete-style strings of *jizz* looped around a *grumble flick* actress's face.

Burberry apes *n.* Designer-clad football hooligans.

Burberry shitbomb *n.* The delightful smell of perfume in the water closet after one's girlfriend or wife has been in to *drop the kids off at the pool.* Air freshener on lead guitar and vocals with excrement on bass and drums.

burbulence *n.* The uncomfortable alimentary rumbling which precedes the breakage of wind. *'Over Nova Scotia I finished the last of my egg sandwiches. Half an hour later I hit a pocket of burbulence, and had to fasten my seat belt and extinguish all lights.'* (from *'My Flight Across the Atlantic'* by Amelia Earhart).

burglar's dollop *n.* An episode of trouser soiling through fear or nerves. *'Iain Duncan-Smith takes the stand for his keynote address to the Blackpool Conference. It's a real burglar's dollop moment for the Tory leader.'* (Andrew Marr, *'BBC News 24'*).

burial at sea *n.* The dignified delivery of a stool, without *splashback.* The opposite of a *depth charge* or *belly flopper.*

burly *n. Bum wipe,* toilet paper, *chocolate shark bait, turd tokens.*

BURMA *acronym.* Secret code used on military correspondence -

Be Upstairs Ready My Angel.

burn bad powder *v. arch. milit.* Of *trouser trumpetry,* to *light a tyre,* emit a *fyst.*

burn out the arse clutch *v.* To fail to avoid defecating into one's *hoggers* whilst standing up having a *piss.*

burnt tyre *n.* An acrid, black, semi-vulcanised *Peter O'Toole* passed through the *back body* following a night on the Guinness.

burp the worm *v. Bash the bishop.*

burtains *n. medic.* labia majorcas. *Gammon flaps.* From the contraction of beef + curtains.

bury a quaker *v.* To dispense with the contents of one's rectum. *Crimp one off,* release a payload from the *bomb bay.*

bury the hobbit *v.* To lose *Bilbo Bellend* in the *wizard's sleeve.*

bus driver's knob *n. medic.* A state of almost permanent semi-priapism suffered by bus drivers who sit on a vibrating seat all day, eyeing up female passengers. A long lasting *semi-on.* A *Varney's teacake.*

bush *n. Gorilla salad, ladygarden, mapatasi.* Female pubic hair.

bushcraft *1. n.* Survival techniques employed in the Australian Outback. *2. n.* Recreational techniques employed in the *Tasmanian Outfront.*

bush meat *n.* Meat found under *bushes.*

bush pig *n.* A slightly more polite term for a *swamp hog.*

bush tents *n.* Ladies' *knickers.*

bushell *1. n.* A measure of hay. *2. n.* A hairy *cunt.*

bushman's hankie *n. Aus.* Term given to the process whereby mucus is expelled from the nose by placing a finger over a nostril and blowing. Popular amongst professional footballers. A *single barrelled snot gun.*

bushmonk *n.* A saucy chap who hides or secretes himself in an item of shrubbery for the purposes of *boxing the Jesuit,* especially near the bowling green in Heaton Park, Newcastle upon Tyne.

bushtucker *n.* Anything on the menu when *eating out* in Tasmania.

bushtucker challenge. *n.* Particularly unpalatable *hairy fish and chips.*

busker's hat *n.* The pocketful of change left over from a night *on the lash,* that feels like about £12, but when emptying it into one's hand to buy Lucozade the next morning, turns out to be about 36 pence worth of 1 and 2 pees.

bust off *v.* To masturbate.

butcher's daughter 1. *n.* A woman who has had unlimited access to the pasty counter. A *salad dodger.* 2. *n.* A woman who has had more than her fair share of *sausages,* eg. her late Royal Highness, Princess Margaret. A *slapper.*

butcher's dishcloth *sim.* Descriptive of the *drip tray* of a lady's knickers when *the fleet is in.*

butcher's dog, to lie like a *sim.* Descriptive of the bedtime arrangements of a married man. To sleep within reach of the *beef* whilst forbidden to touch it.

butcher's dustbin *n.* A sight grimmer than a *butcher's window.*

butcher's kiss *n.* Evidence left on the bedsheet that a fellow has been *doing it* to his wife during *cricket week.*

butcher's string *n.* Skimpy underwear on a fat lass.

butcher's turd *sim.* Descriptive of

the richness of something. *'Do have some more gateau, Mr. D'Arcy.' 'Well perhaps just a little slice, Mrs. Bennet. It's as rich as a butcher's turd.'* (from *'Pride and Prejudice'* by Jane Austen).

butcher's window *n.* An appetizing display of female genitalia.

butfer *n.* An amusing term for the female perineum. The *carse,* the *tinter. 'NORFOLK: Anon, Sir. She has the most agreeable butfer. BISHOP: The butfer, my liege? Wherefore is it called thus? NORFOLK: Why, Sir, butfer that, thou wouldst be in the shit.'* (from *'The Merry Readers' Wives of Windsor'* by William Shakespeare).

butler in the pantry *n.* A polite *turd* which knows its place, remaining below stairs, occasionally coughing discreetly until summoned.

butler's cuff *n.* A tightly-buttoned vagina, the opposite of a *wizard's sleeve.* A *fanny like a mouse's ear.*

butler's revenge *n.* A silent but deadly *fart.*

butler's ringpiece *adj.* Descriptive of something that is nipping clean. *''What can you see, Holmes?' I expostulated, as the great detective peered into his microscope. (I need not remind you of how in the past, he had solved the mystery of the Pope's cap when he found gibbon's tooth marks on the cardinal's walking stick.) 'I'm examining the handle of this dagger of unusual oriental design in the hope of finding a speck of tobacco, only available from one shop in London, or a hair from a rare species of Patagonian chinchilla,' He replied. 'However, I fear our murderer has wiped it as clean as a butler's ringpiece.''* (from *'The*

Brown Hatted League' by Sir Arthur Conan-Doyle).

butt cutlet *n*. A wholesome organic *loaf* cooked up in the *dirt bakery*. A vegetarian's *turd*.

butter your cheeks *v*. To *fart* and *follow through*.

buttered bun *n*. A well-used *snatch*. A *box of assorted creams*.

butterface *n*. A woman with a great figure, but the face of a darts player's wife. From the phrase 'A good body, but her face...' A *bobfoc*.

buttflood *n*. The *squirts*, the *Earthas*.

butt nuggets *n*. *Annabels*.

buttock broker *n*. A controller of prostitutes, a pimp. A *titty farmer, pussy farmer, gash baron*.

buttock hall *n*. *Meat market*. Pub or club frequented by *slappers*.

buttock jig *n*. A close horizontal dance that takes place after chucking out time.

button *n*. *Clitty*. The *devil's doorbell*.

button groove *n*. *Hairy axe wound*, the *snapper*. The vulva.

button view *n*. The tantalising sneak-peak of a woman's *ta tas*

and/or *titpants* viewed through the gap in between the buttons of her shirt or blouse.

butt plug *n*. A medical appliance used to prevent water from the bath going up your *arse*.

butt slammers *n*. *US*. Members of the gay community. *Turd burglars*.

butt sneeze *n*. *US*. *Fart*.

butt's fizz *n*. Celebratory *bubble poo*.

buy a headache *v*. To purchase a strong alcoholic beverage.

BVH *abbrev*. Blue Veined Hooligan. A hard, six-inch tall, one-eyed, skinhead.

BWR *abbrev*. Beeps When Reversing. Code used between men to identify, yet save the feelings of, a lady who has failed to achieve the correct level of thinness. A *barge arse*, a *double sucker*.

Byker plug *n*. An anally-inserted wad of *bog paper* reputedly favoured by habitual drinkers of Newcastle Brown as a means of preventing spontaneous bowel evacuations.

Byker tea cake *n*. A *Glasgow kiss*. A head butt.

Cc

cabbage fart *n.* An *old dog's alarm clock.* A *fart* that smells of rotting vegetation.

cabbage gas *n.* Naturally-occurring renewable fuel used to power *Dutch ovens.*

cabbage *n. coll.* Girls, *totty, blart.* 'What-ho, Jeeves. I've just been down to the Pink Flamingo club. Never seen so much cabbage in all my born pecker.' (from 'Achtung, Jeeves', by PG Wodehouse).

cabbie's doorbell *n.* A car horn, used to inform a street that their neighbour's 3.00am taxi has arrived.

cab hookers *n.* Taxi drivers who walk the streets outside nightclubs in the early hours soliciting for business.

cable laying *n.* The excretion of solid stools.

cab man's rests *rhym. slang.* Bristols, thrupenny bits.

caboose *n.* The *anchor man* in a *bum train. Lucky Pierre's* rear attendant.

cacafeugo 1. *n. prop.* A Spanish ship captured by Sir Francis Drake on March 1st 1579. 2. *n. Shit fire.* Red hot *squirts*, often experienced following a delicious curry from the Curry Capital, formerly the Rupali Restaurant, Bigg Market, Newcastle upon Tyne.

cack 1. *n. Shit*, excrement, *feeshus.* 2. *v.* To *papper*, usually one's *trolleys.* Also *cacka, cak.*

Cadbury alley *n. Bourneville Boulevard.*

cafe hag 1. *n.* A popular brand of decaffeinated coffee. 2. *n.* A *fit* woman whom, upon returning to your flat for coffee following a night out, looks neither *fit* nor womanly under the harsh fluores-

cent lights of one's kitchen whilst waiting for the kettle to boil.

cajooblies *n. Oomlaaters.*

cake detector *n.* A portly person. One who does need to ask directions to the bakery. A *salad dodger*, a *piabetic*, a *double fare*, a *barge arse.*

call down for more mayo *v. Jack the beanstalk.*

call Huey *v.* To vomit, *puke.* Also *call Ralph, call Ruth.*

calve *v.* To have a difficult delivery on the toilet. To attempt to pass an exceptionally toublesome stool where, in extreme cases, it may be necessary to tie a rope around it and get someone to pull it out.

camel's foot *n. Twix lips.* See *beetle bonnet.*

Camillas *n.* The bowels. Named after equine-featured former Prince's *spunkbucket*, now her Royal Highness the Duchess of Cornwall and Queen-in-waiting Camilla Parker-Bowels.

camp *adj.* To be as butch as Kenneth Williams.

Campbell's condensed *n.* A small volume, double-strength *fart* which, when diluted with air, can feed a whole room.

can 1. *n. US. Bottom.* 2. *n. US.* A quantity of *Bob Hope, marijuana.* 3. *n. US.* Prison. 4. *n. US.* Toilet, *shithouse.* 'They put me in the can after I was caught in the can sticking a can up my can.'

canary killer *n.* A *fart* that smells like a 60s cokeworks.

cancer shop 1. *n.* A charitable retail outlet selling corpses' trousers, Mantovani records and damp, mouldy copies of 'Readers' Digest'. 2. *n.* A high street tanning studio.

cancer veranda *n.* The al fresco area

around an office door to which *snoutcasts* are exiled.

c and c *abbrev. Clips and cunts.* Generic term for any television programme consisting of nothing but clips from other televison shows/films/ads/videos interspersed with hilarious, insightful and profound comments from assorted *cunts* whose only reason for existing appears to be appearing on *c and c shows.*

candy floss *1. n.* A large, fluffy fairground snack which is impossible to finish, damages the teeth and invariably leaves one feeling slightly nauseous. *2. n.* A large, fluffy *bush* which is impossible to finish, damages the teeth and invariably etc etc.

cankle *n.* On a lady with a lovely personality, where the calf is indistinguishable from the ankle.

cannonball *v.* Of a fortunately flexible gentleman, to perform a *thirty-four and a halfer.* To administer *self-horatio.*

cannon wheels *n.* The testicles. *'Are you in yet?' 'Aye, I'm in up to me cannon wheels you cheeky cow.'*

can tan *n.* The healthy, bronzed skin tone achieved by gentlemen who sit outside all day, supping from tins of 9% lager. *Tramp's tan.*

captain *1. n.* Penis. *'Don't be shy, love. Go below deck and say hello to the captain.'* **to do a~** *2. v.* To display one's *buttocks* through the back window of a coach, usually to a couple of nuns in a Morris Minor. To do a *moonie.*

Captain Caveman *n.* A yodelling *biffer.*

Captain Hogseye *n.* Curly bearded seafarer with a shiny, bald, purple head who trawls in *cod cove.* And

spits a lot.

Captain Oates, to do a *v.* To altruistically leave the pub early when struggling with the pace, so as not to hold your fellow drinkers back.

Captain's pie *1. n.* Tasty *slice* caught fresh by Captain *Hogseye.* *Haddock pastie. 2. n. milit.* Of naval catering, that pie which belongs to the captain.

capuccino fanny *n.* When the *furry cup* has reached its maximum froth.

caramel keg *1. n.* A much-loved self-explanatory chocolate in a box of Cadbury's Roses. *2. n.* A lady with a *pint glass figure,* eg. her with the red face and the glasses who used to show off at the front of Les Dawson's Roly Polys tap-dancing troupe.

carbon dibaxide *n.* Chemical name for *arse gas.*

car bootylicious *adj.* Descriptive of those rough *bints* one sees in *saggy-arsed* velour tracksuits and *bingo clink.* Also *aldilicious.*

cardie muffins *n. Tits* of the sort you would expect a librarian to have.

cardinal's cap *n. medic.* A swelling and reddening of the *herman* brought on by chronic *bishop rage.* *Fireman's helmet.*

card table *n.* A position whereby a lady engages in simultaneous oral/vaginal pleasures with two gentlemen who, should they wish, could play a game of cards on her back. A frankly unlikely scenario. A *spit roast.*

cargle *v.* Of a *dirty lady,* to gargle with a gentleman's *erotic spendings.* Like they do. From *cum* + gargle.

cargoyle *n.* A lady with such *a lovely personality* that all dates with her are spent in the car to avoid the possiblity of being spotted in her company.

Carling darling *n.* A lady whose attractiveness only becomes apparent after one has had a few. A *ten pinter.*

carnival *n.* A sexual game where a woman sits on a man's face and he has to guess her weight.

carnival knowledge *n.* Biblical phrase meaning to have sex. *'And it came to pass that Mary was up the spout, yea though Joseph had not lain with her, and certainly had not carnival knowledge of her.'* (from *'St. Paul's Letters to the Gas Board'*, Chapter 6, vv. 3-5).

Carolgees' cuff *n.* Having one's *wanking spanner* wrist deep in a *biffer.*

car park, to *v.* To kick the *brad* out of someone. To *take them outside.*

car park karaoke *n.* A post-drink entertainment where women *pissed up* on Bacardi Breezers take to the *purple-headed microphone.*

carpenter's dream *n.* A sexually promiscuous woman. From the fact that she is 'flat as a board and easy to *screw.*' A *boot.*

carpet duster *n.* A dense, heavier-than-air *fart* which forms a thin layer over the whole floor surface.

carpet muncher *n.* A lady who enjoys *gorilla salad*, but turns her nose up at *meat and two veg.*

carpet tiles *rhym. slang.* Haemorrhoids.

carrot knackers *n.* Affectionate term for a ginger-haired fellow. *'Oi, carrot knackers. There's a picture of you in a nazi armband on the front of the Sun.'*

carry out, to have a *v.* To *cack* oneself and have to walk to the nearest convenient spot for a *scrape out.*

carse *n.* The female equivalent of the *barse.*

Carsten Janker *rhym. slang.* A *wanker.* From the bullet-headed footballing kraut who taunted the crowd after putting Germany 1-0 ahead at the start of their 5-1 trouncing by En-ger-lernd, En-ger-ernd, En-ger-lernd! En-ger-lernd, En-ger-lernd, En-ger-lerrr-ernd!

cartman *n. medic.* A small *stool.* From the little shit in the popular children's cartoon series 'South Park'.

carwash *n.* View of the vagina whilst performing *cumulonimbus.* The hair of the *muff* looking like them big whirly brush things.

Casanova's rubber sock *n.* Condom, *blob, French letter, Coney Island whitefish.*

cashanova *n.* One who doesn't waste his money, but spends it wisely on prostitutes. A chap who pays for his love. A *punter*, a *John.*

cash crash *n.* A deliberate car accident intended to enrich the perpetrator by insurance.

cashpoint cripple *n.* See *video cripple.*

casting Churchill's reflection *euph.* A political impression involving a porcelain bowl with water in the bottom, your *arse* and a *bum cigar.*

cat 5 1. *abbrev. RAF.* Classification of an aircraft that is considered beyond repair following a crash. 2. *abbrev. RAF.* Classification of a *chod bin* that is considered beyond use following a *crap.*

catbab *n.* A snack containing unidentifiable meat of questionable provenance, usually sold out of the window of an old ambulance.

catcher's mitt *n.* A contraceptive diaphragm, a *fuck-plug*.

cat flaps *1. n.* Means by which a cute little pussy can enter the house. *2. n.* Means by which a *cock* can enter a cute little *pussy*. Labia minora, *beef curtains*.

Catford bunch *n.* An inexpensive floral offering to a ladyfriend, hand made from the flowers taped to the railings and lamp-posts of South London in memory of the recently-stabbed.

cathedral *sim.* Describing an over-sized vagina which is too echo-y for a satisfactory *organ recital*. A *bucket fanny*.

catholic tastes *1. n.* Wide-ranging interests, from the word 'catholic' meaning 'universal'. *2.n.* Narrowly-focused interests, specifically those pursued by certain members of the left-footed clergy which revolve principally around the contents of choirboys' surplices.

cat on the bed *euph.* Descriptive of the sensations transmitted through the mattress that a gentleman feels when his fellow bedlady is *playing the invisible banjo. 'Can you feel something, your Majesty?' 'It's just a cat on the bed, Mr. Fagan. Now go back to sleep.'*

cat scarer *n.* An unsuccessful hair-cut. A coiffure so bad that the victim's cat doesn't recognise them and runs off.

cat's face *n.* Mrs. Slocombe's *cunt*.

cattle *rhym. slang.* To engage in coitus. From cattle truck = *fuck*. Also *trolley* (& truck), *Friar* (Tuck) or *Russian* (duck).

cat with a strawberry-flavoured arse, like a *sim.* Descriptive of the happy demeanour of those who cannot believe the extent to which Heaven appears to have smiled upon them, eg. A rollover lottery winner, a dog with two *cocks* or whichever ne'er-do-well is currently *banging* Charlotte Church. *'Ever since I heard that Sir Mark Thatcher might get 15 years in prison, I've been walking round like a cat with a strawberry-flavoured arse.'*

caught white handed, to be *v.* To lose a game of *rushin' roulette*.

cauliflower *1. n.* Sex. *'Hey! Your missus gave me a bit of cauli-flower while you were at work last night.' 2. n. 18thC.* Lettuce.

cauliflower biff *n. medic.* A *clout* that has had a right good *banging*. A lady rugby player's *fanny*.

cauliflower cheese *n. Smegma.*

cavalier *n.* An uncircumcised penis. With a big feather stuck in the top.

cavalry caviar *n.* A highly-prized, piquantly-flavoured salty delicacy, traditionally served in armed forces circles on a digestive biscuit or cream cracker. *Officer's Mess.*

caviar *1. n.* Expensive delicacy made from fish periods. *2. n.* Web-speak for scatalogical *grumble*, apparently.

cedar burp *n.* A small outbreak of *chocolate thunder*. A *fart*.

cervix charge *n.* The hidden costs incurred in the *getting over of one's leg,* eg. flowers, meal, taxi home, changing locks, etc.

CF Bundy *abbrev. medic.* Doctors' shorthand written on the charts of terminally ill patients. Completely Fucked But Not Dead Yet.

CGI *1. abbrev.* The City and Guilds Institute. *2. abbrev.* Cunt Gap Index. A measurement on a scale of finger widths of the size of a woman's *Toblerone tunnel*.

Chalfonts *rhym. slang.* Piles, *bum grapes*. From the town of Chalfont St. Gemerroids, Buckinghamshire.

challenge oneself *v.* To engage in a bit of *five against one*. To masturbate.

champagga *n.* A fight fuelled by expensive beverages, as opposed to Special Brew. A brawl one may see once in a blue moon outside a brasserie.

champagne corks *n.* Bullet-hard *nipples* that pop out of the *tit pants* with enough force to take your eye out.

champagne shit *n.* A sit down toilet visit where one strains for some time to *pop a cork*, but once it goes it is followed by a magnum of fizzy brown liquid. A *champoo*.

change ammo *v. milit.* To empty one chamber of the *mutton musket*, readying the firing piece for the next shot. To take a last minute *gypsy's kiss* prior to a *poke*.

change at Baker Street *v.* During intercourse, to decide to *play the B-side*. From the only station on the London Underground where it is possible to change from the Pink line (Hammersmith & City) to the Brown line (Bakerloo).

change lanes *v.* To switch, mid-romp from vaginal to anal penetration or vice versa. *'Just like when on the road, when on the job it is good practice to signal one's intentions before changing lanes so as not to take anyone by surprise.'* (from *'The Joy of Sex'* by Dr. Alex Comfort).

change rain *n.* A shower of coins which falls from the trouser pockets when a gentleman is attempting to undress quietly and not wake his slumbering wife.

chap *1. n.* The *charlie*. *2. v.* To gently slap your *chap* in the face of your sleeping wife, girlfriend or party guest, take a Polaroid photograph and leave it in a place where they are bound to come across it, eg. fridge door, car windscreen, internet.

chapel hat pegs *sim.* Large, erect *nips*. *Pygmy's cocks, Scammell wheel nuts, JCB starter buttons.*

chapkin *n.* A protective cloth placed over a fellow's stomach and chest in order to soak up any salty spillages which may accidentally occur for any reason whilst he is lying on his back.

chapstick *n.* An implement with which a lady moistens dry lips.

charity work *n.* The altruistic act of buying a drink for, or flirting with, an aesthetically challenged woman out of pity. *'Where are you off to, John?' 'I'm just going to go on the dance floor to do a bit of charity work with fat Lisa from accounts.'*

charlie *1. rhym. slang. Cunt.* From 'Charlie Hunt'. *'You look a right charlie'. 2. n. Showbiz sherbert. 3. n. Hampton Wick,* the penis.

Charlie Cairoli's hat *n.* A lady's *minge*, brimful of *spoff*. From the erstwhile clown's blancmange-filled bowler.

Charlie Dimmock's nipples *n.* Term used by vicars to describe the hat-pegs in their chapels.

charlie in the chocolate factory *n. Bolivian marching powder* snorted in a public *shithouse* eg. the *crappers* at the Groucho Club.

Charlie Potatoes *n.* One who labours under the misapprehension that he all that when he ain't. Someone who thinks he's the *bollocks,* eg. Richard Blackwood,

Chris Moyles. *'Look at that cunt swaggering about like he's Charlie Potatoes.'*

charlies *n.* 1970s *tits.*

charlies' angels *n.* See *tit fairies.*

Charlie two-dinners *n.* A gentleman whose glands eschew salads in favour of pies, sausages and more pies. A *double sucker.*

charms *n.* In British tabloid journalism, the breasts. Usually prefixed 'ample'.

charva cava *n.* Substandard *trampagne.* White cider.

charver 1. *v.* US. To have sex, *shag.* 2. *n.* Boy, lad, adolescent. 3. *n.* Aerosol-snorting, be-tracksuited *twocker, borstal boy, car radio removal mechanic.* 4. *n.* A 10-year-old mother of several *pastie babies.* Also, *charva, chav.*

chase the dragon 1. *v.* To 'snort' a syringe full of marijuana cigarettes through a burnt spoon. 2. *n.* To attempt to get a good whiff of one's own *fart,* in an attempt to acheive the ultimate high.

chasing the cotton mouse *adj.* To have the *painters in, flags out, surf the crimson wave,* be *up on blocks.*

chastity patch *n.* A small smear of excrement surreptitiously wiped on the back of one's girlfriend's neck before she goes on a lasses' night out, the aim of which is to deter any would-be suitors.

chauffeur's glove *n.* A tight-fitting *flunkey.* Possibly with three buttons on the back.

chav *n.* A member of the lower orders. The sort of person who would be unlikely to turn up on *'Ask the Family'* in the 1970s.

chavalanche *n.* A terrifying Burberry-clad cascade of *scratters.*

chavalcade 1. *n.* A town centre procession of souped-out, clapped-up Astras, Corsas and XR3is driven by a motley assortment of *scratters, neds, pogs, ratboys* and *Burberry apes.* 2. *n.* A pram-pushing convoy of the above on their way to Greggs.

chavellers' cheques *n.* Giros.

chaviar *n.* Supermarket own-brand 'value' baked beans.

chavrolet *n.* Urban underclass motor vehicle, normally a lower-end production model souped up to *fuck* with alloy wheels, blue downlights, spoilers, tinted glass, laughably loud sound systems etc.

cheapies *n.* Schoolboy sexual thrills. *'Miss Pollard bent down to pick up the chalk and gave William his cheapies.'* (from *'William Stirs Below'* by Richmal Crompton).

chebs *n.* *Tits, norks, headlamps.* Breasts.

check the oil *v.* To put one's *cock* in some bird's *dirtbox* before pulling it out, inspecting, it and wiping it with a cloth.

check the roast *v.* To see if what you've been baking is ready to come out. To go for a *shit.*

cheddar apple *n.* A very large, cheesy *bell end.*

cheek flapper *n.* A *fart* which registers highly on the *brap scale.* A *clapper rattler,* a *drive on the cats' eyes.*

cheese cracker *n.* A savoury, pungent *custard tart.* An air *snack* rather than a *buffet.*

cheese-cutter *n. medic.* A rogue *pube* caught in the *fiveskin,* whilst still attached to the body. Results in two-fold agony; it simultaneously cuts into *Captain Picard's head* whilst trying to tear itself out at the root.

cheesepipe clingfilm *n*. Condom, *rubber Johnny*.

cheesepipe *n*. The tubular organ that secretes *chucky cheese*.

cheese ridge *n*. The fertile area of the *cheesepipe* where *knob cheese* is matured for weeks and months. The *brim* of the *lid*.

cheese whistle *n*. The marvellous musical instrument kept in a fellow's tweeds.

cheesy wheelbarrow *n*. A self-explanatory sexual position utilised by two *uphill gardeners*.

cheezer *n*. That which is a cross between a *chick* and a *geezer*, eg. Julian Clary or Richard Branson.

chef's arse *n*. An uncomfortable, perspiring, smelly *bum cleft*. From the condition's prevalence amongst catering professionals, eg. Gordon Ramsay, Anthony Worrall-Thompson and Nigella Lawson.

chef's special sauce *n*. *Spunk*. *'Here is your steak, Mr. Winner. And chef wanted you to know that he enjoys your Esure adverts so much, he's put you an extra helping of his special sauce on there.'*

Chelmsley Wood foreplay *n*. Any form of domestic violence or spousal abuse. Named after the Chelmsley Wood area of Solihull, West Midlands, which is known to be somewhat rough.

Chelmsley Wood lie detector *n*. A West Midlands Police Force truncheon.

Chelmsley Wood pill *n*. Anal sex. *UTBNB*. One up the bum, no harm done. A *Colchester condom*.

cheps *n*. *Chebs*.

Cherie Blair *n*. A mouth conducive to group fellatio. A *Carly Simon*, a *three-dick gob*.

Cherie Blair's cake hole *n*. A strangely convoluted, and frankly scary *fanny*.

cherry *n*. An intact *virgin string*. One that has not been *popped*.

cherry boy *n*. A crimson, hormone-filled adolescent male with an intact *virgin string*.

chest furniture *n*. *Tits, hooters, sweatermeat*.

chestnuts *n*. *Stits, juglets*.

chest pillows *n*. *Chebs* again.

chest tuners *n*. The symmetrical dials on a lady's *frontage* that enable a gentleman to find Radio Luxembourg. *Nips*.

Chewbacca after a fight *sim*. Descriptive of a particularly untidy *biffer*.

Chewbacca's calling *exclam*. A long, protracted *fart* similar to the strangulated guttural mewings of the famous *'Star Wars'* dog.

Chewbacca's growl *n*. The involuntary shrieks and groans released when one passes a *bum spud* as *wide as a footballer's tie knot*.

chewie *n*. An act of *horatio*, a *sucking off*, a *gobbie*.

chewing a toffee *v*. During perambulation, descriptive of the unpleasant sensation of anal chafing and squelching following insufficient wiping of the *freckle*.

chewing on a brick *v*. Of *logs* and *logging*, that desperate point when the *turtle's head*, and indeed *shoulders* protrude, and the *arse* is left *'chewing on a brick.'*

Chicago shuffle *n*. A sexual act whereby a lady traps a gentleman's *member* under her arm before shuffling a pack of cards. A *Las Vegas bagpipe*, an *Monte Carlo musclefuck*.

chichis *n*. *Mex*. *Tits*, breasts.

chicken *n*. Young gay male. A *botter's apprentice*.

chickenhawk *n*. The time-served *botter*, to whom several *botter's apprentices* are apprenticed.

chicken skin handbag *n*. Scrot, nadbag.

chicken wings *n*. *medic*. The anatomical spare skin underneath the upper arms of a *Duchess of Giblets*, so called as they resemble the contents of a KFC Zinger burger. *Bingo wings*.

chill the husband's salad *v*. Of a lady, to position herself such that a cold blast from the air conditioning goes up her skirt, thus keeping her *lettuce* crisp and fresh. The opposite of *warming the husband's supper*.

chimney sweep 1. *n*. A soot-covered man who cleans your chimney. 2. *n*. A soot-covered man who *bangs* you up the *dirtbox*.

chimney sweep's brush *n*. Dick Van Dyke's penis.

chimping *n*. *Spanking the monkey* whilst grinning from ear to ear. And having a cup of PG Tips.

chimp oneself red *v*. To furiously *relax in a gentleman's way*, to have *one off the flipper*.

chimps' fingers *n*. Particularly dry, thin stools, often with distinct knuckles. *'Twenty six days at sea, and the men are wracked with stomach cramps. Regular bowel motions are naught but a memory. I myself have not passed solids for nigh on two weeks, and that was but a couple of chimps' fingers 200 miles SSE of Christmas Island.'* (from *'The Journal of William Bligh'*, 1765).

chin airbag *n*. A phantom double chin on a non-fatty. Usually associated with pissed, impromptu group photographs on a night out, especially common late on during wedding receptions when wearing a collar and tie and leaning slightly backwards. A *pelican's beak*. *'Fucking hell! It's a great photo of everybody, but look at me! Looks like my chin airbag has gone off.'*

Chinese algebra, harder than *sim*. Descriptive of the magnificent tumescence of a right *diamond cutter*. *'You're a lucky lady tonight, love. This bugger's harder than Chinese algebra.'*

Chinese fire drill *n*. A scene of utter disorder and pandemonium. *'Emergency services were today called out to the Dover branch of Netto after staff reduced to price of own brand baked beans to 1p a tin. In the Chinese fire drill that followed, 17 people were trampled to death and another 68 were detained in hospital suffering crush injuries'.* (*'BBC News 24'*, Jan 3rd).

Chinese firework *n*. The *cock* of a *one pump chump*, ie. one that *goes off* almost instantaneously.

Chinese gravy *n*. Something that tastes foul. *'I was dining at the Y the other night and my fish supper tasted worse than Chinese gravy.'*

Chinese helicopter pilot *sim*. A bloke sitting up and operateing his *chopper*.

Chinese junk *rhym. slang*. Jitler.

Chinese mouse, hung like a *adj*. Opposite of *hung like an Arab stallion*.

Chinese singing lesson *n*. A *gypsy's kiss*. A *piss*.

Chinese tool *n*. A feeble penis, ie. one that is barely up to the job in hand.

chin rest *n*. *Duffy's bridge*.

chinstrap n. The small piece of skin which holds the *German helmet* safely in place. The *banjo*.

chin splash *n*. Condition caused by trying on a *pearl necklace* in a clumsy manner.

chin tinsel *n*. *Sloom*-based decorations dangling from the mandibles of a *messy eater*.

chin varnish *n*. *Sloom*.

Chip Pan Alley *n*. The sort of High Street which only contains chip shops interspersed with the occasional tattoo parlour.

Chipperfield *n*. A proper leathering you get off a bouncer for no good reason.

chippie's toolbag *n*. Of women's *bodily treasures*, the *labia majorcas*. The *beef curtains, mutton shutters, Deputy Dawg's ears*.

chippopotamus *n*. A generously-proportioned lady who honestly just eats like a mouse but whose glands scoff vast quantities of deep-fried spuds.

chip shovels *n*. The hands of a fat lass.

chips 'n' hame *phr*. *Scot*. The observed state of someone's failure to *score* and their resulting departure from the pub or club. *'Wee Angus has had nae luck the neet.' 'Aye, Hamish. It's chips 'n' hame for him.'*

chirp on *n*. The sort of good-natured, non-threatening erection that Kenneth Connor would have got in *'Carry On Cruising'* when Liz Fraser bent over to pick up a quoit. A *stiffy* that causes one to slap the back of one's neck.

choad *n*. A *cock*, specifically one that is wider than it is long.

chocnose *v*. A traditional end of party trick whereby a guest drops his trousers and rubs his *arse* on the nose of a comatose friend for the amusement of the other guests. *'August 3rd. Opening night party for 'Cavalcade' at The Savoy. Kit (Hassall), Gerty (Lawrence) and Fanny (Brice) were all in attendance. Ivor (Novello) passed out on the chaise longue after drinking far too much Bolly, and Jimmy (Clitheroe) chocnosed him, poor dear. How we laughed!'* (from *'The Diary of Noel Coward'*).

chocolate cha-cha *n*. Unlikely-sounding rooftop dance in the style of Dick Van Dyke, but performed by *chimney sweeps* of the *chocolate* variety.

chocolate chimney sweep *n*. A soot-covered man who is not interested in cleaning ladies' flues.

chocolate eclair *n*. A *Cleveland steamer*.

chocolate eye *n*. The *bumhole*.

chocolate fountain *n*. A spectacular, anal, upside-down firework ignited in the lavatory to celebrate having a belly full of beer and a dodgy curry the night before.

chocolate iceberg *n*. Giant *turd* sitting in the pan, nine tenths of which remains below the surface. A *growler*.

chocolate knob, to have a *v*. Of a fortunate fellow, to experience little or no difficulty in persuading ladies to perform *horatio*.

chocolate quilting *n*. The considerate lavatory practice of covering a floating *Bullimore* with a duvet of toilet tissue so as to avoid startling the next occupant.

chocolate sandwich *n*. A sexual act performed in the presence of Arthur Lowe in the film *'Oh Lucky*

Man!' involving a black man and two white lady strippers.

chocolate speedway *1. n. Bumhole, poop chute.* ~**rider** *2. n.* Purple-helmeted star of the *dirt track.*

chocolate starfish *n. Rusty sheriff's badge, Bovril bullet hole.* The *arse.*

chocolate thunder *n. Tail winds,* a *trouser typhoon.* Also *under thunder.*

chocolate wink *n.* A gentleman's cheeky treat for the special lady in his life whereby, when exiting the shower, he bends forward, reaches back and parts his buttocks, momentarily exposing his *nipsy.*

chod hop *v.* To move with increasing desperation from cubicle to cubicle in a public lavatory searching for an acceptable toilet to use, ie. one which is not covered in diarrhoea, has no *piss* on the seat, has a lock on the door, etc.

choir of angels *n.* A cloud-parting zephyr of heavenly *wind* that rises in pitch, timbre and volume, bringing a lump to the throat and a tear to the eye.

choke a brown dog *v.* To apply the *bum brake* too early. To nip a *shite* halfway through.

choke the chicken/goose *v.* To masturbate.

chommie *n.* The *barse.*

chooza *n. NZ.* A *choad.*

choozies *n. Aus.* Breasts.

chop *v.* To practice karate whilst holding a weapon in the hand. To *turn Japanese.*

chopper *1. n.* Penis. *'That (insert name of striker currently having a run of bad form) couldn't score in a brothel with a £50 note wrapped round his chopper.' 2. n.* Fancy orange bike that fat kids owned in the 1970s. *3. n.* Helicopter. *4. n.*

Axe. *5. n.* Nickname of anyone with the surname Harris.

choreplay *n.* Tiresome pre-sex ritual required by selfish women. *Frigmarole.*

chorus from Mama Jo's bongos *n.* An early morning *fart* that sounds like someone from *'Scooby Doo'* running on the spot before scarpering from the ghost. *Morning thunder.*

Christmas spirit *n.* An essentially altruistic approach to oral sex adopted by ladies who believe it is better to give than to receive. *'Henry rather liked his new bird as she displayed the Christmas spirit in abundance, noshing him off three times a day and never asking for anything in return.'*

chrome-dome *n. Slap head, baldy.*

chubblies *n.* Fat bird's *choozies.*

chuck flick *n.* An artistic cinematographic production that eschews plot and dialogue in favour of action, eg. *'European Cum-Bath 26'.* A *stick vid,* a *grumble flick.*

chuckle vision n.The stirring view of rolling *cuntryside* experienced whilst taking a breather during an act of *cumulonimbus* on a fat lass.

chuck out special *n.* Large quantities of leftover fried chicken that have been sweating all day, which are available for next to no money from USA Fried Chicken in Witney, Oxfordshire at around 2am.

chuck salt *v.* To masturbate oneself dry.

chuck up *v.* To vomit, *honk up, barf.*

chuck your muck *v.* To *lose your mess, spend your wad.* To ejaculate.

chuckies *n.* Balls.

Chuckle Brother *n.* Either of the

male participants in a *spit roast*. From the children's TV comedy northerners' catchphrase *'To you, to me.'*

chucky cheese *n.* Vomit-inducing tangy cheddar matured in unwashed *brims*.

chudleighs *n. Chuds, chebs, charlies, charms, chichis, choozies.* Ladies' *tits*.

chuff 1. *v.* To *pass wind, shoot a bunny rabbit. 'Oops! Best open a window vicar. I've just chuffed'.* 2. *n.* Vagina, lady's *front bottom*. 3. *n. zoo. Anus* of a gnat.

chuffage *n.* coll. A *rats' banquet, bangers and mash, Radcliffe's sleepers.* Railway track faecal detritus.

chuff chowder *n.* A pungent soup served as a first course when *dining at the Y.* Hopefully without croutons.

chuff mountain *n.* Surplus of *cabbage* at a party.

chuff muncher *n.* A *woman in comfortable shoes*.

chuff-nuts *n. Dangleberries.*

chuffdruff *n. Muffdruff.* Residual flakes of desiccated *mess* and *fanny batter* found on the *mapatasi.* Pubic equivalent of *mammary dandruff.*

chufflink *n.* A piece of over-elaborate *clitoral* ironmongery often sported by loose women in *bongo vids.*

chuftie plug *n. Cotton pony.* Tampon.

chug *v. Choke the chicken, spank the monkey, burp the worm.*

chugger *n.* A clipboard-wielding charity collector who stalks Britain's pavements wearing a luminous bib and relieving passers by of their valuables, loose change,

spare time etc. From charity + mugger.

chugnuts *n.* Extremely big piles. *'A cushion, Mrs. Bennet, a cushion! I fear the frivolities at Lady Marchmain's ball has brought down my chugnuts no end.'* (from *'Pride and Predudice'*, by Jane Austen).

chumbawumbas *onomat.* A rather predictable use of a pop group's name as slang for breasts. Also *Bananaramas* (penises), *Wurzels* (testicles) and *Bee Gees* (hairy twats).

chumblies *n medic.* Nuts, knackers.

chumley warning 1. *n.* The signal a gentleman gives to a fussy *nosher* to tell her that *Elvis is about to leave the building*. 2. *n.* The signal a lady gives to a *nosher* to warn him that she is about to *step on a frog*.

chunder *v. Aus.* To *chunk*.

chunderbirds *n.* Binge-drinking teenage girls full to the brim with *tart fuel* and screwtop wine, who stagger around parks and town centres vomiting and crying. *'It's seven pm on a Friday and Chunderbirds are GO!'* (voiceover from Police surveillance video footage of Chappelfield Park, Norwich on Fair night).

chunk *v.* To vomit. Also *blow chunks.*

Churchill bulldog *n.* An ugly, overweight *10-pinter.* After her resemblance to the TV Insurance advert canine. A girl who loves to say 'Oh, yes' in the back of a car.

churns 1. *n.* Breasts. 2. *n.* Testicles. 3. *n.* Seemingly any vessel containing white fluid.

chutney Chuckle brother *n.* A *dirty Sanchez.* Also *Stinky Selleck.*

chutney ferret *n*. A *chocolate speedway rider*.

chutney locker *n. medic*. The *bomb bay*, rectum. Also *date locker*.

cidercafe *n*. A town centre bench or war memorial from which *ciderspace* can be accessed.

ciderspace *n*. A virtual multidimensional world, accessible to tramps.

cider visor *n*. *Beer goggles* for the younger street drinker.

cigarbutts *n*. *JCB starter buttons, Bruce Lees*.

cigar clipper *1. n*. An exceptionally tight *clopper*. A *mouse's ear*, a *paper cut. 2. n*. The *nipsy*.

circle jerk *n*. A communal *hand shandy* session. A *milk race*.

cistern chapel *n*. The porcelain font where *Meatloaf's daughter* is baptised.

clabby *adj*. Exceptionally pink. Used to describe *bacon strips*.

clacker *1. n*. One half of a dangerous, finger-breaking 1970s toy. *2. n*. The *fanny*.

clackerbag *n*. A leathery receptacle for *clockweights*.

clacker lacquer *n. medic*. Shameful secretion from the *blip tap* up a lady's *snapper*. *Lovejuice, moip, fanny lube*.

clackervalve *n*. The *nipsy*, the *ringpiece*, the *arsehole*. *'Porphyria was powerless to resist. His eyes burned into hers like sapphires. His muscular arms enfolded her body as she felt herself being swept away in a whirlwind of passion. Tenderly, Sven lay her down on the ottoman, whipped off her scads and stuck his thumb up her clackervalve.'* (from *'The Lady and the Football Manager'* by Barbara Cartland).

clackweed *n*. Perennial pubic hair.

Clacton chinwag *n*. The oral intercourse that takes place between a man and a kneeling woman who has had a couple of bottles of *tart fuel*. A *blow job*.

clagnet *n*. A net-like tangle of *arse cress* which forms over the *freckle*, leading to a sensation similar to that felt when one defecates through a pair of fishnet tights. One would imagine.

clagnuts *n*. *Dangleberries, tagnuts*.

Claire Goosebumps *n*. Smashing *Gert Stonkers* of the type sported by the popular *'Casualty'* actress. *Tits* which are capable of *'Waking the Dead'*.

clamateur *n*. A naive male inexperienced in the workings of the fairer sex's *farmyard apparatus*. *'Honestly Jet, it was nothing. He had no idea what he was doing down there. He was a total clamateur.'*

clamchop *n*. The tasty cut of fish-like mutton found in a lady's knickers.

clam dunk *n*. A spectacular shot at the *furry hoop*. A *break for the border*.

clamembert *n*. Female equivalent of *helmetdale*. *Fanny cheese*.

clam jousting *n*. A *fanular* encounter between two ladies afflicted with lesbism. Also *velcro fastening*.

clamouflage *n*. Thick, impenetrable *bush* which makes the target impossibly hard to spot at first glance. The *pubes* on a *biffer*.

clam ram *n*. A *gut stick, cock*.

clam shandy *n*. A lady's version of a *hand shandy*. A few scales on the *invisible banjo*.

clam smacker *n*. A *bean flicker*.

clankers *n. onomat*. The same as

clinkers, only louder.

clap *n. medic.* Any sexually transmitted disease, but usually gonorrhoea. *Cockrot.*

clapometer *n.* Imaginary medical instrument used by doctors to diagnose the *clap*. *'Don't touch her. I hear she scores ten on the clapometer.'*

clappers 1. *n.* In *farting*, the buttocks. *'Christ! That one didn't half rattle the clappers.'* 2. *n.* That part of a bell like which a lady *goes*.

clapping fish *n.* Female genitalia.

Clara Dawes *n.* An extremely hairy *mott*. From the parts of the actress playing the part of Clara Dawes in the recent TV adaptation of *'Sons and Lovers'*.

claret mouse *n.* A *Dracula's tea bag.* A spent *jamrag.*

clarts *n.* Tacky excrement, such as would cling to the lavatory bowl above the water line rather than slip below the surface.

clarty goalmouth *n.* A *muff* one could lose a boot in.

Clattenburg *n.* Heavily-edited hardcore pornography ie. where it obviously *goes in,* but you don't see it. Named after the hapless referee in the famous Mendes goal incident, where it obviously went in, but he didn't see it.

claw, the *n.* The bizarre contortions of a semen-covered hand that a fellow is forced to employ in order to avoid spilling any *splinkle* onto his mum's soft furnishings whilst making his way to the toilet following a successful bout of *self help.*

claypit *n.* Source of the raw material for making *coil pots.* The *arse.*

clean the au pair's teeth *v.* To receive the oral sex.

clean workspace *n.* A shaven *fanny.*

clear the custard *v.* To have a long overdue *wank.* *'I've got ten minutes before I have to take mass. I'll just nip upstairs and clear the custard.'*

clems *n.* The *clockweights, swingers, nads, cods.* Testicles.

Cleveland steamer 1. *n.* A merchant cargo vessel operating on Lake Erie. 2. *n.* A sexual act much favoured by the Hun that doesn't bear thinking about. A *chocolate éclair.*

climb on *v.* The culmination of a romantic evening. *'Lavinia was powerless to resist. His eyes burned into hers like rubies. His strong arms enfolded her tender body as she felt herself being swept away on a tidal wave of passion. Then he dropped his trolleys and climbed on.'* (from *'The Lady and the Gentleman'* by Barbara Cartland).

clinkers *n. onomat. Aus.* Difficult to remove *poo* particles, *toffee strings, winnets, kling-ons, dangleberries, bum conkers.*

clit and run *n.* A light-hearted indecent assault whereby one makes a playful grab for *Captain Caveman's nose* followed by a swift getaway into a crowd.

cliterati *n.* A dazzling array of *grumble vid* starlets.

cliterature *n.* One-handed reading matter.

clitler *n.* A fashionable clitoral moustache, as seen on female *grumble* artistes who leave a daft little tuft. A *toothbrush muff.*

clitty litter *n.* Vaginal detritus in the *drip tray* of a lady's *dunghampers.*

clock *n.* One who swings like a pendulum do. A *happy shopper,* a *switch hitter, half rice half chips.*

'Birthdays: David Bowie - musician, artist, film actor and right fucking clock, 55.' (*'The Times'*, 8th Jan 2002).

clock springs *n.* Very strong, curly pubic hairs usually found around the *clockweights* or coiled tightly around the top of the *belltower*. Often found stuck onto bars of soap.

clockweights *n.* Large, metal, adjustable testicles that have to be *cranked* at least once every eight days.

clodge *n.* The vagina.

clogmaker's hammer, arse like a *sim.* Descriptive of the buttocks of a 33rpm gentleman who appears to be *banging* his ladyfriend at 78.

clopper *n.* A romantic term for the female genitalia. *'Ocarina was powerless to resist. His eyes burned into hers like topazzes. His strong arms enfolded her body as she felt herself being swept away on a hailstorm of passion. 'Take me, Abdul, take me', she gasped. 'I'm fizzing at the clopper''.* (from *'The Dowager and the Sheik'* by Barbara Cartland).

close the deal *v.* To *scuttle* a bird.

close-up pink *n.* Medically-explicit *cliterature.* Erotica that wouldn't look out of place in a gynaecology textbook.

clot mops *n.* Feminine napkins.

cloth tit *n.* The least far a gentleman can get in a sexual encounter with a lady. *Outside tops.* *'Did you fuck her?' 'No, I only got my cloth tit.'*

clout 1. *n.* Clunge. 2. *n.* South African lesbian rock band.

cloven hoof *n. Camel's foot, camel's mouth, camel's lips.* In fact, any part of a camel.

clowns' buckets, spunk *v.* Of single gentlemen who have spent the day *challenging themselves* repeatedly, to eventually conjure forth nothing more than a wince upon ejaculation.

clown's hat *n.* A *bald man in a boat.* A *clematis.*

clown's pie *n.* A very, very wet *clodge.* *'Finding ourselves alone in the shooting lodge at Balmoral, Her Majesty bade me descend to her ladygarden. After fifty years of widowhood, I found her to be be considerably aroused. It was like being hit in the face with a clown's pie.'* (from *'The Memoirs of Queen Victoria's Ghillie'* by John Brown).

clown's pocket *sim.* To describe the bigger, baggier and perhaps yellow and red checkered vagina. *'May I introduce my wife, Your Worship. She has a fanny like a clown's pocket.'*

clown's smile *n.* Facial make-up donned when performing at the *red ring circus. Mexican lipstick.*

clubbed seal, raw as a *sim.* The state of a bird's *nether pelt* after she's been *banged* senseless with a substantial *giggle stick.* *'Bacteria was powerless to resist. His eyes burned into hers like gallstones. His muscular arms enfolded her body as she felt herself being swept away by a Bex-Bissell of passion. Suddenly, the train whistle blew and she knew their stolen weekend of love was finally over. 'I wish you didn't of have to go back to the front,' she said, choking back her tears, 'but apparently World War One will all be over by Christmas.' Stephen laughed bitterly. 'It's hell out there, darling. But even if I don't make it all the way through to 1918, we'll always* have last night, won't we?' he said. 'You're not kidding,' winced Bacteria. 'Me poor clopper's as raw as a clubbed seal.' (from 'Birdlime' by Sebastian Faulkandles).

cludger n. A lower class lady from the northwest of England, specifically Bolton.

cludgy n. Shitehouse, lavatory, thunderbox.

clump n. coll. Blart, fanny, tussage. 'I tell you what, Mother Superior, this place is absolutely fucking crawling with clump.'

clumper n. The nipsy.

clumsy beekeeper, face like a sim. Descriptive of a lady with a lovely personality. She with a face like a stripper's clit.

clunge n. A clout, a furry hoop.

clusterfuck 1. n. A group of people unable to make a simple decision, e.g, friends standing on a pavement outside a pub wondering where to eat, or a group of PC World salesmen on a team-building course trying to construct a raft. 2. n. A gang bang.

coal hole n. Any grubby little aperture around the back of something. A popular entry point for burglars and tradesmen.

coal scuttle, polish the v. To indulge in a foul act of self-pollution, bleed the hydraulic system, stab the cat etc. To have a wank. 'Bless me holy father, for I have sinned. On Friday, I committed the sin of envy when my brother bought himself some new shoes. On Saturday I committed the sin of sloth when I fell asleep during the qualifying session for the Grand Prix. Then this morning I'm ashamed to say I had impure thoughts about polishing the coal scuttle over the bra pages of the Freeman catalogue.' 'Sorry my son, what was that again? I was just busy polishing the coal scuttle over the bra pages of the Freeman catalogue.'

coat hangers n. Large erect nipples that can double up as an emergency car aerial.

cob on n. A foul temper, usually displayed by werecows. A blob strop.

cobblers ryhm. slang. Bollocks. From cobbler's awls = balls.

cobs n. Nads, pills, pods. Testicles.

cock 1. n. Penis, willy, knob. 2. n. A person to whom a chirpy cockney wishes to speak, often prefixed by 'Wotcha...' 3. n. A gentleman chicken.

cock-a-doodle-poo n. The shit that, needing to come out, wakes you up in the morning.

cock-a-fanny n. The act of hiding one's wedding tackle between one's legs to give the appearance of having female genitals. Popularised by Captain Sensible and East German female shot-putters of the 70's.

cock block n. Shag slab, bed. 'I wouldn't mind lying that on me cock block.'

cock book n. Literature which encourages one to whip up a quick cheese-based white sauce.

cockbuster n. A video shop, or indeed work colleague, specialising in the commercial hiring of blueys.

cockchops n. pej. A pernicious, malicious, seditious fool. A fuckwit, an idiot. 'Armstrong: 'That's one small step for man, one giant leap for mankind.' (Beep) Aldrin: 'Oi, cockchops. That should have been 'one small step for A man.' I knew they should of let me go fog out the rocket.'' (from NASA transcript of Apollo 11 mission, 1969).

cock clamp *n.* A *'v' clamp*, a *mouse's ear.* A tight *muff.*

cock collar *n.* The *fiveskin.*

cock drops *n.* *Blueys.* Viagras.

cock duster *n.* A handlebar moustache of the sort sported by the leather-clad *'Village People'*-style *puddle jumpers* who people Richard Littlejohn's fevered imaginings. Also *scrotum tickler.*

cock eggs *n. medic.* *Clems, swingers, clockweights. Testicles.* Also *knob eggs.* *'Vasectomy is a simple routine procedure. The surgeon makes a small inscision in the scrotal sac, through which he severs the cock eggs from their clacker strings. All this is carried out under a local anaesthetic.'* (Family Planning Leaflet, The Marie Stopes Foundation).

cockfest *n.* A pornographic film featuring quantities of *skinclad tube.*

cock hair *n.* Imperial unit of measurement used in engineering, equivalent to 2.32 *gnat's cods.* *'It seems that the O-ring failed 45 seconds after take off, allowing a jet of superheated gas just a cock hair wide to penetrate the main solid fuel booster, leading to the loss of the Challenger.'* ('*NASA Official Accident Inquiry Report*', 1987).

cock heavy *adj.* Descriptive of a drinking establishment blighted with a serious lack of *blart.*

cock holster *n.* A romantic term for a lady's mouth. *'Felicity was powerless to resist. His eyes burned into hers like sapphires. His strong arms enfolded her tender body as she felt herself being swept away in a whirlwind of passion. Then, she knelt before him and he stuck his eight-inch charlie into her cock holster.'* (from *'The Officer and the Gypsy Duchess'* by Barbara Cartland).

cock in a top hat, sticking one's *v.* Unfulfilling *futtering* in a slack *snapper.* *'How was it for you, Mr. Deayton?' 'Like sticking my cock in a top hat, you whore. Now slag off.'*

cocking her into it *v.* The gentleman's art of cajoling a lady with whom he is sharing a bed into coitus by means of persistent and relentless nudging and frottering. To annoy a woman with one's genitals so much that she eventually lets one *on the nest.* *'She told me she had a headache, but I managed to cock her into it anyway.'*

cockjaw *n.* The open-mouthed expression adopted by porn queens after they've quaffed a gobful of *manpop.*

cock knocker *n.* A gentleman who *bangs* at the *back door.*

cock knot *n.* The machine head of the *one stringed banjo,* the *frenum.*

cockless pair *n.* A particularly athletic looking lesbian couple.

cock lodger *n.* An idle man who persuades a gullible single mum to let him move in and sit on her sofa all day watching DVDs in exchange for the odd *scuttling.*

cock mess monster 1. *n.* A *grumble flick* actress, transformed by a small fortune in *money shots.* A *plasterer's radio.* 2. *n.* A cryptozoological beast occasionally sighted floating round the bath after *playing up periscope.*

cock monkey 1. *n.* A lady who does a lot of jumping about, squealing and general circus-like activity in the *fart sack.* 2 *n.* A film set technician who keeps the gentleman lead erect during set changes, drug runs, *spunk* mopping etc. A *fluffer*.

cockney *1. n.* A pearly-buttoned, colourfully opinionated person born within the sound of Big Ben, who either drives a taxi or sells fruit on a market. *2. n.* A person of indeterminate gender. From *cock + fanny*.

cock nostril *n.* A term for the *Jap's eye* for the more politically correct.

cocknuckle *n.* The sixth knuckle, that always comes at the top of the deck in a *five knuckle shuffle*.

cockoholic *n.* One addicted to cockohol.

cock patience *n.* A game whereby one whiles away the hours with one's favourite *Gash 'n' Gary* mags arranged in a circle around oneself.

cockpit *n.* The piece of skin between the *devil's bagpipes* and the *German shepherd's winkhole*. The *barse*.

cock porridge *n.* Messy load fired from the *porridge gun*.

cock puppet *n.* A petite lady. A *throwabout*.

cock rock *1. n.* A variety of popular music performed by *rock poodles* such as *'Whitesnake'*, *'Van Halen'*, etc. *2. n.* The substance that *knobs* are made of that is able to go from marshmallow limp to diamond hard at the thought of a pair of *tits*.

cock rot *n. medic.* VD, a *dose*.

cock smoker *n.* A lady who doesn't mind a puff on one's *Whitehouse cigar*. A *fellatrix*.

cock snot *n.* Semen.

cock sucker *n.* A motorist who cuts you up.

cocksucker's doormat *n.* Facial hair

growth favoured by the ageing male attempting to hide his jowls. A goatee beard.

cock tease *n.* A woman who wears *fuck me shoes* and then changes into *fuck off slippers* when you get back to her place.

cockumentary *n.* A serious-minded factual film exploring issues surrounding the adult entertainment industry broadcast at 11 o'clock on Channel 5 in order to educate and inform the viewers. While they *wank*. A *masturmentary*.

cock venom *n.* Spaff, spodge, spooge, etc. *Spunk*.

cockwash *n.* Vagina. *'My charlie's absolutely filthy. I think I'll stick it through the cockwash on Sunday morning.'* See also *token for the cockwash, municipal cockwash*.

cockwasher *n.* A *fellatrix* who takes it to the *biffin bridge*. A *deep throater*, a *pork sword* swallower.

coco-pops *n.* *Winnets*, known briefly as Choco Krispies.

cocoa sombrero *n.* Mexican *brown hatter*.

coconut husk *n.* In erotic photography and nude police work, the soft mound of *clocksprings* which becomes visible when a lady *assumes the position*.

coconut minge-mat *n.* Pubic hair you could wipe your feet on.

cod *adj.* Extremely *swiss*. Fucking rubbish.

cod cove *n.* Fish mitten.

cods *n.* Balls. Often prefixed *'a kick in the'*.

cod's wetsuit, wetter than a *sim.* Descriptive of a woman's *bits and bobs* when she's *dripping like a fucked fridge*. Also *otter's pocket*.

coffee turtle *n.* The first *turd* of the

day, powered on its way by the first cup of Nescafe of the day.

coffin-dodger *n*. Affectionate term for an incontinent, elderly relative. An *oxygen thief*.

coitus interruptus *n*. *Lat*. Method employed by God to prevent the birth of *Meatloaf's daughter* whereby the Jehovah's Witnesses ring the doorbell just as you are laying the foundations of a *log cabin*.

coins of the realm *n*. Trouseral *piss spots* of various sizes sported by gentlemen leaving public house lavatories.

Colchester condom *euph. milit*. Anal sex, *one up the bonus tunnel*, as used by squaddies in the garrison town. *'Please be careful, Field Marshal'. 'Don't worry, sweet tits, I'll be using a Colchester condom when I meet you behind the skip.'*

cold tea bag *n*. The feeling one gets in one's underpants a couple of minutes after a badly-diagnosed *fart*.

collar and cuffs *euph*. Matching hair colour, up top and down below. *'See that blonde? Do you reckon her collar matches her cuffs?'*

colly wobbles *n*. The strange, unnerving feeling that one is being watched whilst having sex. Possibly by a *wanking* ex-Premiership footballer.

colon burger *n*. A *shit*.

Columbo's mac *n*. A rumpled *five-skin* that is much too long for the *one-eyed bobby* it covers. *Delaney's overcoat*.

Colwyn Bay *1. n*. Welsh seaside resort famous for its multi-storey Safeway's and its elephant-less zoo. *2. rhym. slang*. Homosexual.

'This is your cellmate, Lord Archer. Try not to drop anything on the floor, only he's a bit Colwyn.'

combustoflatulation *n*. Anal flame-throwing. *Pyroflatulation*.

come *1. v. Cum. 2. n. Cum*.

come in Tokyo *n*. To manipulate both a lady's breasts at the same time in the manner of a World War II radio operator. *Finding Radio Luxembourg*.

come like a bishop *sim*. Of a man, to ejaculate in an explosive style, as one would imagine someone celibate does every now and again.

command module *n*. *Bell end*, glans.

committee shitty *n*. A *motion* that is seconded after the paperwork is complete. A *council dump*.

community chest *n*. A pair of *tits* that the whole estate has had a go on.

compliment the chef *v*. To *drop one's guts* after a meal.

compose one's thoughts *euph*. Polite phrase often used by snooker commentators to describe the actions of players who leave the table in between frames. To defecate, take a *shit, drop the kids off at the pool, light a bum cigar, crimp one off* etc. *'It's all square in the Embassy World Snooker Championship finals and you could cut the atmosphere here at the Crucible with a knife. And as referee Len Ganley prepares the table for the all-important deciding frame, Ray Reardon's just leaving the arena for a moment to compose his thoughts. Let's hope he washes his hands after he wipes his arse.'*

con *n. Fr. Cunt, fanoir*.

con artiste *n. Fr*. A *cunning linguist, muff diver*, a *Jacky Danny*

Cousteau, a *puba diver*.

concrete donkey *n*. A *horse's handbrake*, a *diamond cutter*.

cones *n*. Pointy, orange, dayglo breasts found alongside the M25.

cones are out *euph*. ie. only one lane in use. *Rag week*.

conflatulations *n. interj*. A term of praise accorded one by one's friends following the *stepping on* of a spectacular *duck*.

congrafellation *n*. The act of giving a lucky lady an appreciative pat on the head after she has performed a decent *blowjob*.

conjaptivitis *n. medic*. Occlusion of the male urethral opening due to a deposit of ossified *spangle*.

conkers *n*. See *hairy conkers*.

conkers deep *adj*. To be in a state of total intromission.

conker water *n*. *Spangle, spooge, spadge, gunk*.

continental shelf *n*. Feature of foreigners' barbarian design *jobby engines*, providing a place where one's *royal decrees* can pile up to be admired before being flushed away.

convent porridge *n*. Hot, steaming *spunk* ladled out of a cauldron by a smiling Mother Superior. *Nuns' porridge, jizz*.

convicts' shuffle *n*. The 'chain-gang'-style gait one adopts when looking for *bumwad* whilst manacled by one's *grundies*.

convoy cock *n. milit*. A squaddie's *travel fat*.

cooch *n. US*. A Yankee *fanny*.

cooint *n*. A variation on the popular rude word *cunt*, used in the quaint picture postcard village of Barnsley, South Yorkshire.

cooking lager *n*. Utility pub booze. *Wallop*.

cooter *1. n. prop. US*. A character from *'The Dukes of Hazzard'*. *2. n*. The visible contents of Daisy Duke's shorts in the *'Dukes of Hazzard'*.

cooter cutters *n. US*. The type of shorts worn by Daisy Duke in *'The Dukes of Hazzard'*.

cop a feel *v*. To get one's *tops* or *fingers*. Or *tops and fingers*.

copper bolt *v*. A very heavy or dense *sweaty morph*. With a clockwise thread.

copper wire *n*. A stray pube appearing in a handful of loose change.

copy twat *n*. An acquaintance that always gets the same clothes, car, phone, bird etc. as oneself.

cordless bone *n*. A *bobby's helmet* without the *roll-neck* and *cheese-slicer* apparatus.

corgi *1. n*. A high class hound, such as those that accompany the Queen. *2. n*. A high class *hound*, such as the one that accompanies Prince Charles.

corked *1. adj*. Of wine, to be contaminated with bits which render it unpalatable. *'Mr. Winner's sent his 1978 Montrachet back. He says it's corked.'* *2. adj*. Of *spaff*, to be contaminated with bits which render it unpalatable. *'Mr. Winner's sent his soup back. He says the spunk in it is corked.'*

corks *1. n*. Nipples. *2. exclam*. 1950s schoolboy cry of surprise. *"Corks', cried Darbishire. 'I've just seen Matron's corks. Anyone for a daisychain?"* (from *'Jennings and the Sticky Sheets'* by Anthony Buckeridge).

corn *rhym. slang*. The *chopper*. From corn on the cob = *knob*.

cornbeef cudgel *n*. Short, thick *trouser stick* the 'taking up' of which relieves *gentlemanly tensions*, and so aids restful sleep.

cornbeef lighthouse *n*. Big thing that flashes to attract sailors.

cornbeef sandwich *n*. The contents of Daisy Duke's *cooter cutters*.

cornhole 1. *n*. *US*. Brass eye, ring, balloon knot. 2. *v*. To shove one's *cock* up the same.

corn on the cob *n*. A *spitroast*, where two gentleman revolve the lady in a shallow dish of melted butter.

corn on the nob *n*. A *niblet* on a *bottsman's lid*.

corybungo *n*. *Arse*, backside.

cosif *n*. *medic*. The *tinter*, the *taint*. The perineum. 'Cos if it wasn't there, her guts would fall out.

costume drama *n*. The frantic behaviour of a woman who cannot decide what to wear for a party.

cottage *v*. To visit a thatched public lavatory with climbing roses round the door looking for a bit of *Colwyn Bay* action.

cottage cheese pastie *n*. A well-*shagged fanny*.

cottage kex *n*. Type of gentlemen's trousers with an elasticated waist, enabling them to be lowered or raised at extremely short notice and with the minimum of fuss. Favoured by men who are *good with colours*, for whatever reason.

cotton bullet *n*. A tampon.

cotton mouse *n*. *Jam rag*, *chuftie plug*.

cotton pony *n*. A *fanny mouse*.

cougar *n*. *US*. Sexist and offensive American slang term for a predatory older *slag*, usually sporting *tit tattoos* and bleached hair. Typically to be found reeking of alcohol on a bar stool near the men's room.

cough a dead rat *v*. To *drop a gut*, to

step on a duck. To flatulate.

cough and drop nurse *n*. A comprehensive school health visitor who checks whether or not one's *nuts* wobble whilst one is clearing one's throat.

cough cabbage water *v*. To tread on *the gloy bottle*, to ejaculate.

cough your filthy yoghurt *euph*. A romantic expression for ejaculation. To do a *money shot*. *'Ursula was powerless to resist. His eyes burned into hers like sapphires. His strong arms enfolded her tender body as she felt herself being swept away in a whirlwind of passion. Then he dropped his trolleys and coughed his filthy yoghurt in her hair.'* (from *'The Gentleman and the Lady'* by Barbara Cartland).

council 1. *n*. The *bumhole*. From *council gritter*. 2. *adj*. General purpose dismissive term for anything or anyone deemed somewhat lacking in class. *'Mummy, can I go and play with Jade and Kylie?' 'No, sweetheart, you can't. They're a bit council.'*

council cock *n*. A genital which is unemployed and living on handouts.

council diamonds *n*. Sparkling pavement residue found, for example, following a collision between a *Vauxhall Chavalier* and a telephone box.

council gritter *rhym. slang*. *Gary Glitter, apple fritter, pint of bitter, shitter*.

council pop *n*. Water. Also *tapoline*.

council tax *n*. A weekly levy paid in manageable £1 installments over the fag counter at the newsagent. Lottery ticket money.

council twat *n*. A scraggy, utility

clout. Not very good quality, but it does the job.

court Madam Knuckle *v.* To woo your right hand. See *Madam Palm and her five daughters.*

Covent Garden nun *n.* A *fuckstress.* A *Fulham virgin.* A *ho'.*

covered wagon *1 n.* The method of holding the *tassel* in which the thumb is on the underside of the *shaft* and the fingers form a canopy like the top of a cowboy's wagon. A style much favoured by the street-urinating drunkard. *2 n.* To drive your old cow under canvas after you've had a bellyful of beans. A *Dutch oven.*

cowboy walk *n.* Broad, rolling gait required when walking to the *bog* with the *turtle's head.*

cowgirl *n.* A sexual position popular with the choreographers of American *grumble flicks,* involving a lazy man and a bow-legged woman. A *fucking bronco.*

cow parsley *n.* The salad first course eaten by a *barge arse* as an antidote to the three cake blowout she will have for dessert.

cow's stomachs *n.* the effect of an ill-fitting bra on an over-endowed lady, giving the appearance of four *tits* instead of two.

coyote *v.* A woman who you would chew your own arm off to get away from in the morning.

crabe *n.* A measure of *shite,* thought to equal about two crates full.

crab ladder *1. n.* The *gut stick,* penis. *2. n.* The hairy line that links the top of the pubes to the belly button. *Crab trellis.*

crab paste *n.* A deposit of *fanny batter,* especially on a cucumber.

crabs *n. Bollock jockeys,* pubic lice.

crack *1. n. Minge, fanny.* 'Close your legs honey, folks will see your crack.' (Ronald Reagan at his presidential inauguration, 1980). *2. n.* Pointless *bollocks* spoken after four pints of Guinness in Irish theme pubs. *3. n.* The cleft of the *arse* cheeks.

crack a fat *v.* To achieve a *bone on.*

crack a moistie *v. Aus.* Of a *rude lady,* to become aroused in the *downstairs department.* To get a *wide on.*

crack a stiffy *v.* To *crack a fat.*

crackerjacks *n.* Testicles. *'It's Friday, it's five to five, and I'm off upstairs to whack me crackerjacks.'*

crack hanger *n.* The inverted coat hanger-shaped triangle of thong visible on women bending over in hipster jeans. Also *top triangle.*

crackler *n.* A particularly satisfying *dump* that crackles as it exits the *nipsy.*

crackling *n. Totty, talent.*

crack maggot *n.* See *man overboard.*

crack one's back *v.* To commence a long overdue *Ingrid* ie. where one's spine sounds like it is breaking up and is about to emerge through one's *clackervalve.*

crack one's nuts *v.* To *break one's eggs.*

crack the flags *v.* A vigorous, no nonsense *gut drop* that makes a fresh, crisp sound.

craddock *1. n.* A *cock-a-fanny. 2. n.* An old *cunt* with wonky, bright red lips. Named after the famous TV chef of the 1960's and 1970's, Fanny Craddock, who was an old *cunt* with wonky, bright red lips.

CRAFT *1. acronym. medic.* Doctor's notes terminolgy for a geriatric patient exhibiting symptoms of the onset of senile dementia. *Can't Remember A Fucking Thing*. **2.** *acronym.* Term used by educationalists to describe the the learning potential of their less academically-gifted pupils on school records.

crafty ant *n.* Awkward instantaneous occurrence of *ringpiece* itchiness which happens at the exact moment when it would be most unsuitable to give it a good scratch. Generally occurs the morning after eating a mixed kebab from Abdul's, Manchester.

crafty butcher *n.* A male homosexual, ie. a man who likes to *take his meat* around the back.

crafty fisherman *n.* An hermaphrodite, ie. one who carries around a spare set of *tackle*.

cranberry dip *n.* A special sauce for sausages available only during *rag week*.

crane operator *n.* A *stick vid* actress with a *gut stick* in each hand, the motion of which gives the appearance that she is positioning a crane or wrecking ball. Also *Madam two-swords, downhill skier.*

crank *1. n.* Penis. *2. rhym. slang.* To have a *wank* in the style of someone attempting to start a vintage car. A *ham shank.* *3. n.* A bathroom multitasking exercise. A *crap* and a *wank* performed simultaneously by someone with an extremely busy schedule. *4. v.* To cry and *wank* at the same time.

crap *1. n. Shit. 2. v.* To *shit..*

craps *n. US.* A shit game with dice.

craparazzi *n.* Photographers assigned to the *shitterati*, eg. snapping former *'Big Brother'* contest-ant Cameron Stout leaving a launderette in Arbroath for a six page spread in *'Heat'* magazine.

crap flaps *n.* The doorstep of the *nipsy*. The insides of the buttocks of the *arse.*

crapidation *n.* In a public lavatory, the fear of the appalling horrors about to be exposed when lifting the lid. *'With a trembling hand and much crapidation, Roderick made to lift the lid. What he saw plastered in the bowl made the blood freeze in his veins. It was a sight that was to cast a black shadow over his soul for the rest of his life.'* (from *'The Fall of the Shithouse of Usher'* by Edgar Allan Poe).

crapier mâché *n.* Those little bits of *bumwad* that gather around one's *dot* after a severe wiping. A *wasps' nest.*

crapitus *n. Lat. medic.* The creaking noise emitted by overstretched or broken *farting strings* as *Meatloaf's daughter* exits the *chamber of horrors,* sounding similar to the noises made by a galleon at anchor.

crapkins *n.* Fast food restaurant paper serviettes which, when pilfered in handfuls, act as free toilet paper. Popular amongst students.

crap nap *n.* An alcohol-induced siesta taken in a pub gents cubicle, when one is overcome with sudden tiredness at the effort of pulling down one's trousers and sitting on the *throne. Shitwinks.*

crapper *n.* Lavatory. Named after the inventor of the self-cleaning water closet, Thomas Shitehouse.

crappuccino *n.* A particularly frothy form of diarrhoea which one gets abroad. See *kexpresso.*

craptain Webb *n*. A long *turd* that 'dips its toe' in the water before diving in.

crash mat *n*. A *pap baffle*, a *turd raft*.

crash one's pants *v*. To momentarily lose control of one's *motions* leading to a *pile up* in one's *garnies*. *'I was so scared when Derek went into his trance, I nearly crashed my pants, I can tell you.'* (Yvette Fielding, *'Most Haunted Live'*, Living TV, Oct 31st 2003).

crash the yoghurt truck *v*. To *shed one's load* at the *Billy Mill round-about. Empty the wank tanks.*

crazy log *n*. A little *shit* that produces an annoying crescendo of high-pitched *farts*.

cream *v*. To *crash the yoghurt truck*, esp. in your pants. To *milm*.

cream rinse *n*. A bubbly hair-care product that is often provided gratis with a facial. A *spermanent wave*.

cream tea *n*. A couple of generously -proportioned *nipplecakes*, topped off with a healthy dollop of *squirty cream. Iced baps.*

cream tea *n*. A posh *bird's* cuppa into which one has *jaffed*. Over the back of a spoon.

crème de la femme *n*. *Moip*.

crème de month *n*. Bi-fortnightly *moip* that tastes anything but refreshingly minty.

crepitate *v*. To discharge a noxious fluid accompanied by a slight explosive sound. How Stephen Fry would describe a *follow through*.

crescent wank *n*. To arrange one's favourite *jazz periodicals* in a half-moon display, before kneeling down to perform a five finger exercise on the *spunk trumpet*.

cricket week *n*. A five day test, when a gentleman must *bowl from the Pavilion end* while his wife is *padded up*.

crimp off a length *v*. *milit*. Naval slang for *curling one off*.

crimson wave *n*. Also *crimson tide*. See *surfing the crimson wave*.

crinkle cuts *n*. *medic*. The large, crenellated *scallop lips* that protrude from a salty *bag. Real McCoy's, Nicki Lauda's lugs, turkey's wattles.*

cripple crapper *n*. A *chod bin* designated for the exclusive use of persons of restricted mobility. *'Fuck it. Look at the queue for the shitters. I'll just nip into the cripple crapper.'*

crone bone *n*. A state of somewhat unsettling sexual arousal brought on by an unlikely stimulus, eg. a picture of Camilla Parker-Bowles in jodhpurs.

crop spraying *v*. See *pebble dashing*.

crotch crickets *n*. Crabs.

crotch eggs *n*. Hairy *knackers*.

crouching tiger, hidden dragon *n*. Ancient Chinese sexual position. *Doggy-style* sex with a woman so *fugly*, that one can't bring oneself to look her in the face.

crouton *n*. An erection that floats in one's soup.

crow *1. n. US*. That *muck* which has been *chucked*, esp. onto the *map-atasi*. Post-*porking* residue on the *hairy clam. Muffdruff. 2. n.* Nostril carrion. A *bogie, greb, greenie.*

crowbar *n*. An erection which is hard enought to force a sash window with. A *jemmy-on*.

crowd pleaser *n*. Unusual or noteworthy stool which one feels an urge to show to someone before flushing.

crown jowls *n*. The baggy bit of excess skin that hangs off the end of the *grub screw. Kenny's hood*. The *fiveskin*.

crow's nest *n*. A particularly ramshackle *snatch*. Up a tree.

cruiser and tug *n*. The common phenomenon of a stunning female who is always accompanied by her ugly little fat friend.

crumpet *1. n*. A traditional Scottish cake made of soft, light dough, eaten toasted and buttered, and much craved by the late Sid James. *2. n*. 1970s *blart*.

crumpet batter *n*. Gentleman's erotic spendings.

crumpeteer *n*. A fellow who has a way with the ladies. An expert in the science of *crumpetology*. *'Birthdays: Curtis Mayfield, soul musician and corpse, 58; Charles R Drew, physician and blood plasma pioneer, 96; Allen Ginsberg, beardy poet, 74; Tony Curtis, actor and veteran crumpeteer, 75.'* (from *'The Times'*, June 3rd 2000).

crunchie *1. n*. A tasty confectionary snack. *2. n*. A brittle sock worn the day after one has *wanked* into it.

crunk *n*. The *taint, barse, tintis, tinter*.

crusties *1. n*. Dog-on-a-string owning soapophobes. *2. n*. Over-worn *bills* somewhat lacking in 'April freshness'. *Dunghampers* with a dirty *drip tray*.

Crystal Gayle *1. n. prop*. Longhaired, lightweight US country performer of the 1970s. *2. n*. A prison-based sexual act which may (in fact, almost certainly will) 'make your *brown eye* blue'. *'He walked into the shower block / Of Reading's dreadful gaol / And stooping to pick up the soap / The prisoner's face turned pale / As a voice behind him whispered / 'How about a Crystal Gayle?''* (from *'The Ballad of Reading Gaol'* by Oscar Wilde).

crystal maze, go *v*. To find oneself unable to perform a simple task due to pressure, eg. a learner driver being unable to get the car out of reverse gear during a test, Eamonn Holmes being unable to competently present a television programme when the cameras are on. To go all *cunty booby*.

CSB *abbrev*. Default hairstyle setting for young lady *scratters*. From Chav Scrape Back.

Cuban wank *n*. A *diddy-ride*, a *Bombay roll*. A *tit-wank*.

cubism *1. n*. A French school of painting typified by the works of Picasso and Braque which amalgamated multiple viewpoints into a complex surface of geometrical planes. *2. n*. A harmless gentleman's hobby which involves sneaking into a cubicle in the female toilets of a pub, club or department store and listening in to the action in the neighbouring 'cubes'.

cuckold *n*. A man whose wife allows another man to lay his *cock eggs* in her.

cuckoo *n*. A scoundrel who moves in on a bird's *nest* when one has nipped to the bar after doing all the groundwork.

cuff the dummy *v. US. milit*. To *wank, scrub the cook*.

cuff stinks *n*. The malodorous end result of an unfortunate sleeve mishap suffered when wiping one's *nipsy* following a *Brad*.

cum *1. v*. A sexiness-enhancing misspelling of *come* used by the authors of *bongular* literature to describe male ejaculation. 2. *n*. A sexiness-enhancing mis-spelling of *come* used by the authors of *bongular* literature to describe male ejaculate.

cumbeard *n*. A white, coagulated sperminiferous goatee beard worn by a lady who has helped herself to a double portion of *spangle*.

Cumberland 1. *n*. A long *turd* which forms a spiral in the *pan,* in the style of the popular helical pub grub sausage. 2. *n*. A gentleman's *porky banger.*

Cumberland gap 1. *n*. A repetitive, annoying skiffle song by Lonnie Donnigan which topped the hit parade in 1957. 2. *n*. The triangular gap at the top of a lady's thighs which arouses curiosity as to whether the old *Cumberland* could fit through. The *Toblerone tunnel*.

cumbrella n. A *jubber ray*.

cumchugger *n*. A *bird* who enjoys guzzling *spadge*.

cumdown *n*. That feeling of soul-crushing worthlessness that follows a *sherman,* as inevitably as night follows day.

cumster *n*. A small hamster-like female who fills her cheeks with your *nuts*.

cum to mind *v*. Of a person or favoured memory, to appear as a mental image in the imagination of one embarking on the *vinegar strokes. 'These days I find it's often Kylie Minogue who cums to mind when I'm poking the missus.'*

cum to one's senses *v*. To experience feelings of self loathing and disgust immediately upon ejaculation, when wearing the girlfriend's lingerie, *poking* a Bangkok *ladyboy* or *wanking* into Carol Decker's wardrobe etc., no longer

seem a such a good idea.

cumulonimbus *n. Lat*. Oral sex. Tongular stimulation of a lady's *clematis*.

cunch *n*. A satisfying midday snack furnished by, or comprising of, the secret *girly parts* of an obliging ladyfriend. Derivation unknown.

cunker *n*. Romantic term for one of a lady's *bodily treasures*. The *snatch*.

cunnifungus *n. Lat*. Female equivalent of *knob cheese*.

cunnimingus *v*. The act of orally pleasuring a lady with personal hygeine issues. *Licking out a nine volter.*

cunny *n. Lat. Fadge*, vagina. From cunnus = *shagpipe*.

cunnylicious *adj*. Descriptie of any woman or part thereof, demanding to be eaten.

cunshine *n*. The frustrating reflections which invariably hinder full enjoyment of the glossy *whacknicolour* photographs in *art pamphlets*. Also *porn glare, razzle dazzle*.

cunt 1. *n. 14thC. medic*. Polite term for lady's genitals. 2. *n. 21stC*. Impolite term for lady's genitals. 3. *n*. A traffic warden.

cuntbitten *adj*. Of a gentleman, to have contracted *VD* from a dirty lady. To be struck down with a *dose* of clappage.

cunt book *n*. The *dog house*. '*16th August 1945. Went down the Feathers with Joe and Dwight to celebrate winning the War. Back to Downing Street 4am. Lost keys. Climbed up drainpipe and fell into bins. Woke kids up. Clementine came down to let me in. I reckon I'm in the cunt book for at least a fortnight.' (from 'The Diary of Sir*

Winston Churchill').

cunt bread *n.* A yeast infection on a lady's *ninja's toe.*

cunt bubble *1. n.* An air lock up the *fanny*, often leading to a *Lawley kazoo.* 2. *n.* A traffic warden.

cunt buster 1. *n.* An enormous erection. A *diamond cutter.* 'Olivia was powerless to resist. His eyes burned into hers like sapphires. His strong arms enfolded her softly yielding body as she felt herself being swept away in a whirlwind of passion. Then he dropped his trolleys revealing a right cunt buster.' (from 'The Lady and the Gypsy' by Barbara Cartland). 2. *n.* A large baby.

cunt corks *n.* A term used in chemist's shops when one is too embarrassed to ask for a box of *women's things.*

cunteen *n.* A number which is larger than twelve but smaller than twenty, and is used to describe the size of a group of something one dislikes, eg. 'There were cunteen fucking TV chefs.'

cunt guff *n.* The *dropping forwards of a lady's hat.*

cunt hook *n.* Any stylish car such as a VW Lupo or Daewoo Matiz with oversized wheels, blacked-out windows and rear spoilers, which impresses discerning ladies. A *fanny magnet.* 'Fiesta XR2, red, D reg, 312k, 1 new tyre, some history, MOT October, a real cunt hook £120 ono. First to see will buy. No tyre kickers.' (Advert from 'The Banbury Cake').

cuntinental *n.* Anyone who sits outside a cafe in Britain drinking coffee and eating croissants whenever the drizzle lets up for ten minutes.

cuntitude *n.* A *cuntish* attitude.

cuntlashed *n.* Twice as drunk as *shitfaced.*

cuntlifters *n.* An elderly lady's *dunghampers. Granny's bills.*

cunt ruffler *n.* A man who enjoys provoking ladies who have *fallen to the communists* because he finds their mood swings amusing.

cunt rug *n.* A *muff*, a *merkin.*

cunt scratchers *n.* Humorous term for hands. *Wanking spanners.*

cuntsman *n. US.* A *cocksman, stickman.* A Don Juan type, highly skilled in the pursuit of *poontang.* 'Today's birthdays. Rod Stewart, singer, song writer, cuntsman, 73.'

cuntstruck *adj.* Besotted, hopelessly in love.

cuntwank *n.* A one-sided, loveless, no-nonsense bout of intercourse. A *hand's free.* 'I've just seen that Victorian lesbo drama on the telly. Phwooar! So I'm off upstairs for a cuntwank off the missus.'

cuntweep *n.* The custard-like mess found in a lady's *alans* after she has sat in the office all day chatting about Paolo di Canio's legs.

cunty booby *adj.* To be in a state of confusion. 'I don't pretend to understand the universe - when I start thinking about it I go all cunty booby, me.' (from 'Latterday Pamphlets Number 6', by Thomas Carlyle).

cupcake *n.* Small quantity of *fart* gas caught between the palms of the hands and released in a person's face.

Cupid's toothpaste *n.* Oral *gunk.*

curd *n. Jizz.*

curl one off *v.* To carefully deliver a *mudchild.* See also *three coiler.*

curler 1. *n.* A lump of excrement. 2. *n.* Something in your wife's hair. 3. *n.* A lump of excrement in your wife's hair.

curry hurry *n.* The increasingly-hasty homeward bound trot of one who has recently partaken of some sort of exotic foodstuffs which are already *touching cloth* in high-temperature semi-liquid form, for example a tasty meal at the Curry Capital, formerly the Rupali restaurant, Bigg Market, Newcastle-upon Tyne.

curryoakie *n.* An enthusiastic but tuneless *fart* performed after a gallon of bitter and an Indian meal. A *blanket ripper.*

curry slurry *n.* The mixture of semi-liquified excrement, intestines and internal organs left in the pan of the *chod bin* the morning after a particularly hot madras. *'I'd give it ten minutes if I was you, dear. I just did a bit of a curry slurry in there. Oh, and can you call an ambulance. And a priest.'*

curtain call *n.* A return to the lavatory for an *encore dump.* A *second sitting.*

curtain drop *n.* *Cat flap* length, size of a woman's *beef curtains.*

curtain rings *n.* Labial ironmongery.

curtain twitchers *n.* Lesbians.

curvy *adj. uk. journ.* Of women, to have large breasts and/or *arses.* *'Curvy Nigella Lawson cooked a right royal supper of cod and green ended chips for foreign dictator George W Bush when he recently visited the queen and her brood of bi-sexual children.'* (*'BBC Good Food Magazine'*, November 2003).

cushion creeper *n.* An upholstery-muffled *Exchange & Mart.*

custard 1. *n.* A sweet sauce made from eggs and milk that goes well with rhubarbs. 2. *n.* Someone who is simultaneously a bit of a *cunt*

and a bit of a *bastard*, eg. Paul Daniels, Tim Henman. 3. *Rhym. Slang.* A *bakewell.*

custard cannon *n.* *Lamb cannon, mutton musket, pork sword*, etc, etc, et fucking cetera.

custard cousin *n.* The relationship one has with those who have shared the same *slice* of *pie.* eg. Brian Ferry and Mick Jagger are *custard cousins*, as are Liam Gallagher, Ally McCoist, Jim Kerr and the 14th Batallion of the Royal Scots Dragoon Guards.

custard muscle *n.* Subcutaneous body fat.

custard pie *n.* A pre-*spoffed fadge.* Referred to in various blues songs, including 1947's *'Custard Pie Blues'* by Brown McGhee. Also forms the basis of the Led Zeppelin song *'Custard Pie'* which opens their 1975 double album *'Physical Graffiti'* in which Robert Plant exclaims: 'Save me a slice of your custard pie', apparently implying that he would like to re-*poke*, and indeed chew on, his bird's aforementioned *jitler*-filled *clopper* later.

custardy tart *n.* An arrested woman who *sucks off* the duty sergeant, or performs similar act in lieu of bail.

customer service 69 aisle x *exclam.* Phrase called out over supermarket tannoys to alert male staff of the presence of a fit *bird* in aisle x, so they can go over and run a price check or look at some tins or something.

cut 'n' shut 1. *n.* A second hand car, skillfully engineered from the front and back of two insurance write-offs. 2. *n.* A woman, seemingly constructed of two ill-matched donor women, eg. a fantastic body, but a *minger*, a cutie, but built like a bus, or a flat chested bonebag sat on a big *arse* and tree trunk legs.

cut a rug 1. *v.* To take to the dancefloor and impress onlookers by jitterbugging energetically, especially with an American airman. 2. *v.* To *split a kipper, part the whiskers* etc. To make penetrative love to a lady.

cut price spice *n.* A lady who models herself on Victoria Beckham, but does so on a much tighter budget. Accompanies *David Peckhams* on trips in his *estate car*.

cut the cheese *v.* To *fart*. Also *cut the brie, open the ham*.

cut the cord *v.* To break the link between one's *arsehole* and an invisible, yet highly noticeable cloud of recently expelled *gut gas* by means of rapid, short wafting motions of the hand.

cut through the red tape *v.* To ignore received wisdom and *swim when the red flags are flying*.

cuzza *n.* A *Ruby Murray*.

cybertranny *n.* Man or woman who pretends to be of the opposite sex in internet chat rooms, eg. 16-year-old Brenda turns out to be a 35-stone tattooed American man called Jim-Bob. With his dead mother in a fridge.

Cyclops *n.* A legendary purple-headed monster with the eye of a hog. And two big hairy *bollocks* underneath.

Cyprus manoeuvre *n.* To remove the penis during *doggy sex* and re-enter 'accidentally' up the *bonus tunnel*. The *Limasol slip*. Invented in 1972 by scientists in Cyprus.

Dd

dab the wound *v.* Of a lady, to *gusset type.*

dad dressed as Brad *n.* The male counterpart of a *Whitney dressed as Britney.*

daddaries *n.* Gentleman's version of the mammaries which are found on ladies' chests. *Mannery glands, mantits. 'Phwoar. I bet you don't get many of those daddaries to the pound, Lord Owen.'*

Daddy's sauce *n.* Baby gravy, pineapple chunk.

Dagenham handshake *n.* Sexual practice whereby the gentleman inserts a finger in the *pink,* a finger in the *brown,* then uses a third to ring the *devil's doorbell.*

Dagenham smile *n.* Builder's bum.

dags *n.* Shepherd-speak for sheep's *dangleberries.*

dairy bags *n.* Proper old-fashioned *churns* of the sort Nurse Gladys Emmanuel would have stuck in Ronnie Barker's face whilst plumping up his pillows, causing him to blow his cheeks out and blink amusingly.

daisy chain *n.* Series circuit of *AC* or *DC* sex. The sort which only occurs in *bongo films* and Stephen Fry's public school dormitory.

daisy cutter *n.* A heavyweight *fart,* in breach of the Geneva Convention, that leaves nothing standing within a wide radius.

dakkery doo *n.* A relaxing concurrent *shit* and cigarette. From the German word Dak = cigarette. *'His Holiness will be with us presently, Cardinal. He's just went for a dakkery doo.'*

dalek *n.* An erection reminiscent of a forehead-mounted sink-plunger.

daltons *n.* The *nuts.*

dance the blanket hornpipe *v.* To perform a sailor's jig, *below decks.*

dancer's lance *n.* An unwelcome *dalek* that appears when dancing closely with a lady. A *Saturday night lever, St. Vitus pants.*

dancing bear *n.* A grizzly brown monster that stands on its end in the *pan* and refuses to be flushed away unless hit with a stick.

dancing with the captain *v.* To masturbate. Wearing a bowler hat. See *grandma's party.*

dang 1. *n.* Penis. 2. *exclam.* US. Expression of annoyance. *'Dang them pesky Al Qaeda varmints.'* (George W Bush, State of the Nation Address, 2002). 3. *n.* A word which, together with ding and dong, features prominently in the lyrics of Eurovision Song Contest entries.

dangermouse *n.* A tampon.

danger wank *n. Self-abuse* whereby you shout your parents from downstairs, and then try to *blow your tanks* before they get to your bedroom. A *dangerous spurt* for an adrenaline *jizz-junky.*

dangleberries *n. Winnets,* excrement adhering to the *arse cress* around an inefficiently-wiped *ringpiece. Fartleberries, toffee strings, bead curtains, kling-ons, clinkers.*

dangler *n.* A dangling *donger.*

danglers *n. Hairy conkers.*

dangly ham *n. Beef curtains, bacon strips.*

Danny Fishcharge *n.* Spooneristic vaginal *gleet.*

darb *v.* To *shag, bonk, bang.*

dark star *n.* Black, or rather brown hole from which the *pink Darth Vader* might emerge wearing a *shitty* helmet.

darned hole in a jumper *sim.* Descriptive of a tightly-gathered *ringpiece.*

Darth Vader's hat stand *n.* A sinister, six foot tall, wheezing *cock.*

Darth vulva *n.* The act of eating a *fish supper* with such gusto that it makes a sound not unlike Darth Vader trying to eat a squid without taking his helmet off.

dash for gash *n.* The desperate last half hour before chucking out at a night club.

date locker *n.* Rectum, *bomb bay.*

Dave Narey *rhym. slang. Scot.* A woman who would benefit from a major *waxing session*, eg. Anne Robinson and her who did '99 Red Balloons'. Named after the Dundee United footballer who famously scored with a 25-yard toe-poke against Brazil in the 1982 World Cup.

David Peckham *n.* A young man who aspires to look like the England captain, but lives a very different lifestyle. ie, he has bleached, slicked-up hair, but wears *Armani and Navy* and drives a G-Reg Astra.

dawn horn *n.* Early morning *tent pole, bed flute.* See also *big cock day.*

daylighting *1. n.* Construction industry term describing the appearance of a tunnelling machine or driven pipe from a soil face. *2. n. Touching cloth.*

dead heat in a zeppelin race *sim.* Large *tits, knockers, bazookas, oomlaaters, Gert Stonkers.*

dead heat *n.* The situation whereby the urge to defecate comes to glorious fruition at the exact moment when the buttocks touch the *bog seat.*

dead otter *n.* A single stool of immense proportions.

dealt a Beadle, to be *v.* Whilst playing cards, to receive a totally *shit* hand.

death by chocolate starfish *1. n.* An incredibly disgusting *fart. 2. n.* A chronic attack of the *Earthas.*

death row *1. n. US.* A section of a prison where Texan authorities keep simple-minded black men prior to their execution for crimes which they have usually not committed. *2. n.* A retirement home or sheltered housing complex.

death star *n.* The *nipsy.*

decrapitation *n.* The act of cutting the head off a *Richard the Third,* in order to answer the door, get the phone or present *'Midweek'* on Radio 4.

defarture lounge *n.* The vestibule of the *dirt bakery*, where *exhaust gases* gather in order to build up to maximum pressure. *'Fuck me, Your Majesty. I've got a right beauty brewing up in the defarture lounge, I don't mind telling you.'*

deflate *v.* To *suck off. 'Oi, Gillian. Deflate this for me, will you?'*

de-ice the flaps *1. v.* In aeronautical circles, to carry out various procedures on an aeroplane which ensure that ice deposits on the wings do not impair the operation of the control surfaces and mechanisms. *2. v.* Of a frigid lady, to make use of her *muff* after a substantial lay-off.

Deirdre's neck *n.* The strings supporting the *nadbag* that are under immense tension.

Delhi belly *n.* Delicate stomach condition leading to the *Eartha Kitts.*

Delia *n.* At a social engagement, the cringeworthy performance of an embarrassingly loud and drunken partner. From tired and emotional TV chef Delia Smith's motivational half-time address at the Norwich versus Man City game on February 28th 2005. *'Oh Christ. She's had half a dozen Bacardi Breezers on an empty stomach. Give it ten minutes and she'll be doing a Delia on me.'*

dell *1. n. 16thC.* Prostitute, *tom. 2. n.* Original Hampshire venue of Southampton F.C.'s annual relegation battle.

Denis Norden, do a *v.* To chat up a piece of *clump* in an unnecessarily long-winded and tiresome way instead of just asking for a *poke*. From the way that the *'It'll be Alright on the Night'* host bores the liver out of everyone for ten minutes before each batch of funny clips.

Deptford wives *n. Ankle chaingang* of women of uncertain breeding, staggering under the weight of their *bingo clink* on a night out. Often to be seen lifting their tops to expose their *noinkers* for the cameras of Bravo TV's hard-hitting documentary series *'Booze Britain'.*

depth charge *n.* A large or heavy stool, *copper bolt.* Also *belly flopper, Admiral Browning.*

derection *n.* The opposite of an erection, usually obtained by thinking about Moira Stuart.

derren *n. medic.* Of a man, to be sterile. From the mentalist magician Derren Brown who, in a TV Russian Roulette stunt, was found to be *firing blanks. 'No, we don't need a blob, love, I'm derren. But if you're really worried I'll slip it in your brown pocket.'*

designer vagina *n.* Any *muff* which has been trimmed into an unusual shape, eg. a heart, a *Hitler tash* or Craig David's beard. *Armani fanny, Versnatche.*

desk lifter *n.* An attractive lady teacher who, on bending over to pick up some chalk can cause 30 desks to be raised simultaneously.

devil's bagpipes *n.* A gentleman's *meat and two veg.*

devil's chimney *1. n.* Geological tourist attraction in the absence of anything else to look at on the Isle of Wight. *2. n.* The *shitter.*

devil's dumplings *n.* The breasty attachments found on ladies' fronts.

devil's evacuate *n.* Piping hot *bum slurry* fermented in the depths of Hell. Diarrhoea.

devil's handshake *n.* A roman Catholic *wank.* A means of gauranteeing oneself a place in the eternal lake of fire.

devil's inkwell *n.* A gentleman's post *bust off* navel, brim-full with his onanistic yield.

devil's kiss *n.* A *fart* released during sex in the *69* position. *Hell's mouth.*

devil's kitchen *n.* The *chamber of horrors.*

dew on the lily *1. euph.* A lubricated *flange. 2. n.* Knob glaze, pre-*cum. Perseverance soup.*

DFKDFC *abbrev. medic.* Used in patients' notes during diagnosis - Don't Fucking Know, Don't Fucking Care. *'Patient: Female. Age: 72. Presented: Hot flushes, swollen tongue, racing heart, low blood pressure, tingling down right side, loose finger nails. Diagnosis: DFKDFC. Treatment: Amoxyl 3 times a day.'*

diamond cutter *n.* The hardest erection known to man. *Pink steel.*

diamond in the muff *n*. A genuinely attractive woman in a *grumble flick*.

Diana, to do a *v*. To collide at a spot between two *tunnels* when having sex. To hit the *taint* with one's *bell end*.

dibble 1. *v*. $14^{th}C$. To *shag*. 2. *n*. Cartoon police officer in 'Top Cat'. 3. *v*. To playfully prod around at the *hangar doors*.

Dibnah dick *n*. A sudden loss of erectile strength causing the *skin chimney* to collapse. Can be brought on by catching a whiff of badly-wiped *arse* when *changing at Baker Street*.

dick 1. *n*. *US*. Penis, *pud, plonker*. 2. *n*. Idiot, *plonker*. 'Rodney, you fucking dick.' ('Only Fools and Horses' Christmas Special, 1955) 3. *v*. To *fuck*.

dick-do *n*. *US*. Light-hearted epithet used to describe a *salad-dodger*. Based on the assumption that 'their gut probably sticks out more than their dick do'. 'Deaths; Peter Ustinov, polyglot dick-do, 82.' (from 'The International Herald Tribune', March 29th 2004).

dick docker *n*. A rabbi.

dick duster *n*. A hairy top lip on a lady.

dick head *n*. Fool, *idiot, joskin, brain donor*.

dickie dido *n*. Something on a lady, the hairs on which come down to her knees.

Dickinson holiday *n*. A bottle of fake tan which makes the wearer look like a fucking satsuma. Named after bright orange cheeky ex-con TV auction wideboy David Dickinson.

dick skinners *n*. *medic*. *US*. *Wanking spanners, cunt scratch-*ers. Hands.

dick splash *n*. Urine on trousers or suede shoes caused by shakage or *splashback*. See also *forget-me-nots*.

Dick Turpin's hat *n*. A good old-fashioned three-cornered hairy *blurtch*.

dick van dyke *n*. A strap-on cockney. A lesbotic *twat* rattler, a dildo. A *Mary Pop-in*.

dick weed *n*. *US*. Goldang *melon farming fuckwit*.

dick wheat *n*. Male pubic hair.

dickwit 1. *n*. Probably a character from a Charles Dickens novel. 2. *n*. A bloke who thinks with his *charlie*. 3. *n*. A foolish fellow.

diddies *n*. *Scot*. Ladies' *tits*.

diddy ride *n*. *Scot*. A deep-fried *sausage sandwich*.

diesel dyke *n*. *US*. A butch or masculine lesbian, *fanny nosher*. Also *bulldyke*.

diet fart *n*. A loud clearing of the *nether throat* that sounds dangerous but actually has no smell and is harmless. 'No need to open the window, Your Majesty. It was just a diet fart.'

difficult brown *n*. Tricky option in *bum games*. 'I'd rather take the easy pink than the difficult brown.' See also *Irish, snookered behind the red*.

difficult child *n*. One who, once *dropped off at the pool*, refuses to go into the water and clings onto the side.

Digby *n*. A big, ugly woman. From the 70s children's film 'Digby, the Biggest Ugly Woman in the World'.

dig in the whiskers *n*. *Aus*. A spot of beard-splitting. 'Fuck me, look at that Sheila. She's worth a dig in *the whiskers, wouldn't you say, Rolf?'*

dildo *n*. Practice version of the *pork sword*. A *bob*, a *neck massager*.

dill *1*. *n*. An unpleasant thing put in burgers by the staff at McDonald's. *2*. *n*. A type of pickle.

dillberries *n*. *Dangleberries, wufflenuts*.

dilm *n*. Unpleasant-tasting spermicidal lubricant on a *dunkie*.

dilmah *n*. *Aus*. An amusing party trick whereby the performer of the trick bounces his *knackers* on the forehead of the first person to fall asleep. Named after an Australian brand of tea bag and the similar dunking action associated with them.

Dimmock *1*. *v*. Of a lady, to create a *water feature*. See *squat 'n' squirt*. *2*. *v*. Of a lady's nipples, to pop out like a car cigarette lighter.

ding-a-ling *n*. Chuck Berry's *cock*. With two silver bells hanging off it.

ding! dong! *exclam. arch*. Caddish expression of delight when Terry-Thomas spotted a woman with *dunce's hats*.

dingleberry roast *n*. A lighted *fart*, an *afterburner, a blue streak*.

dinner lady's arm *1*. *n. medic. Bingo wings. 2. sim*. A large, but nonetheless unhealthy-looking *cock*.

dinner masher *n*. A *botter*.

dipping a worm in a bucket *v*. Engaging in unsatisfying sexual congress. *The last hot dog in the tin*.

dip 'n' dazzle *n*. A humourous epithet used to describe one who's ocular organs are so far out of whack to be reminiscent of badly-adjusted headlights, eg. Marty Feldman. An *Isiah*.

DIPS *acronym*. Vic Reeves's car wing mirrors. Drunken Impact Protection System.

dip your wick *v*. To put one's *dill* in the *hamburger*.

director's commentary *n*. The disconnected, self-obsessed ramblings of bitter-sodden tramps under their breath.

director's cut *n*. The point in an 18th generation *jazz video* where a previous *Chinese helicopter pilot* has inadvertently pressed 'record' instead of 'pause', leaving the viewer with a 4-second clip of *'Panorama'* circa 1994.

dirt bakery *n*. That part of the human anatomy where *holemeal loaves* are freshly manufactured around the clock.

dirtbox *n*. *Date locker, chamber of horrors*. Rectum.

dirty Beppe *n*. A *dirty Sanchez*, but with coverage extended to the chin.

dirty bomb *1*. *n*. A crude explosive device containing radioactive material designed to contaminate an area, making it uninhabitable. *2*. *n*. A *dropped back*, the fallout from which makes the immediate vicinity uninhabitable for the foreseeable future, eg. one dropped by Jocky Wilson at a cocktail party. *3*. *n*. A *shit explosion* that peppers the bowl with bio-hazard shrapnel.

dirty Bristow *n*. A sexual act performed by a lady whereby she kneels behind a standing gentleman and licks his *anus* whilst reaching through his legs to stimulate his penis. Occasionally stopping to swig a pint of lager. *Tromboning*.

dirty dentist *n*. *Fanny mechanic, snatch doc*. A gynaecologist. *'I'm* having a bit of bother with me clopper, love, so I'm off to the dirty dentist for a scrape.'

dirty fart n. A fart with delusions of grandeur. A follow through.

dirty lolly n. A girl whom one is tempted to pick up and lick, but who is probably covered in germs.

dirty Sanchez n. To stick one's finger up a lady's back bottom during doggy style sex. Then one draws a moustache on her top lip, apparently.

dirty spine, snip a length of v. To lay a cable, drop a copper bolt.

dirty water n. medic. A medical term for seminal fluid. Bollock bile.

disco fanny adj. The full strength flavour achieved by a vigorous evening of giving it six nowt on the dance floor.

disfabled adj. To be claiming invalidity benefit on dubious grounds, eg. that copper who was off work with stress, but bravely managed to referee a Premiership football match.

dishonourable discharge n. milit. The shameful result of knocking the little general's helmet off.

display model n. A bit of morning wood that's just for show and, despite everyone's best efforts, refuses to go off.

ditch pig n. An affectionate lighthearted epithet for an ugly fat girl.

divot n. A particularly hairy placket.

DIY euph. A single-handed job done around the house at the weekend using one tool and a bag of nuts.

Dizzy Gilespie n. A formidable blast on the spunk trumpet where the lady's cheeks puff out like a bullfrog's.

dizzyade n. Beer. Also dizzy pop.

do v. To give someone one. 'No kissing, just cold, hard sex. And absolutely no simulation - these birds are really being done.' (from an advertisement for erotic videos, 'Daily Express').

do a Southampton sim. To score and stay up when you haven't really got it in you.

dobber 1. n. A rubber johnny. 2. n. A semi-erect dill. A lazy lob on. 3. v. To cheat someone out of something, to rip off. From a bloke called Dobber Bailey from Coventry who, twenty years ago got ripped off buying an engine for his Triumph TR7.

dobgob v. To spooge up when only half stonked. Also dobglob.

dock 1. n. Arse. The polite term by which horsey types refer to their steeds' fudge tunnel. 2. v. To shag. Up a horse's arse.

docker's omelette n. A glistening gobbet of rubbery phlegm with remarkable anti-traction properties. A gold watch, a rolex prairie oyster.

docker's tea break sim. Descriptive of something very long. "Oh, what a tiny little man,' laughed Verruca Salt as she saw the Oompa Lumpa. 'He may be small,' cautioned Mr. Wonka as he turned briskly on his heel, 'but he'll have a cock as long as a docker's tea break." (from 'Charlie and the Chocolate Sandwich' by Roald Dahl).

docker's thumbs n. Nipples so hard one could hang a soaking wet duffle coat off them. Scammell wheelnuts, JCB starter buttons, Dimmocks.

docking n. The rolling of one's five-

skin over another chap's hat. A *clash of heads*.

dockyard cat, fanny like a *sim.* Descriptive of a particularly unkempt semi-feral *snatch. Terry Waite's allotment.*

dockyard rivets *n.* Cigarbutts, pigmies' cocks.

doctor's signature *n.* A particulary wiggly pair of *beef curtains* resembling a GP's scrawl at the bottom of a prescription.

Dodd job *n.* A *nosh* administered by the more toothsome lady, or perhaps one who likes to bite. *'Fancy another Dodd job, Normski?' 'No thanks, Janet. By the way, have you seen the TCP anywhere?'*

dodd *v.* To *shit* oneself in public. Named after a certain James Dodd who *shit* himself on the way to work and then phoned in to say he couldn't come in because he had *shit himself.*

dodger's conscience *n.* The ridiculous purchase of a diet drink after a *Duke* or *Duchess of Giblets* has ordered a large pie and chips, two pickled eggs, a battered sausage and 'a saveloy while I'm waiting.'

dog 1. *n.* A woman who fails to reach an acceptable standard of attractiveness. A *steg.* 2. *n.* A male prostitute. 3. *v.* To hang around in car parks at night, in the pretence of walking a dog, in order to spy on courting couples and watch it *go in.*

dog beers *n.* Any ale drunk by one who is unable to handle their beer. Drinking one *dog beer* leaves the average *two pot screamer* feeling and looking like he has drunk seven.

dog catcher *n.* A man who goes looking for unwanted *hounds* in a

nightclub after all the pedigree *blart* has been collared. A *munter hunter.*

dog eating hot chips *sim.* A crude and voracious, yet effective *horatio* technique. *'Lusitania was powerless to resist. His eyes burned into hers like garnets. His muscular arms enfolded her body as she felt herself being swept away in a force 10 gale of passion. Slowly, she fell to her knees and unzipped Giuseppe's breeches and went at his cock like a dog eating hot chips.'* (from *'The Countess and the Lion Tamer'* by Barbara Cartland).

dog eggs *n. Turds*, often laid on the pavement.

doggie chalks *n.* White canine excrements. *Poodle shit.*

doggies *n.* Intercourse in the position adopted by dogs, usually near some dustbins.

dogging *n.* The saucy behaviour of one who *dogs*.

dog handler *n.* Offensively sexist term for a man who is prepared to go out with a right *fugly* old *steg*.

dog in a bath *n.* A bedroom game like *rodeo sex. 'The missus was setting the video last night and I was on me vinegar strokes when I called her by her sister's name. It was like trying to keep a dog in a bath.'*

dog lime *n. Dog eggs*, canine faeces.

dog-locked *n.* To be stuck in a compromising position due to muscular spasm, usually in the back of a car in a *'Confessions of...'* film. Also, *dog's lock-in.*

dognose *v.* To disturb one's slumbering wife following a *slash* in the small hours by touching her on the leg or buttocks with a cold, wet *bell end.*

dog slobber *n. Electric spaghetti.*

dog slug *n.* The act of licking around, and indeed inside, another person's *rusty sherrif's badge.* A *trip round the world,* a *rim job.*

dog toffee *n.* Tacky pavement deposit that readily adheres to the sole of a shoe or supports an upright lollipop stick.

dog toss *n.* Grinding against a woman's leg in an over-eager fashion whilst dancing at a night club, school disco, or wedding reception.

dog track *n.* A song (usually *'Lady in Red'*) played at ten to two in a nightclub, that precipitates a last attempt mad dash onto the dancefloor by all remaining *hounds.* A *desperate dance.*

dog with two dicks *sim.* Descriptive of a *tomcat with three balls.* To be incredibly pleased with oneself. *'That's one small step for man, one giant leap for mankind. I'm on the Moon and I'm as happy as a dog with two dicks, me.'* (Neil Armstrong, July 1969).

dog's arse *adj.* To be troubled with wind. *'Excuse my wife. I'm afraid she's got a dog's arse today, Your Holiness.'*

dog's back *n.* See *Bilbo Baggins' foot.*

dog's bollocks *n.* Bee's knees, *donkey's knob, monkey's nuts, cat's knackers* etc.

dog's legs *n. medic.* Temporary weakness in the male thighs following a spot of *back-scuttling* with a *dirty lady.*

dog's lipstick *n.* A shimmery pink retractable cosmetic favoured by magicians' assistants.

dog's marriage *n.* A *back scuttle.*

dog's match *n.* A sexual encounter

in a public place, eg. in a bush, doorway, taxi queue or casualty.

doley's blackout *n.* A mid-afternoon session of *self-abuse* snatched during a lull in daytime television. Achieved by shutting the curtains after *'Quincy'* for a quick *tug.*

dolly dagger *n.* A *bob,* dildo.

dollymop *n.* An amateur or inexperienced prostitute.

dolphin skin *n. medic.* The epidermis of the *herman gelmet.*

Don King in a headlock *sim.* Descriptive of a foreign lady's armpits.

Donald *rhym. slang. Fuck.* From Donald Duck.

donger *n. Whanger, pork sword, dill.*

donkey kisser *n.* An inexperienced osculatrix. A lady who *snogs* like a donkey chewing an apple.

donkey punch *n.* Of *bum games,* to knock your partner out cold with a blow to the back of the head whilst in the *vinegar strokes.* Said to have the same aphrodisiacal effect as slamming a goose's neck in a drawer whilst committing bestiality. Don't try either.

donkey rigged *adj.* Blessed with a sizeable penis.

donkey's earhole *n.* A particularly large, flappy, twitching vagina. A *hippo's mouth,* a *clown's pocket.*

Donkey style, do it *v.* To copulate in the *wrong 'un.* ie, in the *ass.*

donkified *adj.* To have a *horse's handbrake,* to be in a state of *tumescence.* To be *on the bonk.*

donner *n.* An unattractive woman, a *ten pinter.* ie, someone one wouldn't fancy too much when sober.

donor *n.* See *benefactor.*

doofa *n.* A *ten-to-two-er.* From the phrase 'She'll 'doofa' me'.

Doomsday book *n. Toilet literature* perused between sobs whilst suffering an apocalyptic rectal breakdown.

doonicans *n.* Assorted *claps*, NSUs and *doses*. From the initials of the bejumpered Irish rocking chair croonster Val.

doorbell *n.* A small button above the *snail's doorstep* that is so difficult to find, that it is often easier to use the *knockers*. The *clematis*. Also *devil's doorbell*.

doorman, have a word with the *v.* To butter up the *bald headed bouncer* in order to be allowed into the premises he is guarding. To *cumulously nimbate* the *clematis*.

doormat basher *1. n.* One who whacks their partner's *fanny* on the back yard wall to get the dust off. *2. n.* A *lesbo*.

doos *n. Tits.*

dopper n. A *dork*.

doppleganger dick *n.* A *hard on* of such intensity, that one's own face is seen reflected in the shiny head, affording it the appearance of a miniature double.

dork *n.* A *dopper*.

Dorothy Perkins *n.* DP = Double Penetration. Of a lady, to simultaneously have *gentlemen callers* in her front and back pockets. Also a *man at C&A*, a *double decker*. *'In the cinema, one so-called film featured a man using disgusting sexual language. Another showed a lady baring her bosoms in the most provocative manner. A third film showed two well-hung men giving a woman a right Dorothy Perkins whilst she repeatedly took the Lord's name in vain. I was so disgusted that I vomited into my handbag. I think Mr. Muggeridge*

next to me felt ill too, as he was groaning and rummaging frantically in his trouser pockets for a handkerchief.' (Mary Whitehouse's report on a fact-finding trip to Amsterdam's Red Light District, 1968).

do the decent thing *v.* Of a lady who is *up on blocks*, to dutifully empty her husband's *bins* by means of an act of *horatio*.

double adapter *euph.* AC/DC man equipped with a *one pin plug* at the front but also having the benefit of a fully-functioning *single pin socket* at the back. A *switch hitter*.

double Barker *n.* A woman blessed with the body of Sue, but cursed with the face of Ronnie. A *bobfoc*.

double bassing *v.* To have sex from behind, fiddling with the lady's left nipple with your left hand and her *clematis* with your right - a position similar to the one adopted when playing the bass viola, although the sound is completely different. To perform *charlimingus*.

double booked *adj.* Of a lady, to be romantically entertaining two gentlemen at the same time.

double bouncers *n.* Value for money *tits* that resonate at twice the frequency of the woman's gait. ie. two bounces per step taken.

double cuffs *n.* The excessively-large *chinstraps* on a *bear trapper's* hat.

double dipper *n.* One who, unable to decide between *rice and chips*, has half a portion of both. A *switch hitter*, a *happy shopper*. A bisexual.

double doors *n. Beef curtains, cat flaps*.

double dragback *1. n.* An impressive football trick as perfected by the likes of David Ginola. *2. n.* A painful *wanking* accident whereby an inexperienced masturbatrix loses rhythm, resulting in one downward stroke being immediately followed by another, thus causing severe *banjo* trauma. Causes an effect similar to being *tossed off* by Ringo Starr.

double fare *n*. One whose fat *arse* takes up two seats on a train or bus. A *salad dodger, barge-arse*.

double header *n*. Of *grumble flick cliterati*, the intriguing act of performing simultaneous *horatio* on two *gut sticks*.

double the melt *v*. To give a lady not one, but two portions of hot cheese in her *hamburger*. To supply a second portion of filling to a *vertical bacon sandwich*.

double yolker *n*. A pornographic actor blessed with the elusive ability to fire off two consecutive *pop shots* without pausing for a sit down and a cup of tea in between. It is not known whether this happens in civilian life.

doughnut puncher *n*. A *dinner masher*.

dowel 1. *n*. In carpentry, a piece of wood that fits exactly into a hole. 2. *n*. In sex, a piece of *wood* that fits exactly into a hole.

down to one's last bead *adj*. To have an empty *sack*, to be bereft of *men's spendings*. To be *wankrupt*.

downhill skier *n*. See *skiing position*. A *crane operator*.

downtime *n*. The period which elapses between ejaculation and rearousal. In most men, downtime is around 20 minutes, though in the case of Cliff Richard it is 39 years and counting.

dowsing rod *n*. A *gut stick* that involuntarily twitches when approaching an area of great wetness.

doxy *n. arch*. Whore, *slag*.

D'Oyley *rhym. slang*. D'Oyley Carte = *fart*.

DP *acronym*. Double Penetration. Especially *one up the arse, one up the fanny*. Often leads to a *Newton's cradle*.

Dracula's tea bags *n*. Used tampons.

dragging like a seal's ringpiece *sim*. Descriptive of something that seems to last forever, eg. being held captive in Beirut, watching an *'Only Fools and Horses'* Christmas special.

dragon food *n*. Chocolates bought for her indoors when one is in the *cunt book*. *'Shit, I've been out on the piss for three days. I'd better stop by the garage and pick up some dragon food before I get home.'*

dragon's nostril *n*. The state of the ringpiece after a hot *Ruby Murray*. *'If you fancy giving yourself a dragon's nostril, then korma along to the Curry Capital, formerly the Rupali Restaurant, Bigg Market, Newcastle upon Tyne.'* (Press release from Abdul Latif, Lord of Harpole).

dragon's snout *n*. A particularly grotesque *turtle's head* which is accompanied by blasts of fiery breath, and may cause maidens to swoon.

drain your spuds *v*. To micturate. To have a *gypsy's kiss*.

draw an ace *v*. On wiping one's *arse* thoroughly, to eventually have an unsoiled piece of paper which indicates the process is complete.

draw mud from the well *v*. To *follow through*.

drawn-on durex *n*. A biro line drawn around the base of the penile shaft which fools a drunken lady into thinking one has taken sensible precautions.

drayhorse's bottom lip *sim*. A big, floppy *snatch*. Full of carrots.

dreadnought *n*. Even bigger than a *dead otter*.

dream topping *n*. Night *spongle*, whipped up in the *farmer's hat* during pornographic REM sleep.

dress-messer *n*. A gentleman with a *hair trigger*.

drink from both taps *v*. To be bisexual, *bend both ways*. See *double adapter*.

drink my kids *exclam*. Informal variant of *'suck my penis'*, usually used in a comedic or insulting sense, rather than a genuinely sexual one.

drink on a stick *n*. A *suck-off*.

drink under the dartboard *v*. Of a lady, to posess a face that does not conform to classical standards of beauty.

drip tray *n*. The often crusty sump in a pair of lady's *dunghampers*.

dripping like a fucked fridge *sim*. Of a lady, to be sexually aroused. *'I'm in the mood for love / Simply because you're near me / and whenever you're near me / I drip like a fucked fridge.'* (Song lyric, *'The Mood for Love'* by Cole Porter).

dripping like a George Foreman grill *sim*. Descriptive of a bird who is *fizzing at the bunghole* or *dripping like a fucked fridge*.

drive from the ladies' tee *v*. Of a man, to sit down in order to have a *slash*.

drive stick *v. US*. To be a lady in uncomfortable shoes, to not *like tennis*. To be a non-*lezza*.

drive the porcelain bus *v*. To pay a kneel-down visit to the lavatory during which one holds the rim like a steering wheel and does some *psychedelic yodelling*.

driving on the cats' eyes *v*. To emit a long, low, rumbling *fart* that sounds like it's going to damage one's suspension.

driving range *n*. The perineum. Where one hit one's *balls* when practising with one's *wood*.

drop a clot *v. medic*. To menstruate. *'It was D'Arcy who spoke first. 'Your disdain takes me somewhat aback, Miss Bennet. I fear I might have acted in some way inappropriately to cause you such offence.' 'No, Mr. D'Arcy, your behaviour has been impeccable, and the fault lies with me. I am dropping clots at the moment and find myself in the foulest of humours' she replied'.* (from *'Pride and Prejudice'* by Jane Austen).

drop a gut *v*. To *shoot a bunny*.

drop a pebble *v*. To erroneously emit a *rabbit tod* whilst attempting to *break wind*. See also *follow through*.

drop a tadpole in her beer *v. Aus*. To make a lady pregnant. *'Her Majesty the Queen is pleased to announce that after several years of trying, HRH Prince Edward, the Duke of Wessex has finally suceeded in dropping a tadpole in the Rt. Hon. Sophie, Countess of Wessex's beer.'* (Official notice, Buckingham Palace Gates, May 2003).

drop anchor in bum bay *v*. To arrive at the *rear admiral's* favourite port of call.

drop fudge *v*. To *pinch a loaf, crimp one off*.

drop her yoghurt *v.* Of a lady, to have an orgasm in her *parts* for whatever reason.

drop one *v.* Let off, *chuff.*

drop one's back *v.* To float an *air biscuit.* To enflatulise the atmosphere around one's *gammon ring.*

drop one's Revels *v.* To suffer an unfortunate *follow through* experience whilst *clearing one's nether throat. 'It's no good. I can't finish this Olympic Marathon, I've dropped me Revels.'*

drop one's yop *v.* To ejaculate messily in a manner not unlike that of a bottle of the popular drinkable yoghurt being dropped onto the tiled floor of a petrol station. *'What's the matter, Cliff?' 'I just dropped my yop, Sue. Best get the Vax out.'*

dropout *n.* Underpant condition whereby a *knacker* protrudes from the bottom of the *shreddies,* or famously in Peter Beardsley's case, football shorts.

dropped pie, face like a *sim.* To resemble one who has been bobbing for chips in a deep fat fryer.

dropping the shopping *euph.* See *drop the kids off at the pool.*

drop the kids off at the pool *euph.* To defecate in the toilet.

drop your guts *v.* To break wind. *"Fossilised fish hooks', croaked Venables. 'Which one of you beanfeasters has dropped his guts?"* (from *'Jennings Makes a Daisy Chain'* by Anthony Buckeridge).

drop your hat forwards *v.* To *fanny fart, muff chuff.* To play the *Lawley kazoo,* blow a *Harry Ramsden's raspberry. 'Just as I was donning the beard, she dropped her hat forwards'.*

drop your hat *v.* To *fart.* Also *drop a bomb, drop your handbag, drop a gut.*

drown a copper *v.* To sink a *dreadnought,* give birth to a *dead otter.*

drown a duck *v.* To float an *air biscuit* whilst in the shower. Descriptive of the noise produced by a quivering *ringpiece* in the presence of flowing water.

drown some kittens *n.* To pass a litter of small stools which nobody wants to give a home to.

drown the chocolate slugs *v.* Alternative to *light a bum cigar* for those anticipating a looser stool.

drug smuggler's wait *n.* An interminable period of lavatorial pandiculation which involves sitting on the *bog* waiting for one of them *shits* that take ages to come down, like when you've ate too much meat.

drugs bust *n.* Simultaneous entry of two *bobbies' truncheons* through the front and back doors. Also *police raid, SVSA.*

druncle *n.* A male relative who generally stinks of *refreshment. 'Do something, dear. Your Druncle George has just dropped the baby onto the barbecue again.'*

dry bob 1. *n.* A public schoolboy who doesn't row. 2. *v.* Fully-clothed sex, leading to *milmed kex.* 3. *n.* A bankrupt *money shot,* a *spaffless stack blow.*

dry docked *adj.* Lack of lubrication situation where a low tide of *blip* prevents the *skin boat* sailing into *tuna town.*

DSB *abbrev.* Dangerous Sperm Build-up. To have two tins of *Fussell's Milk. 'I'm sorry, Sir Cliff, but you are suffering from DSB. As your doctor, the only course of treatment I can prescribe is an*

ADW.'

DSL *abbrev*. Dick Sucking Lips.

duck butter *n. Aus*. Assorted smegmalogical effluviums accumulating under the *fiveskins* of the unclean.

duck sandwich *n*. Prominent *pudenders* visible through the tight leggings of fat-thighed ladies.

duck sausage *n*. A filling gourmet meal which is best eaten in a crouched position. *'I'm glad you got to meet Val Doonican after the concert, nan.' 'Aye, but I had to have three portions of duck sausage off the roadies to get backstage.'*

duck's breakfast *n. Welsh*. Early morning *sausage* and *split kippers*. Accompanied by gentle quacking and a flurry of feathers.

duck smuggler *n*. A *Glen Miller*, one who produces a *string of pearls*, as if trying to smuggle a duck past customs by hiding it up his *arse*. One who *farts* whilst walking.

duckwalk *1. n*. A unique dance pioneered by virtuoso guitarist Chuck Berry. *2. n*. In *farting*, the process of letting out little pockets of gas in time with each step. An *ugly duckling*, a *string of pearls*.

duel fuel *n. Fighting water*.

duel with the pink Darth Vader *n*. A *Hand Solo*.

duelling banjos *1. n*. A female dormitory *wank race*. *2. n*. The vigorous double-tug motion of a *meat vid crane operator*.

duff *1. n*. Bum, arse. *2. n*. Fadge, minge, twat, clopper.

duffy's bridge *n*. The *biffin bridge, tinter, taint, barse*. The perineum.

DUFTO *acronym*. Any old *bird* at a film premier with a whiff of mothballs around her, eg. *'Carry On Breathing'* star Barbara Windsor. Dug Up For The Occasion.

duggle *v*. To receive or perform an act of oral *horatio* whilst *crimping off a loaf*. To take part in a *blumpkin*.

dugs *n. Baps, paps*. Olde worlde version of *jugs*.

Duke of giblets *n*. A *salad dodger*.

dukes *rhym. slang*. Haemorrhoids. From Duke of Argyles = piles.

dump *1. n*. A 40-minute reading session in the *dunny*. *2. v*. To *curl one off*.

dump and burn *1. v. milit*. RAF term for the act of jettisoning fuel behind engines on afterburn, resulting in a spectacular display of rumbling noise and flames. *2. n*. Going for a *tom tit* after consuming unhealthy levels of spicy food, resulting in rumbling noise and flames.

dumpling *n*. A solitary, suety *turd* floating in a pan of *bum stew*.

dumplings *1. n*. baby *dumps*. *2. n*. Particularly filling breasts that go well with *meat and two veg*.

dump station *n*. The *chod bin*.

dump valve *1. n*. A thing that a reader of *'Max Power'* might somehow fasten to his car engine. *2. n*. The *nipsy*.

dunce's hats *n*. Them conical pointed *tits* found underneath woollen sweaters in 1950's America. *Twin peaks*.

dung dreadlocks *n*. Haile Selassie's *beaded curtains*. Laid-back *tagnuts*.

dung funnel *n. medic. Fudge tunnel*.

dunghampers *n. Undercrackers, trolleys, bills*.

dung lung *n. medic*. Descriptive of one who has been *necking turds*. A halitosis sufferer.

dung puncher *n.* A gentleman homosexualist. A *doughnut puncher.*

dunk 1. *n.* To dip a biscuit in a cup of tea. 2. *n.* to dip one's *wick* into a *fanny.*

dunky *n.* Protective sheath to prevent the penis going soggy and falling off into the *hairy goblet* during dunking.

dunny *n. Aus.* Toilet, *netty, cludgie, shite house.*

dunny budgie *n. Aus.* A fly buzzing round an Australian *bog.*

dustman's library *n.* An archive of vintage recycled *niff mags* usually found in the cabins of dustcarts, or the portacabin at the local civic amenity site.

dust the duvet *v.* To *hitchhike under the big top*, to *starch the sheets.*

Dutch *n. Sausage sandwich, tit wank.* Also *Dutch fuck.*

Dutch Alps *n.* Small breasts, *fried eggs, stits, patsies.* Also *Lincolnshire Cairngorms.* As scaled by a *Dutch mountaineer.*

Dutch arrow *n.* A shot up the *bonus tunnel.*

Dutch bellows *n.* A *blanket ripper.*

Dutch blast *n.* Bellows effect achieved at the open end of the duvet when one wants to sample or indeed share the fragrant fruits of a bedtime solo on the *botty bugle.*

Dutch blindfold *n.* When in the 69 position, with the woman on the bottom and the gentleman's *clockweights* fitting nicely in the eye sockets.

Dutch boy *n.* A lady in *comfortable shoes*, a *tennis fan*, a lesbian. ie, one who always has their finger in a *dyke.*

Dutch Breakfast *n.* Something one

has after *awakening the bacon.*

Dutch brylcreem *n.* A glutinous product that you don't particularly want in your hair. *Gunk.*

Dutch cap *n.* An extremely tight fitting rubber hat worn in Holland.

Dutch door *n.* A *bird* who *swings both ways.*

Dutch floor polish *n. Spunk.*

Dutch hand grenade *n.* A *beefy eggo,* caught in the hand and then detonated under an unsuspecting person's nose. A *cupcake.*

Dutch Marathon *n.* The hasty, yet seemingly never-ending walk home after purchasing a new selection of *fleshmags* from a specialist newsagent.

Dutch miracle *n.* The magical appearance of *art pamphlets* under a mattress or on top of a wardrobe in a hotel bedroom.

Dutch oven *n.* The act of cooking one's partner's head beneath the bedclothes using *cabbage gas.*

Dutch oyster *n.* An exotic mouthful of the contents of one's own *winkle.* The possible consequence of a *Swiss kiss.*

Dutch salute *n. Irish toothache.* An erection.

Dutch satay *n.* The epilogue of a *stick vid* where the starlet sucks on the leading man's rapidly softening phallus after she's been *front* and *back fucked* with it, and had it smear *spunk* all over her *tits.*

Dutch sauna *n.* The provision of a fruity *parp* to one's spouse whilst in a hot shower cubicle. An aquatic *Dutch oven.*

Dutch souvenir *n.* A little something brought back in the urethra to surprise the wife and help you remember Amsterdam.

Dutch strawberry *n.* The *herman*

gelmet. With all pips stuck on it.

Dutch teabreak *n*. The act of *relaxing in a gentleman's way* whilst at work. A *monkey's fag break*.

Dutch tug *n*. A no-nonsense paid-for *hand-job*. Do not pay more than £10.

Dutch wink *n*. The flashing of the *bacon rasher* when crossing and uncrossing the legs. *'The film has action, drama, suspense and a superb Dutch wink from Sharon Stone.'* (Barry Norman, reviewing *'Basic Instinct'*).

DVDA *abbrev*. Double Vaginal, Double Anal. The Holy Grail of *bongo video* acts, presumably involving four India-rubber men and one uncomfortable woman.

dyke *n*. Lesbian, *tuppence licker, carpet muncher, three wheeler*, a *woman on the other bus*. See also *diesel dyke, bulldyke*.

dyke differential *n*. The notable discrepancy between the attractiveness of the sort of lesbians depicted in *grumble vids, seed catalogues* etc., and the sort actually encountered in real life.

Dylan *n*. A tangled, matted, unkempt mess of a *bush*, resembling the hairstyle of grizzled singer-songwriter Bob. A *Terry Waite's allotment*.

dyson *n*. A bird with a right good suck on her.

Ee

ear pie *n*. A right *bollocking* a woman gives a man when he stays too long in the pub, forgets her birthday, *fucks* her sisters, etc.

earlids *n*. Invisible, soundproof flaps of skin which descend over a gentleman's ears when conversing with his lady wife.

early morning dip *n*. To make love to a woman whilst she is still asleep. A romantic act that can carry a 15-year prison sentence.

earn brownie points *v*. Of a gentleman, to perform selfless acts of kindness, like doing the dishes or a spot of ironing in the hope that one's partner will express her gratitude with a game of *mud darts*.

Eartha Kitts *rhym. slang. Shits*, diarrhoea. Also *Brads*.

Easter Island statue with an arse full of razor blades *sim. Aus*. A permanently grave, sour expression. First used by Paul Keating to describe Malcolm Fraser when in opposition, but actually describes Jimmy Nail to a T.

eat breakfast backwards *v*. To *drive the porcelain bus*.

eat cockroaches *v*. *18thC*. To engage in the filthy, disgusting act of *self-pollution*.

eat fancy cakes *v*. Of a gentleman, to have a tendency towards the craftier end of *butchery*. To *jump puddles*, to be a *ginger beer*. '*Popstar Stephen Gately shocked Boyzone fans today when he announced at an awards ceremony that he eats fancy cakes.*' (Trevor McDonald, '*News at Ten*' headline story, June 2000).

eat humble cock *v*. Of a lady who has been involved in a disagreement with a gentleman friend, to acknowledge in the time-honoured manner that she may not have been right after all.

eating sushi off a barbershop floor *sim. Cumulonimbus*.

eat one's greens *v*. To do something one would really rather not do just to earn *brownie points* from a female partner, eg. listen to her go on about her day, putting some shelves up.

eat out *v*. To *lap fanny*, to *dive muff*, to *cumulonimbulate*. To *lick out*.

eau de colon *n*. *Rusty water, fizzy gravy*.

ebdon slide *1. n*. In snooker, the positioning of the fingers on the table whilst cueing. *2. n*. In sex, the positioning of the fingers on the lady's *bits* in order to expose the *clematis*.

EC flag *n*. Nipple.

Eccles cake *n*. A casually discarded *Eartha*. Named after local newspaper hack (name removed following legal advice) of the '*Sussex Express*' who, after a night on the strong cider, *shat* himself in the pub and shook it out of his trousers before ordering another pint of Biddenden's 9-percenter.

Eccles snake *n*. A penis with warts.

eddie *n*. See *stobart*.

Edinburgh *rhym. slang*. A *fur burger*. From Edinburgh Fringe = *minge*.

e-dophile *n*. A world wide web chat room *nonce*. An internet *diddler*.

Edward Woodward *onomat*. A bathtime *fart*. A *bottle of olives*.

e-gasm *n*. *Web-grumble*-assisted *stack blow*.

egg-bound *adj*. Blocked of *dung-funnel*, constipated.

egg Mcwhiff *n*. A particularly sulphurous mid-morning *air buffet* produced after breakfasting at a fast food restaurant.

egg white canon *n*. A 4-inch *blue-veined blunderbuss* loaded with two *balls*.

eggy soldier *n*. The result of taking a *dip* whilst the *red flag is flying*.

e-gret *adj*. A feeling of self-reproach experienced following any ill-considered internet trans-action. *'E-grets, I've had a few.'* (Pete Townshend, song lyric).

e-gypsy *n*. One who can't make up their mind which ISP to use, resulting in one's e-mails to them always being returned. A nomad on the information superhighway.

Egyptian PT *1. n. milit.* Sleep. *2. n.* Masturbation.

Eiffel Tower, do the *v*. Of a pair of professional footballers engaged in a *spitroast* with a lucky young lady, to make eye contact and exchange a high five, thus creating the char-acteristic outline of the famous Parisian pylon.

eighteen spoker *n*. A particularly hairy woman's *arsehole* resembling a tiny bicycle wheel.

eighteen wheeler *n*. A *turd* of such length that it runs a significant risk of jack-knifing in the *pan*.

elbow bender *n*. A *bar fly*, a *boozer*.

electric chair *1. n.* A device used by the state of Texas to kill education-ally subnormal black men. *2. n.* The last resort seat in a pub next to the most crashing bore in the establishment.

electric lemonade *n*. A hallucino-genic, West-country scrumpy cider. Also known locally as *Tone Vale Tonic*, after the former mental institute that housed many of its devotees.

electric spaghetti *n*. *Spunk*.

electric twitch *n*. Involuntary jerk

of the head displayed by *grumble flick* starlets upon receiving a face-ful of *jitler*. Named after the similar reflexive spasm which can be achieved by stroking the bars of an electric fire.

elepants *n*. Jumbo-sized ladies' trunks.

elephant man's hat *sim*. Descriptive of a very spacious *fanny*. A *clown's pocket*, a *hippo's yawn*.

elephants *adj. rhym. slang.* Drunk. From elephant's trunk.

elephant's ears *n*. Enormous flappy flaps. Huge *Keith Burtons*.

Ellen MacNomates *n. prop.* Female version of *Billy no mates*, a girl without any friends. Named after popular lone round the world yachtsperson Dame Ellen Mac-Nomates.

Elvis *n*. A *shit* that requires so much effort to force out that one almost has a stroke. The oppposite of a *life affirmer*. *'Are you okay? You look terrible, Your Majesty.' 'I'll be fine, Bishop. That Boxing Day Elvis just took it out of me, though.'*

Elvis's leg *n*. The onset of the *vinegar strokes* whilst *fucking* upright in a doorway, bus shelter or taxi queue. Often accompanied by an 'Uh-huh-huh' vocalisation and involuntary curling of the lip.

embalmer, the *n*. Specialised wrest-ling move whereby one's good lady's stomach gets covered with *sex wee*.

Embassy No. 2 *1. n.* A cigarette/excrement combination performed in workplace toilets up and down the country. *'Keep an eye on run-way six for me, will you? I'm just nipping out for an Embassy No. 2.' 2 n.* An urgent *shit*, usually prompted by the first puff one takes on the first cigarette of the day.

Emmas *rhym. slang.* Haemorrhoids. From Emma Freud, Clement's chimp-eared daughter. Also *Nobbies*.

empty one's back *v.* To *crimp off a tail*, to *lay Al Jolson to rest*.

empty one's beer sack *v.* To go for a *piss* in a pub.

empty the bins *v.* To ejaculate. *'The Holy Father condemns as anathema all artificial means of contraception. The only means of birth control allowable within the Roman church is the practice of ejaculation extra-vagio. That is, to whip the charlie out at the vinegar strokes and empty the bins onto the gunt.'* (Papal Edict, 1988).

empty the caboose *v.* To excrete, pass motions, *drop the kids off at the pool* etc.

empty threat *n.* A terrifyingly loud *fart* that mysteriously fails to assault one's nasal passages. The opposite of an *SBD*.

Ena Sharples' mouth *n.* A disapproving, puckered *rusty bullet hole*. Commonly seen on *grumble mag* models bending over a snooker table. Also *Dot Cotton's mouth*, the *tea towel holder*.

enamel bucket *n.* A big, dry, cold, rattly *fanny*.

Engelberts *rhym. slang. Eartha Kitts.*

English batsman *n. Aus.* Someone who doesn't spend very long at the *crease*. A *two push Charlie*, a *two stroke joke*, a *one pump chump*.

English disease, the *n.* Homosexuality, as defined by the French.

English overcoat *n.* The French equivalent of the English *French letter*. A *Coney Island whitefish*.

engorgement ring *n.* A mythical item of *betrothal jewellery* promised to a lady in return for getting one's *nuts* emptied.

Enochs *rhym. slang.* The guts. From the famous Tory MP Enoch Bowel.

'Enry's 'ammer *n.* A *diamond-cutting* erection of such proportions that it deprives the brain of blood and leaves the owner in a semi-comatose state, as if he had been hit around the head by OAP boxing champ Henry Cooper's trademark left hook. About forty years ago.

Enterprise transporter accident *euph.* A nice looking bird with lousy *tits* accompanied by a ugly bird with great *tits*.

entertainment system *n.* One's ladyfriend's *tits, arse* and *fanny*. *'What's that in your bag, Dr. Von Hagens?' 'Just an entertainment system. I'm taking it home for the weekend.'*

erection section *n.* The top shelf of a newsagents.

Eric *n.* Schoolboy alternative to a *Jake*.

Eros *n.* The pose that must be struck when *pissing* in a toilet with no lock on the door, precariously balancing on one leg with the other holding the door shut.

escape from alcotramp *v.* To spot something fascinating in a shop window across the street when approaching an animated *Harold Ramp*.

escape sub *n.* A technologically advanced brown, sea-going vessel in which an evil hangover makes its getaway. An *alcopoop*.

ESD *abbrev.* Eat Shitty Dick. To *smoke a pink cigar* fresh from *kak canyon*. *Hot karl*.

eskimo's glove *n.* Warm, furry mitten that smells of fish and can accommodate one's whole hand. Not unlike a large vagina.

Essex tartan *n.* Burberry.

etch-a-sketch *v.* To attempt to draw a smile on a woman's face by simultaneously twiddling both of her nipples. *Finding Radio Luxembourg, come in Tokyo.*

Ethel *n. rhym. slng.* An act of *self abuse.* From Ethel Merman = Sherman tank. *'Where is he? He's due on the balcony to bless the crowds in thirty seconds.' 'Don't worry, Cardinal. He's just went in the bog for a quick Ethel over the Daily Sport.'*

Ethelbrown the Ready *n.* A pretender to the *porcelain throne.* A *King Richard* in waiting.

ethics girl *n.* The kind of girl who doesn't *fuck* on a first date, won't do it in a car or shop doorway and wouldn't *swallow* even if one could get her to suck it in the first place. The antithesis of an Essex girl.

eticlit *n.* The observance of rules of correct decorum when *dining at the Captain's table.*

Eton leapfrog *n. Bottery.*

everlasting gobstoppers *n.* The *clockweights* of a gentleman. The *knackers.*

everything but the girl *1. n.* Hull-based 90s duo featuring a woman with a face like a Nicholas Lyndhurst who's been hit with pan. *2. n.* A sophisticated *wank* incorporating low lights, soft music and a bottle of wine.

Excalibur *n.* A magic *turd* of legendary proportions that rises eerily out of the water in a mist-shrouded toilet.

excalibut *n.* Gentleman's Mach 3 razor clogged up with his girlfriend's *trouser twiglets.*

Exchange & Mart *1. rhym. slang.* To *drop a gut. 2. rhym. slang.* A *dropped gut.*

ex files *n.* A *wank bank* folder containing the most filthy memories of sexual depravities enjoyed with previous partners.

exhaust pipe engineer *n.* One who tinkers with *exhaust pipes.*

exhaust pipe *n.* The *Bumhole, fudge tunnel.* Also *tailpipe.*

exhibition position *n.* Variation on *doggy-style* sex. The man takes the kneeling position from behind, places one hand on the lady's back and the other jauntily on his hip. Then turns and smiles at an imaginary audience, pretending to be a moustachioed German porn star.

exit wound *n.* The state of the *freckle* after a particularly fierce *Ruby Murray.*

exorcist *n.* One who is gifted with the power to rid a place of spirits, ie. the top shelf behind the bar.

expecting a harsh winter *euph.* Of a bird, to be putting on weight or over-eating. *'She's stuffing her face with eclairs. She must be expecting a harsh winter.'*

expresso bongo *1. n.* A crap film from the 60s starring Sir Cliff Richard. *2. n.* The fast forwarding through the uninteresting bits of films which almost certainly do not star Sir Cliff Richard.

extras *n.* Something one tentatively asks for whilst winking at a masseuse or osteopath. The *tugging* as opposed to the *rubbing* in a *rub-a-tug shop.*

eye magnets *n.* Lovely *tits.*

eye of Sauron *1. n.* In JRR Tolkein's *'Lord of the Rings'*, a 'lidless eye wreathed with flame' with which the Lord Sauron watched over Middle Earth, and thus 2. *n.* A lidless eye wreathed in flame which is the inevitable consequence of dining at the Curry Capital (absolutely no connection whatsoever to the former Rupali Restaurant), Bigg Market (no, really), Newcastle upon Tyne. A *Johnny Cash, Japanese flag, Wigan rosette.*

eyes like a shithouse rat sim. Descriptive of one with extraordinary visual acuity. *'Check my collar for lipstick will you, Edwina. Only Norma's got eyes like a fucking shithouse rat.'*

eyes like sheep's cunts *n. medic.* Symptom of an extremely bad hangover.

Ff

Fabergé egg n. A large oval *dump* which comes out encrusted in red jewels as a result of *famers* or a ripped *nipsy*.

face fannies n. *Bugger's grips*, sideburns. As sported by the singer out of Supergrass and Anne Robinson.

face grating n. Performing the act of *cumulonimbus* upon a woman with advanced *five o'clock fanny*.

face painting v. To adorn one's spouse with *jelly jewellery*.

fadge n. A cross between a *fanny* and a vagina.

FADS acronym. From the motor trade, descriptive of something worthless, eg. any Citroen over 3-months old. Fuck All Divided by Six.

faecal touch n. Opposite of the Midas touch, ie. everything this person touches turns to *shit*, eg. Clive Sinclair.

FAFCAM acronym. Fit As Fuck, Common As Muck, eg. Denise Van Outen, Suzanne out of Hear'Say.

faff n. A lady's *front bottom*.

fag 1. n. An 8-year-old boy who has to fetch tea, fetch toast and *fetch off* a prefect. 2. n. *Tab, ciggie*, a *cancer stick*. 3. n. *US*. A *bummer*.

fag fireworks n. The brief, but nonetheless impressive night-time pyrotechnic display given to motorists following behind vans.

fag hag n. A wizened old woman who prefers the company of homosexuals.

fagnet n. A man who, when out clubbing, only manages to attract *botters*.

fagnolia adj. The yellowy-creamy-brown colour found on the interior walls of betting shops, pubs and the houses of chain smokers.

fagnostic n. One who either doesn't know or hasn't quite made his mind up which way he wants to swing.

fagriculture n. Uphill gardening and its associated lifestyle.

fail one's driving test 1. v. To prove unable to reach a required level of ability when driving a motor vehicle. 2. v. To prove unable to steer a *fart* around a *brown obstacle*. To *gamble and lose, follow through*.

faint on n. *medic*. A devastating condition affecting certain males who are *hung like rogue elephants*. When a *fat is cracked*, the shaft drains the body of its blood, causing the patient to become light-headed.

fairy hammock n. A *tart's dung-hampers*.

fairy liquid n. *Tart fuel*. Drinks such as WKD and Bacardi Breezers for homos and girls.

fairy wings n. The gossamer tracery of *arse* sweat left on the seat when a lardy chap gets up off the *bog* on a warm day.

fall at Beecher's v. To *come off* before reaching the finishing post. To suffer from premature ejaculation.

fallen off her bike euph. A monthly *cycle accident* leaving a woman bleeding from the *saddle area*.

fallen to the communists euph. Of a woman, to have *fallen off her bike*. 'Any luck last night?' 'No. She's fallen to the communists.'

falling down juice n. Beer. Also *fighting water, dizzyade*.

fall of soot n. The messy result of a failed *dropped hat*. A *follow through*, a *lost gamble*.

family jewels n. Priceless heirloom *knackers*.

fancy wank *v.* To use an ugly bird's *fanny* to save wear and tear on your hand.

fandruff *n. Fanny* dandruff. *Muff-druff, Scurf 'n' turf.*

fanjita *n.* A *tuppence.*

fannanigans *n.* Women's things. From *fanny* + shenanigans.

fannicure *n.* A pampering of the *bush.* A *quim-trim,* a *Hitler tash.*

fanny 1. *n.* UK. *Snatch, snapper, quim, cunt, puh-seh.* Female genitals, ladies' *pudenders.* 2. *n.* US. *Arse, backside.* 3. *n.* Fictitious Great Aunt.

fanny apple *n.* A neonate. A new born baby. *'Births: Smith. At the Portland Hospital. To Evadne and Captain George Everard, a boy, Spartacus, brother to Troy and Elgin. Mother and fanny apple doing well. Deo Gracias.' ('The Times'* Feb 12th 2004).

fannyarse *n.* A *crafty butcher* whose *dirtstar* has been *lubbocked* to the extent that it resembles a lady's *quim.*

fanny badger *n.* See *Blackbeard's ghost.*

fanny batter *n.* The substance which leaves one's chin greasy after a *fish supper. Sloom.*

fanny battering ram *n.* A stout length of *wood* used to burst *Mary hinges.*

fanny bib *n.* A sanitary towel.

fanny bomb *n.* The female organism. *'How was it for you, pet? Did the old fanny bomb go off?'*

fanny farm *n.* A *knocking shop.* A brothel, *trollbooth.*

fanny flange *n.* The vaginal escutcheon.

fanny fright *n. medic.* Nervous condition affecting some macho men who suddenly find themselves unable to have *a bit* when presented with an opportunity.

fanny gallops *n.* In a lady, the early rumblings of sexual excitement at the sight of a Calvin Klein Y-fronts poster. The *hots.*

fanny hockle *n.* The product of a post-coital *fadge cough.*

fanny hopper 1. *n.* A 2-foot diameter inflatable orange vagina with handles at the top. 2. *n.* A gentleman who hops from one *fanny* to another. A *stickman,* a *skippy.*

fanny licker *n.* A small dog, such as a Yorkshire Terrier or Pekingese, which is best-suited to sitting on a lady's lap. *"Oh God. Tricky-Woo's got worms,' wailed Tristram as he put down the phone. 'Tricky-Woo?' I said. 'Who, or indeed what, is Tricky-Woo?' 'My dear James, it's Mrs. Pomfrey's fanny licker,' laughed Siegfried, as he stuck his arm up yet another cow's arse."* (from *'Some Vets Do 'Ave 'Em'* by James Herriot).

fanny magnate *n.* A commercial purveyor of ladies' favours. A *pimp, fanny farmer.*

fanny magnet *n.* Something or someone to which top drawer *blart* is inexplicably drawn, eg. A Ferrari, Rolex watch, Mick Hucknall.

fanny mechanic *n. medic.* One who performs *MOTT* tests, a *box doc,* a *snatch quack,* a *scrape doctor.* A gynaecologist.

fanny nanny *n.* A feminine napkin.

fanny nosher *n.* A *woman in comfortable shoes* who takes the *other bus* to *dine at the Y.* A *tennis fan,* a *lady golfer.*

fanny paddy *n.* A *muff huff,* a *blob strop.* A *Monty.*

fanny rat *n.* A sexually promiscuous

male. A *skippy, a bed hopper.*

fanny swill *n.* The frothy, post-coital substance fashioned by a lady after a good session.

fannytastic 1. *adj.* Anything wonderful to do with the female genitals. 2. *adj.* Descriptive of a thing which is so excellent that it can only be compared with a *fanny.* 'Have you been watching the repeats of *'My Family' on UK Gold?' 'No, and it's been fannytastic.'*

fanny tax *n.* Surcharge paid on drinks in a bar staffed by top class *blart.*

fanny turd *n.* A child. *'Births: Chocmonockly-Ffeatherstone-haugh. On February 17th, at the Portland Hospital. To Rupert and Rowenta (nee Ponfrit-Cake), a 6lb 8oz fanny turd, Parkinson Cowan. A brother for Tefal. Deo Gracias.'* (from *'The Times'* Feb 12th 2004).

fannyversary *n.* The single once-a-year *fuck* to which a husband is legally entitled.

fanoir *n. Fr.* French insult. *'Vous etes une fucking grand fanoir, M. D'Artagnan.'* (from *'The Three Musketeers'* by Alexander Dumas).

FANTA *acronym.* A one night stand. Fuck And Never Touch Again.

fan your arse *v.* To perform a male courtship display, masculine showing off. *'Well you can tell by the way I fan my arse / I'm a woman's man, with a sweaty barse.'* (Song lyric, *'Stayin' Alive'* by The Bee Gees).

farce *n.* The *snot.*

farm bent *adj.* Descriptive of a fellow who finds himself inclined to quadruped romance as a consequence of enforced rural remote-ness. 'GRAMS: Wine bar. Int. Day. FX: Door opens. EDDIE GRUNDY: Nelson! Come quickly! There's trouble in 5 Acre field! NELSON GABRIEL: What on earth...? EDDIE GRUNDY: It's your dad, Nelson. He's gone farm bent. NELSON GABRIEL: Oh no, not again. GRAMS: Dissolve to ext. day. FX: Distressed cow. WALTER GABRIEL: Ooh, yeah. Take that Daisy. You know you want it right up you, you dirty bitch. FX: Particularly loud moo.' (from *'The Archers'*, BBC Radio 4, October 2nd 1983).

farmers *rhym. slang. Emmas.* From Farmer Giles.

farmer sutra *n.* The ancient Dutch treatise on the art of erotic *barnyard love.*

farmer's breakfast *n.* A *shit* and a drink of water.

farmer's broth *n. Spiff, spodge, sprangle,* etc.

farmer's protest *n.* An outbreak of chronic diarrhoea which pebbledashes the *chod bin* bowl with semi-liquid *shit.* From the universal habit of agricultural types who register their objections to unfair bank service charges by spraying thousands of gallons of cow *crap* all over the front of their local branch.

farn't *n.* An *air biscuit* that, no matter how hard one tries, cannot be *floated.* A *fart* that can't.

FARO *acronym.* A gentleman's post-coital afterplay. Fart And Roll Over.

fart 1. *n.* A *bottom burp,* the expulsion of foul air from the *chamber of horrors,* causing the *clappers* to vibrate musically like a tuning fork. A *beefy eggo,* a *poot,* an *air biscuit.* 2. *v.* To *drop one* of the above, *step* *on a duck.*

fartacus *n. prop.* A hero who takes responsibility for a *duck* they didn't *step on.* From the Roman slave Spartacus who was crucified on the Appian way for *letting off* in the presence of Julius Caesar.

fart blanche *n. Fr.* The opportunity to freely *drop a Tommy Squeaker* without fear of detection, eg. in a noisy ham-packing factory, in the pits at a stock car race, or when nursing one's father back to health from a near-death diarrhoea mishap.

fartbreak ridge *n.* The rugged, windswept anatomical scarp that runs from the *anus* to the *nutsack* or *fanny*, upon which *farts* sometimes break. The *biffin bridge.*

fart buffer *n.* The methane safety cushion which presages the *turd* and allows one a little extra time to reach the lavatory. *'I'm afraid I must dash, Your Majesty. I've used up my fart buffer and I'm touching cloth.'* The *turtle's breath.*

fart catcher 1. *n.* Male homeosexualist. 2. *n.* Derogatory term for one who waits on another person, eg. a valet or footman.

farter *n. Aus. milit.* A sleeping bag. *'Tuesday, December 18th, 1912. Ate last of the pemmican in the night. Heavy snow again. Found Bowers dead in his farter. There is no hope for us now.'* (from *'The Journal of Captain Scott'*).

fart funnel *n.* The *arse.*

fart higher than your arse *euph.* To have an inflated opinion of oneself. To think one all that when one ain't, eg. talentless fat *fuck* Chris Moyles.

farticles *n.* The crumbs of an *air biscuit*, often found in the sheets after *breakfast in bed.*

farting against thunder *met. meteorog.* Descriptive of a hopeless task that will inevitably end in failure. eg. Attempting to pay by cheque in McDonald's, saying 'no' to a Pennine Windows telesales person, trying to get Jack Straw MP to give you a straight answer to a question, etc. *Pissing into the wind.*

farting bracket *n.* A device to the left of the clutch pedal found in luxury motor vehicles which enables the driver to lift one buttock and *let one go* without taking his attention off the road. *'Once again, the Mercedes E Class has an extensive range of dealer-fit options. But at this price range, things like air conditioning, farting bracket and CD autochanger really should come as standard.'* (Jeremy Clarkson, *'Sunday Times'* July 2003).

farting clappers *n. medic.* Small, fragile, castanet-like bones up one's *nick* that resonate at particular frequencies, producing an unexpectedly loud 'braaap!' sound in polite company.

farting crackers *n.* Trousers. *'When invited to a black tie function, the correct mode of attire for gentlemen would be ~white dress shirt and collar, cummerbund, black shoes, black dinner jacket and corresponding farting crackers.'* (from *'Debrett's Guide to Etiquette'* by Buckridge Pottinger).

farting sideways *v.* To have a bad case of piles. *"Do please sit down, Mr. Willoughby,' Lady Marchmaine invited. 'Thank you, Madam,' he replied, 'but if it is all the same with you, I shall remain standing. I rode a fox to earth over* *three counties yesterday and I fear I am farting sideways.''* (from *'Sense and Sensibility'* by Jane Austen).

farting strings *n. medic.* Tendons or ligaments in the *lisks* which are prone to snapping during periods of excessive mirth. *'In a landmark court case, a Birmingham pensioner with an IQ of 6 is suing the BBC after snapping her farting strings laughing at the sitcom 'My Family.''* (BBC News report, Michael Buerke).

fart juggler *n.* One gifted with the ability to hold and queue *dropped hats* when in a potentially embarrassing situation, eg. in a lift, and then fire off a *repeater* when at a safe distance. An *air traffic controller.*

fart knocker *1. n. Bum bandit, fudge nudger. 2. n.* One who criticises another's *farts.*

fartleberries *n. Dangleberries, winnets, chocolate raisins.*

fart on one's weetabix *euph.* To spoil one's chances. A less vulgar version of *piss on one's chips.*

fart sack *n.* The bed. *'Malaria was powerless to resist. His eyes burned into hers like Swarovski crystals. His strong arms enfolded her body as she felt herself being swept away on a monsoon of passion. Roughly, Pablo took her by her heaving shoulders, pushed her down and did her on his king-sized fart sack.'* (from *'The Countess and the Matador'* by Barbara Cartland).

fart sauce *n.* A *raspberry coulis* that is served with *arse cress.* The rancid juice accompanying a wet *poot.*

fart sucker *n.* A sycophantic *arse licker,* eg. BBC Royal 'Correspondent' Nicholas Witchell.

fart to a shit fight, bring a *v.* In a competitive situation, to be seriously overmatched.

farty winks *n.* A flatulent and refreshing post-prandial nap usually taken on a Sunday afternoon in order to let one's guts settle after a big dinner. *'Jesus. Is the dog ill?' 'No, it's your dad. He's just having farty winks in front of the Grand Prix.'*

fasturbation *n.* Emergency, hurried *self abuse.*

fat bird's shoe, full as a *sim.* Descriptive of a something or someone which is stuffed to bursting point, eg. a former glam-rock star's hard disk, a postman's wardrobe, Jim Davidson's skin. *'More spooge, Marc?' 'No thanks, lads. I'm as full as a fat bird's shoe'.*

fat lass sarnie *n.* A shameful, yet hugely satisfying sandwich that must be consumed out of the view of one's mates on account of its embarrassing nature, eg. a crisp, mayonnaise and tomato ketchup bap.

fat rascals *n.* Playful *titties.*

fatty *n.* Something that causes much hilarity in the school showers. An erection.

fatty clappers *n.* Large, Granada Men & Motors-style *knockers.* The sort of *devil's dumplings* that would make steam come out of Robin Askwith's collar.

faux-pwa *n.* A slip of lap-dancing club etiquette. To *milm* one's *kex* when fishing for a tenner to stuff in a bored dancer's *dunghampers.*

fawn *v.* To *come,* to *reach the Billy Mill Roundabout. 'Felicity was powerless to resist. His eyes* *burned into hers like sapphires. His muscular arms enfolded her body as she felt herself being swept away in a whirlwind of passion. Then he whipped out his charlie and fawned all down her dress.'* (from *'The Lady and the Cossack'* by Barbara Cartland).

feather spitter *n.* An over-enthusiastic *pillow biter*.

feck *exclam. Ir. Fuck*. Popularised by Fathers Ted and Jack.

feeding me rabbits *euph.* Having a *wank*. From the character Lucien in Liverpudlian sitcom *'The Liver Birds'*, who would stay home alone all day and answer the door looking dishevelled, explaining *'I was just feeding me rabbits'*.

feed it a bun *phr.* Term used to emphasise the enormousness of a male member. *'I didn't know whether to suck it or feed it a bun.'*

feed the beavers *v.* To *drop a log* into the pan.

feed the ducks *v.* To *wank*. From an apparent similarity in hand movements when on a park bench *wanking*.

feed the fish *v. nav.* To vomit over the side of a ship, *bury one's biscuits* at sea. A nautical *honk*.

feed the pony *v.* To *frig* a lady's *front bottom*.

feel like Andy Warhol looks, to *v.* To *feel Welsh*.

feel Welsh *v.* To be hungover, to feel none too chipper.

feeshus *n.* Excrement.

felch *v.* The tender act whereby a gentleman orally retrieves his *spoff* from his partner's *arsehole*. *'Birds do it / Bees do it / Even educated fleas do it / Let's do it / Let's felch some spunk.'* (Song lyric *'Let's Do It'* by Cole Porter).

felchmeister *n. Ger.* A man in lederhosen with a shaving brush in his hat who is particularly adept at *felching*.

felmet *n. medic.* The point where the *fiveskin* is connected to the *bell end*. The *bobby's chinstrap*, the *banjo*.

felt tip *n.* A marker pen *stool* that protrudes from the *nipsy* and keeps drawing lines on one's *bumwad*.

fem *n.* A highly photogenic species of lesbian. Commonly found in pairs on TV porn channels. Also *femme*.

femtex *n.* Hormone-based explosive which becomes dangerously unstable once a month.

fenchested *adj.* Of a lady, to be sadly lacking where it counts. To have *Dutch Alps*. Named after the horribly flat fenland area of eastern England.

fent *n.* The erotic perfume of a woman's *clout*. If a worn pair of ladies' pants is draped over a steaming kettle, the room will be filled with the alluring aroma of *fent*.

fentilator *n.* A pair of birds' used *grundies* worn on the head whilst *boxing the Jesuit*. A *musk mask*.

fertle *v.* To *feed a lady's pony* through her *bills*.

festival flange *n.* Extra premium strength *minge*. *Disco fanny* that has been baked in the sun and hasn't been washed for two days. the Special Brew of *twat*.

festival hot dog *n.* A hand-held *pap baffle*.

festival knickers 1. *n.* The undergarmentry effected by young ladies at open air pop concerts, ie. crispy *shreddies* with a long weekend's worth of excitement evident in the gusset. 2. *n.* The undergarmentry effected by young ladies at open air pop concerts, ie. none at all.

fetching off *v.* The gentle art of *tipping your concrete* into a lady's knicker drawer whilst she's out of the room.

FFTBBB *abbrev.* The inevitable converse of a *bobfoc.* A girl who possesses a face pretty enough to be rendered by a Renaissance great, but who has a body resembling a medieval vision of Hell. Face From Titian, Body By Bosch.

fiddler crab 1. *n.* In the world of human *relaxation*, a gentleman who has *relaxed* so much that one forearm is the size of Popeye's whilst the other has practically withered away. 2. *n.* In the world of marine biology, the South eastern Atlantic crustacean *Uca pugnax, Uca pugilator* or *Uca minax*, distinguished by the fact that one of its arm nipper things is much larger than the other, possibly as a result of too much *wanking*.

fifth Marx brother *n.* Faecal residue left on the gusset of the *undercrackers* as a result of insufficient wiping. From Ginger Marx.

fig *n.* A lady's pudendum.

fight a turkey *v. Choke a chicken.*

fighter pilot's thumbs *n. Chapel hat pegs, pygmies' cocks.*

fighting water *n. Falling down juice, wreck the hoose juice,* Spesh.

filf *n. acronym.* The object of a *chubby chaser's* affections, a *bird* that gives a gentleman *Victoria wood.* Fatty I'd Love to Fuck. Also *filfy.* 'That Fern Britton's well *filfy*'.

fill your boots *v.* (pref, **go on son~**) To make the most of a sexual opportunity.

fillet-o-fish *n.* A *fanny* that is on the menu, but for which one has to wait four minutes whilst it is prepared.

filthy Ned *n. Dirty Sanchez's* brother.

final whistle *n.* A *fart* that comes in three loud, controlled blasts, causing the assembled crowd to jump up and cheer.

finding a peanut in a kebab *euph.* Descriptive of the difficulty encountered when a gentleman attempts to locate the *wail switch* during foreplay.

finding nemo *n.* The performing of an act of oral *cumulonimbus. Dining at the Y, licking out.*

finger blessing *v. Ferkyfoodling* sans *dunghampers.*

finger of fudge *n.* The consequences of *breaching the hull.* A *taxi driver's tan.*

finger pie *n.* A *handful of sprats*, a *pony feeding session.*

fingers *n.* Sucessfully gaining digital access to one's *bird's snatch.* "Smell them!', cried Jennings 'Pwoar!' sniffed Darbishire. 'What an ozard ronk. What have you been up to?' Jennings grinned conspiratorily. 'I just got my fingers off Venables' sister in the prep room and I'm never going to wash my hand again."* (from 'Jennings and the Strange Urges' by Anthony Buckeridge).*

fingersmith 1. *n.* A disgusting *self-polluter* of either gender. 2. *n.* Piss-poor BBC costume drama about Victorian *carpet-munching*, which disappointed thousands of sofa-bound *fingersmiths* across the country.

finisher *n.* The favourite page of an

art pamphlet saved for the climax of a *cat stabbing* session.

Finnegan's wake *n*. Descriptive of one's face upon waking in the morning after a heavy session *on the turps* and a poor night's sleep. Characterised by grey pallor and puffyness around the eyes.

Finsbury bridge *n*. The *barse*.

fire down below *exclam*. An announcement used by a gentleman signifying the discovery of a genuine redhead.

fireman's blanket *n*. A precautionary *turd*-catching mat of *shit rag* laid on the *bog* water surface, with the intention of preventing noise and/or *splashback*.

fire one across the bows *v*. A *navel engagement* whereby the *pirate of men's pants* withdraws from the battlezone just before the *egg white cannon* shoots its payload.

fire snakes *n*. Venomous post- curry or chilli stools that rattle out the *arse* at a fair old lick.

fire, throw a log on the *v*. To *shit* oneself whilst attempting to light a *fart*.

firey surprise *n*. To receive a brand spanking new electric fire that one never knew about.

firing blanks *v*. Post-*snip spoffing*. *'You can put the ticklers away love, I'm firing blanks.'*

firkin 1. *n. arch.* A measure of ale capacity, equal to nine gallons or half a kilderkin. 2. *n*. The *fuckwitted* epithet for half the pubs in Britain.

firkyfoodling *n. arch.* Tudor foreplay. *'Dearest Maid Miriam. Until lately did my husband Henry be a most wonderful and caring lover. But forsooth I am most sad to relate that of recent times he wan-teth naught but most hasty coupling with me. He spendeth no time on the firkyfoodling. Yea I fear that my tastes for the courses of love hath declined as a consequence. And now he hath vouchsafed to cut my head from my shoulders. Five wives hath he taken already before me, and of two hath he separated their heads from their shoulders. What am I to do? Pray, pray, pray help me. C. Parr, London.'* (Letter to 'Daily Mirror', 1545).

first impressions *n*. Breasts.

first load *n*. That which is flushed down the *chod pan* prior to that second round of lower intestinal grumbling which heralds the arrival of a bonus *drop of shopping*.

first mud *n*. The *popping* of a *brown cherry*.

first two inches are cold, the *exclam*. A cry to indicate the urgency with which one requires a lavatory. *'I answered the urgent hammering on the door. It was Holmes, in the guise of a Greek Admiral, and posessed of a wild expression the likes of which I had never seen before. 'What is it, Holmes?' I expostulated. 'Why, it's three in the morning.' 'No time for explanations, Watson,' he gasped as he pushed past me towards my water closet. 'The first two inches are cold.'* (from 'The Case of the Great Big Shit', by Sir Arthur Conan Doyle).

firtle *v*. To cut a hole in a poster of one's favourite pop star or film actress, and *fuck* it.

fish 1. *n*. prop. Lead singer out of 'Happy Shopper Genesis' pop band Marillion. 2. *adj*. Not very good. 'That lead singer out of

Marillion is fish'. *Crap, swiss, pants, mouse, fucking rubbish.*

fish box *n.* A lady's *twat.* *Billingsgate box, fish mitten.*

fish drowner *n.* A *clown's pie.*

fisherman's jumper *n.* A damp, overly-hairy *clopper*, smelling not too dissimilar to a deep sea trawler captain's wool sweater after hauling in a net full of haddock. *'Having been accustomed all my life to ideals of a feminine nakedness gleaned from classical antiquities, I was somewhat taken aback on my wedding night to find that my young bride had a right old fisherman's jumper between her legs.'* (from *'The Memoirs of John Ruskin'*, 1819-1900).

fisherman's sock, pull on like a *sim.* No-nonsense method of sexual intercourse. *'Concertina was powerless to resist. His eyes burned into hers like zirconium. His muscular arms enfolded her body as she felt herself being swept away on a tsunami of passion. They stood before each other naked, until he could wait no longer. Roughly, he grasped her by the waist and pulled her on like a fisherman's sock.'* (from *'The Lady and the Cheesemonger'*, by Barbara Cartland).

fisherman's swig *n.* A well deserved sup from the *hairy goblet.*

fish from the other bank *v.* To be *on the other bus*, to *jump puddles*, to be *good with colours.*

fish fryer's cuff *sim.* Descriptive of a pair of well-worn knickers with a heavily-*battered* gusset.

fish-hook shit *n.* A *turd* containing a sharp object that snags the *nipsy*, eg. a peanut, a filling, the wife's *clit ring.*

fish mitten *n.* A *muff* that keeps the fingers and thumb of one hand warm.

fishmitten's bark *n.* An audible release of *clam gas*. A *queef.* A *fanny fart.*

fish supper *euph.* 1. *n.* A Friday night feast with the tang of the sea and plenty of batter. 2. *n.* Fish and chips.

Fishwick 1. *n. prop.* A small Scottish village 4 miles west of Berwick upon Tweed. 2. *n.* The bit of braided string that hangs out of a *kipper* that has *fallen to the communists.*

fist 1. *v.* Of boxers, to punch someone in the ring. 2. *n.* Of homosexuals, to punch someone in the *ring*. 3. *n.* Of heterosexuals, to punch someone in the *quim*.

fist magnet *n.* Someone who attracts punches to his face, eg. Jimmy Carr.

fist of fury *n.* Of a gentleman with a restricted *wank window*, for example whilst his missus has just nipped next door for a cup of sugar, a mindlessly violent act of *self abuse* carried out in a sort of masturbatory red mist. An *armbreaker, bishop rage, power wank.*

fist rape *n.* Taking advantage of your clenched hand after inviting it back to your place for a coffee and a flick through a *meat mag*. *Knuckle glazing.*

fit *adj.* Attractive, worthy of *one.*

fitbin *interj.* The rudest word in the English language, so rude that its meaning has been encased in 500 tons of concrete and dumped in the Irish Sea.

five against one *n.* A very one-sided but nonetheless enjoyable game of wrestling in which *Madame Palm* *and her five sisters* attempt to *strangle Kojak*. The game ends when one *makes the bald man cry*.

five finger spread *n*. Counter-productive attempt to suppress *upchuck* with the hand. A *chuckspreader*.

five knuckle shuffle *n*. *One-handed workout* to a Geri Halliwell yoga video.

five o'clock fanny *n*. A stubbly *ladygarden*. A *Flintstone fanny*, a *face grater*.

five pee fifty pee *sim*. Anal/numismatical comparison descriptive of the rapidly-alternating diameter of one's rectal sphincter at moments of extreme nervousness. *'Did you see the match last night?' 'Yeah, the last ten minutes were proper five pee fifty pee.'*

five-pinter *n*. A very ugly woman who one would only happily chat up after five pints of *dizzyade*. A *St. Ivel lass*.

fives *n*. A traditional Etonian game played with four fingers, a thumb and a *cock*.

fiveskin *n*. *Fourskin*.

five-to-two-er *n*. Five minutes uglier than a *ten-to-two-er*.

fizzing at the bung hole *adj*. Descriptive of effervescent sexual arousal in a woman.

fizzle *n*. A gentle or quiet *arse firework*.

fizzy gravy *n*. Diarrhoea, *rusty water*.

fizzy knickers *n*. A *wide on*.

fizzyjizz *n*. Aerated semen caused by over-enthusiastic *cat stabbing*. *Bubblecum*.

flaccid flashback *n*. A ghastly, inappropriate, unerotic memory, eg. nan burping after eating too much stuffing, topless uncle mowing the lawn, Olive off *'On The Buses'*, that pops into one's head during sex, causing one to deflate like Richard Branson's balloon.

flackets *n. medic*. *Beef curtains*.

fladge and padge *abbrev*. Of *rub-a-tug shop* services, *Mr. Whippy* off a whore in a nurse's outfit. From flagentry and pageantry.

flags are out *exclam*. *Wet paint* warning, when the fixture list shows *Arsenal are playing at home*.

FLAME *abbrev*. Fanny Like A Mouse's Ear.

Flamingoland *n*. A watering hole with a high density of *Yorkshire flamingos*.

Flanders poppy *sim*. A *ringpiece* that has been through the wars, ie. is bright red and shot to pieces.

flange 1. *n*. A *fish mitten. Muff, beaver, minge*. 2. *n. coll*. Not a word to describe a group of baboons. 3. *n. coll. Fanny, blart, tush*.

flangina 1. *n. medic*. Any form of physical or emotional pain caused to a man by the nagging of his female partner. *'I know I said I'd be back by ten and now it's Tuesday, but for fuck's sake give it a rest will you, woman. You're bringing on my flangina.'* 2. *n. medic*. Women's things.

flannelled *adj*. The state of one's face after *going down* on a *fish drowner*.

flap a herring *v*. To *fart* in a wet and audible manner, such that the *cheeks* of the buttocks clap together.

flap dabbling *n*. In the world of *masturbating* ladies, to *gusset type* in a disinterested fashion. From *flap* + dabbling.

flap-flops 1. *n*. The shoes commonly worn by old ladies in naturist resorts. *2. n.* The *tits* commonly worn by old ladies in naturist resorts.

flapjack *1. n.* A dense, syrupy cake that has pretentions to healthiness. *2. n. medic.* A *quim quack's* tool for jacking *flaps* apart. A speculum.

flapmates *n.* A pair of *curtain twitchers*. *Tennis fans.*

flapmonger *n.* One who mongs *flaps*. A *tart farmer*, a *pimp.*

flappocks *n.* The confusing yet strangely intriguing in-between-style genitalia of a *trolley dolly* who is half way through a programme of gender reassignment surgery, in either direction.

flap snack *n.* A quick *fish burger* or *bacon sandwich*. Elevenses at *the Y.* Token *cumulonimbus.*

flap snot *n. medic.* A *fannular discharge. Lizzie dripping, clam jam. Gleet.*

flaptulence *n.* The *dropping forwards* of a *lady's hat. Queefage, fanny farting.*

flash *v.* To treat a lucky lady to a surprise private viewing of one's *fruitbowl.*

flasher *n.* A gentleman who frequents parks wearing a mac, beret, little round glasses and trouser bottoms tied round the knees with string.

flash in the pan *n.* A *spooge*-free male orgasm. A cashless *money shot.*

flash the ash *exclam.* A gentle reminder of a person's social responsibility to share his cigarettes with others in his peer group. *'Oi, fuck face! Flash the ash, you tight-fisted cunt.'*

flash the upright grin *v.* To expose the female genitals, *flash the gash.*

flat as a kipper's dick *adj.* Descriptive of unleavened *baps.*

flative *adj.* Of food, that which induces flatulence, eg. cabbage, *musical vegetables.*

flat Stanley *n.* A sexual encounter involving a very large lady.

flat, straighten up the *v.* Of a closet *puddle-jumping* couple, to hang a *'Hollyoaks'* calendar on their wall in order to disguise the *whiff of lavender* in the air.

flatty, crack a *v.* To suffer an unfortunate erectile dysfunction in the *trouser department.*

flatulence *n.* The whole kit and kiboodle of *farting*. From the Latin *flatus* = to start & *lentus* = a cold tractor.

fleemail *n.* A rapidly-scribbled note of thanks, including a false name and address, left on the pillow of a *munter* by a long gone *fanny hopper* who woke up without his *beer goggles* on.

flembrandt *n.* A distinctive piece of pavement art seen adorning much of London's walkways. *Lung paint.*

fleshbombs *n.* Two large wads of *jubbly gelignite* packed in a woman's *titpants.*

flesh lettuce *n.* Lady bits.

flesh wallet *n.* The *hairy cheque book, pubic purse.* Somewhere to put one's *money shots.*

fleshy flugelhorn *n.* Tuneful variation on the *bed flute, pink oboe.*

flex, to have a *v.* To *bust off.*

flick finger *n. medic.* The finger with which a woman *flicks herself off.*

flies' dinner gong *n.* A *fart.*

flik *n.* Dried up *spoff* found on curtains, furniture, foreheads, shrouds etc. *'I felt so betrayed when the President denied we had had a relationship. Then my friend Linda Tripp reminded me that I still had the dress with his flik all over it in the cupboard.'* (Monika Lewinsky, Statement to the US Senate Impeachment Committee, 1999).

flinge *n. coll. Blart, tussage, flap.* From *flange* + *minge*. *'Come on. Let's go and find some flinge.'*

flingel *rhym. slang. Cunt.* From the instrumental hit *'The Rise and Fall of Flingel Bunt'* by The Shadows.

flinging in the rain *n.* The act of masturbating in the shower.

fling string *v.* To *jizz* via air mail. To *lob ropes.*

flipper *n.* A Taiwanese *ladyboy* that fools the gagging punter to the extent that he thinks: *'Fuck it. I've paid me money, I'll just flip her over'.*

flipping pancakes *n.* The practice of loosening up one's *batter* prior to sending it arcing up into the sky. On a Tuesday.

float an air biscuit *v.* To release a *tree monkey* from captivity.

floater 1. *n.* A *turd* in the pan which will not flush away. 2. *n.* A member of the crap 70s soul band, eg. Larry (Cancer), who likes a woman that loves everything and everybody.

flock of pigeons *n.* The sound of a loose bowel movement.

flog pocket *n.* The front flap of a pair of Y-fronts, useful when a fellow needs rapid access to his *old chap* for whatever reason.

flogging on *v.* Accessing the internet in search of *left-handed websites.*

flog the log *v.* To *whup one's wood, spank the plank.*

floordrobe *n.* The clothing receptacle most used by students, teenagers and men home from the pub.

flop out *n.* Condition whereby the flaccid penis protrudes through the bottom of the underpants, this often occurring during the transfer from a sitting to a standing position.

floppy red cup *n.* The *Hairy goblet.*

flop to pop *n.* A standard interval used to measure the quality of *horatio* techniques. The time taken to ejaculate from a flaccid start. *'Egbert was powerless to resist. Her eyes burned into his like sapphires. Her ladylike arms enfolded his masculine body as he felt himself being swept away in a whirlwind of passion. Then she knelt down in front of him and took him from flop to pop in three minutes flat.'* (from *'The Officer and the Gypsy'* by Barbara Cartland).

Florida fartbox *n. US.* An *abnormal load. Orlando dirtbox.*

florins *ryhm. slang.* The *shits.* From pre-decimal 'florin' coins known as *two bob bits.*

flossing the squirrel *v.* Of a lady, to be sporting a thong-styled underpant.

flub 1. *onomat.* The sound of a *fanny fart.* 2. *v. Fuck* in flowerpot man language.

fluff *n. nav.* A maritime *blow off.*

fluffer *n.* In a *bongo vid* studio, a *fellatrix* employed between takes to ensure the tumescence of the male actors.

fluffit *n.* The sweetest name in common use for the *cunt.*

flum *n. Ladygarden, cunt rug, pubes.*

flump 1. *n.* A cylindrical marshmallow sweet. *2. n.* An offensive and hurtful term used by sexist women to describe the flaccid penis of a man who, for all they know, may be suffering from serious medical problems.

flunkey *1. n.* A Royal slave, one who fawns on a *nob. 2. n.* A *dunky.*

flush puppies *n.* Dalmatian-spotted suede shoes that have been standing too close to a urinal.

flushstration *n.* The sense of increasing annoyance felt when a *faecee* one has just excreted refuses to disappear down the U-bend, despite repeated cranks on the handle.

flute player's lips *n.* Descriptive of the *ringpiece* ejecting last night's curry and beer.

flux capacitor *1. n.* The invention that allows a 35-year-old Michael J Fox to play a teenager in the *'Back to the Future'* trilogy. *2. n.* The Y-shaped vein on the shaft of the *tallywhacker.*

fly feast *n.* An al fresco act of *cable laying*, usually up an alleyway or behind some bushes.

fly sheet *n.* A *fiveskin.*

flying pastie *n.* Excrement wrapped in newspaper and thrown into a neighbour's yard for whatever reason. See *pyropastie.*

flying scotsman *n.* A highly complicated sex act that doesn't sound like it's worth the bother.

flying squirrel *n.* Genital manipulation amusement. *Farmyard* animal impression involving the stretching of one's scrotal leather almost to breaking point, in the style of the wing-like membranes on the popular airborne rats of the genus *Pteromys.*

fly's eyes *n.* A gentleman's party trick whereby the shorts or bathers are pulled tight between the legs so that the *clockweights* bulge out on either side of the *gusset. 'August 6th. We all go down to Cliveden for the weekend. Gerty (Laurence) and Fanny (Brice) were there as usual. Ivor (Novello) entertained us all by singing King's Rhapsody by the pool, and followed it by doing fly's eyes. How we all shrieked. Benjamin (Britten) laughed so much he shat himself, poor dear.'* (from *'The Diaries of Noel Coward'*, 1938).

fly's graveyard *n.* The *nutsack* netherworld situated on the dorsal side of the *chicken skin handbag* which remains unseen by human eyes.

fly the flag *v. NZ.* To *zuffle.*

fnarr! fnarr! *exclam.* Suppressed childish exclamation of amusement uttered after a double entendre.

foaming at the bunghole *adj. Frothing at the gash. Glistening.*

foggles *1. n. R.A.F.* Wrap-around glasses used in pilot instrument training, which are frosted except for a section at the bottom, so as to restrict the pilot's view to his instrument panel only. *2. n.* A phenomenon whereby, on meeting a lady, one's attention is focused on the lower features to the exclusion of anything above shoulder level. *'She was a blonde, or perhaps a brunette. She might have been ginger. I can't remember. I had my foggles on.'*

fog up *adj.* Of *train pulling*, to be the driver, as opposed to the *porridge stirrer* in the *guard's van. 'Bagsy me fog up. I don't want any of you lot's sloppy seconds again.'*

folder *n*. One whose good breeding, manners and culture have instilled in them the proper way of preparing toilet paper for smudging the *chocolate starfish*.

follow through *v*. To accidentally soil one's *undercrackers* whilst attempting to *fart*. To create *russet gusset*, *drop a pebble*.

fomp *v*. *US*. To engage in sexual foreplay, to *firkyfoodle*.

fond of shopping *euph*. Male homosexuality.

fond of walking holidays *euph*. A *woman in comfortable shoes*, a *tennis fan*, a *tuppence licker*.

fondleberries *n*. Testicles.

food in the beard *euph*. A symptom of insufficient wiping after a *tom tit*. To have *winnets* in the *crackers*.

food's ghost *n*. An invisible, eerie presence accompanied by a low humming sound and the stench of death. A *McArthur Park*.

foop *n*. *onomat*. The sound of a penis being removed from an anal passage, presumably a bit like when you blow across the top of an empty milk bottle.

footballer's tie-knot *sim*. An expression that describes something that is wider that it ought to be. *'Thank you, Your Holiness, but I'd rather not sit down. I had a cak this morning and the bastard was as wide as a footballer's tie knot, believe me.'*

footstool *n*. *Pavement toffee, barkers' eggs*.

footwell flavour *n*. The soul-destroying aroma of *dog's egg* that appears three minutes after turning on the car heater.

force field *n*. A thick *fart* that clings to the warp and weft of one's *duds*, preventing anyone from coming within six feet for a good ten minutes. A *Velcro guff*.

FORD *abbrev. medic*. Casualty doctors' notes terminology. Found On Road Drunk.

foregasm *n*. A *stack* which is *blown* whilst still trying to *light the fire*. When a gentleman *spends his money* before he's even got *into the shop*. Going *up and over like a pan of milk* before the niceties of *frigmarole* have been satisfactorily completed. A *Pope-shot*.

foreploy *n*. Any gambit used to get a woman into bed, eg. claiming to be an airline pilot, member of the SAS, employee of the month at McDonald's etc.

foreporn *n*. The token, exaggerated, wooden acting preceding the *spaff candy* of a *grumble vid*. Usually viewed on fast forward.

foreskinzola *n*. A pungent, unappetising, mature *knobcheese*.

forget-me-nots *n*. The final notes in a *Chinese singing lesson*. Droplets which form a tiny but embarrassing wet patch on your trousers. *Dicksplash*.

forgetiquette *n*. To inadvertently forget one's manners, eg. when taking a mobile phone call during Earl Spencer's speech at Lady Di's funeral, scratching one's *arse* and sniffing your fingers just prior to shaking the Queen's hand backstage at the Royal Variety Performance.

fork lift truck *n*. An exotic sexual position performed in back alleys and shop doorways, whereby the female participant is hoisted clear of the ground by the thighs in order to keep her *arse* clear of *piss*, vomit, broken glass and spent *jubbers*.

form 1. *n*. Means of judging horses by statistics. 2. *n*. Means of judging *birds* by statistics. *Fitness, fuckability*.

fort knockers *n*. Highly reinforced and practically impenetrable bras of the sort that nuns, librarians and Anne Widdecombe might wear.

Forth bridger *n*. An irritable and cantankerous woman who seems to *have the painters in* all year round, eg. Germaine Greer, Roseanne Barr, Bjork.

fough *n*. An inadvertent *dropping of the guts* when clearing one's throat. Derivation unknown. Possibly from Frank + Bough.

foul Paulo *n*. An Italian *Dirty Sanchez*. A faecal moustache.

four-man bob *n*. A large, speedily-ejected *turd*. Possibly rocking backwards and forwards 2 or 3 times before coming out.

four minutes *rhym. slang*. Haemorrhoids. From four minute miles = piles.

Foyston Gap *n*. The space at the top of a woman's thighs, a term peculiar to Greatfield, Kingston upon Hull, East Yorkshire. The *Toblerone tunnel*.

frampton 1. *n. prop*. An overrated 1970s singer with a voice like Steven Hawking. 2. *n*. A *fanny fart*.

Francis *n*. US. A lady's *arse*.

franger *n*. Condom.

Frankenstein's feet *sim*. The illusion of having someone else's feet stiched onto one's legs caused by the serrated indentations on one's ankles left by tight socks.

Frankie *rhym. slang*. Porn, *scud* material. From Frankie Vaughanography.

frap *v. onomat*. To *fart*.

freckle maggots *n*. Rolled-up pieces of 3-ply *shit ticket* which congregate around the *tea towel holder* after it has been given a right good wipe.

freckle *n*. Aus. Arse, brown eye, chocolate starfish.

Fred *n. rhym. slang*. Sperm. From the famous golfer Fred Funk, whose name rhymes with *spunk*.

freemason's handshake, fanny like a *sim*. A tight vagina, particularly one which applies unusual pressure to the second knuckle of one's right hand.

free the tadpoles *v*. To liberate the residents of one's *wank tanks*. To have a *tug*.

French *n*. Popular coital position whereby the man sits astride a bicycle selling onions while the woman perches on the handlebars and inflates his testicles.

French accordian player *n*. A gentleman inexperienced in the art of romancing a lady, who believes the best way to go about things is to press and squeeze everything he can find as quickly as possible.

french horn 1. *n*. Brass orchestral instrument, distinguished by its rotary valves, narrow conical bore and large, flared bell. 2. *n*. Sexual position in which the female sits on the male's lap and he gets a mouthful of *tit* and four fingers in her *letterbox*.

French letter *n*. *English overcoat, jubber ray*. Prophylactic sheathage.

French polish, to *v*. To *buff up one's wood* till it gleams. And all *spadge* comes out the end. To have a *Tom Hank*.

French safe *n*. A secure *box* that can be cracked open by fiddling with a little button at the top. Usually found behind a hinged oil painting on the front of a woman's *trolleys*.

French sickness *n*. Any *cockrot* caught from prostitutes advertising their services in phone boxes for £20 or less.

French snuff *n*. The pungent particles of *shit* which are inhaled from the end of the index finger after it has just scratched the *rusty bullet hole*.

French wank n. A *posh wank*.

French week *n*. A long and demanding day at work which is probably equal to the amount of effort expended by our gallic cousins from Monday to Friday. *'How was work today?' 'Crazy, I put in a French week.'*

frenchy *n*. Rubber carrying case for a *French horn*.

Freudian slip *n*. An inadvertent slip of the tongue revealing subconscious sexual desires. *'Would you like a piece of my two foot black cock up your arse, Vicar? Oh, I'm sorry, I meant a piece of my home-made sponge cake.'* Named after crack-headed, *motherfucking* psychoanalyst Sigmund.

friar's chin *n*. To tuck one's vest/shirt/jumper under one's chin to keep it out of harm's way whilst *pulling the Pope's cap off* over a *Tijuana bible*.

friar's weeds *n*. A holy unkempt garden of 13 *amp fusewire*.

Friar Tuck *rhym. slang*. An act of coition. A *Donald Duck*.

friction bairns *n*. The offspring of a homosexual. So called because the *lavender* father shoots his load solely as a result of friction. *'Ere, did you know that Julian Clary's missus has just had twins?' 'Friction bairns, them.'*

Friday foal *n*. One who, late on a Friday evening, proceeds to take on the ambulatory characteristics of a new-born baby deer. A *beer Bambi*.

Friday night gamble *n*. To reject the advances of a perfectly acceptable bit of *tussage* on the chance that one might pull something better later on in the evening.

fridge magnet *n*. A man whose successive girlfriends' sexual appetites are a source of disappointment. *'Trish won't take it fudgeways either. What am I, a fridge magnet?'*

fried eggs *n*. Small *baps*, *titterlings*, *stits*.

friend of Dorothy *n*. Politically correct terminology for a *fudge nudger*.

friendly fire 1. *n. milit*. The actions of US armed forces against journalists, ambulances, wedding parties and anyone who fights alongside them. 2. *n*. An unexpectedly powerful *jizz bolt* that overshoots the belly and hits the *self-abuser* in the face. 3. *n*. Of a gentleman *jazz flick* actor, to be caught in the line of fire of a fellow thespian's *pop shot*. 4. *n*. Small residue of urine ejected from the penis when one is trying to put it back into one's flies following a *scoot*. Usually when wearing light-coloured trousers.

frig *v*. To *wank*, esp. of women.

friggonometry *n*. The precise science involved in selecting and arranging one's fingers at the correct angle whilst *diddling* a rude lady's *devil's doorbell*.

frightened skydivers *sim*. Descriptive of stools that are reluctant to exit the *bomb bay doors*. *'I think I'm going to have to try All Bran. My turds are like frightened sky-*

divers.'

frigment of one's imagination *n*. A subject conjured up in the mind to oil the wheels of *self abuse*.

frigmerole *n*. Unnecessarily time-consuming foreplay performed on a missus.

fringe-parter *n*. A gusty *fanny fart* during a session of *cumulonimbus*. A *lip rattler*.

fritter *1. n.* NZ. A hot, *batter-coated morsel*. *2. n.* An item of food cooked in a frying pan.

frock *n*. Cosmetic husband in a *lavender marriage*. The male equivalent of a *beard*.

Frodo *n*. An annoying little *turd* that clings to the *ring*. One that forces one to *tap the ash*.

frog, catching the *n*. The act following a successful *peel and polish*, whereby a lady cups her hands to collect her manfriend's expelled *baby gravy*. The resultant characteristic pose of clasping one hand on top of the other whilst desperately trying to contain said *spooge* is nostalgically evocative of slightly more innocent times spent by a pond striving to hold onto captured amphibians.

frog's chin *n*. The saggy *bag of tripe* that hangs over and obscures the *furry bike stand* of an unacceptably curvaceous lady. The *gunt*, the *poond*, the *fupa*.

frombie *n*. A lady who is blessed with such a *lovely personality* that the only way a gentleman could bring himself to do her would be *'from behind'*.

frontal forelimb *n*. A prehensile *dobber*. A *middle stump, third leg*.

front bottom *n*. Ladies' *parts of shame*.

front bummer *n*. A woman in com-fortable shoes.

front loaded date *n*. A social engagement where the male party's sophisticated and gallant veneer gradually slips away, until by the end of the evening he is revealed in all his boorish glory.

frostitute *n*. A lady of the night who gives her clients a service without a smile.

frothing at the gash *adj*. *Fizzing at the bung hole, gagging for it.*

frottage *v*. The act of deriving pleasure by rubbing one's clothed genitals on any convenient surface, eg. a door jamb, fridge, woman's *arse* on a crowded tube train.

frottage cheese *n*. The sticky end product of a successful act of *frottage*.

frotterer *n*. One who indulges in *frottage*, ie. one who *frotts*.

frube *v*. After an act of *self harm*, to squeeze the remaining drops of *spodge* out the end of one's *giggle stick*, as one would the fromage frais from one of those yoghurt-filled tubes.

fruit bowl *n*. Two plums and a banana. The collective term for a gentleman's *wedding tackle*.

fruit feeler *n*. A gentleman who is *light on his feet*.

fruit fly *n*. *Fag hag*.

fruit salad *n*. A small lady with generous *tittage*, ie. a small *peach* with a large *pair*.

fruit up *v*. Public school *firky-foodling*. *"What's going on in here?' thundered Mr. Wilkins as he burst into the showers. 'Please, Sir', announced Venables. 'I gave Jennings a ten shilling postal order to fruit me up. Now he says he's sprained his wrist during Latin prep, and he won't give it back."*

(from *'Suck THIS, Jennings'*, by Anthony Buckeridge).

frum *v.* To *frig* a *bum*.

fruttocks *n.* The cheeks of the spare *arse* that certain *salad dodging* ladies possess around the front. The *fupa*, the *poond*, the *gunt*, *bilge tanks*. Front *buttocks*.

frying chips *n.* The sound a lady makes when she is seated on a *thunderbox, splitting her whiskers* and *putting out a fire*.

FTSE *1. abbrev.* Financial Times Stock Exchange. An index of the performance of the top 100 companies that allows people with pension funds to work out how much they have lost that day. *2. abbrev.* A *pappering of the kex*. Follow Through, Shit Everywhere.

fubes *n.* 13 amp, usually ginger, *pubes*. Contraction of *fuse-wire pubes*.

fuck *1. n.* An act of copulation. A *bang. 2. v.* To *have it off, poke*, copulate. *3. v.* To beat someone in fisticuffs, esp. a member of the constabulary. *'Come on, let's fuck a copper!' 4. v.* To break, damage something beyond repair. *'Fucking hell. You've fucking fucked the fucking fucker'. 5. v.* To dismiss something with contempt, esp. for a game of soldiers. *6. interj.* Exclamation of surprise or disappointment. *'Oh, fuck!' 7. exclam. interrog.* Slightly stronger version of 'on earth' when used in a question. *'What the fuck happened here?' 8. exclam. rhet.* A forceable refutation. *'Did you fuck my wife?' 'Did I fuck!'. 9. n.* That which is given by a person who cares. *'Isn't it dreadful about the Queen Mum dying?' 'No. I couldn't give a fuck'.*

flying~ *10. n* That which one who doesn't care could not give to a rolling doughnut.

fuckabulary *n.* Those twenty words which, skilfully combined and recombined, make up the entire dialogue of all the porn movies ever made. Also *cockabulary*.

fuck all *n.* Nowt. *'Did you fuck her last night at all?' 'Did I fuck. I got fuck all all night.'*

fuck all in a five-year plan *adj. Can.* An attempt to justify an extravagant purchase. *'I know strictly speaking we don't need a subwoofer on the stereo, but 800 quid is fuck all in a five-year plan. Now put them scissors down, love.'*

fuck an air fanny *v.* To *relax in a gentleman's way*.

fuckanory *exclam.* An extension of the word *fuck*, used to express extreme shock, disappointment or annoyance.

fuckard *n. arch.* Someone who was no rocket scientist 500 years before rockets were invented. A 15th Century *Johnny No-Stars*. A *dolt*, a *fuckwit*.

fuck butter *n.* KY jelly.

fucker *1. n.* A disagreeable, person, often prefixed 'big fat'. *2. n.* Anything at all. *'Fucking hell, look at the size of that fucker!'* (Sir Christopher Wren on seeing the dome of Saint Peter's in Rome).

fucking the night *sim.* Copulating with a *yeti's welly*. *'How was it for you, Andrew, darling?' 'It was like sticking my cock out the window and fucking the night, Sarah.'*

fuck juice *n. Jitler.*

fuck me shoes *n.* Footwear worn by a *boot*.

fuck off *1. exclam.* A request for someone to leave. *2. adj.* Of a price, quote or estimate for goods or services, an over-inflated figure intended to put the customer off when the supplier doesn't want the business. *'He wants me to clean his gutters out, but I'm not going up there. I'll give him a fuck off price, £250'. 3. adj.* Anything that is exceptionally large or intimidating. *'He came to clean me gutters out, and turned up with a big fuck off ladder. And he only charged £250. Well you wouldn't catch me going up there for that money.'*

fuck 'n' chuck *n.* A lady with whom a gentleman has had a *whirlwind one-night romance,* who does the decent thing by leaving alone afterwards. A *hump 'n' dump.*

fuckpond *n.* A little post-coital pool that forms in a depression on the bottom sheet, usually full of tadpoles. A *fuckpuddle.*

fuckpouch *n.* The overhanging lump of *ladyflesh* which casts a shadow over the main event. The *poond, gunt, fupa, fat hat.*

fuckshitfuckshitfuckshit *exclam.* Phrase uttered when driving a car through a particularly tight space at too high a speed.

fucksock *n.* The sort of condom one's granny would knit.

fuck stick *n.* A short, stout stick used for *fucking* something. A penis.

fuckstrated *adj. US.* To have a severe case of *DSB.*

fuckstruck *adj.* Cuntstruck.

fuck the dog *v. Can.* To do absolutely nothing. *'Busy day at the office, dear?' 'Not really. Made a few calls in the morning, went to the pub at dinnertime, fucked the dog in the afternoon.'*

fuck trophy *n.* A baby. Usually applied to the progeny of ugly couples who need proof of their ability to achieve congress.

fuck truck *1. n.* A 'UK Amateurs' film production that is unlikely to win Best Movie at this year's Academy Awards. *2. n.* A filthy van with a mattress in the back, used for location filming in 1.

fuckwit *n.* A simpleton, a fool, one of little intelligence, a *bollock brain, Johnny No-Stars.*

fud *n. Scot.* Berkeley Hunt. A *flingel.*

fud slush *n.* Scottish *fanny batter,* usually smeared on the face whilst eating a *haddock pastie.*

fudge *v.* To lie in the spoons position with one's partner, and *fart* so that it vibrates onto their person.

fudge packer *n.* One who packs fudge.

fudge tunnel *1. n.* A tunnel made out of, or for the underground transportation of, fudge. *2. n.* The *arsehole.*

fuggit *exclam.* Ancient Egyptian curse uttered when denied a British passport.

fugly *adj.* Fucking ugly.

FUKT *acronym.* Post Office acronym for any parcel marked 'fragile', which has come open as a result of being played football with by bored sorting office staff. Failed Under Kinetic Testing.

Fulham handshake *n.* A friendly greeting exchanged between two gentlemen in a public lavatory cubicle. A *WC Handy.*

fullbeams *n.* Ladies' *headlamps* which really ought to be dipped in order to avoid dazzling oncoming gentlemen.

full cuntal lobotomy *n.* A loss of reason found in men when presented with open *pissflaps.* The nervous system shuts down and all actions are controlled by the *hairy brain*.

full English breakfast *n*. A very untidy vagina that is frankly too much to face first thing in the morning.

full Nelson *n*. When *wrestling one-self*, a hold involving one hand, one eye, and a funny-shaped hat.

full throttle for take off *exclam*. The only way of having a *gypsy's kiss* when in possession of a *diamond cutter*.

fumble bags *n*. Good value *knockers*.

fun bags *n*. Breasts, *knockers*, *thruppennies*.

funbagtastic *exclam*. Upon seeing a glorious pair of *fleshbombs*, one might utter *'Funbagtastic!'*

fun boy three 1. *n*. Novelty pop act of the early 1980s. 2. *n*. The *fruit bowl* of the male. The *meat and two veg, fishing tackle*.

funburn *n. medic*. Painful reddening on the skin around the elbows, knees and buttocks, consequent upon bouts of sex on cheap nylon carpets.

funch *n*. Sex during your lunch hour, from *fuck* + lunch. A *nooner*.

fun cushions *n*. *Dirty pillows*.

funderwear *n*. Erotic but impractical lingerie. Purchased at great psychological expense by red-faced husbands, only to be returned to the shop the next day by thunder-faced wives. *Gash garnish*, any clothing bought from Ann Summers.

fun extractor *n*. A sour-faced woman sitting in the corner of a room, sucking all the enjoyment out of the atmosphere. *'Jesus, we went round to Tez's but he had the fun extractor turned on and it was a shit night.'*

fun junction *n. medic*. The area in a young lady's *soft undercarriage* between the *front* and *rear bottoms*. Upon arrival, a gentleman might exclaim: *'Which way along the fun junction today?'*

funky hammer juice *n*. The *clam bisque* which, it is rumoured, sometimes sprays from a *dirty lady's clopper* whilst she is being *nimbed* on her *cumulus*. *Oyster juice*.

funky spingers n. Spooneristic knuckle glitter.

fun size *n*. A very small *turd*. A *miniature hero*.

funt *n*. The kind of advertising executive that came up with the recent 'Do You Speak Micra' campaign.

funtan *n*. A short-lived, healthy glow in the face of a gentleman following a spot of *self-discipline*.

FUPA *abbrev*. Fat Upper Pussy Area. The bloated lower belly of a woman. A *gunt*, a *poond*.

fur burger *n*. *Minge, hairy pie, vertical bacon sandwich*.

furgle 1. *n. prop*. Christian name of 'The Undertones' lead singer. 2. *v*. To copulate rudely, crudely or noisily.

furry bicycle stand *n*. A *fanny* set into concrete outside the library.

furry hoop *n*. *Furry bicycle stand*.

furry letter box *n*. An eight inch wide, spring-loaded horizontal *clapping fish*. That traps the postman's fingers.

fusewire *n*. A ginger person's *gorilla salad*.

Fussell's Milk 1. *n*. A thick, sweet condensed milk. 2. *n*. The contents of the male *churns* after prolonged abstinence from sexual activity. 'A *sackcloth shirt in place of silk / My nads like tins of Fussell's Milk.'* (from *'The Ballad of Ford Open Prison'* by Jonathan Aitken).

futtering *v.* A *trip to hairyfordshire.* A bout of *front door work.*

futurehead *1. n.* In popular music, any member of the eponymous Sunderland-based 4-piece beat combo. *2. n.* The tungsten-tipped head of a *Thora* which announces its impending arrival by burrowing through the *nipsy.*

futz *n. US.* The vagina.

fuzzbox *1. n.* A guitar effects unit popular in the late seventies. *2. n.* A *minge.*

fyst *n. arch.* A 15th century foul-smelling *fart.*

Gg

Gabrielle *n.* A semi-successful *Velma*. A *King Harold*.

gag *1. n.* A pre-*spew* spasm, often cause by a blockage in the throat - what Mama Cass did on a sandwich, but Linda Lovelace didn't do on a *cock*. *2. v.* What women are doing *for it* when they want it up 'em.

gak *n. Jizz, mess, springle.*

galloping knob rot *n. medic.* VD, any painful social disease resulting in the production of *gleet* and the *pissing* of razor blades.

gallop the lizard *v.* To *relax* in a *gentlemanly manner.*

gam *1. n. US.* Lady's leg. *'Hot Diggety! Check out the gams on that broad, Bub.'* *2. v. abbrev. Gamahuche.*

gamahuche *v.* The act of *cumuloing* one's partner's *nimbus. French.*

gamble and lose *v. US.* The secret vice of a *man of the cloth.* To *fart* and *follow through.*

gammon and pineapple *n. Ham-on-ham.*

gammon flaps *1. n.* Hole in a farmhouse door through which pigs come and go at will. *2. n. Beef curtains, gammon goalposts.*

gammon ring *n.* The *nipsy.*

gander's neck *n.* An extremely long, thick *gut stick* which hisses menacingly if one gets too close.

gang bang *1. n.* A *shit* song by 'Black Lace'. *2. n.* A sexual free-for-all in a tastelessly decorated living room.

gap lapper *n.* A lesbian. Or possibly one who runs circuits around a clothes shop.

gaping gill *n.* The state of an unfortunate *grumble flick* actress's *ringpiece* just after the male lead has withdrawn his *cock*. Named after the famous North Yorkshire pot hole, that is 50m across and 200m deep. But not full of *spunk*. Also *granny without her teeth in, gaper.*

garbonzas *n. Gazungas.*

garboon *n.* One who *snurges.*

Gardener's Question Time *1. n.* Achingly dull Radio 4 programme on which middle-aged women from Harrogate ask Eric Robson whether their compost needs pruning if there's going to be a late frost or something. *2. n.* A series of discreet enquiries made of a certain type of street gentleman by a herb enthusiast in the hope of purchasing a certain type of home-grown foliage which is a popular filling for roll-up cigarettes.

garlogies *n. Bell end* bogies.

Garrity dance *n.* The action of moving straight to the landing, knees together, after taking a *Brad* and finding nothing to wipe your *balloon knot* with. Named after the stupid dance popularised by the lead singer of Freddy and the Dreamers.

Gary Glitter *rhym. slang. Shitter, anus.*

gaseous clay *n.* A bowel movement in which the sufferer passes flatulence-assisted stools which look like something from a school pottery lesson and which, upon hitting the pan, 'float like a butterfly'. However, because of their high exit velocity, they also 'sting like a bee'.

gash *1. n. Hairy axe wound* between a woman's *lisks.* The vulva. *2. n. coll. Totty, blit, bush, talent, blart.*

gash and Gary *n.* Of *jazz periodicals*, a comprehensive *below stairs* photograph of a lady in which both her *front* and *back doors* are on display.

gash baron *n*. A merchant trading in women of questionable repute. A *tart farmer*, a pimp.

gash card *n*. A female only method of payment for goods and services. Accepted by taxi drivers, milkmen and pizza delivery boys.

gash crash *n*. A motor accident, usually in early spring, caused by drivers distracted by appealingly-attired females. A *rear end cunt*.

gash mark six *n*. A state of arousal in ladies. *'A lady's hairy oven must be heated to gash mark six before the gentleman slams in his lamb.'* (from *'Bedroom Management'* by Mrs. Beeton).

gash matter *n*. Remnants of a *fish supper* on the chins of *diners at the Y*. An *11 o'clock shadow*.

gash pasty *n*. A particularly flaky vagina. *'She was so dry down there it looked like a gash pasty.'*

gash plaster *n*. A feminine napkin, a *jam rag*.

gashtray *n*. The *gusset* of a lady's *farting crackers*.

gashtronome *n*. A connoisseur of *haddock pasties*.

gastight *adj. naval*. Of a *stick vid* actress, to be simultaneously bunged up in all available orifices.

gay *1. adj.* Limp of wrist, tending to ask others to shut doors, critical of the 'dust in here'. *2. adj.* Of retired colonels who write to the *'Daily Telegraph'*, a perfectly good word for happy or brightly coloured.

gaydar *n*. A remote imaging process developed during the war at Bletchley Park which is able to detect leather caps and Judy Garland records at substantial distances.

gaylord *n*. A good-natured term of homophobic abuse used by schoolboys to refer to anyone who is not gifted at sport or who wears glasses.

gazoo *n. Arse, bum.*

gazungas *n. Gert Stonkers.*

gearbox *n*. The *anus*. *'Molly was powerless to resist. His eyes burned into hers like anthracites. His strong arms enfolded her body as she felt herself being swept away on a squall of passion. Then, in a single move Buzz pulled down her clouts, bent her over the ironing board and stuck his charlie up her gearbox.'* (From *'The Cornish Milkmaid and the Astronaut'* by Barbara Cartland).

geek *n*. Someone who knows too much about a subject that it isn't worth knowing anything about, eg. computers, PlayStation cheat codes. A *human rhubarb*.

geetle *n*. The little pointed bit of *shit* that hangs outside one's *nipsy* after one has had a *Gladys*. A *bumbob*.

geeze bag *n. Wind bag, fartpants*, prolific *pump* artist.

geezerbird *n. Gadgy wife, half-a-gadge*. A butch-looking woman.

gender bender *n*. An effeminate, flowery male of indeterminate or obscure sexual orientation, eg. Boy George.

gender blender *n*. A person whose physical and facial appearance offer no clue as to which sex they belong to, eg. the man/woman who drove the 47 bus into Nottingham in the early 1980s.

genie rub *n*. Buffing up a *skin lantern* until you are granted three sticky wishes.

genital floss *n*. A skimpy bikini bottom. *Arse floss*. A thong.

genitalia failure *n*. Marshmallowing of the *cock*. The *droop*.

gentleman's excuse me *n*. A popular *meat flick* scenario in which several blokes take it in turns to *push a lady's guts in*.

gentleman's gel *n*. A soothing facial/breast cream for ladies which doubles as a hair styling product.

gentleman's reading room *n*. The one room of the house where one may comfortably relax and peruse the *'Autotrader'* from cover to cover. The *shitter*.

gentleman's relish *n*. A polite term for *jizz*, such as what might be used by society folk at a Buckingham Palace Garden Party.

gentleman's toe pump *n*. The frantic but pleasurable wiggling of the toes, about 15 seconds after the *jester's shoes*, that helps out the last drops of *jitler*.

gentleman's wash *n*. A hurried washing of the male genitals (usually in a pub toilet sink) in anticipation of forthcoming sex.

George Best undercoat *n*. The pint of milk drunk 'to line the stomach' prior to going out on a drinking binge lasting several days. *'I can't be over the limit, officer. I may have necked 10 pints, but I had a George Best undercoat before I came out.'*

George *v*. *US*. To *roger*.

German *n*. A sexy romp involving *shitting* on each other like pigs.

German ambassador *n*. A *pastry chef*. From the amusing fact that the German word for an ambassador is Botschafter.

German cornflake *n*. A herpes scab on one's *herman gelmet*.

German eyebath *n*. A *spoff monocle*. A *Gabrielle*.

German rigger *n*. Theatrical term for one who prefers his *rigging* done in the German fashion.

German's eye *n*. *Jap*. How the *Jap's eye* is referred to in Japan. So called because 'it never smiles'.

gerotica *n*. What one gets indelibly burned into one's hard disk the moment one logs onto www.horny-grannies.com. *'Honestly officer, it's just a little bit of harmless gerotica. Someone must have downloaded it onto my laptop as a joke.'*

gertie 1. *n*. *Fanny, minge*. 2. *n*. *coll*. Women, *blart*.

Gert Stonkers *n*. *Gonzagas*.

get *n*. *Bastard, twat*. Often applied to children, prefixed *'You cheeky little...'* and accompanied by a swipe to the back of the head.

get a click *v*. To *score, pull, tap off*, with a view to *getting boots*.

get boots *v*. *US*. To *get it on, get your end away*.

get it on *v*. To *get off, get it up* and *get your oats*.

get it up *v*. A significant part of *getting your end away* after *getting off*.

get off *v*. Of teenagers, to *get a click*, first step towards *getting your oats*.

get off at Edge Hill *v*. To do a *coitus interruptus*, to withdraw before *spangling*, (from Edge Hill, being the last railway station before Liverpool Lime Street) Also (Edinburgh) *Haymarket*, (Newcastle) *Gateshead*, (Leeds) *Marsh Lane* etc.

get one's sovereigns on *v*. Whilst preparing for a *pagga*, to adorn one's hands with cheap *clink*, thereby creating a budget knuckle duster effect.

get some blood in it *v.* To have the early stages of a *bonk-on, half a teacake.*

get up them stairs *v.* A gentleman's instruction to his wife which indicates that he has finished eating, drinking and watching football, and now wishes to retire to the bedroom to make an ungainly and flatulent attempt at sexual intercourse.

get wood *v.* To attain a state of tumescence. *'Quick, Heinz! Roll the camera. Gunter's got wood.'*

get your end away *v.* To *get it on.*

get your oats *v.* To *get your end away.*

GFS *abbrev. medic.* Doctor's notes terminology used to indicate that the patient may be talking out of their *arse*. Gesticulating From Sacrum.

Ghandi's flip flops *1. adj.* Descriptive of the dryness of a nun's *cunt. 2. n. Spaniel's ears.*

ghee whizz *n.* A buttery, sludgy *piss* taken by a chap stricken with a urinary tract infection.

ghost jizz *n.* The non-existent result of a *flash in the pan.* A *map of Atlantis.*

ghost shit *n.* Stool or *dump* of which there is no trace when one stands up and turns to admire it.

gib *1. v.* To *bullshit. 2. v.* To gatecrash. *3. v.* To stick your *old man* up a goose's *arse* and slam its head in a drawer.

gibbon gristle *n.* Penis.

giblets *n.* A *club sandwich*, a *ragman's coat.*

gick *n. Ir. Shit.*

gigglers *n.* Suspender belt. *'Get past there and you're laughing'. Giggle band.*

giggling pin *n. Gibbon gristle.*

gilbo *n.* The kind of phlegm eructated during a cold, or after drinking cream soda. *Gold watches, dockers' omelettes.*

GILF *acronym.* Granny I'd Like to Fuck. A sexually-alluring older woman, eg. Marie Helvin, Kathleen Turner, Thora Hird.

gimp *n.* A giant masked *bummer* kept in a box in the basement of a gun shop.

ginger beer *rhym. slang.* A *pinch of snuff.*

gingle *adj.* The forlorn state of being ginger and single.

gink *n. Geek.* A short-sighted Colonel in a checked suit and bowler hat.

Ginster's finest *n.* A *twat* that looks, smells and tastes like an out-of-date Cornish pasty.

ginvalid *n.* One who has tragically lost the use of their legs following a long battle with the Gordons.

gip *n.* The sensation at the back of the throat heralding the arrival of *Hughie and Ralph.*

gipper *1. n.* Legless American footballer played by former late US president Ronald Reagan (now deceased) in the inspirational film 'Bedtime for Bonzo'. *2. n.* A bird who is as filthy as the bait bucket on a fishing boat.

giraffe piss *n.* The standard method of urination when in possession of a *panhandle*, ie. to stand with one's legs wide apart and angle the *tent pole* down towards the bowl in the manner of a long-necked cameleopard drinking at a water hole.

giraffe shit *n.* Any stool passed, which causes one to stretch one's neck to get away from the smell.

girlpop *n. Moip, blip, fanny batter.* Secretions of the *Bartholin's gland.*

giro jolly *n.* The euphoric mental state attained by the unemployed on Thursdays.

gisp *n. medic.* A term used by doctors in North Wales to describe the bit bet-ween the *balls* and the *arsehole.*

give Ronaldo a rub down *v.* Celebrity slaphead *wanking* terminology. *Strangle Kojak, take Captain Picard to warp speed.*

give the dog a bone *v.* To sexually satisfy a female before one goes rolling home.

Gladys *rhym. slang.* To defecate. From Gladys Knight = *shite.*

gland grenades *n.* Hairy, wrinkled *spunk* bombs that have a tendency to *go off* in one's hand if they are not *tossed* far enough.

glandlord *n.* The owner of a property who prefers his tenants to pay the rent with their *hairy chequebook.*

glandstand *n.* A Saturday afternoon erection, starting 5 minutes before *World of Spurt.*

glandular fervor *n. medic.* A disease affecting men which causes them to masturbate like nobody's business.

glarsefibre *n.* The bad-matted yet rust-proof *shite/arsecress* matting effect achieved on a catastrophically ineptly-wiped *freckle.* From the resultant disaster area's resemblance to a crudely-repaired body panel on a crashed vehicle.

Glasgow postman *n.* A thief. After the remarkable frequency with which birthday cards, parcels and giros go missing in the Glasgow postal system.

Glasgow salad *n.* Chips.

Glasgow shower *n.* A quick swipe of underarm deodorant used as an alternative to washing when in a hurry or Glaswegian.

glassback *n.* A person with a poor health record at work. One whose constant illnesses keep them from work, but don't prevent them going to the pub at night or refereeing Premiership football matches at the weekend.

Glastonbury tailback *n.* The uncanny ability of some people, usually women, to *squeeze their fig* for five days when lavatorial conditions are not quite to their liking.

Glaswegian siesta *n.* A night in a police cell.

glaze a knuckle *v.* To *wank.*

glebe end *n. Lincs.* A quaint colloquial expression for the *herman gelmet,* the origins of which are lost in the mists of time.

glee *n. Spoff, spadge, spunk.* *'Blimey, when that Trinny from 'What Not To Wear' comes on telly, I can hardly contain my glee.'*

gleet *n. medic.* Unpleasant mucopurulent discharge caused by *cockrot.*

Glist 1. *n.* Julie Walters's favourite dishwasher tablet. 2. *n. Ball glaze.*

glistening *adj.* Of a lady, to be sexually aroused. *"And we know for a fact, that Lady Marchmaine could not have killed the Bishop,' added Miss Marple waspishly. 'She had ridden from Barnchester to the Manor House in twenty minutes. When she arrived she was glistening for it and spent the afternoon with Brigadier Lewerthwaite in his quarters. So YOU, Nurse Hatpin, must be the murderer!"* (from *'Ten Pairs of Knickers'* by Agatha Christie).

glitterati *n. coll.* Celebrity paedophiles.

glob *v.* To emit a viscous fluid slowly and rhythmically out the end of the *giggling pin*.

globes *n.* Hanging objects of joy.

gloke *n.* A woman who exhibits pseudo-blokish behaviour such as watching football, drinking beer, farting etc, in the mistaken belief that this will result in her being regarded as one of the lads, eg. Sara Cox. A *ladette*.

glory hole *n. US.* In a *cottage*, that hole made by *bosching*, through which The Bishop of Durham could touch a farmer's *cock* nearly 40 years ago.

glory wipe *n.* The token single sheet polish required after passing the rare but pleasant stool which slips out *like an otter off the bank*, leaving no trace of *Sir Douglas* on or around the *balloon knot*.

Gloy *n. Mess*, semen. From the paper glue used in schools. *'Oops! I think I've just trod on the Gloy bottle.'*

gluebook *n.* A well-read *art pamphlet* that is no longer openable.

glue gun *n.* Tool used to stick the pages of *niff* mags together.

Gnasher's loot *n.* A promiscuous woman's sexual history, ie. a long string of *big sausages*.

gnomon 1. *n.* Obscure word known only to the likes of Stephen Fry and Robert Robinson, describing the little sticky-up bit which casts a shadow on a sundial. 2. *n.* The little sticky-up bit which casts a shadow on an under-endowed man, eg. The Rt. Hon. Jack Straw MP.

gnosh *v.* To suck a penis in an enthusiastic and extremely noisy fashion.

go ahead London *exclam.* A humorous term used to break the ice when tweaking the nipple of a woman one has only just been introduced to.

go all the way to Cockfosters *v.* To have a *full portion of greens* with plenty of *summer cabbage*. *'I thought I'd have to go home via the Billy Mill roundabout, but she took me all the way to Cockfosters.'*

gock *n.* The male version of the *gunt*. Unsightly lower abdominal protuberance filled with residual beer and pies. From gut + *cock*. *'What's that on the top of your head, Gillian?' 'It's your gock, Geoff.'*

goalmouth scramble *n.* A hugely exciting writhing mass of arms and legs which includes lots of intimate contact, but doesn't end up with anyone actually *scoring*. Frantic *heavy petting*.

gob 1. *n.* The *North and South*. 2. *v.* To spit, *hockle*. 3. *n.* A body of *lung butter* so propelled. A *greb*, a greenie.

gob job *n.* A *chewie*, a *sucking off*.

gobbie *n.* See *gob job*.

gobble *n.* Noise made by turkeys.

gobbler *n.* An eager *fellator/fellatrix*.

gobbler's cough *n. medic.* Condition arising from the build up of genital detritus in the throats of over eager *noshers*. *White owl pellets*.

gobshite *n.* Someone who talks *crap*. eg. Stuart Maconie, Andrew Collins or Liverpudlian hotel staff in fly-on-the-wall documentaries.

go commando *adj.* To *freeball*. To go out *undercrackerless*.

go cunt up *adj. Arse over tit.* Pear-shaped, badly awry. *'Houston, Houston, we have a problem. There's blowback in Challenger's solid rocket boosters. It looks like things could go cunt-up.'* (Silus T. Oysterburger, Mission Controller, KSC Florida).

Godzilla *n.* A ferocious burp, accompanied by clawing motions with the hands.

go faster stripe *n.* A *fanny bush* shaved into a more aerodynamic design. *Pires's chin.*

going down *1. v.* Doing the oral sex. *2. exclam.* Expression often used to describe the imminent movement of a lift.

going for a McShit *v.* Visiting the bogs in fast food restaurants when one has no intention of buying the food. If challenged by a suspicious manager, the assurance of a food purchase after the toilet visit is known as a *McShit with lies.*

going live *1. n.* A former Saturday morning children's TV programme starring prostitute dungeon visitor Jamie Theakston. *2. n.* Sex performed without a prophylactic appliance. *Riding bareback,* a *bath without wellies, skinnydipping.*

going to the judges *euph.* An indeterminate end to a bout of drunken sex.

gold watch *n.* A small clock or chronometer, made of precious metal which leaps from the throat after a cough. A *docker's omelette, greb, sheckle, prairie oyster.*

golden bogey *n.* A nose-stud.

golden deceiver *n.* A blond who looks gorgeous from behind, but is actually a right *dog* from the front. A *backstabber,* a *back beauty.*

golden rivet *n. naval.* The *freckle,* the *dot,* the apple of the *captain's* eye for sailors who *polish the other end of the deck. Spice island.*

golden shower *n.* To be *pissed* on by a big German for a saucy treat. *Water sports.*

golden slumbers *1. n.* A slightly over-the-top Beatles song sung by Paul McCartney on the Abbey Road album. *2. n.* The act of bed-wetting, as commonly practised by the under-5s, the over-80s and *wankered* men the world over.

golden ticket *1. n.* In Roald Dahl's *'Charlie and the Chocolate Factory',* the magical token which allowed Charlie Bucket and his aged grandfather to visit Willie Wonka's fantastic confectionary works, and thus *2. n.* In a sexual relationship, permission to enter the wife's mysterious and exciting *chocolate factory,* though preferably without an elderly relative in tow.

goldfrapp *n.* A *Jonathan* executed whilst wearing a *jubber ray.* A *posh wank,* a *boil in the bag,* a *birthday bash.*

golf ball *n.* An oversized, pock-marked *clit* discovered lying in an area of rough.

golf ball arse *n. medic.* Condition of the *buttocks* after sitting for too long on a beaded car seat.

golf tees *n. Bruce Lees.*

golfer's divot *n.* A shapeless clump of *pubage.* With all soil underneath it.

gonad glue *n. Gloy, gunk.*

gonga *n.* A *docker's omelette* that occasionally has to be swallowed rather than served up on the pavement.

gonk *1. n.* A *shit* fairground prize, made out of stolen cats, that looks like a miniature cross between Gail

Tilsley and Don King. 2. *n.* A *rub-a-tug shop* punter.

gonzagas *n.* *Guns of Navarone.*

Gonzo's nose *sim.* Descriptive of a gentleman's sorry looking, unresponsive penis. Named after the 'Muppets' character. *'I'd love to give you one, darling, but I've had ten pints and I've got a cock like Gonzo's nose.'*

gonzo vid *n.* Low budget, unscripted pornography where the cast wait until the cameras start rolling before going to the toilet. An acquired taste.

goober *n. Aus.* Antipodean term for *cock venom.* *'Strewth, Rolf, what the billabong have you been doing? My underwear drawer's full of goober.'*

gooch *n.* The *barse, tintis, Finsbury bridge.*

good cop, bad cop *n.* Of two gentlemen, to be faced with the classic fit *bird*/ugly mate combination at the bar: they must chat up both, knowing one will achieve a good 'cop', the other a bad one.

good listener *n.* A man who is *good with colours, light on his feet.* One who *likes shopping.*

good time *n.* Street prostitute parlance for a fucking awful time.

good with colours *adj.* Of a gentleman, to be adept at *jumping over puddles.*

gooey in the fork *n.* Of a lady, to be not far short of *dripping like fucked fridge.*

Goofy's ears *n.* Dangling labia, particularly pendulous *gammon flaps.*

goo gargle *n.* A hot protein mouthwash, which is spat out as opposed to being swallowed.

google *n. Spunk* produced as a result of internet porn.

goo gun *n.* A *pocket paste dispenser, jizz stick.*

goolies *n.* The colloquialism for testicles least likely to offend a grandparent.

goose *n.* A light-hearted sexual assault, often taken in bad spirit by po-faced lesbians.

goose, shit like a *v.* To suffer from a loose motion in the *back body.* *'Don't drink that cloudy pint, Kirsty, or you'll be running off to shit like a goose all the way through 'Newsnight Late Review.''*

gorblimey *adj.* A type of trouser popular among council tenants in the 1950s.

gorilla autopsy *n.* A large, untidy and hairy *clout,* such as the one on Lindsey from the Tartan Arms, Lloret de Mar, circa 2002.

gorilla salad *n.* Ladies' pubic hair. *Twat thatch.*

gorilla's armpit *n.* A *fanny* which would daunt all but David Attenborough.

gorilla's breakfast 1. *n.* A *shit* that smells good enough to turn around and eat again right out of the *pan,* as gorillas do in the wild on winter mornings. 2. *n.* An affectionate name for an early morning *pan cracker.*

gorillas in the mist *n. Boilers* who, through an alcoholic fog, take on siren-like qualities. Can lead to *dances with wolves.*

go through the gears *v.* To perform a *fart* of continuous melody, going up in pitch every few seconds, making a sound like a London bus pulling away.

got mice *adj.* Of a lady, to be *visited by Aunt Flo.* To be *up on blocks.*

go to Barnsley *v.* To *do the tradesman's entrance* of a lady. Named after the famous South Yorkshire *shit hole*.

gouch *n*. The *biffin bridge, chin rest, taint, tinter*.

go ugly early *v*. A nightclub or party gambit. To settle for a keen *swamp donkey* rather than chasing something better and risking ending up with nothing. *'Good piss up last week, Gaz. I saw you went ugly early.'* To *stick at 15*.

grace period *n*. The few precious hours after a hot *cuzza* during which one can *tread on a duck* without the fear of *following through*. *'I tried Abdul Latif's Curry Hell, reputedly the hottest curry in the world. Upon the first taste, my eyes melted and my throat burst into flames, and with a grace period of just forty-five seconds I was straight off to the lavvy. On my 2-mile journey home I had to stop the car on 173 occasions, each time not knowing which end to point at the gutter.'* (Jonathan Meades, *'The Times Magazine'* Restaurant Review).

Graham Norton's hair *n*. Descriptive of one's *barnet* after being *seagulled* by a gentleman, or after walking under Status Quo's hotel room balcony.

Grand Old Duke of York *n*. An unconvincing erection, a mix of duty and apathy, one that is 'neither up nor down'. A *lard on*, a *dobber*.

grandad erector *n*. A sight so sexually stimulating that it could raise the dead.

grandchav *n*. One who is blessed with grandchildren whilst still young enough to fully enjoy the experience.

grandma's party *n*. A bout of mas-

turbation. Wearing a bowler hat. See *reggae like it used to be*.

grandma's perfume *n*. The smell of piss. *Eau de toilette publique*.

grandma's Wolsley *n*. The greying *minnie-moo* of an old dear which hasn't given anyone a *ride* since the 60s. A *mothballed fanny*.

gran flakes *n*. The contents of a nursing home hoover bag.

granny batter *n*. KY jelly.

granny magnet *n*. A male who, having had no luck finding a ladyfriend of his own age, is forced to *cop off* with a right old *slapper*, eg. The *blotto* one with the incontinent laugh being held up by her mates in the kebab shop.

granny's elbow *n*. An unpleasantly elongated *ball sack*. A *rantallion*.

granny's hat, muff like your *sim*. Descriptive of a particularly hairy *otter's pocket*, possibly smelling strongly of mothballs and damp.

granny's kiss *n*. From a gentleman's perspective, the experience of performing *cumulonimbus* on a badly- maintained *clopper*. Not unlike receiving a smacker from one's sloppy, pucker-lipped grandmother sporting a *'Magnum PI'* moustache and tasting like she's just eaten a gammon butty.

granny's mouth *n*. A saggy, loose-lipped, whiskery *cunker*.

granny's oysters *n*. Elderly female genitalia.

granny's purse *n*. The condition of one's *clappers* after a comprehensive bowel evacuation, ie. firmly snapped shut.

grape smugglers *n*. Tight gentlemen's briefs, as worn by *grumble flick* stars in the 1970s.

grappling hooks *n*. The unyielding fasteners on a lady's brassiere.

grassy knoll 1. *n.* Site where the second gunman stood during the assassination of JF Kennedy. 2. *n.* A *ladygarden*.

grated carrot *n.* Coarse, ginger-coloured *gorilla salad*, suitable for a *vagetarian* diet. Rusty *fusewire*.

grating the cheddar *n. medic.* To accidentally scrape one's *lid* along the zip of one's *flies*. *"I say, Jeeves. Could you take these trousers to my tailor and have him replace the zip fastenings with good old buttons,' I croaked. 'I only bought them last week and I've grated the cheddar four times. My poor cock end is ripped to pip, don't you know."* (from *'Swallow it All, Jeeves'* by PG Wodehouse).

grattan 1. *adj.* Descriptive of a state of ill-health. *'Shut the curtains will you, love? I must have had a bad pint last night and I feel right grattan.'* 2. *v.* To masturbate over desperate material in the absence of anything better to masturbate over, eg. the bra pages of your mum's catalogue.

grave-sniffer *n.* A senior citizen. A *coffin-dodger*.

greasebox *n.* A *quim*.

greasy waistcoat pocket *n.* A shallow, well oiled *fanny* large enough for a thumb to be inserted. Or a gold watch.

great escape *n.* A *fart* that is planned well in advance and released surreptitiously over a period of time. And probably shaken nonchalantly from the bottom of the trouser legs whilst whistling.

Great Yarmouth gnomes *n.* Washing machines, broken tellies and *pissed* mattresses used as garden ornaments in the *shit* Norfolk town.

Greek *n.* Any sex games where the *rusty bullet hole* is the main arena. *Swedish*.

Greek sauna *n.* A *Dutch oven*.

Greek tip *n.* A stray pubic hair adhering to coinage that is handed over in shops, restaurants, etc.

green wings *n.* An unwanted accolade. Sex with a *clappy slapper*.

Greggs' dummy *n.* A chicken and mushroom filled pacifier used by teenaged mums to soothe their teething infants.

Greggs' revenge *n.* Descriptive of the delightfully rich aroma produced when one *steps on a duck* after consuming a Greggs' Steak Bake.

greyhound 1. *n.* A very short skirt, ie. one that is only one inch from the 'hare'. 2. *n.* An hilarious heterosexual changing room impression involving an erect penis and a champagne wire.

grimble *n.* Glossy, American marshmallow-hard pornography, usually shown on Channel 5 on Friday nights.

grime bubble *n.* A *fart, air biscuit*.

grimsby *n.* A mingsome *minge*.

Grimsby meal *n.* An unpleasant northern *fish supper*.

grimshits *n.* A portmanteau term for faeces distinctly lacking in cohesion. *Fizzy gravy, bubblepoo* and *bicycle chains* are all *grimshits*.

grind *v.* To have sex with all the fervour of an old bus going up a steep hill in Lancashire. ie, if one stopped, one would be unable to start again.

gripper *n.* More light-hearted heterosexual changing room horseplay, this time whereby somebody grabs hold of one's *arse cress* and gives it a great big yank.

gristle thistle *n*. Persistent purple-headed weed, commonly occurring in *moss cottage* gardens.

groaner *n*. A *turd* so big that it cannot be expelled without vocal assistance. A *U-blocker*.

grogan *n*. *Scot.* A *log*, a *turd*.

groin grease *n*. The sweat that builds up around the inner thighs and *knackers* of a *salad dodger* on a hot day. *Arse feta*.

grolsch *n*. An under-lubricated *snatch*, ie. one that is 'not ready yet' and needs another minute's brisk rubbing.

grommet *n.1950s Totty*.

gronk *n*. *RAF.* To have a *shit*. *"Bandits at three O'clock!' ejaculated Algy. 'Great!' replied Biggles. 'I've got half an hour to have a big smelly gronk!"* (from *'Biggles Drops his Fudge'* by Capt. WE Johns).

gronk board *n*. *milit.* A panel where photographs of the ugliest women *banged* by sailors are displayed for the amusement of the entire ship's crew.

groodies *n*. How *charms* are referred in the film 'A Clockwork Orange'.

groovy legs *n*. *med.* Post prolonged *doggy-style* sex leg wobbly numbness. *'I wasn't sure how long I was back scuttling her, but it must have been ages, because when I stopped I had my groovy legs on.'*

G-rope *n*. A *G-string* for the fatter lass.

grope fruits *n*. *Shirt potatoes*.

grotdog *n*. A lower-grade hotdog, of the sort which might be purchased at Walthamstow Dog Stadium, to pick a location entirely at random.

grot slot *n*. The married man's 30-minute long internet pornography download window which occurs whilst his wife is at the shops.

grotter *n*. The *snatch*.

groundhog lay *n*. A depressingly familiar intercourse routine between a man and his long term girlfriend.

groundhog wank 1. *n*. A dismal attempt at *self abuse* which repeatedly peters out, leaving the *wanksmith* with no choice but to start again. 2. *n*. The overly-familiar *tug* sequence of a *pornigamist* who only owns one *art pamphlet*.

ground zero *n*. The *freckle* the morning after an evening of heavy *refreshment*.

grow a tail *v*. To defecate, *build a log cabin. Snip a length of spine.*

growl at the badger *v*. *Scot.* To noisily *nosh* a *beaver*. To loudly *nod at a stoat*.

growler 1. *n*. The sort of meat and potato pie sold from one of the various catering outlets inside the ground at Gigg Lane, Bury, in the mid-1980s. So-called because within 30 minutes of eating the pie, one's stomach would begin to growl. A *Cornish nasty*. 2. *n*. The *shithouse*.

grown-up book *n*. *Bongo mag, self-help pamphlet, jazz mag.*

grub *n*. *Barse cheese*.

grubscrew 1. *n*. An act of intercourse performed at work during a lunchbreak, perhaps in a store room or on a photocopier. 2. *n*. A tiny, shrivelled penis, found on Egyptian mummies, Siberian nudists and the Rt. Hon. Jack Straw MP.

grumbelows *n*. A retail purveyor of *seed catalogues*. A *bongo store*.

grumbilical cord *n*. The sturdy wire that links one's satellite dish to one's Sky box, allowing ladies' *grotters* to appear on one's television screen.

grumble 1. *rhym. slang.* The vagina, *quaynt, placket, Berkeley.* From grumble and grunt = *cunt.* 2. *n.* Any form of porn featuring *tits, arses and grumbles.*

grumble bee *n.* A *tugster* who is unable to select a favourite *art pamphlet,* and so flits from one to another.

grumbled 1. *adj.* Of *tescosexual* gentlemen, the state of being caught mid-way through an act of *jazz*-fuelled onanism, when their spouse returns unexpectedly early from a shopping expedition. 2. *adj.* The unfortunate situation when one's mother/wife stumbles across one's stash of *art pamphletry.* To be caught in possession of pornography. *'Mrs. Baddiel: 'I was cleaning your room, David, and I found 56 tons of hard core anal pornography.' David Baddiel: 'Oh, no! I've been grumbled!''*

grumblehound *n.* A creature whose nose, upon entering the newsagent, can be seen twitching in the direction of the top shelf.

grumble in the jungle *n. Rhythmic cliterature* found whilst taking the dog for a walk in the woods. *Grummer.*

grumbleweed 1. *n.* A Sid Little lookalike, usually the director's brother, who manages to poke a selection of *cliterati,* who would normally not even wipe their *arse* with him. 2. *n.* A miraculous patch of undergrowth where discarded pornography can reliably be located. 3. *n.* One who has masturbated so many times in one session, that he can no longer muster the

strength to lift the pages of his *scud mag.* One who has *wanked* himself into enfeeblement. 4. *n.* A token *fluff tuft* on an otherwise clean-shaven porn starlet's *snatch.* A *clitler.* 5. *n.* Any member of the West Yorkshire-based comedy combo, specialising in gasmask-related songs and disturbingly accurate impressions of Sir Jimmy Savile.

grummer *n. abbrev. Grumble mags, art pamphlets.*

grump on *n.* Reluctant *wood.* An erection that has to be cajoled to tumescence. Prevalent amongst *jazz* actors, *slag night* strippers and men married to Janet Street-Porter.

grundle *n. US.* The *barse.*

grunties *n. Jobbies,* faeces, *poo.*

grunts *n.* The type of *fugly boots* whose blurred Polaroid pictures appear on the readers' wives pages of *grumble mags.*

guard dogs *n.* A pack of fierce hounds that accompany their attractive friend, preventing any bloke from trying his luck.

guardsman's hat, fanny like a *sim.* Descriptive of an enormous black, hairy *snatch* that could, if one wasn't careful, slip down over one's eyes. Also, *fanny like a busby.*

guard's parcel *n.* A present that turns out to be a disappointment. Derived from the advice given to those who live near a railway line frequented by freight trains, ie. never pick up what looks like a discarded package near the tracks, it may contain the guard's excrement if he's been taken short. *'Pulling up Beattock, the guard needs a shite / But there's no bogs till Glasgow, much later tonight. / In* *time-honoured fashion he empties his arsehole / Into brown paper to make a guard's parcel.'* (from *'The Shite Train'* by WH Auden).

guard's van *n.* When *pulling a train*, the least desirable position in the queue. *'Bagsy I'm not in the guard's van fellas'.* The last *pink carriage* into *fanny* station.

Guatemalan taco *n.* A sexual act which makes a *Cleveland steamer* seem positively salubrious.

gubbed *adj. Trousered, wankered.*

gubbs *n. Thruppenny bits.*

guck *n. Muck, spod, gunk, mess.*

guff *v.* To *fart, let off.*

guff cloud *n.* The noxious, green vapour produced by *dropping one's hat.*

guided muscle *n.* Penis.

Guinness rope *n.* A length of stout, dense *cable* which blocks the *pan* after a heavy feed of the black stuff. It takes 119 seconds to lay the perfect length of *Guinness rope.*

guinnets *n.* Jet black *dangleberries* that cling to the *arse* after a night drinking the famed stout. *Buoys from the black stuff.*

gums around the plums, get your *v.* An irresistible romantic overture made by a male to a female.

guns of Navarone *n. Whoppers, tits, fleshbombs,* large breasts.

gunt *n. Can.* Of the larger woman, when the gut and *cunt* become one indistinguishable bulge below the belt. A *super-poond.*

gurgler *n.* The toilet, *shite pipe,* drain. *'Have you got a coat hanger? Only I was spewin' up last night an' I coughed me fuckin' falsies down the gurgler'.*

gurk 1. *v.* To burp. 2. *v. Aus.* To *guff.*

gurkha's sword *n.* A *hard on* which has to be used before it can be put away. From the not necessarily true belief that a member of the tough Nepalese regiment must draw blood with his kukri before he is allowed to return it to its sheath.

gurning chimp *n.* A particularly expressive *fanny.*

guru Palm and the five pillars of wisdom *n. Madam Palm and her five lovely daughters.*

gusset 1. *n.* The bottom of the pants area of a woman, the *fairy hammock's drip tray.* 2. *n. coll. Flange, totty, fanny, blart.*

gusset graze *n. medic.* The friction burn on the side of one's *old man* incurred when administering *a bit of the other* to a young lady whilst tenderly riving her nethergarmentry to one side.

gusset icing *n.* The decorative crust which has fallen off a *clown's pie. Fanny batter.*

gusset nuzzler *n.* A *fanny nosher,* a *lady golfer,* a *lesbian.*

gusset pianist *n. Invisible banjo* player. *'I've heard she plays the gusset piano'.*

gusset sugar *n.* Tooth-rotting *muffdruff. Batter bits.*

gusset typist *n.* A *bean flicker,* a female *merchant.*

gustbin *n.* A rather charming term used to describe the nether regions of a rather large lady.

gut grunt *n.* A burbulent rumbling, or any subsequent anal emission.

gutted hamster *n. Gutted possum, gutted rabbit, giblets.*

gutter's shed 1. *n.* A dockside building where fish are filleted. 2. *n.* A particularly mingsome *minge.*

guttocks *n.* The rolls of fat that obese women get on their stomachs which, when turned through 90°, look remarkably like their *arse.*

guyrope *n.* The flap of skin connecting the *flysheet* to the *tentpole*. The *banjo*.

guzunda *n.* A potty, or *pisspot*.

gwank *n.* A girlie *wank*. A lady's bout of masturbation.

gwibble *n.* A dribbly, underpowered ejaculation, opposite of a *pwa*.

gym buddah *n.* An overweight woman in sportswear, with *over-blaaters* and a huge *gunt*.

gymsniff *n. prop.* A gentleman who attends the gym and who prefers to use the apparatus directly after sweaty *birds* in order to sniff the seat.

gynaecolumnist *n.* Any female journalist who uses her newspaper to bang on about *women's things*, eg. Julie Burchill.

gypsy clit *n.* A nomadic *clematis*.

One which, despite a fellow's best efforts to find it, never seems to be in the same place two nights running. A *Flying Dutchman*, a *Scarlet Pimpernel*.

gypsy's *rhym. slang. Piss.* From gypsy's kiss.

gypsy's curse *n.* The loss of *wood* before insertion, as a result of failing to buy some pegs at some point in the past 20 years.

gypsy's dog, like a *sim.* Descriptive of someone who looks like he could do with a square meal. *'Feargal Sharky? He's like a gypsy's dog, him. All ribs and bollocks.'*

gypsy's eyelash *n.* The rogue *clockspring* in the *Jap's eye* that causes the *piss* to go everywhere but in the *bog*. Common cause of *pan smile* or *Queen Mum's grin*.

Hh

hack off a lump *v.* To *crimp off a length*. To defecate.

haddock pastie *n. Hairy pie*, a *Grimsby meal*.

had the dick *adj.* Descriptive of something which is broken beyond repair. *"What-ho, Jeeves,' I exclaimed. 'Fetch the Frazer-Nash round to the front door, there's a good chap. I feel like taking a spin.' 'I'm afraid that may not be possible, sir,' he replied. 'Your Aunt Millicent drove it to Ascot and back with the handbrake on, and I fear it has had the dick."* (from *'For Fuck's Sake, Jeeves!'* by PG Wodehouse).

haemogobbling *n. Dining at the Y* when the house wine is *moon juice*.

haemogoblin *n.* A gentleman who has a fish supper at the *all-night sushi bar*, despite the fact that it is closed for redecoration.

hag *n.*An ugly woman, *boiler, boot, steg, swamp donkey*.

haggis *1. n.* Unappetising object consisting of meat and oats stuffed into a veiny skin bag. *2. n.* Unappetising object consisting of meat and oats stuffed into a veiny skin bag.

haggis rag *n.* A small piece of fabric, esp. towelling, used for wiping clean or drying the *haggis* after a bout of exercise.

hail damage *n.* The vile, unsightly, dimpled skin found on the thighs of middle-aged celebrity women and brought to the world's attention by gleeful paparazzi. Cellulite.

hairache *n.* The mother of all hangovers.

hair trousers, to be wearing *v.* To be naked from the waist down.

hairy axe wound *n.* Vertical *gash*.

The *mingepiece, quim, cock socket*.

hairy beanbags *n.* Pink 1970s style seating provided within the underpants for the exclusive use of the *bald man, Spurt Reynolds, Kojak, Captain Picard*, etc. Testicles.

hairy brain *n. medic.* The small wrinkled organ, about the size of two plums, that governs a gentleman's thought processes.

hairy cheque book *n. Gash card, furry purse*.

hairy conkers *n.* Knackers.

hairy cornflake *1. n.* An affectionate name for *shit* DJ Dave Lee Travis, coined and used exclusively by himself. *2. n.* Affectionate name for a small, dried crust of *poo* stuck firmly to the *arsecress*. *2. n.* An hirsute breakfast cereal.

hairy cup *n. Hairy goblet.* A *fanny*.

hairy doughnut *n.* An occasionally jam-filled confection, often dusted with *gusset sugar*.

hairy goblet *n. Hairy cup, front bottom*.

hairy handshake *n.* A firm five-fingered greeting that costs £10 from a woman behind a skip, after which there are no hard feelings.

hairy knickers *n.* Descriptive of when a lady removes her *farting crackers* and her *minge* makes it appear that she has yet to do so. An extremely well-carpeted *barber's floor*, a *Terry Waite's allotment*. An extreme *biffer*.

hairy mits *rhym. slang.* Tits. *'Look at the hairy mits on that! I could do her through a hedge backwards.'*

hairy pants *n.* See *hairy knickers*.

hairy pie *n. Kipper, velcro triangle*.

hairy pint *n.* An unsuspecting person's alcoholic beverage that has been discreetly spiked for the amusement of onlookers with a small quantity of *pubes*.

hairy raisins *n*. Hunchback spiders.

hairy saddlebags 1. *n*. Knackers 2. *n*. Pissflaps.

hairy scallops *n*. The furry shellfish eaten when *bearded clams* are out of season.

hairy swingers *n*. Hirsute *man-sacks* containing the *clockweights*.

hairy toffee *n*. Dangleberries, klingons.

half a crown thru'penny bit *sim*. Pre-decimal version of *five pee fifty pee*, used to describe the rapid flexing of the *nipsy* during moments of severe anxiety.

half a jaffa *n*. That which may be glimpsed in the crotch area of a young lady wearing tight jeans.

half a lemon *n*. A paradoxical form of lesbian who only fancies women who look like blokes.

half a nasty *n*. A *podge-on*.

half a teacake *n*. Not quite a *fatty*, the beginings of an erection. The state you would like your *fruitbowl* to be in when a new woman sees it for the first time.

half babies *n*. Spunk.

half caff *n*. The strength of a fellow's *spooch* immediately post-vasectomy, ie. before he's *crashed his yoghurt truck* the requisite twenty times to ensure he's completely *decaff*.

half Elvis, to do a *v*. To fall asleep whilst having a *shit* on the toilet. Usually done by one in an advanced state of *refreshment*.

half leapfrog *v*. To have sex in the *doggie position, set the video*.

Halfords hero *n*. Motorist behind the wheel of a *noughtomobile*, who has kitted out his bottom-of-the-range hatchback with several hundredweight of expensive tat, including alloy wheels, ludicrous spoilers, an extremely loud stereo and an exhaust pipe like a fucking coal scuttle.

half rice half chips *adj*. Descriptive of a *witch hitter*, one who *drinks from both taps, bowls from both ends. AC/DC*.

half time talk *n*. In a *spitroast grumble flick*, the token dialogue which occurs between the two leading men whilst they change ends.

hamburger *n*. Of the female anatomy, that which can be seen in a *hamburger shot*.

hamburger hill *n*. The large tor that frequently casts *stoat valley* into shadow on ladies of advancing years. A *gunt, a fupa*.

hamburger shot *n*. A rear view in a *scud mag* displaying a *vertical bacon sandwich*. A *reverse peach*.

ham fisted *adj*. To be *wanking*. 'My mum came in and caught me ham fisted the other night. I didn't know where to look.'

ham howitzer *n*. A *lamb cannon*.

Hamish blue *n*. Ripe, azure-tinted *knobcheese*, found north of the border and south of the sporran.

hammock *n*. Panty liner, *jam rag, sanitary towel*.

ham-on-ham *n*. Descriptive of the delightful sight of two ladies going at it *hammer and tongues*.

Hampton *rhym. slang. Dick*. From Hampton Weenis, a village in Essex.

ham shank *rhym. slang*. A *Barclays*.

hamshank redemption *n*. A discreet bout of *male pleasure* whilst trying not to waken up one's cellmate.

hand Chandon *n*. A high class *hand*

shandy off a posh bird, who *pops your cork* with her thumbs under the *brim* of your *lid*.

hand cock's half hour *n.* A 30-minute *armful*.

handful of sprats *n. 1950s.* A fistful of *fish fingers*.

hand job *n.* Manual relief, one of the cheaper *extras* available at the *rub-a-tug shop*, or in the pub car park.

hand love *n.* The sordid act of *self-pollution*.

hand pump *n. milit.* Wanker, nut juggler etc. *'Oi! Windsor, you fucking hand pump. Get them fucking boots back on, Your Royal Highness.'*

handruff *n.* Flaky deposits consisting of an amalgam of dried *potato fat, perseverance soup* and *helmetdale* found on the palms, thighs and soft furnishings of bachelors who have been watching a few episodes too many of *'Desperate Housewives'* without occasionally pausing to give the inside of the *farmer's hat* a wash.

hands free wank *n.* See *fancy wank*.

hands like cows' tits *sim.* Descriptive of one who is dextrously inept. An alternative to butterfingers. *'I'm terribly sorry, Mrs. Johnson, but I accidentally cut through a major blood vessel near your husband's heart and he didn't survive the surgery. I'm afraid I was on the pop last night and I've got hands like cows' tits this morning. The nurse will show you out. Good day.'*

hand shandy *n.* A frothy one, pulled *off the wrist*.

hand solo *n.* A solitary *hand shandy*.

hand to gland combat *n.* A three-

minute, one-man bout of gladiatorial combat involving a *spam javelin*.

handycrap *n.* A *shit* taken by an able-bodied person who goes into *arse labour* only to discover that all the other toilets are occupied, out of order or blocked with *bangers and mash*, and is forced to avail himself in the disabled facilities.

hang a rat *v.* To go to the lavatory for a *number two*. *'Where is he? He's supposed to be on the balcony blessing the multitude.' 'Keep your fucking hair on. He's just went to the khazi to hang a rat.'*

hanging bacon *n.* A *club sandwich* which hopefully isn't held together with a cocktail stick.

hanging basket *n.* Dangling area of foliage which can look nice when properly tended but attracts flies if allowed to run to seed.

hanging brain *n.* A *coffin dodger's clockweights*, dangling out the leg of his shorts.

hanging chod *n.* A semi-detached *turd*.

hanging out the back of *v.* Doggy-style sex. *"What am I to do, Jeeves?' I blustered. 'I've got myself engaged to Agatha AND Marjorie. This really is the the worst pickle of my entire puff.' 'Don't worry, sir,' soothed the sage retainer. 'I shall arrange for it that Miss Wegg-Prosser walks in and finds you hanging out the back of Miss Lola la Titz from the Prince of Wales Theatre's burlesque production 'Woof! Woof!'"* (from *'Gott In Himmel, Jeeves!'* by PG Wodehouse).

hanging salad *n.* Wedding tackle, fruit bowl.

hangman's noose *n.* A large vagina,

big enough to push your head into. A *wizard's sleeve*, a *clown's pocket*.

hang ten *1. v.* In surfing slang, to stand on the front of the board with all of one's toes curling over the edge. *2. v.* To be *masturbatricized* by one's partner using her feet rather than the more traditional *wanking spanners*. *'Riding waves is really sweet / Catching tubes a real good treat / But best of all is hanging ten / With me knob between the missus's feet.'* (from *'Wankin' USA'* by the Beach Boys).

hang your hole *v.* To *moon*.

hanky panky *n. Slap and tickle, the other.* Light-hearted sex.

Hannibal Lecter's breakfast *n.* The feast which awaits a man performing *cumulonimbus* on *Billy Connolly's beard*, and the ensuing *Thompson's tidemark* it leaves on his face.

ha'penny *n.* Vagina. A *tuppence*.

happy camper *n.* One who is gay, yet treats their predicament light-heartedly, eg. Graham Norton, Duncan Norvelle, Peter Tatchell.

happy Harry *n.* A semi-erect penis. A *dobber*, a *lard on, half a teacake.*

happy Havana *n.* A firm, rectilinear *turd* of such pleasing proportions that it could almost have been rolled on the thigh of a sultry temptress, and which requires little or no wiping to boot.

happy lamp *n.* The *sixth gear stick. 'I'm horny. Think I'll give my happy lamp a quick genie rub.'*

happy paper *n.* Beer tokens, folding money.

happyrash *n. medic.* A light-hearted dose of the *pox*. Any non-fatal *STD.*

happy sack *n.* The scrotum, *hairy saddlebags.*

Happy Shopper *1. n. prop.* A cheap 'n' cheerless grocery brand. *2. n.* A bi-sexual - one who *shops on both sides of the street. Half rice half chips.*

harbour master *n.* A man who has piloted the course of a few *tug-boats* in his time, he can tell you. A *stickman.*

hardbore *n. Grumble* that promises to be a real *meat vid* on the box, but when you get it home you find it's got Robin Askwith, Bill Maynard and Doris Hare in it.

hard on *n. Wood*, a *bone on*, a *bonk-on.* A fully-tumescent gentleman's part.

hariolae *n.* The hairs that foreign ladies cultivate around their nipples.

Harlem shuffle *n.* The facial gurning and involuntary neck spasms that beset a gentleman during the *vinegar strokes*, making him look like 'Sir' Mick Jagger strutting about on stage. *'Quick, camera two, a close up of Gunter's cock. He's doing the Harlem shuffle.'*

Harley Davidson *n.* An act of lavatoryless defecation, in which the dumper is forced to cling to trees or railings in order to steady himself, thus adopting a position similar to that used when riding an American motorcycle. A *fatboy.*

harlot *n.* A scarlet woman.

Harlow pub quiz *n.* Entertainment regularly held at the Essex town's popular nightspots. The quizmaster usually asks one of two questions: 'What the fuck are you looking at?' or 'Do you fucking want some?', to which all the possible answers are wrong.

149

Harry 1. *rhym. slang. Jizz.* From Harry Monk = *spunk*. 2. *rhym. slang.* Hobo. From Harry Ramp = tramp 3. *rhym. slang.* Cigarette. From Harry Rag = fag. 4. *rhym. slang.* Cheese sandwich. From Harry Rees-Bandwich.

Harry Rampsdens *n.* Discarded fish and chips, as feasted upon by homeless fellows. *Tramps' truffles.*

Harry Ramsden's raspberry *n.* The combination of smell and sound to be endured during a dirty girl's *fanny fart.*

Harry Redknapp's eyelids *sim.* Descriptive of particularly hangdog *beef curtains.*

Harry's challenge *n.* A daunting *fish supper* that is too big for one man. A big *fanny.* From the menu at the Yardley branch of Harry Ramsdens which offered a meal of that name, where one was granted a certificate is the portion was finished.

Harvest Festival *n.* Domestic state of play for the bachelor gentleman when , following a fortnight *on the lash*, he is reduced to living on out-of-date tinned food from the back of the cupboard.

harvest festivals 1. *n.* One-night stands, ie. ploughing the field before scattering. 2. *n.* A pair of well fitting but comfortable underpants where 'all is safely gathered in.'

hatching eggs *v.* To remain seated on the *chod bin* long after the last *turd* has been dropped.

hat rack *n.* Someone who's head is only of any use for the storage of hats. A *Johnny No-Stars*, a *shit-for-brains.* eg. Bez out of The Happy Mondays.

hatstand adj. Descriptive of one who has mental health issues.

hatties *rhym. slang.* Delirium tremens. A *turps nudger*'s shakes. From *'Carry On'* Actress Hattie Jelirium-Tremens.

have a go at oneself *v.* To *stab the cat, feed the ducks.*

have it off *v.* To get *a bit*, have a *portion, give* somebody *one.*

have one's arse in one's hand *euph.* To be in a bad mood, to have a strop on. *'He's BACK!... and this time he's got his arse in his hand!'* (Advertising poster for *'Terminator 3'*).

Havers, on the *adj.* Descriptive of the way certain blokes smarm up to members of the opposite sex in an overly charming way, eg. kissing their hands, etc. in the style of middle-aged charmer Nigel Havers.

have the painters in *v.* To menstruate, be *on the blob. Fall to the communists.*

Hawaiian muscle fuck *n.* The act of *bagpiping.*

Hawaiian sunrise *n.* A glorious and uncomfortable orange, red, blue and purple aurora, which can be seen around one's *ringpiece* early in the morning after consuming spicy foodstuffs, for example a Vindaloo Special Tandoori Chingiri from the Curry Capital, Bigg Market, Newcastle upon Tyne, the previous evening.

Hawaiian waft *n.* To disperse the aroma after *stepping on a duck*, using an exotic hula-hula motion.

Hawick *onomat.* To *puke.* After the Scottish border town. *'I think I'm going to Hawick'.*

he-dam *n. Knobcheese, helmetdale, purple Leicester* etc.

head *n.* Something which is given by women to men, and is afterwards described as 'good' by the recipient when talking to friends. A *chewie.*

head for the hills *exclam.* To be forced to hide your *soldier* in the *Dutch alps,* because the *redcoats are in the valley.*

head in one's top pocket, to have *v.* To be so copiously-*refreshed* that one's head cannot balance on one's neck any more and seems to be falling into the top pocket of one's shirt. An extreme form of *nodding.*

headlamps *n. Bristols.* '*Phewf! I wouldn't mind giving her headlamps a rub.*'

head off a nun, like trying to get *met.* Descriptive of something very difficult to achieve. *Finding a pube in an afro. 'And I fully intend to bring in legislation on asylum that will make getting British citizenship like getting head off a nun before the next parliament.'* (David Blunkett addressing the Labour Party Conference, 2003).

heavage *n.* A *Bristol Channel* that is only there thanks to cleverly designed *titpants.*

heave *v.* To vomit, *make a pavement pizza,* release a loud *technicolour yawn.*

heave a Havana *v. Grow a tail,* take a *dump, light a bum cigar, cast Churchill's reflection.*

heave-ho *n.* The *arse.*

heavy dick *n.* The very first stirrings of erectivation. The beginnings of a *semi-on. 'Hey, I don't like admitting it, boys, but that tranny off There's Something About Miriam has given me a bit of a heavy dick.'*

heavy shooter *n.* One whose *money shots* tend to be *pwas* rather than *gwibbles.*

hedge coke *n.* Plastic bottles filled with fluid too pale to be true cola, discarded on roadside verges by lorry drivers in order to tempt thirsty runners or cyclists in need of refreshment. *Trucker's tizer, kidney cider.*

hedgehog *n.* A *fanny* shaven 5 days ago. A *face grater.*

hee *1. n. Thai. Minge, hairy cheque book. 2. interj.* One of a series of noises made by laughing gnomes/policemen.

hefty-clefty *n.* A *welly top,* a *horse's collar,* a *melted welly.* A very wide *Mary.*

Helena Bonham *rhym. slang.* The *anus.* From the English rose actress Helena Bonham-Carter = *farter.*

helicopters, attack of the *n.* Drunken spinning of the head, a sudden reminder that you need to make an urgent call on the *great white telephone.* The *whirlies, wall of death.*

hello Cleveland *exclam.* Phrase uttered by a gentleman who is *doing* a lady from behind and inadvertently *pots the brown* rather than the *pink.* From the scene in '*Spinal Tap*' when the band find themselves in the wrong tunnel.

helmet *n.* The *bell end.*

helmet *n.* A quantity of *fellatio.* An amount of *blow jobs. 'My nan wanted to meet Roger Whitaker, so she had to give the roadie some helmet to get backstage.'*

helmetdale *n.* A strong-smelling, mature *knob cheese.*

helmet mag *n.* A *stroke periodical,* an *art pamphlet.*

helmet pelmet *n.* The *Fiveskin, Kojak's roll-neck.*

helmetscale *n.* Fully-ossified *knob-*

cheese that has to be chipped off the *bishop's hat* using a toothpick. Found only on the most determined opponents of genital hygiene.

helmet, to give it some *v.* To engage in an activity with some gusto. To give it *rice*, give it *welly*, give it *six-nowt*. *'It may be necessary to apply a considerable amount of torque in order to loosen the wheel studs. Indeed, you may have to give the wheel brace quite a bit of helmet before they begin to yield.'* (from the *'Austin Maxi Haynes Manual'*, 1978)

Hendrix on the high notes *sim.* Descriptive of the facial contortions of a gentleman in the final throes of coitus, reminiscent of the late plank spanker in full axe frenzy. The *vinegar strokes*.

Henman *n.* An impotent fellow. Named after the British tennis sensation Tim, who never manages to make it past the *semi* stage.

Henrietta Street 1. *n.* An old, narrow, twisty thoroughfare in Whitby and thus 2. *n.* An ageing, serpentine *clunge* with a strong aroma of kippers.

Henry Moore 1. *n.* A large pile of *shit* in a public place. 2. *n.* A large reclining dog *turd* on the pavement.

herbert pocket *n.* The pocket that the *herbert* slips into. The *arsehole*. From the name of the character in *'Great Expectations'*, being played by Sir Alec Guinness, and given to police upon his arrest for *cottaging*.

Herbie's bonnet *n.* The *beetle bonnet*, *camel's lips*.

Hershey highway *n. US.* Transatlantic *Bourneville boulevard*,

Cadbury alley.

Hershey highwayman *n. US.* An *ass bandit*.

Heskey *n.* A girl who *goes down* at the slightest touch.

hibernating grizzly *n.* A big hairy brown *shit* asleep in the *claypit* that one would be foolish to rouse from its slumbers.

hickies *n. Slapper*-speak for love bites, *shag tags*.

hickory dick *n.* A *cock* so hard it would bend any nails one attempted to drive into it.

hide the salami *n.* A bedtime game for two players, one *sausage* and a *hairy pie*. Also *sink the salami*, *bury the bratwurst*.

hiding policemen's helmets *adj.* Of a lady, to be *nipping out, smuggling peanuts*.

high miler *n.* An old banger who looks like she's been round the clock a few times, but is still running, eg. Joan Collins.

high pressure vein cane *n.* The penis, *prick, tallywhacker, Hector the meat injector*.

Hilary *n. rhym. slang.* A *five knuckle shuffle*. From US actress Hilary Swank. *'I just seen that Carol Vorderman flogging loans on the satellite and I knocked out a quick Hilary there and then.'*

hillbilly's hat *n.* A particularly dishevelled *cock socket*.

hill start *n.* The painstaking task of pleasuring oneself after a heavy drinking session, when reaching *biting point* can take hours.

Himalayas *n.* Gentlemen who *garden* on very steep inclines.

hingoot *n. Scot.* A lady of easy virtue, a *slapper*, a *prossie*, a *good time girl*. Literally, a woman who has enjoyed so much *cock* that her fanny is *'hinging oot'*.

hippo's ear *n*. A *hippo's mouth*. A *donkey's yawn*. A *fanny* like a *bucket*.

hippo's mouth *n*. Anotgher large, unsightly, gaping vagina.

hippo's saddle *n*. Something big, grey and leathery in a lady's *knickers*.

hippocrocapig *n*. Anne Widdecombe if you set her head on fire and put it out with a shovel. A *rhinocerpig*.

hipposuction *n*. Optimistic cosmetic surgical procedure carried out on the larger lady.

hip tits *n*. The large pair of flabby rolls of stomach blubber that hang down around the waists of fat Americans, as seen waddling around Disneyland.

hissing Sid *n*. One's *one-eyed trouser snake*.

hit and miss *rhym. slang. Piss.*

hit and run *v*. To indulge in sexual intercourse with a *boiler* despite one's better judgement, and leg it before she wakes up.

hitch-hiking under the big top *n*. Of *wanking chariots* and their owners, shifting into *sixth gear, polishing the tent pole*.

hitching to heaven *n*. More meaty *hand to glans* combat.

Hitler piss *n*. A braced, Nazi salute position from which to have a drunken *Chinese singing lesson* at the pub toilet trough.

Hitler tash *n*. A *clitler*, a *Lambourghini*.

Hitler wank *n*. An act of *self-pollution* performed in a shower with the left arm lodged firmly against the cubicle wall to prevent loss of balance.

HMP *abbrev*. A lady for whom only the finest things in life will do.

High Maintenance Pussy.

hobbit *n*. A small hairy thing.

hobbit dick *n*. A *penis* that is wider than it is long. A *tuna can cock, Welshman's cock, choad*.

hobgoblin *n*. A *bumgoblin*.

hobnail boots, that one wore *exclam*. A phrase shouted loudly in order to make the most of a volubly-*dropped gut*. *'In polite company, following another's audible act of flatulence, it is permissible to offer a comment. If the wind breaker was the wife of a Governor General, one might say 'One-nil to you, Your Excellency'. If the younger son of a Duke has farted, a comment such as 'Fuck me, that one wore hobnail boots, My Lord, would be perfectly acceptable.'* (from *'Debrett's Etiquette'*, 2003).

hobnob *n*. A big, dirty *ringpiece*, barnacled with such an excess of *winnetry* that it takes on the appearance of the much-loved family biscuit.

hockmagandy *n*. The one day of the year when Scotsmen *fuck* their wives.

hoeing the HP *v*. Uphill *gardening* on the *brown sauce allotment*.

HOFNAR 1. *n*. prop. A mid-nineties Seattle-based college band. 2. *acron. US*. Hard On For No Apparent Reason.

hog's eye *n*. The serving hatch through which *perseverance soup* arrives.

hog's eye hairpiece *n*. *Aus*. That long, piss-combed tuft of hair that seems to grow out the end of a dog's *unit*. Like on the top of Woody Woodpecker's head.

hogans *n*. *US*. *Charlies, Gert Stonkers, Norma Snockers*.

hole *n*. Anything you can stick

something up.

hole in one *n.* Successful penetrative sex without using the hand for guidance.

holiday money *n.* Male genitalia, the *family jewels, meat and two veg,* the *fruit bowl.*

Hollyoats *n.* A leisurely Sunday afternoon bout of *personal pollution* enjoyed whilst watching the omnibus edition of the blonde-heavy Chester-based soap. Careful control is required to avoid emptying one's *saddlebags* as Mr. Cunningham appears on screen, or when it cuts back to Vernon in the 'T4' studio.

Hollywood *n.* A completely depilated *mingepiece.* A *Barthez.*

Hollywood ending 1. *n.* A satisfying cinematic denouement in which good triumphs over evil and everyone goes home happy. 2. *n.* A *shit* that needs no wiping.

Hollywood loaf *n.* A *podge-on, half a teacake.* So named because of its popularity with male actors called upon to perform in the nude.

holy trinity *n.* To engage in anal, oral and vaginal sex in one session.

homburger *n.* A vegetarian fast food option.

home brew *n.* Laser-print quality *grumble mags* made from *cyber scud.*

hommage *n.* Act of devotion performed in a kneeling position.

homnambulist *n.* Chap who gets an inexplicable urge to go walking about on Hampstead Heath in the wee small hours.

homoclaustrophobia *n.* Possibly irrational fear of being trapped in an enclosed space with a *bummer.*

homosexual *n.* A man or woman sexually attracted to members of his or her own sex. Often at bus stops. From the Greek homos = lifter, sexualos = togas.

homversation *n.* Of males, the discussion of anything at all except cars and football, but particularly 'Coronation Street', clothes, hair and cottaging anecdotes.

honesty box bargain *n.* A *five fingered discount* available to the value-conscious shopper at railway station newsagents. Named after the express counter thoughtfully provided for the use of passengers who are in a hurry not to pay.

honey altar *n.* The *muff diver's* object of worship.

honeypot *n.* A *fanny* surrounded by bees. Winnie the Pooh's *bird's twat.*

honkies *n.* Big *muckspreader* round back.

honk up *n.* Hoy up, bowk.

Honore de 1. *n. prop.* First name of the famous French novelist responsible for such works as 'La Comedie Humaine', ie. Balzac and thus 2. *n.* The scrotum. 'Jean-Pierre a vomi sur le trottoir du Champs Elysée quand Josephine l'a frappé avec ses grands Docteur Martens sur son Honore de.' (from 'La Comedie Humaine' by Balzac).

hooberstank *n.* The first, and usually biggest, *fart* of the morning. *Morning thunder, reveille, dawn chorus.*

hoobs 1. *n.* A bizarre set of aliens which appear on Channel 4 in the mornings. 2. *n.* A particularly impressive set of *funbags.* From huge + *boobs.*

hoodwink 1. *v.* To deceive, or mislead by falsehood, eg. when selling endowment mortgages or pension schemes. 2. *v.* The act of squeezing the *fiveskin* over the *Dutch straw-berry* in order to encourage the last few drops of *piss* to exit the *blow hole*.

hooker *n*. US. A *ho'*, a *pro*.

hooking fish *v*. *Feeding the ducks, stabbing the cat*.

hoop *n*. A *hole*.

hoop flogger *n*. A lady who is *on the batter*.

hoop stretcher *n*. A *crafty butcher* who hides his *salami* in a *tea towel holder*.

hootchie *n*. US. *Totty, blit, muff*.

hootchie cootchie *n*. *Hanky panky, how's your father*.

hooter *n*. Conk, *neb, sneck*. Nose. Not the singular of *hooters*.

hootermammy *n*. A former *Miss Lincolnshire* who receives a visit from the *titty fairy* during pregnancy. eg. Kerry out of Atomic Kitten. One who has *collected the baby bonus*.

hooters *n*. Bazookas, *baps, head-lamps*. Not the plural of *hooter*.

hoover up *v*. To try, usually unsuccessfully, to 'sniff up' the smell of a recently dropped *fart* when one sees an attractive woman approaching.

HOP *acronym*. Hang Over Poo. Giant, exceedingly loose stool, the noisy passing of which is a significant milestone in the recovery from a hang over. An *alcopoop*, an *escape sub*. '*Ahh! I feel much better after that hop. Anyone fancy a pint?*'

hop into the horse's collar *v*. Nip to the *cock wash*.

hopper arse *n*. A *forty guts*, a *salad dodger*.

horatio *n*. Posh Latin term used by doctors, lawyers and police to describe a *chewie*.

horizontal jogging *n*. Hilarious euphemism for sexual intercourse, esp. '*a bit of the old~*'.

horizontally accessible *adj*. To describe a *slag, bike, yoyo knickers*.

horn, the *n*. Ceremonial symbol of a man's affection for a woman, paradoxically given by the woman to the man.

hornbag *1. n*. A bag for keeping horns in. *2. n*. An extremely attractive woman, ie. one who gives you the *horn*.

horndog *n*. An extremely unattractive woman, ie. one who loses you the *horn*.

horny *adj*. The state of a man whilst in possession of *the horn*.

horse eating oats *sim*. *Feeding the pony*. '*And David went unto the house of Bathsheba and she had not known her husband Naboth for ages. And David did put his hand down her knickers and lo, it was like a horse eating oats.*' ('*Deuteronomy*' Ch 6, v 23).

horse's collar *1. n*. Vagina. *2. sim*. To imply generous proportions. Also *cathedral, clown's pocket, hippo's mouth*. '*She's got a fanny like a horse's collar.*'

horse's doofers *n*. Superlative *mutt's nuts, dog's bollocks*, bee's knees, The *donkey's knob*.

horse's handbrake *n*. A *diamond cutter*, a *concrete donkey*, a raging *bone on*.

horse's head, sitting on a *v*. Of queues for the *dunny*, to be suffering from a more extreme case of the *turtle's head*. '*Hurry up will you, I'm sitting on a horse's head out here.*'

horse's nose *n*. The early stages of a *shaven haven* being allowed to grow out. Noticeable when *feeding the pony.*

hosebag *n.* Woman of loose morals. She with a *fanny* like a *billposter's bucket. A boot, slapper.*

hose job *n. Blow job, chewie, horatio.*

hose monster *n.* An ugly woman who cannot get enough hosepipes.

hospital button *n.* A particularly unhealthy looking *gold watch.*

hot *adj.* Condition which, in conjunction with *horny,* is often used to describe ugly, fat, bored women waiting on the end of expensive telephone sex lines, eg. *'Hot and horny bitches thirsty for your love seed. £1.80/min.'*

HOTBOT *acronym.* The expression of one's desire for a *dog's marriage.* Hang Out The Back Of That.

hot dog *1. n.* An egg delicacy famously enjoyed by the cult actor Divine in the film *'Pink Flamingoes'* (Children's Film Foundation, 1977). *2. v.* To eat said morsel, freshly laid by a poodle. *3. v.* To slap one's *sausage* into a lady's *buns.*

hot fish yoghurt *n.* Cream sauce filling for *hairy pie.*

hot hello *n.* The warm trickle down her leg that reminds a lady of the deposit that was recently made into her *special bank.*

hot karl *n.* Post-anal sex *horatio.*

hot lunch *n.* See *Cleveland steamer.* Or better still, don't.

hot meat injection *n.* An inoculation with the *spam syringe.*

hot monocle *n.* Half a *Velma.* A facial ejaculation which reduces one's *bird's* ability to see by fifty percent. Or in the case of Gabrielle, one hundred percent, fifty percent of the time.

hots *n.* Reciprocal gift for a girl after she's given one *the horn.*

hotty *n.* US. *Totty, blart.*

hound *n. Dog, steg, boiler.*

hound cable *n. Barker's rope. Dogshit.*

Howard's Way *rhym. slang.* Gay. From the shit BBC TV drama of the same name.

how much? *exclam.* Amusing mock-shocked utterance from one who has just *broken wind.*

how's your father *n.* Sex. Often prefixed *'Fancy a quick bit of... ahem...?'*

hoy *v.* To throw, lob, chuck, esp. beer down one's neck.

hoy up *v.* To *throw up, barf, spew.*

HPS *abbrev.* Horizontal Payment Scheme. Female method of remuneration favoured by taxi drivers, traffic wardens and drug dealers. Also *hairy cheque book, gash card.*

huby *n.* A semi-erect penis, a *dobber, half a teacake,* a *lob on.*

huffle *v.* To *bagpipe.* To take part in an *Hawaiian muscle-fuck.*

Hughie Green *n.* A swift *wank* taken when 'opportunity knocks'. *'Mr. Pickwick closed the door behind Mrs. Fezzyfelt, sat down behind his old oak desk, and took the turnip watch from his waistcoat pocket. 'Odds bodkins,' he shouted. 'Five minutes until Mr. Sticklebrick arrives. Time enough for a swift Hughie Green.'* (from *'The Pickwick Papers'* by Charles Dickens).

hulk spunk *n.* Snot.

hum *1. v.* To *ming,* stink. *2. v.* To sing with the lips closed, or as near to closed as possible during a *hum job.*

hum job *n.* Vegetarian oral sex involving no meat, just *two veg.*

accompanied by simultaneous humming of the musical variety.

Humber Bridge 1. *n.* Suspended estuary crossing which connects Grimsby to Hull and thus 2. *n.* The thing on a lady which links the *fishy bit* to the *shitty bit*. The *taint, tinter, carse*.

humble grumble *n.* Poor man's porn, eg. Women's Health Week leaflets pressed into service as *monomanual literature. Paupernography*.

humdinger *n.* A *fart* which makes the wallpaper peel.

hummer 1. *n.* A large, butch military vehicle favoured by Californian hairdressers and Arnold Schwarzenegger. 2. *n. Arse, bum.* 3. *n.* A *humdinger*.

hummingbird, hung like a *adj.* To have a *cock* like a *Chinese mouse*.

hummingbird's wing *sim.* Descriptive of the speed of a naughy lady's fingers whilst interferring with her *bodily treasure*. '*I come home from the pub last night and caught the missus playing her banjo to an Enrique Iglesias video. Her fingers were going like a fucking hummingbird's wing, I can tell you.*'

hump 1. *v.* To *shag*, have sex in the style of an old Labrador with its *lipstick* out. 2. *v.* To carry heavy amplification equipment to and from a live music venue whilst one's *arse* sticks out the back of one's jeans.

humpty *n.* The act of *humping*.

hunchback spiders *n.* Hairy ladies nipples.

hungry arse *n.* Condition afflicting women whereby their *bills* disappear up the *crack* of their *hummer* as they walk.

hunt for brown October *n.* The act of seeking out and destroying a *U-bend U-boat*. With a bog brush or a stick.

hurl 1. *v.* To *hoy*. 2. *v.* To *hoy up*.

hurt yourself *v.* To vigorously *relax in a gentleman's way*. '*Thanks for that new porn, mate. I'm going to go home now and hurt myself.*'

hush puppies *n.* Breasts so impressive that all men are rendered speechless in their presence.

hussy *n.* A shameless woman, a drunk and an unfit mother.

hymen climbin' *v.* The act of being the first felow to plant his *flagpole* up *Mount Venus*. Plucking a *bird's virgin string*.

Ii

IBM *1. n. prop.* A large computer company. *2. abbrev.* Itty Bitty Meat. A small penis. *3. abbrev.* Inches Below Muff. The units in which a *greyhound skirt* is measured.

I can't believe it's not batter *n.* KY Jelly, *granny batter*.

ICBM *acronym.* Of modern day state-of-the-art trouser weaponry, an Inter Cuntinental Ballistic Missile.

iced fingers *n.* Bakers' confectionery-speak for the results of *glazing the knuckle*.

ice the cake *v.* To decorate a *tart* with *cream*. Often seen in European *grumble flicks*. *'Gunter! There's only thirty seconds of tape left in the camera. Quick, ice that cake!'*

ice the log *n.* An environmentally sound toilet visit where one has a *wank* after a *shit*, thereby saving water on the flush.

Iggy popshot *n. Whacking off* on a TV's *ass*.

Ikea bulb *n.* A lady that *blows* first time one *turns her on*.

Imperial barge *n.* The male member. A particularly majestic *skin boat*. *'You should have seen how Mrs. Eisenhower's eyes lit up when my nine-inch imperial barge heaved into view.'* (from *'The Memoirs of Winston Churchill'*).

impersonate Stalin *v.* To perform oral sex on a woman, *don the beard, eat hairy pie*. *'Hold tight up there love, I'm just gonna do a quick impersonation of Stalin.'*

Indian mustard *n.* Diarrhoea.

Indian rope trick *n.* An impressive erection attained under seemingly impossible circumstances, eg after 12 pints and/or 6 *wanks*.

indoor fishing *v.* A coarse form of *angling for tadpoles*. A gentrified *wank*.

indoor hobo *n.* One who lives inside, but looks like they should be living in a doorway, eg. Johnny Vegas, Ricky Tomlinson, Tracy Emin. A *tramp's mate*.

Ingrid *rhym. slang.* An act of anal excretion. Named after the luscious 'tits out' *'Hammer Horror'* actress Ingrid Pitt.

inheritance *n.* A miasmatic bequest bequeathed to a toilet-goer by the previous occupant.

injury time *1. n.* The dying seconds of a football match where the losing side throw caution to the wind and take a shot at anything in a desperate attempt to score. *2. n.* The last song of the evening in a nightclub.

Inman's twitch *n.* The brisk, staccato, buttock-clenched walk to the toilet when one is attempting to prevent *turtle* egress. From the gait adopted by 1970s sitcom actor John Inman.

inside job *n.* A game of *pocket billiards*. Vigorously and rhythmically looking for change in your front pockets at a sophisticated lapdancing establishment. An *IPW*.

interior decorating *n.* Slapping a bit of white emulsion about the womb using the *naughty paintbrush*.

interrogate the prisoner *v.* To *box the Jesuit, strangle the parson, choke the chicken, bash the bishop, pull the Pope's cap off, have a five knuckle shuffle, pull your pud, spank the monkey* etc. To interfere with oneself in the *farmyard area*. *'Richard, come down and get your tea.' 'I'll be right down, Judy. I'm* *just interrogating the prisoner. Into your shoe.'*

in the club *adj.* Up the duff, pregnant, preggers. From *in the pudding club*.

in the hockey team *adj.* Descriptive of a lesbidaceous woman. Or *lady golfer*.

Ipswich smile *n.* A *pasata grin*.

IPW *acronym.* The act of rummaging for change in one's trousers whilst in a lap-dancing establishment. In-Pocket Wank, an *inside job*.

Irish 1. *n.* Heterosexual anal sex, supposedly as a means of contraception. *UTBNB*. 2. *rhym. slang.* Toupee. From Irish jig = wig.

irish luggage *n.* Politically incorrect phrase used to describe the life's accumulations of a *paraffin*, traditionally carted about in a picturesque knotted hankerchief on the end of a stick slung over his shoulder, but more usually in an old supermarket trolley filled with *shitty* bundles of carrier bags.

Irish shave *n.* A *dump*.

Irish toothache *n.* An erection, bone. *'Is that a gun in your pocket, or have you just got Irish toothache?'*

iron *rhym. slang.* A *crafty butcher*. From Iron hoof = *poof*.

IRS 1. *abbrev. US.* The yankee tax-man. 2. *abbrev.* Itchy Ring Syndrome. Irritating anal affliction caused by insufficient wiping of the *chocolate starfish*, or by inflammation of the *farmers*.

I say! *interj.* Caddish expression of delight upon seeing a pair of *dunces' hats*.

Isle of Wight 1. *n.* A UK holiday destination made popular by Queen Victoria. 2. *rhym. slang.* A load of rubbish. From Isle of Wight = pile of shite. *'That holiday we had on the Isle of Wight last summer was a complete Isle of Wight. We're going to Wales this year.'*

isnae *n. Scot.* The *taint*, the *tintis*.

itch *n.* The feeling of sexual attraction towards his wife which a married man gets on average once every 7 years.

Itchypoo Park *n.* The area around *spice island* during a bout of *IRS*.

it's a knockout *n.* An amusing pub game where an individual with *legs like snapped candles* has to attempt to carry three brim-full pint glasses through a jostling, crowded hostelry from bar to table without spilling any.

I've loved in it *exclam.* Humorous staff version of the popular fast food advertising jingle, usually sung whilst preparing or serving *McDonald's special sauce*.

Jj

jackage *n. coll. Jazz, grumble, grummer, Frankie Vaughan* etc. or more generally, any materials used by a fellow for the purposes of *jacking off to, at, on* or *over*.

Jack Douglas *1. n. prop.* British film and television performer notable for wearing dungarees and a cap, whose Alf Ippatitimuss character was prone to sudden, spasmodic physical tics and hence *2. n.* Any violent, involuntary recoil from something, eg. a pint of milk which has gone off, a blocked train lavatory swimming in urine and faeces, or Shane McGowan's breath.

jacked up *adj.* To be celibate whilst suffering from a *dose*.

jack off *v.* To *whack off, choke the chicken, jerk the gherkin*.

jack roll *1. n. SA.* A gang bang. *2. n. US.* A mugging.

jack shit *n. Bugger all, sweet FA,* zero, zilch. Nowt.

jacksie *n.* Polite word for *arse*, especially in the recepticular context. *'You can stick your fucking parking ticket up your jacksie, mate. I'm not paying.'*

jacksie rabbit *n. Muddy funster, Hershey highwayman*.

jacksydent *n.* A trouser mishap, a *follow through*. From *jacksie +* accident. *'Paula Radcliffe has pulled out of the 10,000 metres final, after suffering a nasty jacksydent during the marathon.'*

jack the beanstalk *v.* To attempt to pull up the *purple-headed gristle thistle* by the roots.

Jack the ripper *n.* A hard, thick, bloodthirsty *turd* that does its evil work in one's *back passage*. A *ring splitter*.

Jacky Danny *rhym. slang. James Hunt*.

jacobs *rhym. slang.* Testicles. From Jacobs crackers = *bollocks*. Generally kept close to the cheese.

Jade yawning, a fanny like *sim.* A *clown's pocket*.

jaff *v.* To *wank*. In Norfolk.

jaffas *n.* The *nuts* of the *fruit bowl*.

jail bait *n.* Worms dug up by tunnelling prisoners and later, after their escape, used for fishing.

jake *1. n.* A columnar monument erected in memory of a nice pair of *jamboree bags* one once saw, or a notable scene from a *meat vid. 2. n. Scot.* An ugly woman, *horndog, lumberjill*.

jamboree bags *n. Funbags*.

jambush *n.* A *blobstrop* that comes out of nowhere.

James Hunt *rhym. slang. Jacky Danny*.

jammer *n. Carib.* A *pud*. See also *windjammer*.

jammet *n. Carib.* A West Indian term for a *slapper*.

jammy dodger *n.* A lady who uses the fact that the *tomato boat has docked* to avoid performing her wifely duty.

jammy todger *n.* A *barber's pole*.

jampax *n.* A lady's hygiene product, a *fanny nanny*.

jam rag *n.* A tampon, *fanny mouse, chuftie plug*.

jam raid *n. Crimson tidal* movement which leaves *tuna town* inaccessible by *skin boat* at certain times of the month.

jam session *n.* An improvised ragtime duet.

Jane *1. n.* A ladies' lavatory. *2. n.* A *fanny*.

jang *n. Dong*.

janitorial pleat *n.* An unexpected *stiffy* or *tent pole*, named after the unique and unusually-positioned design feature found only in the work trousers supplied to lecherous old school caretakers.

Japanese flag *n.* Appearance of the *arsehole* when blighted by *ring sting. Arse of the rising sun.*

Japanese teardrop *n.* An unexpected single drop of *merry monk* that turns up ten minutes after the *bolt* has been shot, regardless of how thoroughly one mops the *herman*. The *missing fish.*

Jap's eye *n.* The male urethral opening, *hog's eye.*

jarred *adj. Pissed, sloshed, wankered.*

J. Arthur *rhym. Slang. Wank.* From the British film distributor J Arthur Rasturbation.

jaywank *v.* To cross the *Billy Mill Roundabout* without due care and attention. To *wank* without regard to the consequences.

jazz *1. n.* Improvised music characterised by syncopated rhythms. *2. n.* The *fadge, mott. 3. n.* Sex, intercourse, *the other. 4. n. Frankie Vaughanography.*

jazz drummer, go at it like a *sim.* To hunch over one's plate and shovel food into one's mouth at an unseemly speed.

jazz egg *n.* A little *spodge* of *spadge.*

jazz festival *n.* The purchase of two or more *Noddy books* at one time.

jazz fusion *n.* The process by which the pages of a *scud mag* are cemented together.

jazz mag *n.* Printed volume of pornographic material, gentleman's interest journal. *Art pamphlet.*

jazz magnate *1. n.* A porn millionaire, one who who has benefited from a series of wristy investments. *2. n.* A short, blind, hairy-palmed man who owns a substantial stash

of *scud mags.*

jazz talc *n. Bolivian marching powder, showbiz sherbert, Keith Richards' dandruff.*

jazz trumpeter's cheeks *sim.* Descriptive of a lady's well-rounded *arse.* Dizzy Gillespie's face-style buttocks.

jazz vocalist *n.* One who encourages himself with erotic one-sided conversations (ooh, baby, yeah! etc) with the girls in *art pamphlets* whilst practising *self-pollution.*

JB *n.* See *Jodrell.*

j-cloth *n.* A teenager's phenomenally-absorbent underbed sock, used for cleaning up adolescent spillages.

Jebbs *1. n.* Manufacturer of crash helmets and hence *2. n.* Big round *knockers* which carry a BSI kitemark and comply with BS 6658.

Jedi *rhym. slang.* A *turd.* From Jedi Knight = *shite.*

Jehovah's stiffness *n.* An unwelcome erection which arrives at the most inconvenient times and then refuses to leave. A *tiffter, Jake.*

jelly hammock *n. Drip tray.*

jelly jewellery *n.* The earrings, nose studs, fancy spectacles and other facial adornments a lady sometimes receives when she was expecting her partner to give her a *pearl necklace.*

jelly roll *1. n. US. Fanny, muff, totty. 2. n.* Getting fucked by a jazz pianist who died in 1941.

jelly water mangos *n.* Large *knockers, gazunkas.*

Jenny *n. US. Boris, minge.*

jerk *n.* A stupid, dim or dull person.

jerkin' the gherkin *n.* Jiggling a small cucumber round on the end of a string.

jerk off *v. Jack off.*

jerkolator *n.* An extremely noisy *blow job*, performed by someone who comes back for coffee.

jerkwad *n. US. Tosser, fuckwit, wankipants.*

Jersey Royals *euph.* Smallish, but pert and firm, *shirt potatoes* which are particularly good boiled with a bit of butter on. *Sara Cox's orange pippins.*

jester's shoes *n. medic.* The involuntary upward curling of the toes that herald the onset of the *vinegar strokes*, whilst lying on one's back wanking. *'Zoom in on Gunter for the money shot, camera two. He's got the jester's shoes.'*

jeweller *n.* A gifted manufacturer of *jelly jewellery* and *pearl necklaces.*

jewels *n.* See *family jewels.*

jibble *n.* The final, sad, leaking tears of *spangle* which drip out of one's *hog's eye* in those *wangst*-ridden moments of spiralling despair and self-loathing which apparently follow a bout of *self help.* From *jizz* + dribble.

jig-a-jig *n. It, how's your father.*

jigger *n. 18thC.* That tool with which a man commits *jiggery pokery.* The *fuckstick.*

jiggered *adj.* In a state of fatigue. *Buggered, knackered, shagged out.*

jiggery pokery *n. Shenanigans,* assorted sexual goings on. *'I'll have no jiggery pokery going on under my roof.'*

jiggle ring *n.* The larger lady's *muffin top* lifebelt, shaken to attract the attention of prospective partners. *'Don't look now, but that munter at the bar is offering you her jiggle ring.'*

jiggle show *n.* A titillating, but *chest tuner*-free early evening TV show,

eg. *'Baywatch', 'Charlie's Angels'.*

jiggle the jewellery *v.* To *jack off* the *Jimmy Wonkle.*

jigglypuff *n.* A man who watches female television programmes, such as *'EastEnders'* and *'Emmerdale'* of his own free will.

jill off *v.* Female equivalent of *jack off*, to *paddle the pink canoe.* Until it leaks.

Jimmy Edwards *n.* Tufts of *pubage* protruding either side of a bikini bottom, resembling the handlebar moustache of the late *'Whacko!'* star.

Jimmy Riddle *rhym. slang.* Vicar-friendly term for a *piss.*

jimmy sack *n.* School lavatory high jinks. During an act of urination, the *fiveskin* is pinched shut, creating a high-pressure bag of *piss* at the end of the *penis.* This can be used to chase people as, when released, a *jimmy sack* can be explosive.

Jimmy White's brother *n.* The most boring member of any group of lads who turns up every night at the pub to sit in abject, oppressive silence. From the urban legend that when Jimmy White's brother died, his friends broke into the undertakers to take the corpse out for one last *piss-up.*

Jimmy Wonkle *n.* The gentleman's *widdle tap.*

Jim Royle's beard *n.* A *Dylan.*

jism *n.* Semen. Also *gism, jissom, jizz, jizzom.*

jitbag *n.* A *dunky*, a *jubber ray.*

jit gel *n. US.* The contents of a used *jitbag* once it has floated across the Atlantic.

jit gel rag *n. US.* Any available object on which you wipe your *cock* after sex, eg. tissues, underpants, curtains, tramp's beard.

jitlag *n.* The slimy, post-coital after-mess that drops out the end of one's *charlie* about 20 minutes after *stack blow.* The *post bolt,* the *missing fish.*

jitler *n. Spunk.*

jizlas *n.* Thin sheets of paper used to mop up *tugwax.*

jizz 1. *n. Jism.* 2. *v.* To *shoot one's load, lose one's mess.*

jizzbags *n.* The scrotum, *John Wayne's hairy saddlebags.*

jizz bib *n.* A sacrificial T-shirt placed over the stomach and chest to prevent seminal claggage of the chest hair during a horizontal *wank.*

jizz bib *n.* A *shirtlifter's* goatee beard.

jizz bolt *n.* A glob of ejaculate that leaves the *hog's eye* with enough force to put the television screen through.

jizzbolt jury *n.* Any group of men watching and discussing the merits of a *stick vid.*

jizz drive *n.* An external storage medium for *left-handed website* downloads.

jizziotherapy *n.* A 3-minute, one-handed massage that relieves stiff-ness for up to half an hour.

jizz jar *n.* Girlfriend. Probably con-sidered derogatory, although one would think they'd take it as a compliment.

jizz juggler *n.* An enthusiastic *wankatrix.*

jizzle *n.* A drizzle of *jizz.* Derivation unknown.

jizzmopper *n.* A member of the hon-ourable profession of peep show *wank booth* hygienist.

jizzmopper's cloth 1. *n.* An absorbent rag used by a *jizzmopper*

in the performance of their daily duties. 2. *n.* Descriptive of a *cock-oholic's* knickers.

jizz off a porn queen's face *sim.* A hardcore version of 'water off a duck's back'. *'Frankly, Clare Short's criticisms of Tony Blair's presidential style of government are like jizz off a porn queen's face to the Prime Minister.'* (Andrew Marr, Radio 4 *'Today'* programme, May 2003).

jizzard *n.* A swirling blizzard of *sticky snow,* sufficient to stop a *train being pulled* in a *grumble flick.*

J-No *n. prop.* A self-deluded bird with a horrible fat *arse* who believes she looks good in tight jeans or hipsters.

Joan Collins' knickers See *tart's window box.*

job *n.* A *feeshus.*

jobby, a big *n. Scot.* A *dreadnought.*

jobby engine *n.* The lavatory or water closet. The *shit pot.*

jobby jouster *n.* A Knight of King *Richard the Third.*

jockeys *rhym. slang.* Nipples. From jockeys' whips = *nips.*

jockey's coffin *n.* An exceptionally small and snug-fitting *fluffit.* A *mouse's ear,* a *paper cut. 'And so it was that Mary was pure and had not known a man and had a snatch like a jockey's coffin, yet she was great with child.'* ('Luke' Ch 1 v4).

jockey's starting position *n.* The well-braced *arse*-in-the-air stance adopted by one who is shortly anticipating a *shot from the starter's gun.*

Jodrell *rhym. slang.* A J Arthur. From the UMIST radio telescope Jodrell Bank.

joff *v.* To *milm* one's *grundies* without even being *tumescent*. Derived from Jizz On Flop. *'I joffed when I found my dad's bootleg 'Night in Paris' vid behind some tins of paint in the garage.'*

jogging behind a gritter *sim.* Descriptive of the face of a woman with a less than peach-like complexion, eg. Susan Tully, Frances de la Tour, Kate O'Mara. *'Jesus Christ! She's got a face like she's been jogging behind a gritter. Where did you find her?' 'She was jogging behind a gritter.'*

John 1. *n.* Percy, Willie, John Thomas. A *cock.* 2. *n.* A *pro's* client, a *Hillman Hunter.* 3. *n. US.* A *crapper.*

John Holmes *n.* A massive marijuana cigarette, named after the legendary saucy actor of the same name who reputedly had a large *tassel.* (Not to be confused with a *Luke Jackson* - a rather small and unsatisfying marijuana cigarette named after Luke Jackson from Sutton Coldfield).

John Lees *rhym. slang. Scots. Tits.* From noted dead blues groaner John Lee Hooker = *sooker.*

John Merrick's cap *n.* A vast, out of shape *fanny.*

Johnny *n.* A *dunky*, a *jubby ray.*

Johnny Cash 1. *n.* £2 for 3. 2. *n.* A *Wigan rosette.* A *burning ring of fire.*

johnny jibber *n.* To lose *wood* upon opening the *flunkey.* Premature ejaculation and *johnny jibber* are thought to affect 1 in 4 males at some time in their life.

Johnny no-stars *n.* A *dolt.* From the 'star rating' system on the badges displayed by staff at McDonald's. One who occupies a place on the lower end of the evolutionary fast food chain.

John Sargent 1. *n.* A *fry-up face.* Refers to anyone with features resembling the ITN journalist. 2. *n.* A great British fried breakfast of which, before commencing, one might say *'Now over to political correspondent John Sargent.'*

John Thomas *n.* The pet name by which Lady Chatterley's lover (horizontal gardener Mellors) referred to his *pink hoe* in the controversial steamy novel by Harry Worth.

John Wayne's hairy saddle bags *n. Jizzbags.*

John Wayne's safety catch, more time off than *sim.* In an office or workplace, descriptive of employees who are constantly ill. *Glassbacks.*

John Waynes *n.* Walking like Mrs. Thatcher, ie. the gait adopted after *giving birth to Meatloaf's daughter.* Makes the walker look like they've been sitting on a horse for three days.

joiner's bag *n.* A battered, capacious *fanny* with all hammers and spirit levels falling out of it.

join giblets *v.* To do *thingy* with a bare lady.

jollies 1. *n. Police.* In constabulary terms, trips to scenes of crimes. 2. *n.* Women's breasts. *'Look at the jollies on that nun, Your Holiness.'*

jollup *n.* A dollop of *jizz.* From Greek *jollopus* = dollop of *jizz.*

jollyrancher *n. US.* One blessed with the cat-like ability to perform self-*horatio*, ie. a man who never leaves the house.

Jonathan *rhym. slang.* A *Sherman tank*, a *Barclays*, from the masturbating TV presenter Jonathan Ross

OBE = *toss*.

joombye *n. Scot. Jism, jizz, McSpunk, vitamin S.*

Joseph's balls *n. medic.* Nuts that have not been evacuated for a long time. From the supernaturally cuckolded biblical carpenter's testicles. *'How's tricks, Cliff?' 'To tell you the truth, Hank, I've not had any since the late fifties, and it feels like I've got Joseph's balls in my pants.'*

joskin *n.* A country bumpkin, a yokel, a *sheep shagger.*

josser *n. 19ᵗʰC. Fuckwit* or parasite. The ideal name for someone who is both.

jostle the chosen one *v.* To *pull the Pope's cap off*, to *box the Jesuit.*

jotter *n.* The *teatowel holder, loon pipe, council gritter, gazoo, balloon knot, raisin, chocolate starfish, Gary, rusty sheriff's badge, freckle, clacker valve, kakpipe, corn dot, ringpiece, crapper, aris, quoit, poop chute, panda's eye* etc. The *arsehole. 'Palmolive was powerless to resist. His eyes burnt into hers like malachites. His muscular arms enfolded her body as she felt herself being swept away in a mistral of passion. "I love you, Alfonso,' she gasped. 'Take me now, I'm yours.' 'Drop your grundies and bend over then, love,' said Alfonso, unzipping his heaving slacks. 'I'll slip you a quick length up the jotter."* (from *'The Lady and the Travel Rep'* by Barbara Cartland).

joy plug *n.* The congealed remnant of a successful *wank* that causes a slight pause at the start of a *hit and miss.*

joyrider's moustache *n.* The light growth of fluffy top lip *bum fluff* popular with teenage delinquents.

joystick *n.* Of *choppers*, the cockpit instrument or *knob*, which gets throttled, *trouser toy, pant plaything.*

joy valve *n.* A lady's *bodily treasure.*

J-pig *n.* An internet *porn monster.*

jubblies *n.* Lovely breasts, *funbags.*

jubnuts *n. Bead curtains, dangleberries, dags.*

judges' eyebrows *n. Spiders' legs.*

Judith *n.* A very dense, dark *fadge*, as sported by the character Judith in *'Monty Python's Life of Brian.' 'Bloody hell, love, you've got a right Judith on you. It looks like you've been hit between the legs with a bag of soot.'*

jugged-mare *n.* A aesthetically-challenged lady who is nevertheless worth a go due to her large *tits*. A *bapdog.*

juggernorks *n.* A huge pair of *Gert Stonkers* that come bearing down on you well ahead of their owner.

juggler's doughnuts 1. *n. prop.* A popular themed fast food store at Alton Towers. 2. *n. Shirt potatoes* when handled in the style of a circus performer tossing balls from hand to hand.

jug jousting *v.* A *bunny rub.*

jugly *adj.* Ugly, but with big *knockers*, eg. Anna Ryder Richardson, Erica Rowe, Lord Owen.

jugs *n.* A lady's *top bollocks*, breasts.

juicy flute *n.* A chewy, salty snack for the ladies. The *gut stick.*

JULF *acronym.* Jumped Up Little Fucker, a pushy *twat.*

jullet *n. medic.* The phenomenon of the breasts, upper chest and chins of a *salad-dodging* lady all being merged into the same wobbling mass of flesh. The antipode of the *gunt.* From *jugs* + gullet

jump *v.* To have sex off the top of a wardrobe. Also *someone's bones*.

jump on the grenade *v.* Of a man, to perform the noble and selfless act whereby he *cops off* with an ugly bird solely to enable his friend to *pull* her fit mate. From the slightly less impressive story from World War I where a Private threw himself on a grenade to protect his comrades from the blast.

jungle juice *n. Blip, moip, fanny batter.*

jungle VIP *n.* A woman with pendulous breasts. From the apposite lines of the song performed by Louis, the orang-utan 'King of the swingers' in Disney's *'Jungle Book'*.

junior *n. US.* Penis, usually used in reference to one's own.

junk *1. n. coll.* The contents of the *fruitbowl.* "*I say, Jeeves. Drat these new fangled flies in my plus-fours,' I blustered. 'Haven't I just caught all my junk in the bally zipper mechanism."* (from *'Ooh, Yes! Just There! Don't Stop, Jeeves'* by PG Wodehouse). *2. n.* The *ejaculate* that lobs out the end of the *cock* part of the *junk.* "Launder these plus fours, Jeeves, there's a fellow," I said. '*I'm meeting Aunt Agatha for tea, and there's dried junk down the front from where Dulcie Wegg-Prosser gave my old chap a strop in the back of the Lagonda."* (from *'Fetch Some Tissues, Jeeves'* by PG Wodehouse).

Kk

kahoonas *n*. Large wobbly bosoms, *golden bodangers, kermungers, Gert Stonkers*.

kak *n*. *Keech, kaka*.

kak klaxon *n*. The *rectal hooter* from which loud anal honks are emitted, together with the occasional *bonus ball*.

kakpipe cosmonaut *n*. He who prefers to *dock* in the *rear unloading bay*.

kama slutra *n*. Exotic repertoire of sexual positions practised in cars, in shop doorways and behind skips etc. on Saturday nights.

kangaroo pouch *n*. A large *granny fanny*, big enough to fit your head in.

kangaroo shagging a spacehopper *sim*. Descriptive of the way a *shit house* door blows in the wind.

Kaplinsky, suffer a *v*. To fail to hear some important information as one's attention is entirely focused upon the thighs or cleavage of the person speaking. Named after Natasha Kaplinsky, whose thighs and cleavage drown out the news on BBC TV's 'Breakfast programme'.

kazoo 1. *n*. A tissue paper-covered aperture which *hums* tunelessly. 2. *n*. A completely unmusical musical instrument.

Keats *n*. A bout of *self abuse* that one has, despite being physically debilitated. Named after the romantic poet John Keats who, struck down in his early years with tuberculosis and consumption, still managed a couple of *tugs* a day.

kebabble *n*. The incoherent mumblings and inept attempts at ordering food endured by the staff of greasy takeaway outlets after the pubs have closed.

kebabe *n*. A woman who looks incredibly tasty when one is *pissed* at two in the morning, but the thought of whom turns one's stomach in the sober light of day.

keck cackler *n*. One with a laughing *kazoo*.

keck cougher *n*. He who *burps backwards*, or emits *under thunder*.

kecks *n*. See *kegs*.

keech *n*. *Crap, kak, kaka, keek*.

keel haul *v*. To drag one's tongue underneath a woman from *lip* to *ring*.

keema naan *n*. A shaved *fanny* with the very tip of the *bacon* sticking out.

keeping it on the clutch *v*. To skillfully work a *wank* just below boiling point to see one through the adverts on Channel 5. *Treading water*.

keep one's powder dry *v*. To feign disinterest in a bout of sex with the wife to ensure one can give it to the girlfriend with both barrels in a later engagement.

keep shouting sir, we'll find you *exclam. milit*. Humorous phrase uttered after someone has *dropped* a particularly loud *gut*. See also 'speak up caller, you're through' and 'a bit more choke and she would have started'.

keep the change *v*. Of a lady, to imbibe the issue of *horatio*, as opposed to expectorating it. To *swallow*.

keepy-uppy 1. *n*. A marathon ball control game practised by schoolboys in the park. 2. *n*. A marathon ball control game practised by Sting in his wife. Tantric sex.

kegs *n*. See *kex*.

keister *n*. *kak hole, arse*.

Keith Burtons *n.* Spooneristic *beef curtains.*

Kelly Brooks *n.* An ill-matched pair of wonky *jugs.*

Ken Dodd *v.* To masturbate into your partner's hair whilst they are asleep, leaving them on waking with a hairstyle similar to that of the scouse comic.

Kennedy *n.* A sexual session which incorporates penetration in all orifices except the ears and nose. From the sex-mad American president John F. Kennedy who once said 'you haven't finished with a woman until you've had her three ways'.

Kennedys, the *n. prop.* The male genitalia; the *fruit bowl, meat and two veg.* Named after the famous US political dynasty, ie. Jack and Bobby, and Ted in the middle with his big head.

kennel maid *n.* The hostess of an inexpensive massage parlour.

Keown surgery *n.* A piece of maxillo-facial reconstruction (commonly a broken nose) performed by a no-nonsense centre-half during a Sunday League football match.

kerbside quiche *n.* A *pavement pizza.*

Kermits, the *n.* Of a gentleman, the unwelcome situation of being constantly stalked and chatted up by a *pig* he would never wish to *fuck* in a million years.

kerrangatang *n.* A large, hairy, heavy metal enthusiast.

Kestrel manoeuvres in the dark *n.* The wayward shuffle of a *Harold Ramp* who has spent the whole day on the *wifebeater.*

kex 1. *n. Shreddies, trollies,* underpants. 2. *n.* Trousers.

kexorcism *n.* The act of driving out an evil, demonic *food's ghost* from one's *chamber of horrors.*

kexpresso *n.* A type of diarrhoea produced by one who needed a *crappuccino*, but couldn't get to the toilet on time.

key dropper *n.* A *bottee.*

keyboard hero *n.* One who is bravely prepared to engage in prodigious acts of personal courage that would normally entail the risk of a thorough kicking if he were not protected by the anonymity of an internet message board.

keyhole surgery *n.* The act of having a vigorous and satisfying dig around a particularly itchy *teatowel holder.*

KFC 1. *abbrev.* Something quick, spicy and filling involving a bit of greasy old *cock* and a *bucket of batter.* Knob Filled Cunt. *'I thought we'd stay in tonight, love. Fancy a KFC?'* 2. *n.* A girl who will cheaply provide a bit of breast, a bit of leg and a *box* to put your *bone* in.

khazi *n. Shitter, bog.*

khaki buttonhole *n.* The *chocolate starfish.*

Khyber *rhym. slang.* Arse. From Khyber Pass. Pass pronounced as in *'~me the cucumber sarndwiches'.*

kick start the motorbike *v.* To lift one's leg prior to popping an anal wheelie.

kick the knackers out of *v.* To complete the majority of a piece of work. *'By the February of 1498, and after two full years of work in the refectory of St Maria delle Grazie in Milan, Leonardo had just about kicked the knackers out of his Last Supper fresco. Accordingly, in March of that year* *he embarked for Florence in order to start inventing the helicopter.'* (from Vasari's *'Lives of the Painters'*).

kick with the left foot *v.* What players who arrive on the *other bus* tend to do, a football equivalent of *bowling from the pavillion end*.

kid's piss *n.* A nightclub toilet act of urination whereby the *kex* and *bills* are lowered onto the shoes at the urinal by someone too *pissed* to attempt a penile extraction through the flies.

kidney cider *n.* A discarded drinks container at the side of the road containing lorry driver's urine.

kidney fizzer *n.* Uncomfortably biological hangover after a particularly heavy night of binge *refreshment*, characterised by bubbling sensations in the lower back. *Alcoseltzer.*

kidney prodder *n.* During an act of sexual congress, a particularly impressive thrust.

kidney wiper *n. Slat rattler.* See also *purple headed womb broom*.

kid with an ice-cream, like a *sim.* Descriptive of the face of a lucky *grumble flick* starlet after a series of well-aimed *pop shots*.

kife 1. *n. coll. Blart, totty, tussage.* 2. *n.* The other.

kilt 1. *n. coll. Birds.* 2. *n. coll. Scot.* Blokes.

kilt lifter *n.* A Scottish fellow who is *good with colours*, a *McQueen*.

kingbast *n.* A sweary term that can be shouted in front of grannies, vicars, nuns etc. without causing offence. Contraction of *fucking bastard*.

King Canute *n.* An enormous *Richard the Third* that blocks the bend and holds back the tide of the flush, causing the toilet to overflow.

King for a day *euph.* To have a bad case of the *Brads*, ie. to spend all day on the *throne*.

King Kong's finger *n.* A *turd* large enough to flatten a car. An *Elvis killer*.

King of the elephants *exclam.* An affectionate chorus, sung humorously in the street whilst pointing at someone with big bones.

kipper 1. *n.* The *Billingsgate box, minge, captain's pie.* 2. *n.* That useful bit of skin that keeps the *plums* safely out of the *arse's* reach. The *barse, tintis, notcher. Perry Como's lip.*

kipper basting *v. Shagging.*

kipper for breakfast *n.* To rise early and go for a *horizontal jog*, ideal cure for *dawn horn*.

kipper's cunt *n.* Even more pungent than an *anchovy's fanny*. The *ne plus ultra* of fish smellyness.

kiss for granny *n.* The hermetically-sealed, tightly-pursed peck one gives one's girlfriend after *crashing the yoghurt truck* in her gob. A *nun's kiss.*

kissing tackle *n.* The north and south, *cakehole*.

kiss the Amish *v.* To perform oral sex upon a particularly *Dave Narey* pair of *catflaps*. To *lick out* a *bear trapper's hat*.

kiss the frog *v.* Of a lady, to perform *horatio*.

kiss the porcelain god *v.* To *talk on the great white telephone*.

Kit-Kat *v.* To stimulate a lady with four fingers at once, using a swift, forward thrusting, karate chop-type motion.

Kit-Kat shuffler *n.* A *masturbatress, weasel buffer, gusset typist*.

kitten hammer *n*. A penis. From the scientific fact well known amongst 12-year-olds that every time they masturbate, a kitten dies.

kitten hammock *n*. *Titpants*.

kitten purse *n*. Charming, feminine term for a lady's *cludge*.

kittens' noses *n*. *Puppies' noses, jockeys*. Nipples.

klatch *n*. *Drip tray* flotsam. *Gusset effluvium*.

kleeneczema *n*. *medic*. The skin condition contracted when tissue sticks to a *wedding-milky* hand.

kling-ons 1. *n*. One of numerous races of *'Star Trek'* alien with Cornish pastie foreheads. 2. *n*. *Winnets, dangleberries*, assorted anal hangers-on.

klutz *n*. A thickhead. From the German *for fuckwit*.

knack 1. *v*. To break. 2. *v*. To hit. 3. *v*. To hurt.

knacker 1. *n*. A single testicle. 2. *n*. A *knobhead*. 3. *v*. To tire out.

knacker barrel *n*. Attractively-packaged *smegma*.

knackernits *n*. *medic*. Crabs, *piss-nits*.

knackers *n*. *Balls, nuts*, testicles. *'Ooyaah! I've knacked me knackers! It fuckin' knacks.'*

knee shooters *n*. Large breasts with downward-pointing *jockeys*.

knee trembler *n*. Intercourse while both parties are standing up. Often in a shop doorway.

knicker bacon *n*. Labial rashers.

knicker bandit *n*. A raider of washing lines, *Daz back doorstep challenger*.

knicker oil *n*. Alcopops.

knicker sausages *n*. Large *fanny lips*.

knickers like Jack the Ripper's hankie *sim*. Descriptive of the *dung-hampers* of a lady who failed to pad up properly during *cricket week*.

knickertine stains *n*. *Skid marks* off an *arse* that is a *heavy smoker*.

knight *v*. To reward a lady with one's *pork sword* in recognition of her outstanding service in the kitchen. To *put to the sword*, to *fuck*.

knob 1. *n*. The penis, *prick, John Thomas*. 2. *v*. To shag. *'I knobbed the arse off her.'*

knob cheese *n*. *Smegma*. Foreskin *feta* found underneath *Kojak's roll-neck* and around the *banjo* or *cheese ridge*. Also *knob Stilton, knob yoghurt, Helmetdale, bell end brie*.

knob chopper *n*. Precariously-balanced lavatory seat which falls down while one is having a *piss* and therefore must be held up manually. A *penis fly trap*.

knobelisk *n*. A square-sectioned penile column that is thick at the base and tapers towards the top.

knob end 1. *n*. The *herman gelmet*. 2. *n*. The extremity of a door handle. 3. *n*. A *knobhead*.

knob fodder *n*. *Blart, flange, tussage, fanny*.

knob head *n*. A *fuckwit*, thickhead, oaf.

knob jockey *n*. Someone who sits on a door handle whilst the door is in motion for sexual gratification.

knob of butter *n*. *medic*. To be affected by *brewer's droop*. *Pele's cock*. Impotence.

knob scoffer *n*. Pejorative epithet implying that an individual likes to *smoke the white owl*.

knob shiner *n*. Someone who is always prepared to polish a *pink oboe*.

knob snot *n. Cock hockle.*

knob socket *n.* Any orifice that a penis could be put into, eg. the neck of an oven ready chicken, a hole in a tree, the wife's *fanny*, etc.

knobstacle course *n.* Attempting sex with a bird whilst in a drunken stupor.

knob throb *n.* The pulsating surge of blood to the genital region which heralds the onset of a raging *diamond cutter.*

knobtical illusion *n.* An excuse given by a man for the apparently pitiful size of his *manhood. 'It only looks small because of the way the bathwater's bending the light. It's a knobtical illusion.'*

knob toffee *n.* Sperm.

knocker hoppers *n. Titpants, rascal sacks.*

knocker jockey *n.* A small woman with very big *tits.* A *midget gem.*

knocker nest *n.* Bra. See also *over the shoulder boulder holder, kitten hammock.*

knockers 1. *n.* Devices for banging on doors. 2. *n.* Breasts. *'What a lovely pair of knockers, Lord Owen.'* 3. *n.* Of football punditry, those who have criticised a player in the past. *'Well Brian, the lad has certainly had his fair share of knockers.'*

knocking shop 1. *n.* Brothel, *rub-a-tug parlour.* 2. *n.* A pub or club where women go to be picked up. A *meat mart.*

knock off the bobby's helmet *v.* To engage in a fistfight with one's *little Kojak.*

knock one in *v.* The female version of *knock one out.* To *play the invisible banjo.*

knock one on *v.* To have sex (with a partner).

knock one out *v.* To have sex (with oneself).

knock the back out of her *v.* Of a man, to have a very energetic *romp* up a lady.

knock the lid off the ark *v.* To release an *arse banshee* of biblical proportions that causes everyone in the room to disintegrate. From the climatic scene of the first *'Indiana Jones'* movie.

knot splitter *n.* A *toilet baby* of impressive, *nipsy*-challenging girth. *'Gerry (alarmed): What was that scream, Margo? Are you alright in there? (Flush sounds. Toilet door opens. Margo appears, holding doorframe to steady herself) Margo: Get me a gin and tonic, Gerry, and make it a large one. Gerry (pouring drink): What's happened? Margo: That's the last time I eat a slice of Tom and Barbara's Broad Bean Flan. I've just done a knot splitter in there that's probably blocked the drains from Surbiton to Thames Ditton. (Tom appears at the French windows in wellingtons.) Tom: Have you just started the extractor fan in your bathroom, Margo? Margo: Yes. Why? Tom: Well, three of my pigs have just fainted. 10 seconds of canned laughter. Cue theme music and end titles.'* (Extract from script of *'The Good Life Christmas Special'*, BBC TV 1978).

know, in the Biblical sense *v.* To have *carnival knowledge* of or to *bang* someone. *'Last year at Club 18-30 I knew about forty birds in the Biblical sense, in eight days! And another six sucked me off.'*

Knowle facelift *n.* Budget cosmetic surgery, whereby bags under the eyes, wrinkles and even eyelids are flattened by the over-enthusiastic application of hair scrunchies.

knuckle glitter *n. Funky spingers.*

knuckle nightcap *n.* A late-night *Sherman* which aids restful sleep.

koala bear's ears *n.* Tufts of female *puberage* sticking out the sides of *dunghampers. Judges' eyebrows, thighbrows.*

Kojak's moneybox *n.* The *herman gelmet.*

Kojak's roll-neck *n. Foreskin.* Based on the slap-headed lolly sucking 1970s TV detective who always wore a cheesy-necked pullover.

KOKO *acronym.* An exclamation coined by the Central Office of Information during World War II for the use of armed services personnel. Knickers Off, Knockers Out.

kosher dill *n.* A circumcised *gherkin.*

Kronenberg *n.* A lady who appears from behind to be about '16', but reveals herself to be about '64' when she turns round.

Kruger *n.* A scary *hand job* from a woman with extremely long fingernails. A *Freddy.*

kumikaze attack *n.* A ruthless close-range facial assault waged by the *jap's eye. Cum bombing.*

kung food *n.* Chinese comestibles.

Kursk *n.* A giant *dreadnought* mouldering at the bottom of the *pan.*

Kuwaiti tanker *rhym. slang.* A *merchant banker.*

kweef *n. US.* A *pump* from the *front bottom*, a *drop of the hat, forwards*, a *Lawley kazoo.*

Ll

labia lard *n. Fanny batter, blip.*

labia majorca *n. medic.* A cheap and popular destination for lads on holiday.

labia minorca *n. medic.* A slightly smaller holiday destination, though just as popular.

labiarinth *n.* A term describing the unnecessarily complex design of a woman's *Hampton Maze.*

lab kebab *n.* Ladies' donner labiums. The *vertical bacon sandwich, fur burger.*

labrador lipstick *n.* A dayglo pink *stalk on.*

lab technician *n.* Someone with a workmanlike attitude to handling *knicker bacon.*

lace curtain *1. n.* An exceptionally long *fiveskin.* *2. n.* A delicate gossamer fretwork of *Helmetdale.*

ladyboy *n. ornith.* A confusing species of *cock bird* with female plumage and *tits.* A *chickboy.* Native to Bangkok and Iggy Pop's hotel room. A *shim.*

Lady Chalk of Billingsgate *n.* Thrush, a yeast yinfection of the vagina. *'I regret to announce that Lady Chalk of Billingsgate is visiting at this present time, Bishop. Could you pass the yoghurt?'*

ladygarden *n.* The fertile patch where a *downhill gardener* plants his seeds.

lady in waiting *1. n.* Actress in a *meat movie* threesome who, temporarily, has nothing to do. A *grumble gooseberry,* a *ballflower. 2. n.* A reclining *grumble flick* actress anticipating the imminent arrival of several short flights from the *Greek Island of Testos. 3 n.* The lady in a *flesh mag,* who is sure to 'do the job', but is held in reserve until the rest of the publication has been thoroughly investigated. A *finisher.*

lady killer *n.* A penis of such extreme length of girth that it could prove fatal. A *cunt buster,* a *kipper ripper.*

lady marmalade *n.* Patti Labelle's *labia lard. Fanny batter.*

Lady Penelope's minge *n.* A *snatch* that is *boiling beetroots,* ie. one with a string attached.

lady's low toupee *n.* A *merkin,* a *cunt rug.* An all-weather *ladygarden.*

lady-tramp *n.* A woman of deceptively sophisticated appearance who lets herself down the moment she opens her mouth, eg. Scary Spice.

lager bomb *n.* A strong-smelling beer *fart,* a symptom of *brewer's flu.*

Lake Wendouree *n. Aus.* Ejaculation. From the very, very small, sticky lake at *Ballarat,* Australia.

lamb cannon *n.* An arms development dating somewhere between the *mutton musket* and the *bacon bazooka.*

lamb hangings *n.* A none-too-appetising *butcher's window* display. *Mutton shutters, beef curtains, gammon goalposts, steak drapes, bacon strips, flackets.* A lady's *labia majorcas.*

Lambourghini *n.* A *cunt 'tache.* A small, pointless tufty outcrop of pubage remaining on a *shaven haven.* A *jazz fanny.* A *clitler.*

landing *n.* The area between the bedroom and the lavatory, or between the *shitter* and the *sack.* The *barse,* the perineum.

landmine *n.* A fresh *dog's egg* hidden in a suburban lawn, which is often detonated by a lawnmower leading to untold misery.

Langball *n*. Type of *dangleberry* which attaches itself to *John Wayne's hairy saddlebags.*

langer *n*. Penis.

langered *adj*. *Lathered.*

lapdog *n*. A Spearmint Rhino dancer with a *lovely personality.*

lapper *n*. *Hairy pie* eater, *bacon sandwich* connoisseur.

lap poodle *n*. A gently-bouffanted *minge*, much in fashion in the 1970s. A *Judith*, a *Jackson.*

laptop *n*. A light, compact, perfectly-formed piece of kit that can be booted up on your lap or table as desired. A *throwabout.*

lardigan *n*. A woollen outer garment worn knotted around the waist by larger ladies in a futile attempt to hide their big, fat *arses.*

lard of the manor *n*. The *piabetic* bloke who lives on your estate.

lard on *1.n*. A porn star's perfunctory *hard on* which does the job, but only just. A *satiscraptory bonk on*. *2. n*. The state of non-sexual excitement felt by a bigger-boned gentleman when approaching a Ginster's display.

lard wimple *n*. A *pelican's beak, chin airbag.*

larse *n*. *medic*. The lateral point of the upper thigh where the leg becomes the *arse*. The bit seen in *jazz mags* that remains white even though the model has spent many hours on a sunbed. '*...the femoral vein ascends behind the semitendinosus, where it joins the great saphenous vein just behind the larse and continues on to meet inferior vena cava half way between the tits and the fanny...*' (from '*Grey's Anatomy*').

lashing strap *1. n*. In the haulage industry, a 3-inch-wide strap and buckle arrangement with a breaking strain of 5 tons, used by lorry drivers to tie down heavy loads onto the backs of their trucks. *2. n*. The choice of thong or *titpants* strap for the fatter lass, eg. Michelle MacManus off '*Pop Idol*'.

lash on, get a bit *v*. To find some female company. '*Howay, let's gan oot an' get a bit lash on.*'

last hotdog in the tin *sim*. Descriptive of penetrative sex with a lady possessed of a *wizard's sleeve. Wall of death.*

last meat supper *n*. Final fling before marriage. It's all *fish suppers* thereafter.

last minute bookings *n*. The desperate and desperately unattractive *blart* that one is free to pull at 1.59 am after the *ugly lights* come up in a nightclub. *Floor sweepings, sediment.*

last orders at the pink bar *euph*. Announcements heralding the onset of the *vinegar strokes*. '*Are you on the pill, love, 'cos it's last orders at the pink bar?*' (Wilfred Hyde-White quoted in the '*Memoirs of Joyce Grenfell*').

last orders *n*. The ring of an *arse bell* that causes a stampede of similar magnitude to that experienced at 10.50pm in pubs up and down the land. '*Stand back, your holiness. I had three scotch eggs and a pint of Bass for lunch, and I've just called last orders.*'

last post *n*. Ceremonial act of taking down one's *bird's knickers* last thing at night.

last resort *n*. A light-hearted pet name for the wife, ie. that which one must reluctantly return to after a failed night *on the pull.*

last week's lettuce *n.* An unappetising lady's *cludge,* from its similarity to an out-of-date salad, ie. brown, limp, sweaty, and sticking to the side of the bag. *'Fancy a lick of last week's lettuce, Charlie?' 'No thanks, Camilla.'*

last whoreders *n.* The chaotic rush for *rashgash* in a club at ten to two. *The witching hour, two o'clock binrake.*

last year's hanging basket *n.* An untidy, straggly *mott. Terry Waite's allotment.*

latch lifter *n.* A borrowed fiver which enables one to enter a public house. *'Lend us a latch lifter till I get my giro.'*

lathered *adj. Pissed, plastered, langered.*

laugh at the carpet *v.* To *park a tiger.* To *vomit.*

laugh at the grass *v. Aus.* To *laugh at the carpet* al fresco. *'Where's Bruce, Bruce?' 'He's outside laughing at the grass, Bruce.'*

launch your lunch *v.* To *hurl one's biscuits.*

lava lamp 1. *n.* A kitsch electrical appliance that was all the rage in the 1960s and again now. 2. *n.* The appearance of the bath after one has *waxed the dolphin* in it.

lava lamp, guts like a *sim.* The unpleasant sensation that big, glowing, waxy bubbles of gas are backing up one's large intestine. Possibly following a night on the pop or a delicious curry from the Curry Capital, Bigg Market, Newcastle upon Tyne.

lavatory *n.* The smallest room, little house, *loo,* water closet, convenience, place of easement, *shithouse, crapper, privy, bog,* latrine, *cackatorium, temple of cloacina,* toilet, *khazi, thunder box, comfort station, meditation room, library, gentleman's reading room.*

lav child *n.* A *turd.*

lavender *adj.* Pertaining to *good listeners.*

lavender marriage *n.* Any matrimonial coupling about which there is a whiff of *lavender.*

lavitation *n.* The yogic exercise performed when hovering over a public lavatory seat so as to avoid direct contact when having a *shit.*

lav train *n.* The swarm of ladies that all go to the toilet together in pubs.

Lawley kazoo *n.* A *hat dropped forwards. Harry Secombe's last raspberry.* A *kweef.*

lawn monkey *n.* The possible consequences of a *split jubber ray.* Also *yard ape, turf chimp, fanny turd.*

lawn sausages *n. Park links, dog's eggs, dog toffee, hound cable.*

lay 1. *n.* Prospective or past sexual partner. *'I knew your wife many years ago. She was a terrific lay.'* 2. *v.* To *fuck* a woman with a small amount of cement and a trowel.

lay a cable *v.* To *build a log cabin, grow a tail, drop a copper bolt.*

lay a cuckoo's egg 1. *v.* A party trick where a foreign *bogie* is introduced into an unconscious reveller's nostril for the amusement of the other guests. 2. *v.* To get someone else's missus *up the duff. 'Have you seen him? Nowt like his brother or his dad. He's fucking ginger. Somebody's laid a cuckoo's egg there, if you ask me?'* (*'Nigel Dempster's Diary'*, 1984).

lay-and-display *n.* A type of European lavatory where the *twinkie* lands on a dry porcelain surface for inspection prior to being flushed away.

lazy lob on *n*. A semi-erect penis, *dobber, half a teacake*.

lazy man's wee *n*. A gentleman's sit-down *piss*, usually taken in the middle of the night when his aim cannot be trusted. A *she-pee*.

lead in your pencil, to have *v*. To be *on the stonk*.

lead the llama to the lift shaft *v*. To point *Percy* at the vagina.

leap of filth *n*. The feeling of blind trust needed when buying *grumble* online. *'I feel badly let down. I made a twenty quid leap of filth and you can't even see it going in.'*

learn *v*. Of a man, to make love to his sweetheart. *'Get on that bed. I'll fucking learn you, you dirty bitch.'*

leather on willow, like the sound of *sim*. A very pleasing *crack*. *'Was her topiary in good order?' 'Leather on willow, mate. Leather on willow.'*

lecher's nightmare *n*. A grisly underwear display given by stilton-thighed elderly ladies when they sit in deck chairs. *Next month's washing*.

left footer *n*. A gay or Catholic person, but ideally one who is both.

left-handed batsman *n*. Someone who prefers his balls delivered from the *Pavilion end*.

left-handed web site *n*. An internet website specialising in *cyberscud*, causing visitors to use the mouse with the left hand.

left legger *n*. A lady who particularly enjoys being *sorted out* on the front passenger seat of a car. Derived from the technique of hanging her left leg out the window, thus affording the driver unhindered access to her *cunker*.

left the lid off the gluepot *v*. To smell of *spunk*. *'Jesus, Your Majesty! Who's left the lid off the gluepot?'*

leg bye *n*. When a delivery of liquid *shite* trickles down leg side for some unexpected *runs*.

leg iron shuffle *n*. The gait adopted by one with the *turtle's head*, trying to make it to the *crapper* without *signing his bills*.

leg lifter *n*. *Benefactor*. Somebody who *breaks company*.

leg man *n*. One who prefers ladies' *gams* to their *tits* or *arses*.

leg necklace *n*. *Cumulonimbus*.

lego hand *n. medic*. A tertiary form of *wanker's cramp*. A condition afflicting the hand of one who has overindulged in *self-pollution*. From the similarity to the rigid empty grasp of the Danish toy figures.

leg over *n*. A *sausage and doughnut situation*. *'Did you get your leg over?' 'No, but I got tops and three fingers.'*

leg tensing *n*. The act of tensing one's leg when having a *toss*. *'This wank is going nowhere. I'd better get a bit of leg tensing in.'*

leg warmer *n*. The *fiveskin* or *peparami wrapper*.

leisure facilities *n. medic*. Breasts.

leisure trove *n*. A veritable Aladdin's cave of *relaxation-oriented literature*, such as might be discovered in the study of a recently-deceased vicar by his startled family.

Lemsip and a wank *n*. A cure for whatever ails you. After listening to one's tale of woe, divorce, sacking etc., a mate might reply, *'Have a Lemsip and a wank and you'll soon feel better.'*

lend *v*. To give, in the *sausage* sense.

'Phwoar! Your mum's a bit of alright. I wouldn't mind lending her one'.

length *n*. An imperial saucy postcard unit of sex, as *slipped* to a woman by a man who works in a lino factory.

Leo Sayer *rhym. slang*. All dayer. *Bender*, prolonged drinking session, all day party.

lesbiany *adj*. Appertaining to lesbianism. In a *rub-a-tug shop* one might enquire *'Any chance of you and your mate doing something lesbiany?'*

lesbionage *n*. The furtive act of watching a couple of *carpet munchers* as they *munch* each others's *carpets*, perhaps whilst up a ladder and wearing infra-red night vision goggles.

lesbo *n*. A *tuppence licker, bean flicker, carpet muncher, lickalotopus, dyke*.

lesbology *n*. The scientific study of lesbian activity. A branch of feminism studied almost exclusively by males and which involves much scrutiny of video footage.

Leslie gash *n*. A luscious-lipped pouting *fanny*. After the comedy-gobbed Homebase ad star.

let off *v*. To *let rip, blow off, launch an air biscuit*.

let one go *v*. To *let off*.

let Percy in the playpen *n*. Of a woman, to consent to intercourse.

let rip *v*. *Let one go*.

let the dog out *v*. To nip home at lunchtime and *feed the ducks* after a frustrating morning surrounded by *office beaver*. *'Hold all my calls, Miss Jones. I'm just nipping home to let the dog out.'*

let the twins out *euph*. Of a lady, to remove her brassiere.

lettuce *n*. The crinkly leaves underneath the *gorilla salad*. The *piss flaps*.

lettuce licker *n*. A *lezza*.

lever arches *rhym. slang*. Haemorrhoids. From lever arch files = *Chalfonts*.

lezza *n*. See *lesbo*.

lezzo boots *n*. Any clumpy, unfeminine footwear worn by women. The opposite of *fuck me shoes*.

libratory *n*. A *crapper* which is well stocked with *shiterature*. From library + lavatory.

lick a bus battery *v*. To commit *cumulonimbus* on a lady who is 2.66 times skankier than a *nine-volter*.

lickalotopus *n*. Scientific name for an experienced *carpet muncher*.

lick both sides of the stamp *v*. To be *AC/DC*, a *happy shopper*, *half rice half chips*.

licker licence *n*. Permission to have a drink from the *hairy goblet*.

licking a nine-volter *n*. The act of *cumulonimbus* on a particularly skanky *snatch*, the effect being the same as placing your tongue across the terminals of a PP3 battery.

lick of paint *n*. *Mexican lipstick*. *Pasata grin*.

lick one's arse and call it chocolate *phr*. Expression used to bring a deludedly optimistic person down to earth. *'Mr. Speaker, my Right Honourable friend the Chancellor has told the house that thanks to his prudent fiscal policies the economy is in a stronger position now than ever. He is entitled to take that view, of course, and he is likewise entitled, should he wish, to lick his arse and call it chocolate.'* (Miss Widdecombe (Conservative) 'Hansard' report, October 2001).

lick out 1. *v.* That which is done by a small child to a bowl of cake mix. 2. *v.* That which is done by a moustachioed porn star to a *haddock pastie*.

lick-twat *n. prop.* One who has the gift of tongues. A *cumulonimbalist*.

lid *n.* The bit above the *brim*. The *herman gelmet*.

Lidled *adj.* Descriptive of a town or district that is in decline, evidenced by the opening of a branch of Lidls. *'Dover, once the gateway to Europe, home of the White Cliffs, now sadly Lidled.'* Also *Nettoed, Aldied.*

life affirmer *n.* *Shit* taken during the worst depths of a hangover or other depression which is of such magnitude that it restores one's vital signs. A *crap* which would make the late Fred Astaire dance down the street, occasionally bouncing his silver-topped cane off the kerb.

lifting the cheek *v.* The sly behaviour of a *cushion creeper*.

lighthouse cat, rank as a *sim.* Descriptive of a gentleman who has experienced an excessively long period without getting his hands on a *bird*. *'Giz a shot on your clopper, Una. I feel as rank as a lighthouse cat.'*

lightning in a bottle *n.* A photographic *art study* which captures the moment a gentleman *expels his custard* in a shot arcing majestically towards the face of a beautiful young lady. Named after the equally tricky task of photographing a lightning bolt.

lilies on the pond *n.* The artistic practice popularised by impressionist painter Claude Monet of laying sheets of toilet tissue on the water surface before giving birth to *Meatloaf's daughter*. A *pap baffle*.

lils *n.* 1950s/60s *Tits*.

lime water *n.* Semen, spunk, spooge, spangle, tweedle.

lineman's pasty *n.* A very full disposable nappy thrown from a train window at loafing, orange-clad track workers.

lingam *n.* Hindu. Penis. From ancient *grumble book 'The Karma Sutra'.*

lion tamer's corpse *sim.* Descriptive of the sorry state of one's *chap* after a *rag week romp*.

lippie *v.* Of a dog, to *frotter* on one's leg with its *lipstick* out. *"Aw. He must like you, Dr. Watson,' expostulated the great detective, sucking on his pipe thoughtfully and adjusting the brim of his deerstalker with the handle of his magnifying glass whilst playing his violin. 'He's trying to lippie your leg, look."* (from *'The Hound of the Baskervilles'* by Arthur Conan Doyle).

lip reading *n.* Observing women in tight pants who have the *camel's foot.* *'If she bends over any more I'll be able to read her lips from here.'*

lip ring *n.* A lipstick line around the *pork sword* showing how far it has been swallowed.

lip ripper *n.* A magnificently girthsome *charlie*.

lip service *n.* A lacklustre act of *horatio* performed by a timid or blocked-nosed *nosher*.

lip sink *n.* The wash basin in the ladies' toilet of a pub in which *birds* have the female equivalent of a *gentleman's wash* when they have *pulled*.

lipstick *n.* A dog's *cock*, available in a variety of shimmery colours.

lipstick lesbian *n.* Glamorous, feminine female homosexual, as found on the Adult Channel but rarely down the pub.

lip stretcher *n.* A particularly girthsome *choad*. A *Pringle tube*. A challenge to a pair of *DSLs*.

liquid bookmark *n.* A homemade means of recording one's place in the pages of a gentlemen's *art pamphlet*.

liquid gold *n.* A cup of tea in Betty's tearooms.

liquid kids *n.* Spooge, spunk.

liquid laughter *n.* Puke, psychedelic yodelling.

liquid rage *n.* Merry monk.

liquor portal *n.* The hole in the space/time continuum found outside pubs which transports the inebriated to the safety of their hallways in the blink of an eye.

Little Ben *n.* A small *Big Ben*.

little death *n. Fr.* In a male, the postcoital feeling of *shagged outity*.

liver lapels *n. Beef curtains, labia majorcas.*

liver sock *n.* The *fanny*.

Livingstone daisies *1. n. Bot.* Attractive flowers that come out when the sun shines. *2. n.* Attractive *knockers* that come out when the sun shines, causing taxi drivers to mount the pavement, milkmen to fall down manholes and vicars to ride their bicycles into fruit barrows.

lizard rag *n. Aus.* A scaly piece of bedside cloth used for wiping excess *spoff* and *moip* from one's *bloodstick* after *popping the turkey in the oven*.

lizard's lick *n.* A feeble ejaculation that barely clears the *hog's eye*, the

unimpressive result of excessive *beauty shivering*. A bankrupt *money shot*. A *gwibble*.

Llewellyn-Bowen's cuff *n.* An overelaborate vagina. A foppish *ragman's coat*.

load *1. n.* 1996 Metallica album. *2. n.* The quantity of *cock hockle* blown, chucked or shot at the point of orgasm. *3. n.* That which is shed by a lorry driver, whilst *wanking* in a layby.

loaded *adj. Aus.* To be in need of a great big *shit*. To be *touching cloth*. *"Curiouser and curiouser' thought Alice, as the white rabbit came scampering past. 'I wonder where he's going in such a hurry.' 'Oh, my dear paws!' he cried. 'Oh my fur and whiskers, I'm loaded. If I don't reach the lavatory soon I shall surely papper my grundies."* (from *'Alice's Adventures in Wonderland'*, by Lewis Carroll).

loaded for bear *1. adj.* Hunting term, indicating that one is packing particularly impressive ammunition. *2. adj. Fucking* term, indicating that one is packing particularly impressive ammunition.

loading the mag *euph. milit. Thumbing in a slacky.* The act of easing a *lard-on* into a *fanny* in a porn film.

load of old shoes falling out a loft, like a *sim.* Descriptive of a heavy bout of loose, lively diarrhoea. A *flock of pigeons*.

load rage *n.* A violent confrontation in which a purple-faced *bald man* is struck viciously with a *wanking spanner*.

lobcock *n.* A large, flaccid penis such as could be *lobbed* onto a pub table by its drunken owner.

lobotomy bay *n.* Semi-mythical destination of any serious drinking binge.

lob ropes *v.* To *jizz* onto something through thin air, eg. a face, some hair, *tits* etc.

locked out, Mrs. Brown is *euph.* Having *followed through.* *'Apologies, Your Excellency, but I really must be excused. I've just opened the back doors and it appears Mrs. Brown is locked out again.'*

log *n. Bum cigar, brown trout.*

logarhythm *n.* The shaking of one's *arse* in an attempt to break the neck of a dangling *turtle.* The working out of a *simple harmonic motion.*

log cabin *n.* A wendy house for *Meatloaf's daughter.*

log fire *n.* The pain experienced in the *back body* the morning after eating a particularly spicy *Ruby Murray. Ring sting.*

log flume *1. n.* To simultaneously defecate and urinate down the same leg of one's kex. *2. n.* A *turd* in a pub pissing trough. *3. n.* A *Thora* splashing down into the pan.

lollipop lady *n.* A woman who is partial to the occasional *slice of cheesecake.*

lolly bag *n.* Scrotum.

lolly stick *n.* Anything pointlessly, but intentionally added to a pile of *shite.* A *turd's barnacle. 'Has anyone seen that Big Brother's Little Brother? What a fucking lolly stick that is.'*

long ball game *1. n.* In football, a series of aimless pokes in the direction of the box in the hope of scoring. *2. n.* In bed, a series of aimless *pokes* in the direction of the *box* in the hope of *scoring.*

longshanks *n.* One who is blessed/cursed with a very low-swinging *chicken skin handbag.* A *rantallion.*

lonk *v.* German. To *shit* oneself on orgasm.

look at *v.* Euphemism for masturbation. *'Did you look at that porn film I lent you yesterday?' 'Yeah, I had a quick look.'*

looking for badgers *v.* To cruise for gay sex. Also, *stretching one's legs.*

loon pipe *n. Anus.*

looniform *n.* Characteristic garb of one who favours screaming at the traffic as an occupation, usually consisting of a 1970s jacket and trousers that clear the ankles by a good three inches.

loop the loop *v.* To order a *vertical bacon sandwich* to *eat out* and a *drink on a stick* for the lady, No.69 on the menu.

loose, on the *adj.* Of a *dirty lady,* to be *frothing like bottled Bass.* To have a *wide on.*

loose at the hilt *adj.* To have diarrhoea, *the Brads.*

loose clacker *n. coll.* A herd of *ten-to-two-ers.* Ropey *cabbage.* The group of girls remaining unspoken for at night club chucking out time.

loose fries in the bag *euph.* Descriptive of a feeling of serendipitous sexual jubilation on discovering the *bird* one is *copping off* with has hidden extras, eg. has a shaved *snatch,* is wearing stockings, is a *swallower.* From the joyous feeling experienced when, on finishing one's McDonald's, one finds extra chips in the bottom of the bag.

loose lips *adj.* Affectionate description of a woman who has been *cocked* more times than Davy Crockett's rifle.

loose sausage meat *n.* A flaccid penis which cannot be funnelled into a condom. *'Sorry love, my sausage meat seems a bit loose.' Stuffing the marshmallow.*

loose shunting *n.* A *dog's marriage* with a *clown's pocket.*

Lord Foulbowel *n.* One whose lower chamber is a rich source of *brownhouse gases*, eg. a Coventry City fan who spends 72 hours farting in a car accompanied by 4 friends as they attempt to visit all 92 football league grounds to raise money for charity.

Lord of the Pies *n.* A *salad dodger*, a *double sucker*, eg. Danny Baker.

Lord Winston's moustache *n.* A particularly hairy and poorly-trimmed *biffer*, named after the exuberant face fungus of the popular ennobled telly boffin, test-tube *fanny apple* pioneer and former leading *twat mechanic* Dr. Robert Winston. Also *Rhodes Boysons, whack-os.*

lorry driver's breakfast, fanny like a *sim.* Descriptive of a *clopper* which is cheap, greasy and requires plenty of sauce before consumption.

lorry driver's lunchbreak *n.* A *shit* in a layby.

lose the marathon *v.* To take a long time to complete a digestive transit. *'That crap took me so long I would've lost the marathon.'* Derivation unknown.

lose your manners *v.* To *fart.*

lose your mess *v.* To ejaculate, *shoot your load.*

losing ten seconds *adj.* Descriptive of one who has a *mole at the counter*. From not Dame Paula Radcliffe's 2005 London marathon run, during which she experienced controversial *traffic calming*

measure difficulties that slowed her down by the specified time interval whenever a 'violent stomach cramp' wracked her scrawny frame.

lotties *n.* Lils, dugs.

loudmouth soup *n.* Beer.

Louis *v.* To force out a stubborn *turd* with such strain that one pulls a face like Louis Armstrong going for a top E.

love bat *n.* During a game of sexual intercourse, the short, stout implement with which the man strikes his wife's *cunker*. See also *slag bat.*

love beads *n. milit.* Road surface farm animal containment provision which provides exceedingly fleeting and intermittent sexual stimulation for squaddies in the backs of 'rumpety-pumpety' army trucks. A cattle grid.

love bumps *n.* Funbags, guns of Navarone.

love cough *n.* The *dropping forwards* of a *lady's hat*. A *queef*, a *Lawley kazoo*, a *frampton*. A *fanny fart.*

love juice *n.* That liquid produced in the *Billingsgate box* upon which the *skin boat* sails. Often referred to as *luv jooz* in illiterate 1970s *scud literature. Blip, moip.*

love palace *n.* The *cunt.*

love puff *n.* Gentle, romantic *air biscuit* launched in the direction of one's partner in bed, often the morning after a *Ruby*, in an attempt to cement the intimacy of the moment.

love sausage *n.* Big pink *banger* served with *hairy love spuds.*

love socket *n.* Vagina, entry point for the *main cable*. Also *rocket socket, serpent socket, spam socket.*

love spuds *n*. Root vegetables found in the *shreddies*.

love torpedo *n*. *Rumple foreskin*.

love tripe *n*. The folds of tender flesh around a bird's *goalmouth*.

love truncheon *n*. *Love torpedo*.

love tunnel *n*. That place in which *Percy* the small pink engine shunts his *load*.

low hanging fruit *1. n. polit.* Funding which can be cut back easily during a budget. *2. n. Nads* that hang out of badly-designed shorts.

low loaders *n*. Saggy breasts with a small amount of ground clearance.

LRF *abbrev.* Low Resolution Fox - a female who appears to be attractive from a long distance, but is in fact unbelievably ugly close up.

lucky dip *n*. The fortunate, final wipe of one's *ring* which reveals a hidden *clod*, thus preventing *pappered pants*.

lucky Pierre *n*. In *botting* circles, the busiest *botting* link in a three man *bum chain*, the filling in a *shirt lifter* sandwich. A *botter* who is simultaneously a *bottee*.

lullage *n*. The overhanging flab seen on fat lasses wearing trousers they fully intend slimming into. A *gunt*, a *poond*, a *muffin top*.

lulu *n*. A lady who is getting on a bit, but is still worthy of *lengthage*. A *gilf*.

lumber *1. n.* A raft of tightly-packed *turds* occluding the toilet water surface in a *chod bin* after an afternoon testing the 'all you can eat'

buffet at an Aberdeen Steak House. *2. n.* A unspecified quantity of erect peni.

lumberjill *n*. A hatchet-faced woman that fells one's *wood*.

lunchbox lancer *n. arch.* Medieval term for a *cocoa shunter*. *'Fear not the French, for their knights are without heart, and their King without wisdom. But keep thine backs as to the wall, for amongst their number thou shalt find more than a few lunchbox lancers, I can tell you.'* (from *'Henry V part III'* by William Shakespeare).

lunchbox *n*. In British tabloid journalism, that conspicuous genital-filled bulge which used to appear in athlete Linford Christie's shorts.

lunching at the Lazy Y *v. Dining out* cowboy style, on *hairy pie*, beans and coffee.

lung butter *n*. Phlegm, *green smoking oysters*.

lungry *adj.* Having an appetite for cigarettes. *'Giz a drag on that, Your Excellency. I gave up for new year and now I'm proper fucking lungry.'*

lung warts *n*. *Stits, fried eggs. Parisian breasts*.

lurpy *n. Can.* Heterosexual *horatio*.

lush puppies *n*. Those grey slip-on brogues or loafers worn with white socks by middle-aged, *turps-nudging* 'oldest swinger in town' types.

lychees *n*. A sweeter, more exotic *knacker*-speak alternative to *plums*.

Mm

M32 *n.* A *titfuck*, ie. the most direct route for *coming* into the *Bristol* area.

Mabel syrup *n.* Old bird's *flange juice.*

mac in the bath, I wouldn't wear my *exclam.* Expression of a gentleman's unwillingness to don a prophylactic sheath on his *cock end.* In the same vein as *'I wouldn't wear my wellies on the beach.'*

mack *n.* Penis, *tadger.*

mackerel *1. n.* Pimp, controller of prostitutes. A *tart farmer. 2. n.* The *tarts* he farms. *3. n. coll. Cabbage.*

mad cow disease *1. n.* Viral disease caught off cheap pies. *2. n.* A monthly hormonal condition causing distress to men's ears. *Rag rage, tammy huff, blob strop.*

Madam Palm and her five sisters *n.* A hand when used for five minutes of harmless fun that will certainly result in its owner being cast into a lake of fire by our infinitely merciful God. A *wanking spanner.* Also *Palmela Handerson. 'I'm nipping off to bed with Madam Palm and her five sisters.'*

Madam Twoswords *n.* A multitasking actress in a *stick vid* or *art pamphlet* who has a gentleman's waxy *charlie* in each hand. A *crane operator,* a *downhill skier.*

mad as a lorry *adj.* About as *radge* as it is possible to be.

Madeley *n.* A bloke who feels comfortable talking about relationships, star signs, *'Sex and the City'*, *'Ally McBeal'* and shit like that.

magician's hankie *1. n.* A *shite* that just keeps on going and going, like the endless knotted cloths pulled out of conjurors' hats. *2. n.* A *botty burp* which, to the surprise of the assembled audience, continues to emerge over an astounding length of time, and in several audibly discrete segments.

magicking the beans *v.* Gareth Hunt's *wanking* action.

magic sheet *n.* An enchanted blanket, often seen in American TV movies which clings to an actress through some invisible force, covering her *knockers.*

magnificent seven *n.* The frankly unlikely scenario of being able to unload one's *weapon* in every available orifice on a woman.

magnificent six *n.* The same act as above, but performed on Daniella Westbrook.

mailed and sent *rhym. slang.* On *the other bus.*

main cable *n.* One's live seed feed into the *love socket.*

make a bald man cry *v.* To masturbate. *'Have you seen Kylie's arse on the front page of the FT today? It's enough to make a bald man cry.'*

make babies *v.* To go *bone jumping,* to fornicate.

make like a Chinese helicopter pilot *v.* To masturbate, *grin like a wanking Jap* whilst *polishing the joystick.*

make the rounds *v.* To have a final grope of all one's ladyfriend's *treasures* before falling asleep.

make the weigh-in *v.* To enter the toilet as a middleweight and come out half an hour later as a welterweight. To have a really big *shit.*

make your shit hang sideways *v.* To be annoying. *'That Matthew Kelly really makes my shit hang sideways.'* (Bernard Levin, TV Review in *'The Times'*).

making nylon *v.* An experiment in

the bath resulting in the creation of viscous, stringy threads that stick to the hairs of one's legs.

mambas *n*. Mammaries, *mumbas*.

Mambo #5 *1. n.* A catchy novelty hit record which contains an instrumental line that sounds like a repetitive *fart*. *2. n.* A repetitive *fart* that has all the makings of an instrumental line in a catchy novelty hit record.

mamfest *1. n.* The stirring sight of a lot of ladies' breasts en masse, eg. at the beach, in a nightclub, through a hole drilled in the wall of a ladies' changing room. Contraction of mammary festival. *2. n.* A particularly fine and well presented pair of *tits*.

mammaries *n*. Mammary glands, *tits, swinging pink milk churns, knockers*.

mammary dandruff *n*. Morning-after residue from a *sausage sandwich*, the remnants of a *pearl necklace*.

mamnesia *n. medic*. A highly specific form of male memory loss. Upon seeing a fantastic pair of *norks*, the sufferer forgets key facts about himself, eg. that he is married, that he has four children, or that he is the presenter of a topical quiz show. Also *penile dementia*.

manberries *n*. Coarse term for the *clockweights, John Wayne's hairy saddlebags, knackers* etc. Testicles, *yongles*.

manberry sauce *n. Gentleman's spendings*.

mandruff *n*. Flakes of dried *lovepiss* found on one's wife's head and shoulders.

man eggs *n*. Sperms.

man fanny *1. n.* A changing room entertainment whereby a bare gen-tleman impersonates a bare lady. A *cockafanny*. *2. n.* A risible goatee beard sported by polytechnic lecturers and 45-year-olds who have just bought a motor bike.

manfat *n*. Semen. Also *man milk*.

manflaps *n*. The tiny flaps surrounding the *Jap's eye*, usually only visible when taking a much needed high pressure *piss*. The *hog's eyelids*.

Manfred *rhym. slang. Jitler, jism, spaff*. From the not particularly famous German philosopher Manfred Bunk = *spunk*.

mange *n*. See *mangina*.

mangina *1. n.* The badly-sewn Cornish pasty-like seam running along the underside of the scrotum that stops one's *clockweights* falling out. *2. n.* The *nipsy* of one who is *good with colours*.

manging *adj*. Minging.

mangos *n*. See *jelly water mangos*.

man handle *n*. The *bone on* that a store detective gets upon apprehending a female shop lifter in anticipation that she may offer to *talk to the judge* in the stock room.

manhood *n*. In British tabloid journalism, the penis.

man in the iron mask *n*. An extremely hirsute *snatch* trapped inside a pair of knickers. From the classic tale by Alexandre Dumas.

man mayonnaise *n. Gentleman's relish, hanging salad cream*. Semen.

man meringue *n*. A light, crumbly nest of dried *milm* found on the inside of a gentleman's well-worn *Bill Grundies*.

mannery glands *n*. A portly gentleman's dugs. *Bitch tits*.

manny *n*. The convincing illusion of womanhood achieved when a gentleman tucks his *giggling stick* and *knackers* back behind his legs. A *cockafanny*. A contraction of man + fanny. See *man fanny*.

man of the cloth *n*. Our *farter*, who, despite fervent prayer, finds that he has besoiled his raiments. A *through-follower*.

man overboard *n*. A *bald man in a boat* whom you fear has become detatched from his mooring, but which turns out to be a pellet of compressed *shit scrape*.

man pop *n*. Spooge, jitler, baby gravy.

mam sandwich *n*. Two amply-proportioned *milkers* with the head of a happy gentleman wedged snugly between them.

manshee *n*. One who could conceivably be a man or a woman.

man trap *n*. Female genitals, the *hairy love pit*.

manwich *n*. To be the lucky chap filling pressed between two slices of ladies.

man with nice nails *n*. One who is *good with colours*.

mapatasi *n*. *Aus. Minge*. From 'Map of Tasmania', the small hairy island that smells of fish off the south east coast of Australia.

map of Africa *n*. The cartographical stain left on the bed sheet and often the mattress below after an exchange of bodily fluids. A splodge of *splooge*. Also *map of Ireland, map of Hawaii*.

marabou stork *n*. A *fixed bayonet, the old Adam*. An erection.

maracas *n*. *Knackers, clackers*, those that swing beneath *tallywhackers* making a rattling sound.

marge *n*. A loose woman. From margarine, which 'spreads easily'. Also *Flora*.

margold *n*. The common male ability to do five *pop shots* in two hours. To do a margold. After a boast by *grumble* thespian Bill Margold on Channel 4' s 'After Dark'.

Marianas trench 1. *n*. The deepest recorded sub-marinal depression on Earth, found in the Pacific ocean and reaching a depth of 35,839 feet below sea level. 2. *n*. A *fanny* like a fucking bucket.

marks of Mecca *n*. Carpet burns on the knees caused by excessive worship at the *hairy temple*.

marks out of two? *interrog*. From one ogling male to another, to cue the reply 'I'd give her one.'

mark your territory *v*. To *drop one's guts* and walk away.

Marley arse *n*. Accumulated *winnetage*, leading to *anal dreadlocks*. *Tagnuts* that have gone to pot.

Marley's chains *euph*. Breasts that, despite having gone south in a big way, must still be carried about by their owner. From the chain-dragging ghost of his former business partner that visits Scrooge in Charles Dickens's 'A Christmas Carol'. Also *Ulrikakas*.

marmalade madam *n*. 17thC. Tom, doxy, flapper, laced mutton. A ho'.

Marmite driller *n*. One who jumps over puddles on the *marmite motorway*.

Marmite kofte *n*. The sort of viscous black *shite* that, instead of dropping into the *chod bin* pan in the traditional manner, chooses to smear itself around the *nipsy* like so much axle grease. The resulting Augean Stables-style cleaning session only ever happens when one is in a hurry to catch a plane, train, last orders or read the closing headlines at the end of the *'BBC Six O'Clock News'*.

Marmite motorway *n*. Anus, arse, back passage.

Marmite pot, arse like a *sim*. A *ringpiece* which, after a particularly sticky *Brad Pitt*, seems to have a never ending supply of *shit* and the wiping of which will never *draw an ace*.

Marmite stripe *n*. Brown stain or *skidmark* found on unwashed *shreddies*. *Russet gusset*.

Mars bar *1. n*. A caramel, nougat and chocolate confection, which when eaten daily is a proven aid to work, rest and recreation. *2. n*. A substantial and impressive *skid mark*.

Marty Feldmans *n*. On certain ladies, the lop-sided *tits*, where the nipples point up, down and all around. Named after the late comedian Marty Feldman, whose distinctive nipples pointed in different directions.

Mary *1. n*. Sponge, *pillow biter, angel*. *2. n*. Bean *flicker, carpet muncher*. *3. n*. A *liver sock*.

Mary Chipperfield *n*. A *wank* ie. a *monkey spamking* session. From the famous circus chimp dominatrix of the same name.

Mary Hinge *n*. Spooneristic *biffer*.

Mary Poppins' bag *n*. A surprisingly roomy *fanny*. A *clown's pocket*.

mash *v*. To fondle a lady's *shirt potatoes* as if testing them to destruction.

massage parlour wank *1. sim*. Something that is performed quickly and efficiently. *'And the wheel change and refuelling was performed like a massage parlour wank by the Ferrari mechanics and Schumacher should exit the*

pit lane still in the lead.' (Murray Walker). *2. sim*. Something that is expensive and over too quickly, eg. the 'Pepsi Max' ride at Blackpool.

masturmentary *n*. TV programme with a high *tit* and *fanny* count with a token bit of information thrown in to justify its showing, eg. a behind the scenes look at the porn film industry. The staple fare of late night Channel 5.

matelot's matress *n. nav*. A thick piece of bedding material provided to keep *Jack Tars* jolly in their bunks. A Wren.

mathsturbate *v*. To have a vowel and three consonants whilst thinking about Carol Vorderman.

mayor's hat *n*. A *howzat* often eaten by goats.

McArthur park *1. n*. A 1970's maudlin ballad by Richard Harris. *2. n*. A particularly evil *dropped gut* that gives the impression that 'something inside has died'.

McDonald's farmyard *n*. The restaurant area of a high street fast food outlet, filled with sundry dullards, *scratters* and fatties grazing on burgers and fries whilst snorting appreciatively.

McSplurry *n*. The type of *grimshit* one experiences after dining for a week solely at a fast food restaurant. *Bubblepoo*.

McSuck *n*. An *horatio* delivered with a force equivalent to that required to drink a newly poured McDonald's Thick Shake.

MDF *abbrev*. A *dobber*. Medium Density Flop-on. Not quite *wood*.

me *n*. Personal pronoun used at the end of a sentence to emphasise preference. *'For all these wenches are beauteous fair, and I doth admire them all, me.'* (from

'Romeo and Juliet' Act III, Scene 2, by William Shakespeare).

meat and two vag *n.* A *threesome* involving two ladies and a smiling man who keeps pinching himself.

meat and two veg *n.* A gentleman's *undercarriage.* A *pork sausage* and a couple of *love spuds.*

meat balloons *n.* Older boys' playthings, which do not stick to the wall even after protracted rubbing on a jumper. *Mumbas, large tits.*

meat flute *n. Pink oboe.*

meat injection *n.* An inoculation against virginity.

Meatloaf's daughter *n.* A big boned *mud-child.* A *dreadnought.*

meat market *n.* Bar or club where *birds* with short skirts and blotchy legs dance round their handbags, waiting for a *pull.* A *meat rack, buttock hall.*

meat moth *n.* A *spam butterfly* commonly attracted to the bright lights of a *grot mag* photographer's flash.

meat movie *n.* A *grumble flick.*

meat paste *1. n.* Something your mum puts on your sandwiches at school. *2. n.* Something disgruntled chefs put on the burgers at McDonald's.

meat petite *n.* Descriptive of a little *cock.*

meat platter *1. n.* An unappetizing raffle prize on offer in a working men's club. *2. n.* An unappetizing *clopper* on offer in a working men's club.

meat tie *n.* Formal pink neckwear for topless ladies. Tied with a shiny purple knot. With all *spunk* coming out the end. The sausage in a *sausage sandwich.*

mechanic's nails *n.* Finger-end condition cause by *bumwad*

pushthrough. Taxi-driver's tan.

mechanical dandruff *n.* Royal Air Force *crabs.*

medieval fireplace *sim.* A vast, gothic vagina.

medophile *n.* One who has become so accustomed to participating in *saucy mesomes* that it has become his preferred form of sexual activity. One who is no longer *master of his own domain.*

megraine *n.* Intermittent illness afflicting ladies and footballers when they realise they are no longer the centre of attention.

Mekon *1. n. prop.* The chief villain and leader of the Treens featured in Dan Dare's *'Eagle'* adventures of the 1950s, distinguished by his enormous cranium and little body, and hence *2. n.* A badly-poured pint which is 'all head and *fuck all* else'.

melanied *adj.* Drunk, battered, *blatted.* From the surname of All Saints popsie Melanie Blatt. *'I'm sorry Moira, but I can't let you go on air and read the news in that state. You're absolutely melanied.'*

Melbourne *n.* A soft *cock.*

melching *v. Minge felching.*

melon farmer *exclam.* The BBC-authorised, poorly-dubbed version of *mother fucker* used in films such as *'Die Hard'* and the entire *'Beverly Hills Cop'* series. Also *ever-loving, muddy funster.*

melons *n.* Female breasts. A large 'pear'.

melted welly *n.* A poetic term describing a lady's *bodily treasure.* *'Spatula was powerless to resist. His eyes burnt into hers like mamellated chalcedony. His muscular arms enfolded her body as she felt herself being swept away* *on a noctilucent cloud of passion. 'Am I the first?' whispered Dartanyan. 'Sort of,' she vouchsafed in return, her voice quivering with unrequited passion. 'I've not let the other two have a shot on me melted welly yet."* (from *'The Lady & the 3 Musketeers'* by Barbara Cartland).

melvin *v.* To grab by the *balls.*

Melvyn 1. *rhym. slang.* A cigarette. From Melvyn Bragg = fag. 2. *rhym slang.* Sexual intercourse. From Melvyn Bragg = *shag. 'Me and the missus always light up a nice Melvyn after we've had a quick Melvyn.'*

ménage à moi *n. Fr.* A three-in-a-bed romp where the two ladies fail to turn up. A *wank.*

ménage à une *n. Fr.* A saucy *mesome.*

men in the rigging *n. naval.* Small *tagnuts* trapped in the hairs of sailors' *arses. 'Six months since leaving Tahiti and no sign of land. We ate the last of the breadfruit weeks ago. Water and toilet paper strictly rationed. Crew growing restless, complaining of scrofula, scurvy and men in the rigging. Lord help us.'* (from *'The Diary of Fletcher Christian'*, 1789).

men's spendings *n. arch. Jizz.*

men-stool cycle *n.* The happy period of a man's life when his *shit* appears at the same time every day.

merchant *rhym. slang. Kuwaiti tanker.*

merkin *n.* Man-made *mapatasi,* a *stoat syrup, pubic Irish.*

mermaid *n.* A fat *bird* with a pretty face, but nothing worth bothering with below the *tits.*

mermaid's flannel, wet as a *sim.*

Descriptive of a very, very, very wet *fanny.* Also *otter's pocket, clown's pie.*

merry monk *rhym. slang.* The happy result of *pulling the Pope's cap off.*

Mersey trout *n.* A sweetcorn-eyed brown scouse fish.

Merthyr socialite *n.* A South Wales man-about-town who is often spotted in a giddy social whirl flitting between William Hills, The Windham and The DSS offices.

mesome *n.* A *one-in-a-bed romp.* A wank. *'I'm off upstairs for a mesome.'*

MESS *acronym. Spunk.* Named after the chef's secret ingredient in McDonald's Extra Special Sauce.

mess *n.* Semen, *gunk, cock hockle.* That which is lost when one *chucks one's muck.*

Messerschmitt knickers *n.* An easy lady's *scads,* ie. ones which come down without much of a fight.

Mexican aftershave *n.* The acrid tang of chilli and garlic left in the *bog* after a rather nasty night of beer and spicy food.

Mexican picnic *n. SVSA,* a *drugs bust.*

Mexican barbecue *n. SVSASO.* A *Mexican pinic* with a *cock* in the mouth for good measure.

Mexican lipstick *n.* The embarrassing *Thompson's tide marks* often found after *eating out* with a lady who was *up on blocks.* A *pasata grin.*

Mexican screamers *n. medic.* A gastroenterological disorder characterised by fiery liquid excrement. *Tijuana brass-eye, Mexican shat dance.*

Mexican suicide *n.* To die peacefully in one's sleep. *'It is announced* *with deep regret and sadness that Her Royal Highness Princess Margaret committed Mexican suicide at 6.32 this morning at St George's Hospital.'*

mezoomas *n. Pink velvet cushions on which the family jeweller prefers to display a pearl necklace.*

Michaels *rhym. slang.* Piles. From the 1970s TV game show host Michael Miles. *'These nylon trolleys don't half chafe me Michaels.'*

Mickey *n. Irish. Dick.*

middle leg *n.* The penis. Also *middle stump, third leg.*

Middlesbrough accent *n. medic.* A severe cough. *'The patient typically presents complaining of headache, high temperature, a productive Middlesbrough accent and nausea. Treatment - 200mg Amoxyl, three times a day'* (*'Tuberculosis - a Guide for Doctors'* Health Department leaflet).

midget's surfboard *n.* A bachelor/teenager/priest's *spongle*-hardened sock which has become petrified by a plethora of *emissions* and which is on the Home Office's list of approved weapons which can be used against household intruders. Also *Womble's toboggan, Mother Shipton's sock, bachelor's boomerang.*

mid-loaf crisis *n.* Anything that spoils the enjoyment of a good *tom tit*, eg. a doorbell or telephone ringing, a dawning realisation that there is no *bumwad*, or a policeman approaching the shop doorway.

midnight mouth organ *n.* A high-cholesterol instrument played with relish around kicking out time in town centres across the land. A kebab.

midruff *n.* The exposed area of torso between a young lady's cropped top and her low-cut jeans which may have been toned, tanned and firm a couple of years ago, but which now hangs over her waistband like so much uncooked bread dough.

midstool *v.* Act of a chap who is so hopelessly lost in love that he would happily kiss the *clackervalve* of the object of his desire whilst they are half way through *dropping anchor* at *bum bay*. *'FREDDY: You know what, Professor Higgins? Miss Doolittle's the girl for me. I'm head over heels in love with the gel and I don't care who knows it. Dash it, old man, I think I'd even midstool Eliza if she asked.'* (from *'Pygmalion'* by George Bernard Shaw).

mighty Wurlitzer 1. *n.* An enormous organ. 2. *n.* Reginald Dixon's *cock.*

mile 'I' club *n.* Similar to the Mile High Club, but for the solitary traveller. To *spin one's own propellor* in an aeroplane toilet.

MILF *acronym.* Mums I'd Like to Fuck. *Yummy mummies.*

milf float *n.* A pretend sports car, such as the Peugeot 206CC, driven by an attractive young mother in an effort to recapture the carefree spirit of her lost youth.

milkers *n. Dairy bags.*

milkman *n.* That which comes, bringing *yoghurt* in the mornings.

milkman's bonus *n.* An unexpected gift after delivering the *cream* to Mrs. Brown. A *winnet on a stick, shitty dick.*

milkman's gait *n.* The walk adopted by someone who has *overshagged.*

milk of human kindness *n.* See *liquid rage.*

milk race 1. *n.* Adolescent *wanking* game for two or more public school children. 2. *n.* A barrack room *toss-up* to decide who eats the last cream cracker.

milk shake *n.* The uncontrollable quaking caused by imminent *stack blow. Elvis's leg, Cecil Parkinson's disease.*

milk the cow with one udder *v.* To be the only hand in the *farmyard area.*

milk the snake *v.* To practise *self abuse.*

millennium domes *n.* The contents of a Wonderbra, ie. very impressive when viewed from the outside, but there's actually *fuck all* in there worth seeing. Disappointing *tits.*

Mills & Bone *n.* Erotic literature with plot pretensions for the red-blooded bachelor.

milm *v.* To cover something in *jism.* *'Oy, mum, I've milmed me kex.'*

mimsy 1. *adj.* Descriptive of state of the borogroves. 2. *n.* A *clopper.*

minotaur 1. *n.* In Greek mythology, a monster with a man's body and a bull's head. 2. *n.* In nightclubs, a monster with a woman's body and a face like a cow's *arse.*

mince medallions *n. Dangleberries, kling-ons.*

miner's snot *n.* The liquid, stringy black *lav children* that can result from a night spent *sniffing the barmaid's apron.*

miner's sock *n.* A perspiring, debris-laden *fanny* after a hard day's graft.

ming 1. *v. Scot.* To emit a foul smell, to *hum. 'Hoots mon, it's minging in here!'* 2. *n.* A foulsome miasma. *'Gaw, blimey! What's that bloom-*ing ming?' 'I'm afraid Jocky Wilson has done a shit in your shoe, Mr. Bristow'.* 3. *v.* To exude ugliness. *'In the 80s Peter Beardsley's perm was minging.'* 4. *n.* The bill, the *scuffers,* the *bizzies.* 5. *n.* A new marijuana cigarette made up from discarded ends. A tramp's spliff. 6. *n. prop.* The evil Emperor in 'Flash Gordon.' 7. *n. coll.* A quantity of ugly women. *'Don't bother going to Simbas tonight. The place is heaving with fucking ming.'*

Ming the merciless *n.* An exceptionally foul-smelling *Exchange & Mart.*

minge *n. Fanny, quim.*

minge binge *n.* The frantic fish-eating spree of the *gash gannet.*

mingelicious *adj.* A *front bottom* alternative to the more *fat arse*-centric term of approbation *bootylicious. 'That Kylie Minogue is right mingelicious isn't she, Cardinal?'*

minge mat *n. Mapatasi, velcro triangle.*

mingerling *n.* To move and socialise amongst the less obviously attractive ladies in a nightclub after resigning oneself to the fact that one isn't going to pull a *looker. 'Well, looks like all the class blart have been snaffled. Better start mingerling.'*

minge winker 1. *n.* Striptease artist. 2. *n.* She who flashes her *gash,* eg. whilst folding her legs.

minglewank *n.* A surreptitious *tug* performed through the trouser pocket in a crowded place, eg. on a tube train, in a supermarket, at a funeral.

miniature heroes 1. *n.* Small *fudge nuggets* which, even in the face of vigorous wiping, cling tenaciously to the *arse cress*. 2. *n*. Tiny *arse bars*.

minihughie *n*. A mouthful of *spew* that can be discreetly swallowed back down. The *vurp's* big brother.

mini series 1. *n*. A troublesome *log* that requires several flushes to see it off. 2. *n*. A pile of *shite* starring Jane Seymour.

mink *n*. A more up-market name for the wife's *beaver*.

minkle *n*. Hampshire term for a lady's *front pocket*. *'Fuck me, vicar. You can see her minkle.'* *Can also be used as a friendly greeting. 'Hallo vicar, you fucking minkle.'*

mink's minge, soft as a *sim*. Descriptive of something which is very soft, eg. fine velvet, silk pyjamas or Keith Flint out of The Prodigy. *'New Andrex Ultra. 50% longer, 50% stronger, but still as soft as a mink's minge.'* (Ad Campaign, Bartle Bogle, Heggarty, BBD, DDP, Needham).

minky 1. *n*. A French monkey. 2. *n*. A species of whale. 3. *n*. A *hornbag*. An attractive female.

minnie moo *n*. *Minge*.

minute man *n. medic*. One afflicted with the hilarious and shameful condition of premature ejaculation. A *two push Charlie*, a *point and squirt merchant*.

miserbation *n*. The practice of *wanking* over free underwear catalogues, travel brochures and other sundry *humble grumble*, as indulged in by parsimonious bachelors who consider shelling out good money on a copy of *'Razzle'* to be a frivolous waste of money. *Ebenezer spooging*.

miser's shite *n*. A bowel movement,

the wiping of which causes no soiling of the first sheet.

Miss Hastings *n*. An ugly woman who is in fact the least ugly woman in one's environs. From the heavily be-uglywomanned Sussex seaside town.

missionary impossible *n*. A lady with a *lovely personality* who can only be *poked* in the *doggy position*. A *lumberjill*, a *bobfoc*, a *frombie*.

Miss Lincolnshire *n*. Any woman with *spaniel's ears*. *'And this year's Miss Lincolnshire is... Patsy Kensit.'*

Miss Selfridge shuffle *n*. The embarrassed, self-conscious little dance performed by a man left waiting in the lingerie department of a department store whilst his wife is in the changing rooms.

missus button *n*. The control on the front of a PC (often labelled 'reset') which can be hit to remove all the vile, hardcore *grumble* from the screen when one's wife or partner returns home unexpectedly.

Mitchells *n*. Huge pairs of *tits*. Termed after their resemblance to the bald heads of *'EastEnders'* hard boys Phil and Grant. *'Dear Miriam, I found a lump in my left Mitchell and I'm scared to go to my doctor in case she gives me bad news.'* (Problem page, *'Daily Mirror'*, June 2002).

Mobe *n*. Abbreviation of Moby Dick. An epic *turd*, longer than a *mini series*, which may require harpooning with the lavatory brush to see it off.

mobile throne *n*. A portable *shit house* that everyone avoids at pop festivals because the floor is two inches deep in *mocking birds*.

mocking birds *rhym. slang.* *Douglas Hurds.*

mock turtle 1. *n.* A character in *'Alice in Wonderland'* by antique kiddie diddler Lewis Carroll. 2. *n.* Something that feels like a *shit,* but turns out to be a *fart.*

model T fart *n.* A *wind breakage* that sounds like one is about to be run over by Laurel and Hardy.

mod's parka *n.* A young lady's *clopper* of a particularly unattractive mien, resembling a sort of floppy funnel with a bit of flea-bitten fur stuck round the collar. Possibly encountered on Brighton beach whilst a youth in a leather jacket strikes it repeatedly using a length of metal pipe.

mohair knickers *n.* Large, unruly *minnie moo,* one with *spider's legs.* A *biffer.*

moip *n.* Female genital lubrication. *Froth, fanny grease, vagoline.*

moip mop *n.* A gentleman's beard used to soak up *sloom,* in the same way one would use a slice of bread to soak up gravy. *'Short back and sides, please. And could you trim the stray bits off my moip mop.'*

moist and meaty *adj.* Alliterating adjectives used extensively to describe the female and male genitals respectively, as well as dog food.

mole at the counter *euph.* A mammalian *turtle's head.* *"From the imprint of his shoes, Watson, I deduce that our quarry is a left-handed doctor of unusually short stature, who has known prosperity but has lately fallen on hard times. And by the short, irregular length of his stride, it is apparent that he has a mole at the counter,' said Holmes.'* (from *'The Case of the Speckled Bowl'* by Sir Arthur Conan Doyle).

mole's eye *n.* A *fanny* which makes a *mouse's ear* look like a *horse's collar.* *'Consignia was powerless to resist. His eyes burnt into hers like ambers. His muscular arms enfolded her body as she felt herself being swept away on tradewind of passion. "Now, Fernando,' she gasped. 'Take me now. All these years in the convent I've been saving myself for the right man, and now I've found you.' 'Fucking get in," breathed Fernando. 'You must have a snatch like a mole's eye."* (from *'The Nun and the Windowcleaner'* by Barbara Cartland).

molten brown *euph.* An unpleasant, morning-after-Vindaloo-style *digestive transit,* which melts the *balloon knot.* Named in direct contrast to the rather pleasant bathroom cosmetics manufacturer. A *rogan splosh, dump and burn.*

moneymoon *n.* The magical, but all too short period of financial stability which one enjoys after paying one's wages in or taking out a bank loan.

money shot *n.* The moment in a *bongo flick* where the leading man makes a small deposit from *Kojak's money box,* usually into the leading lady's face. A *pop shot.*

mongrel *n.* A *dobber,* a *semi, half a teacake.* A *cock* in a state of semi-turgidity that is neither one thing nor the other. A *knob* which is *on the bounce.*

monkey *n.* Vagina. A *toothless gibbon.* *'Does the monkey want a banana?'*

monkey bath *n.* A bath so hot, that when lowering yourself in, you go:

'Oo! Oo! Oo! Aa! Aa! Aa!'.

monkey cum *n.* Any cream-based *tart fuel*, eg. Bailey's.

monkey feather *exclam.* Bizarre substitute for *m******f****** dubbed into Eddie Murphy films on BBC1 to avoid offending some stupid old cunt. Also *mother father, money farmer, melon farmer, muddy funster.*

monkey pie *1. n.* A chip shop delicacy heated to the temperature of the earth's core which, upon taking the first *Bee Gee's bite*, causes its purchaser to cry out in a series of inarticulate, high-pitched simian shrieks. *2. n.* A hairy, ill-mannered *clopper* that keeps blowing raspberries.

monkey wank *n.* To masturbate oneself or another using the feet. Whilst swinging in a tyre.

monkey's chin *n. Twix lips, beetle bonnet*, a prominent *mound of Venus.*

monkey's fag break *n.* Like slipping out for five minutes for a fag, but for a *ham shank* instead of a *Harry Rag*. A *wank* at work.

monkey's fist *n.* A round, yet lumpy *Richard III.*

monkey's forehead *1. n. velcro triangle, mapatasi. 2. n.* The front top bit of Sunderland manager Peter Reid's head.

monkey's kneecap *n.* A scabby *fanny* one could spend the day picking fleas from.

monkey's tail *n.* A small lick of *turd* on the rear of the seat caused by sitting too far back whilst *dropping the kids off at the pool.*

monkey's toe *n.* A nipple big enough to peel a banana. A *Westminster Abbey hatpeg.*

Monkhouse's Syndrome *n. medic.*

To vomit into the mouth and swallow with a tortoise-like gulp and hand gesture, reminiscent of the late Bob Monkhouse introducing a punchline. *Bob's Full Mouth.*

monk's chain *n. eccles.* A circle or line of friars, public schoolboys or BBC football commentors interfering with each other's *parts of shame.* A *daisy chain*, a *circle jerk.*

monk's chunks *n.* The excess *smeg* build-up of a man who has given up caring any more.

monk's cowl *n.* A *wizard's sleeve.*

monk's hood *n.* A voluminous *Jacky Danny.* A *wizard's sleeve*, a *hippo's mouth.*

monks' trunks *n.* Underpants that are crunchy with dried *spunk.*

monster munch *n. Cunnimingus.* From the comparable olfactory experience of sticking one's face in a bag of the popular pickled onion snack and breathing deeply.

Montezuma's revenge *n. medic. Mexican screamers*, the *shits. Tijuana cha-cha.*

Monty *n.* A *blopstrop, tammy huff.* From the mood swings of Ryder Cup winner and perennial *moanarse* Colin Montgomery.

moo *n.* A name to call one's wife when one thinks the word 'cow' is too offensive. *'Where's me bladdy tea, eh? You fucking stupid old moo.'*

moobs *n.* Flabby breast-like structures sported by non-sporting gentlemen whose only form of daily exercise is to jog past the salad in the works canteen. From~ man + *boobs. Man breasts, mannery glands, bitch tits.*

mooey *n.* A *sausage wallet.*

moomph *1. v. Aus.* To sniff a lady's

bicycle seat. *2. n. Aus.* One who *moomphs.*

moon *v.* A rugby move, where the prop forward sprints around the defending back four to the rear of the bus and presses his naked *arse* up to the back window.

moonie *1. n. prop.* A follower of the Rev. Ying Tong Yiddel-I Moon. *2. n.* An act of *mooning.*

moon juice *n.* The liquid product of a lady's monthly discomfort. The cargo of the *tomato boat. Lunar mess, fanny jam.*

moonwalk *n.* The optical illusion of walking without moving achieved by someone trying to wipe a *dog's egg* off their shoes onto the grass.

moose *n. Boiler, steg.* Often a feminist with hairy armpits.

moose knuckles *n. Can. Camel's feet, Ninja's toe.*

moosetrap *n.* The protracted, often expensive and frankly unnecessary efforts expended when attempting to seduce a right *boot* of a lass when, in reality, a simple 'Fancy a bang?' would probably achieve the same outcome. Inspired by the popular charity shop 1970s children's boardgame *'Mousetrap'*, which featured an overly complicated contrivance for the purpose of entrapping a small plastic rodent that was frankly going nowhere.

moped *n.* A fat woman. Fun to *ride*, but you wouldn't want your mates to know.

more tea vicar? *phr.* Faux-farcical attempt to distract a clergyman after the launch of an *air biscuit,* now widely used to diffuse post-*fart* tension. Other popular post-flatulous remarks include; *sew a button on that, catch that one and paint it blue, good health!, pin a tail on that* and *there goes the elephant.*

morgan *rhym slang. Arse.* From Morgan Stanley Dean Witter = *shitter.*

morgue cheater *n.* A senior citizen. A *coffin dodger,* an *oxygen thief.*

morning glory *n.* The appearance of a *tent pole* first thing in the morning. A *dawn horn.*

morning thickness *n.* A post-slumber state of erectivitation. Also *dawn horn, morning wood, morning glory.*

morning thunder *n.* The first, usually very powerful *fart* of the day.

morning wood *n.* The *dawn horn.*

Morrissey's stag night, like *sim.* Descriptive of a public house peopled entirely by broken men of indeterminate age staring silently at their half-empty pint glasses. *'Shall we go to Yates's instead? It's like Morrissey's stag night in here.'*

mortal *adj. Refreshed* within an inch of one's life.

Moses effect *n.* The effect a seatbelt or bag strap has on a lady's *baps,* ie. causing them to part like the Red Sea.

moss cottage *n.* The ideal home for *John Thomas.*

mothball diver *n.* One who savours *granny's oysters.*

moth boy *n.* The member of a drinking party who, upon entering a pub, proceeds directly to the bandits, attracted by the flashing lights.

Mother Hubbard's dog *sim.* Descriptive of an underused *minge,* ie, drooling and *gagging* for a *bone.* *'It's noo a score and seven years since her beloved Bonny Prince Albert passed awa'. Today, whilst* *oot aside the loch, Her Majesty confided in me that she missed his big wullie affy bad, and that most o' the time, her wee royal badger was akin tae Mother Hubbard's dog.'* (from *'The Life of John Brown, the Memoirs of a Royal Ghillie'*).

mother's love *n.* The quality which alows one to re-enter the *cludgie* after *laying a cable* when others have deemed the smell too evil to tolerate.

motion sickness *n.* Nausea caused by doing a *dump* so foul and evil that it makes one gag.

motion thickness *n. Travel fat.*

motor cycle kick stand *n.* The morning erection that manifests itself whilst one is asleep on one's side, preventing one from rolling over onto one's stomach.

mott 1. *n.* A lady from Cumbria. 2. *n.* Part of a Norman fort from GCSE history. 3. *n.* A *minge, mapatasi.*

mottzerella *n.* A stringy, warm substance with the appearance of melted cheese, found on a *fanny* which has been somewhat neglected in hygiene terms. *Voodoo butter, chodder.*

mound of Venus *n.* The craggy outcrop above *salmon canyon* usually hidden by a dense covering of *bush*. A *beetle bonnet, monkey's forehead, grassy knoll.*

mount *v.* To *hop on* for *a bit.*

mountbattens *n.* Small fragments of shattered *turds* found floating in the toilet.

Mount Fujis *n.* Uncannily conical tits as seen in 1950s American B films. *Twin peaks, sweatermeat.*

mouse *adj.* Descriptive of someone who is poor at what they do. *Swiss.*

'That Eamonn Holmes is a bit fucking mouse, isn't he?'

mouse meat *n.* Cheese.

mouse's ear, fanny like a *sim.* Descriptive of a tight *minnie moo*, a *butler's cuff.*

mouse's tongue *sim.* Descriptive of a very small penis. With cheese on the end.

mousetrap 1. *n.* Agatha Christie play which performs a sort of Care in the Community role for bad actors. 2. *n.* A bin found in the ladies' restrooms where women may discreetly dispose of their feminine hygiene products, such as *jamrags, fanny nannies*, and *chuftie plugs.*

moustaka *n.* A female lady's pubic hair which has been neatly parted down the centre in the style of a Wild West saloon bartender's moustache.

mouth muff *n.* A goatee beard normally sported by someone who mans an IT help desk and likes T'Pau. A *cocksucker's doormat.*

mouth-to-muff *n.* Lesbotic resuscitation technique. Also *quimlich manoeuvre.*

moy 1. *n.* Helmet cheese. *Smegma.* 2. *adj.* Shit. esp. dog's~. *'Waterworld' (1995. Dir. Kevin Costner) starring Kevin Costner and Dennis Hopper. A visually striking futuristic pile of high budget dog's moy.'* (Halliwell's Film Guide).

Mr. Benn, to do a *v.* To get so *mullered* that one goes into a toilet in a pub, and the next thing one remembers is coming out the toilet of another pub, suspecting one has had a little adventure inbetween.

Mr. Blobby 1. *n.* Tidy-bearded annoying *cunt* Noel Edmonds's rubber-suited annoying *cunt* side kick. *2. n.* A gentleman during the one week in four when he has to do without, due to his wife being *Mrs. Blobby.*

Mr. Bond *n.* A particularly buoyant *turd* that returns to the surface of the water even after flushing. *'Ah, so we meet again, Mr. Bond.'*

Mr. Brown is at the window *euph.* To have the *turtle's head.* First used by Queen Victoria. *'Pray forgive us, Mr. Gladstone, but we cannot receive you at the moment. Mr. Brown is at the window, and we fear we may papper our kex.'*

Mr. Flitcroft's woes *n.* Constant reminders that one's relationship is on the rocks, eg. a piece of music, a photograph, a fifty-thousand strong jeering crowd.

Mr. Happy's business suit *n.* A condom.

Mr. Jones *1. n.* 19thC. Penis. *2. n.* A butcher who frequently purports that 'they don't like it up 'em'.

Mr. Sausage *n.* The excitable trouser man.

Mr. Trebus's yard *sim.* Descriptive of a much-neglected, unhygienic and rat-infested *clopper.* From the late *'Life of Grime'* star's shit-filled garden.

Mr. Whippy *1. n.* Semi-viscous ice-cream that comes out of a tap in a van. From 60p. *2. n.* Flagellation, corporal punishment dished out at *rub-a-tug shops.* From £25.

Mr. Whippy's in town *exclam.* Declaration that all is not well in the *chamber of horrors.*

muck *n. Mess, baby bouillon, load.* That which is *shot.*

mucksavage *n.* A *bumpkin*, a *buffle*, a *cabbagehead.* A *joskin.*

muck spreader *n. Arse, bum.*

muck truck *n.* A late night emergency food vehicle parked at the side of the road near a pub or club at chucking out time, where the cuisine is often somewhat less than haute, but looks smashing after a gallon or so of *pop.*

muck trumpet *n.* A tunefully farty *brass eye.*

mucky dip *n.* A *scuttling* up the *coal hole.*

mucky *n.* Any item of a pornographic nature, book, video, etc. *'Have you got any mucky I can borrow?' 'Yes, but don't get any spragg on it this time.'*

mud *1. n.* Excrement. *2. n.* Excrement 1970s pop group.

mud button *n. winnet, dangleberry, tagnut, clinker,* etc.

mudchild *n.* A *sweaty morph.*

mud darts *n. Anal love. Bum sex.*

mudeye *n. Arse, ringpiece,* one's old-fashioned plastic *tea towel holder.*

muddy funster *1. n.* A *botter. 2. n.* A *melon farmer.*

mud hole *n.* That *hole* from which one *blows mud.* The *crop sprayer, cable layer.*

mudlark *1. n.* A horse which enjoys heavy ground. *2. n.* The sort of goings-on enjoyed by foreign sex perverts on the internet.

mud oven *n.* The rectum of the anus. *'Mitochondria was powerless to resist. His eyes burned into hers like haematites. His muscular arms enfolded her body as she felt herself being swept away in a pyroclastic flow of passion. Then he said those words of which she had dreamed so long, yet never dared hope to hear. 'How much to give you one in the mud oven, then love?'* (from *'The Aged Prostitute* *and the 18-year-old Scouse Football Star who has Just Been Signed by Manchester United for Twenty-Eight Million Quid'* by Barbara Cartland).

mudpussy *n.* The *arse,* when used by heathens for purposes for which the Lord did not intend it.

mud valve mechanic *n.* A *brown pipe engineer.*

mud wrestling *n.* A long and messy battle on the toilet, involving much grunting and groaning, which usually ends in either a fall or a submission.

muff 1. *n. Minge, fanny.* 2. *v.* To *shag,* have intercourse with. 3. *v.* To fluff, miss an easy goal-scoring opportunity, eg. *'Oh fuck! Emile Heskey has muffed it.'*

muff diver *n.* A footballer who misses an easy goal scoring opportunity, then falls over in an attempt to win a penalty kick.

muff diver's dental floss *n.* Female pubic hair.

muff huff *n.* Menstruation moodiness or PMT. A *period drama,* a *blob strop.*

muffia *n.* A collection of criminal women, or women married to criminals.

muffin 1. *n.* Flour-based bakery product. 2. *n.* 1960s TV mule whose name remains a source of perpetual hilarity among the elderly and infirm.

muffin tops *n.* The pastry-like midriff overhang achieved by lasses wearing tight, low-slung *kex.*

muffle *v.* The female equivalent of *zuffle.*

mufflinks *n.* Female genital jewellery. Pierced fanular silversmithery.

muff nudge *n.* The light brushing of a female hairdresser's *beetle bonnet* against one's elbows when she leans forward to cut one's hair.

muffocation *n.* The inability to breathe when a *dirty lady* is sitting on your face.

muff riders *n. Birds' crabs.*

mufftash *n.* The stylish, Kevin Webster-style furry residue which adorns the upper lips of those who have but recently been *licking out* a lady's *mimsy.* A *Barnsley moustache.*

muff trumpet *n.* A *fanny fart* that would have a troop of soldiers standing by their beds.

mug stains *n.* Large, dark, flat *jockeys* that often appear during pregnancy.

Mugabe *n.* The frankly silly postage stamp-sized tuft of *muff turf* left above the *fannies* of certain porn actresses and *jazz mag* models.

mule's lip *n.* A large foreskin.

mullered *adj. Langered.*

muller love *n.* The temporary amorous feelings one has towards a right *pig* as a result of being *mullered.* To find someone attractive when looking at them through *beer goggles.*

mullet *n.* Inbreds' haircut favoured by country and western singers and 1980s footballers.

mulligan *n. Aus.* Penis.

mumbas *onomat.* Breasts. If *oomlaaters* made a noise, they would say 'mumbas' in a deep, fruity baritone.

mumblers *n.* Tight women's bicycle shorts through which you 'see the lips move but can't understand a word.'

mummy returns *n.* A *brown zombie* that comes back wrapped in *shit tickets.*

mumph *onamat.* See *flub.*

mumrar *n.* The act of sneaking up behind your mother and shouting 'RAR!'

munch bunch *n.* A gang of *dykes.*

mung *n.* Particularly runny type of *arse feta.* 2. *n.* That smell which emanates from within the fleshsome rolls of a *Duke of giblets.* '*Rik – I like what you did with the song, but I'm not sure that your interlude of vigorous breakdancing during the middle eight was such a good idea. There was a right fucking mung in here by the time you reached the last chorus. Dr. Fox has had to open the window.*'

mungos *n.* Great big sideburns as worn by Jerry Dorsey, lead singer of Mungo Jerry. *Bugger's grips, face fannies.*

municipal cockwash *n. Town bike, box of assorted creams, buttered bun.*

munts *n.* Particularly butch, though not necessarily *lesbotic* ladies, often found amongst the sailing community. From men + *cunts.*

muscle Mary *n.* An extremely wellbuilt *ginger beer.*

mush in the bush *n.* The kind of sex act that Dick Van Dyke might perform on Julie Andrews. *Cockney cumulonimbus.*

musical vegetables *n.* Baked beans, as eaten by cowboys and *trouser trumpeteers.*

musical wank *n.* A *strum* undertaken to the rhythm of some music.

musk mask *n.* To wear a lady's *undercrackers* as a balaclava whilst having a right good *wank.*

mustang *n.* Of *shitty arses,* that stubborn *dangleberry* which cannot be shaken off.

Mutley chunter *n.* The act of voicing disapproval under one's breath when forced to perform an act under duress, in the style of Dick Dastardly's dog. Usually involves muttering 'ratting, dratting, etc' through tightly-clenched teeth.

mutton dressed as kebab *sim.* Ugly women who doll themselves up and make themselves look even worse, eg. Julie Goodyear. Also *mutton dressed as spam.*

mutton musket *n.* A smaller, more portable field weapon than the *lamb cannon.* Also *mutton bayonet, mutton dagger.*

mutton tugger *n.* In a slaughterhouse, one whose job it is to pull the meat off the bones of old sheep.

mutt's nuts *adj.* Descriptive of something which is very good. The *dog's bollocks.*

mycoxafloppin *n. medic.* The principal active ingredient in Viagra.

Myleene *rhym. slang.* The *anus.* From the fat-titted former Hear'Say songstress Myleene Klarsehole.

mystic smeg *n. Erectoplasm.*

Nn

nadbag *n*. The *nut sack, pod pouch, scrot sling*.

nadger *n*. A testicle which has been battered black and blue. *'I tell you what, she loves it rough. She's left me with a right pair of nadgers, Mother Superior.'*

nadgina *n*. A *cockney's pod purse*, which has been refashioned into a *cludge* at the skilled hands of a dextrous surgeon. *'Day forty-four in the house, and Nadia's giving her nadgina a quick rinse in the sink.'*

nad nogg *n*. *Splod*.

nadpoles *n*. *Jizzbag taddies. Spunks*.

nads *n*. *Knackers*, testicles, *plums*.

Nagasaki tan *n*. A sunbed induced glow of such ferocity that it appears that one was present an the detonation of an atom bomb, eg. one sported by Judith Chalmers, Des O'Connor, Jodie Marsh.

name that tune *exclam*. A humorous exclamation called out to draw attention to an amusing breaking of wind at a middle class dinner party.

nana Kournikova *n*. A *bird* who appears to be fit from the back, but who on turning round is revealed to be a pensioner. A *Kronenberg*, a *Toyah*.

nan bread *n*. *Bingo wings*.

nan's grin *n*. A *shaven haven*. A *toothless gibbon*, a *Barthez*.

nan's mattress, as pissed as your *sim*. To be in an extreme state of *refreshment*. *'Ladies and gentlemen, welcome aboard flight BA103 from Oslo. We would advise you to keep your safety belts fastened throughout the flight as it looks like it could be quite a bumpy ride. We're not* expecting *any turbulence, it's just that the captain is as pissed as your nan's mattress.'*

national grottery, win the *v*. To be the lucky discoverer of a massive deposit of porn hidden under a bush, in a skip or a recently-deceased vicar's study.

nature's make-up *n*. A range of black and blue eye cosmetics favoured by the wives of certain British sportsmen and ex-James Bond actors.

naughty Nazi salute *n*. A *bonked-on cock*.

nauticals *rhym. slang*. Piles. From nautical miles.

navigator of the windward pass *n*. A *rear admiral*.

Navy cake *n*. *milit*. Army and Air Force term for the *arse*.

NBR *abbrev*. No Beers Required. A good-looking woman. Opposite of a *five pinter*.

NDL *abbrev*. Nipples Don't Lie. Body language phenomenon that allows anthropologists insight as to how they are getting on when chatting up *birds* in the pub.

Neapolitan knickers *n*. The disgusting state of a proper old *slapper's gusset*. Vanilla, strawberry, chocolate, the lot.

necking turds *v*. Accusation made against one suffering from halitosis. *'Excuse me, madam, I don't wish to appear rude, but have you been necking turds?'*

neck tripe *n*. The unappetizing hanging flesh that adorns the throats of ageing ladies.

neddies *n*. *Nellies*.

nellies *n*. *Knockers, tits, neddies*.

Nelson Mandela *rhym. slang*. Wreck the hoose juice, wifebeater. Stella.

Neptune's kiss *n*. The cold, wet smacker on the *arse* caused by *splashback*.

net curtains *n*. Old ladies' *drapes*, which tend to twitch over to one side when the neighbours come out.

nether eye *n*. That single *unseeing eye*, situated in the *nether region*, which cries brown, lumpy tears.

nether throat *n*. In *farting*, the *poot chute, botty bugle*. *'Pardon me while I clear my nether throat.'*

nettie *n*. Outside loo, *clart cabin, shite house. Dunny, cludgie, growler*.

Netto fabulous *adj*. Descriptive of one who eschews posh jewellers such as Tiffanys and Aspreys in favour of down market *blingmongers* like Price-drop.TV and Argos.

Netto ghetto *n*. A shopping arcade consisting entirely of discount stores, eg. the Loreburn Centre, Dumfries.

Newcastle cup run *euph*. Descriptive of that wistful feeling experienced by gentlemen looking down at their own erections and wishing they could *suck* themselves *off*. From the fact that they know *'it's within reach, but it's never going to happen.'*

Newton effect *n*. When struggling to pass a three *breather ring dreadnought*, the pleasing sensation as the force of gravity takes over.

Newton's cradle *1. n*. A still fashionable, chromed executive toy which, by means of colliding, suspended balls demonstrates Newton's third law of motion. *2. n*. The off-putting and often *timber-felling* image of two *grumble flick* actors banging their *knackers* together as they perform a *DP*.

Newton's revenge *n*. The cruel effect of gravity upon aged *tits*.

NFF FFN *abbrev*. Descriptive of a lady who looks alright from a distance, but is a right *steg* close up. A *Thora bird*, a *golden deciever. Nice From Far, Far From Nice*.

NGTs *abbrev*. National Geographic Tits. Flat, pendulous breasts as sported by old tribeswomen in the aforesaid school library jazzmag. *Spaniel's ears*.

niags *rhym. slang*. Nuts. From Niagra Festicles ~ testicles.

nicely poised *adj*. Of a gentleman, to be prone to *jumping puddles*. To be *good with colours, on the other bus*.

nice piece of glass *n*. Comestible ordered by humorous males at the bar. *'I'll have a nice piece of glass in a Stella sauce, please.'*

nick bent *adj*. Temporarily travelling on the *other bus* whilst staying at Her Majesty's pleasure.

nickles and dimes *1. n*. Low denomination US currency. *2. n*. A low denomination *grumble vid money shot*. A *stick flick lizard's lick*. *'Goddammit, Gunter. That was goddamn nickles and dimes.' 'What do you expect? It's the fifth popshot I've done in two hours.'*

nick one to the wicketkeeper *v*. To fail to avoid the *follow-on* whilst wearing white trousers.

niftkin's bridge *n*. Female equivalent of the *biffin bridge* or *barse*.

Nigella shites *n*. The aftermath of eating upper class fodder.

night watchman *n*. A *copper bolt* that has failed to flush away and is discovered the next morning.

nikey pikey *n*. A white-baseball-capped, XRFord-driving, Reebok Classic-wearing gentleman, such as one from the Central Avenue area of Hayes, Middlesex.

nillionaires' row *n.* Name given to any run down street in one of the country's less salubrious residential areas.

NIN *acronym. medic.* Normal in Norfolk. Doctor's shorthand implying that your physical and mental characteristics indicate that your mother is possibly also your sister, cousin, aunt and perhaps even your father.

nine-bob-note, as bent as a *sim.* *Colwyn Bay.*

nine dart leg *1. n.* The successful completion of a game of darts using the minimum number of throws possible, a feat achieved notably on TV by Phil 'The Power' Taylor during the 2002 World Matchplay Championship. *2. n.* The successful completion of a sexual encounter in the shortest possible time, usually achieved by a *two push Charlie.*

ninja's toe *n.* A *camel's foot.*

ninth finger *n.* The *cock.*

nip and tuck *n.* The act of *nipping off* one of *Bungle's fingers* at the knuckle, with the result that the stump is retracted cleanly into the *bomb bay.* The correct response to a *mid-loaf crisis.*

nip 'n' roll *v.* The dextrous art of relieving an itch in *John Wayne's hairy saddlebags.*

nipnosis *n.* Trance-like state induced by concentrating one's gaze on a pair of bobbing *milkers.* Often only ends when the *nipnotised* subject drives through a red light and broadsides a police car.

nip on *n.* A nippular erectivation. A nipple *hard on.*

nipping Christian *n.* A cutpurse, a

thief.

nipping the turtle *v. Crimping off a length, shutting the bomb bay doors.*

nipplecakes *n.* Appetising breasts that one wouldn't mind *icing.*

nipotism *n.* In the world of business, the discriminatory practice of hiring and promoting ladies on the basis of *first impressions,* to the detriment of the careers of their more flat-chested counterparts.

nipsy *n. medic.* The pincer-like muscle just around *Ena Sharples' mouth* that cuts one's *Bungle's finger* to length when contracted.

nitby *n.* Semi-acronymous term describing a chav baby. Corruption of 'Not in the Baby Book', from the unusual names given to *Greggs' dummy*-sucking nippers, eg. Mercedes, Chardonnay, Beyonce, Scratchcard etc.

nob *1. n.* A hay clarse, hoity-toity person. A toff. *2. n.* A small piece of butter. *3. v.* To *fuck,* penetrate with the *knob.*

Nobbies *rhym. slang.* Haemorrhoids. From 1966 toothless footballer Sir Norbert Stiles = piles.

nobgoblins *n.* Those mythical creatures that make one's *nuts* itch the second one is in polite company.

nob snog *n.* A genteel term for an act of *horatio.*

nob Tarzans *n. medic. Genital guests* who swing from *pube* to *pube* through one's underpant jungle. *Crabs.*

nob turban *n.* A crest of Kleenex adorning one's post-*wank helmet.*

nocturnal emission *n. medic.* The end result of a wet dream.

noddies *n.* The bikini overflow of an unwaxed lady, from its similarity to the effusive *bugger's grips* worn by

1970s rock legend Noddy Holder. *'Cor, look at the noddies on that Bulgarian lass.'*

noddy *n.* Condom, *French letter, cock 'holder'.*

noddy book *n.* Bongo mag.

Noddy Holder's sideburns *sim.* Descriptive of a particularly luxuriant ginger *bush*, the kind that Charlie Dimmock probably has.

nodge *v.* To observe the sexual activity of others. To *voy*, to *dog*.

nodger *n.* A *peeping Tom, voyeur*. A *merchant* who prefers 'live' *grumble* rather than the recorded variety.

no glans land *n.* The nether regions of a lady's nether regions. The *carse, taint, tinter, notcher, snarse* or whatever.

noinkers *n. Jubblies, kahunas, shirt potatoes, boobs, sweater fruit, knockers, cab man's rests, baps, funbags, bumpies, neddies, chichis, mambas, dirty pillows, chebs, charlies, diddies, doos, cajooblies, jugs, bubbies, zeps, bazongers, headlamps, whammies, norks, bangers, tits, dumplings, hogans, thrupennies, assets, churns, whammers, yoinkahs, begonias, mumbas, pink pillows, top bollocks, melons, oomlaaters, nellies, choozies, chubblies, chumbawumbas, blimps, charms, baby's dinners, fun cushions, paps, bojangles, garbonzas, airbags, Gert Stonkers, puppies, Bristols.* A lady's bosoms.

no job *n.* Being *sucked off* by a lady whilst so *pissed* one can hardly feel it. See also *bland job*.

nollies *n.* Word used by posh southern ladies when referring to a gentleman's testicles. From *nuts* + *bollocks* + *goolies*. *'The Archbishop of Canterbury's shoes were so shiny that when he lifted his arms up to crown me Queen of Great Britain and all her Commonwealth Dominions, I could see his big hairy nollies reflected in them.'* (HM the Queen, interviewed by Matthew Wright on *'The Wright Stuff'*, Channel 5).

nollocks *exclam.* A version of b******s which can be used in polite company without causing offence. *'Don't talk fucking nollocks, vicar. Of course you want another cup of tea'.*

nookie 1. *n.* Sex, only a *bit* of which it is advisable to have at any one time. 2. *n. prop.* A humorous name for a ventriloquist's bear.

nooner *n.* See *funch*.

norkelling *v.* When on holiday, the act of wandering along the beach to examine the wares on display. Preferably from behind a pair of dark shades.

nork hammock *n.* Of female fashions, a halter neck top.

norkolepsy *n. medic.* A trance-like state in men caught in the beam of a fantastic pair of *headlamps*, eg. in the office, swimming pool, night club, church etc. *Titnotism.*

norks *n. Tits, knockers*. Also *norkers, norgs, norgers*.

Norman Cook *n.* A measure of alcohol which after being drunk can make a *Fat Bird Slim*. Approximately two *St. Ivels*.

Norma Snockers *n.* Wieldy *bojangles*. See also *Gert Stonkers*.

norton *n.* A *bearded clam*.

Norwegian's lunchbox *sim.* Descriptive of a *clopper* that smells like half a stone of whale blubber marinated in roll-mop herrings and sour milk.

NORWICH *acronym. milit.* Cipher used on military correspondence - Knickers Off Ready When I Come Home. First used during World War I, when Norwich was known as Korwich.

no score drawers *n.* Unflattering ladies' undergarments worn when the *pools panel is sitting* and the dividend forecast is low.

nose, blow one's *v.* To wipe away the post-ejaculation *sprongle* from one's *hog's eye*. *'I had to blow my nose on the back of her dress before pulling my pants back up.'*

nose fruit *n.* Bogies.

nose jizz n. Snot.

nosh off *v.* To perform *cumulonimbus* on a man.

nosh out *v.* To perform *philately* on a woman.

noshtalgia *n.* Fond remembrance of particularly good tunes played on one's *pink oboe* in days gone by.

notcher *n. Biffin bridge.* The area of skin between the *clockweights* and the *starfish*, so called because it's 'notcher' *bollocks* and it's 'notcher' *arse*.

not the marrying kind *adj.* Descriptive of a fellow who is *nicely poised* or *good with colours*. *'Has your Cedric found himself a nice girl and settled down yet?' 'No, well you know my Cedric. He's not the marrying kind.' 'Still a male prostitute then?' 'Yes.'*

noughtomobile *n.* A vehicle that occupies the lowest possible position on the *fanny-magnetism* scale. eg. A souped-up Daewoo Matiz with *'Max Power'* stickers.

NTL *n.* An excessively long stay on the toilet reading the paper, philosophising etc. After the telecommunications company who

spend months *laying* just one *cable*.

nudger *1. n.* Gay male. *2. n.* What a *fudge nudger* uses to *nudge fudge*.

nuggets *1. n.* Testicles. *2. n.* Any inedible part of a chicken or turkey, when coated in batter or breadcrumbs. eg. the *nuggets*.

number one *euph.* A *penny, tinkle.*

number threes *n.* Vomit.

number two *euph.* A *sit down, tuppence*, a *duty*.

nummghh *exclam.* The insulting noise made by pushing the tongue into the lower lip, usually directed at a person of low sense, or one who has inadvertently asked a foolish question. Regionally accentuated by either loose wristed hand waggles or transverse elbow-crested ear slaps.

nunga munching *v.* The ganneting of *hairy pie, licking out* a lady's *clunker* with relish.

nunnery *n.* Elizabethan name for a *rub-a-tug shop* from an age when nuns were widely believed to wear *yo-yo knickers*.

nun's fanny *1. sim.* Descriptive of something that is extremely dry, eg. the Sahara desert, George Best's throat. *2. euph.* Anything that is particularly tight, eg. any space a lady attempts to park in, the glove that OJ Simpson didn't wear when he wasn't murdering his wife.

Nurembergs *rhym. slang.* Haemorrhoids. From Nuremberg Trials = *piles*. Also *Seig Heils, four minute miles*.

nurfing *v. Garbooning, nerding, pooning, shniffle-piffling, snaffling, snarfing, snarzing, snerking, snerdling, snerging.* The presumably very common act of sniffing ladies' bicycle seats.

nut butter *n*. A lightly-salted dairy product served hot from the male *churns* onto *baps*.

nut chokers *n*. Gentlemen's tight *shreddies, budgie smugglers*.

nutcrackers *n*. Unfeasibly tight 'spray-on' *round the houses* sported by *rock poodles* such as Justin Hawkins out of comedy band The Darkness.

nut custard *n*. *Banana yoghurt*.

nut fangle *n*. Pre-*wank* prep work.

Nutkin *n*. Of a man, the worst hairstyle it is possible to have, eg. those worn by Phil Harding (*'Time Team'* yokel archaeologist), Bill Bailey (troll-like comedian) and Terry Mancini (has-been QPR footballer). Named after TV animal trainer Terry Nutkin.

nutmegs *n*. *Balls* that hang down right between a footballer's legs.

nuts *1. n*. A fellow's *Knackers. 'I'm going to shave my nuts.' 2. adj*. Mad. *'Shave your nuts? You must be nuts.' 3. n*. Things that monkeys eat. *'That monkey's nuts. I gave it some nuts and it's rubbing them on its nuts.'*

nut sack *n*. The scrotum, *nadbag*.

nymph *1. n*. The caterpillar of a dragonfly. *2. n*. A sexy young *bird*.

nympho *n*. Sex-crazed *bird* that's *gagging* for it 24 hours a day, 7 days a week. The sort who would *shag* a pneumatic drill and blow up the generator.

NYPD blue *n*. A *poke*, where the *pokee* assumes the position of someone being frisked by New York's finest, against the wall or across the bonnet of a car.

Oo

oats *n*. A *portion* of that which one gets during sex with a Quaker.

OBE 1 *abbrev.* A memorable token of one's evening out, awarded by a nightclub bouncer as one is ejected from his establishment. One Behind the Ear. **2.** *abbrev.* Order of the Brown Entrance. An honour bestowed on a gentlemen for services to his bird's *shitter. Brown wings.*

offer a Jaffa cake *v*. To instigate a homosexual courting ritual involving the popular orange-flavoured biscuit/cake confection. If any male accepts another's offer of a Jaffa cake, then they are tacitly agreeing to partake in an act of anal romance.

officers' laces *n*. Ladies' string-like thongs buffed brown between their *arse cheeks.*

off-piste *n*. Sexual term whereby a gentleman ventures away from the officially sanctioned area into more rugged and challenging terrain. *'Come on, love. I've cooked dinner and even helped with the washing up. How many more brownie points do I need before I can go off-piste?'*

off the team *adj*. To be forbidden from playing on the *furry turf*. To be in your missus's bad books.

off your face *adj. Ripped to the tits* on the demon drink.

off your trolley *adj. Hatstand*, mental.

oil of goolay *n*. A white, sticky type foundation cream which reduces the signs of ageing when applied to ladies' faces out the end of one's *cock.*

oil spill *n*. An *Eartha* that constitutes a health threat to marine life.

oil tanker *rhym. slang*. An *onanist.*

oil the bat *v*. To *polish the pork sword, wax the dolphin.*

oil the truncheon *v*. To buff up the *bobby's helmet, collect kindling, wank.*

oily loaf *n*. A well-baked *turd.*

oily rags *n. rhym. slang*. Cigarettes.

OJ's glove 1. *n*. The state of the hand after *finger banging* a lady during *ragweek*. **2.** *n*. An extremely tight-fitting *liver sock.*

old dog's nose, dry as an *sim*. Descriptive of a *pink wafer*. A *moipless muff*. *'What's up love? I've been tickling your wotsit for three minutes and you're still as dry as an old dog's nose.'*

olden doubloons *n*. The *dunghampers* of a young lady who eschews *clackerfloss* preferring instead *bills* of a more matronly cut. *Elepants.*

oldest toad in the pond *n*. A particularly low, vociferous, grumbling *fart*, usually after eight pints of stout and a bar of Bourneville.

old faithful 1. *n*. A spectacular eruption of hot steam from a hole in the ground in Yellowstone National Park, USA. **2.** *n*. A spectacular eruption of hot *spooge* from the mouth of an inexperienced *cock nosher*, particularly one lying on her back.

old holborn *n*. The frayed edges of the *velcro triangle*, a *pant moustache. Spiders' legs.*

Old Leigh oyster *n*. A particularly viscous phlegm delicacy which requires a sight more chewing than its bivalve namesake.

old man *n*. Penis. Also *old fella*. *'The old man's been out of work for six months. Most days we play pocket billiards to keep him occupied.'*

Old McDonald's combover *n*. Stray

pubage agonisingly trapped under the brim of the *farmer's hat. Bobby Charltons.*

old shocker, the *n.* To surprise one's sexual partner by poking a cheeky *pinkie* up the *chuff* during intercourse. *"I say, Bertie. You'll never guess what,' gasped Piggy excitedly. 'I've just been in a clinch with Marjorie in the rose garden. Just as I got to the vinegar strokes, she popped me the old shocker. Quite took me aback, don't you know."* (from *'Now Start Humming, Jeeves'* by PG Wodehouse).

Oliver *adj.* To be inebriated. From Oliver Twist = *pissed.*

olivia *v.* To have sex with several filthy tramps on a *piss*-stained mattress, all at once.

Olympic village *n.* Any urban area with a disproportionate number of fat, unhealthy inhabitants wearing shitty, polyester-based sportswear.

omelette maker *n. Sp.* A lesbian.

onanism 1. *n.* Incomplete sexual intercourse. *Vatican roulette.* 2. *n.* A posh word what the Queen might use for *wanking* and that.

one *n.* A *poking.* The SI unit of sex, given to a woman by a man and measured from the moment it *goes in* to to moment it *goes off.* Equivalent to 0.6 of a *portion,* and 2.36 of a *bit of the other.*

one cheek sneak *n.* The stealthy approach to *shooting bunnies.* From a sitting position, lifting one *buttock* in order to slide out an aurally-undetectable *air biscuit.* A *cushion creeper, leg lifter.*

one-eared spacehopper *n.* Cliff Richard's genitals. A *panhandle* on someone with *DSB.*

one-eyed pant python *n.* See *one-trouser snake.*

one-eyed trouser snake *n.* See *one-eyed Willie.*

one-eyed Willie *n.* A *charlie.*

one-eyed Willie's eye patch *n.* A condom, *English overcoat.*

one-eyed zipper fish *n.* A *Cyclops, trouser trout.*

one four seven 1. *n.* In snooker, a complete clearance in which the player empties the table in a single visit, scoring maximum points in the process. 2. *n.* In toiletry, a complete clearance in which the toiletee empties his *Camillas* in a single sitting, finishing with a black. *'Watch my pint, boys. I'm going for a one four seven.'*

one-handed mag *n. Jazz magazine, rhythm read, art pamphlet, a grumbular periodical.*

one-holed flute *n.* A *pink oboe,* a *blue-veined piccolo,* a *purple headed* (insert wind instrument here).

one in the pump, to have 1. *v.* To have the *hots* for a female. *'Phoar! I've got one in the pump for her, I can tell you.'* 2. *n.* Drinking parlance for a pint paid for but not yet poured.

one o'er the thumb *n.* A *five knuckle shuffle.* *'Quite satisfied, Scrooge closed the door and locked himself in; double-locked himself in, which was his custom on these occasions. Thus secured against surprise, he took off his cravat; put on his dressing-gown and slippers, and his nightcap; and sat down before the fire with a copy of Razzle for a quick one o'er the thumb.'* (from *'A Christmas Carol'* by Charles Dickens).

one oar in the water *n.* Descriptive of someone unlikely to forge a successful career in rocket science, but who may find gainful employment chasing trolleys round Sainsbury's carpark. *'Doctors feared that after his near fatal quadbike accident, Mayall could have been left with one oar in the water. Amazingly, he made a full recovery, although he will remain on fit pills for the rest of his life.'* (Profile of Rik Mayall, *'The Guardian'*, Sept. 2001).

one off the crossbar *n*. To be just not quick enough in dropping one's *scads* after being caught short by an unexpected visit from *Mr. Whippy*. To *beskid* the waistband of your *shreddies*.

one off the wrist *v*. *Five knuckle shuffle, wank, hand shandy*.

one point five *n*. A toiletry visit product that falls somewhere between a *number one* and a *number two*. A runny *shit*. Or more rarely a lumpy *piss*.

one pump chump *n*. One who *goes off* on the first push. Twice as fast as a *two push Charlie*.

one-man orgy *n*. A long-lasting and elaborate *cat stabbing* session involving assorted stimuli, speeds and positions.

one string banjo *n*. A skin-covered instrument upon which a man might strum to his heart's content.

one-stroke cylinder engine *n*. A *Bakewell* released whilst walking that lasts for several paces. A *string of pearls*.

onepack *n*. A *beergut*.

oneplay *n*. Pre-masturbatory arousal techniques.

oner *n*. The line of condensed *arse cleft* perspiration left on a plastic seat after it has been sat on in the summer months. Upon exiting a taxi and preparing to pay, one might point to the seat and say,

'There's a oner, keep the change.'

oneymoon *n*. A romantic week's break from the missus which affords the married gentleman a welcome opportunity to enjoy an uninterrupted seven day period of luxurious *self abuse*.

oneymoon suite *n*. In an hotel, a room set aside for unaccompanied commercial travellers who do not wish to be disturbed; must include at least two porn channels and a copious supply of quilted toilet tissue.

on her dabs *adj*. Of a lady, to be menstruiferous. To be *boiling beetroots, serving strawberry jam for tea*.

onk, on the *adj*. Of the male generative member, to be tumescent.

on the batter *adj*. Of a lady, to be involved in the practice of showing successive gentlemen good times behind a skip for £5.

on the bench *adj*. After being *off the team*, to be optimistic that you may be given a late chance to *score*. To be in your missus's slightly better books. *'After the shameful episode with the exotic dancer I have alas been off the team these last six weeks. Today I bought my darling Victoria a bunch of flowers from the all-night garage, and I think I am on the bench.'* (from *'The Journal of Prince Albert'*).

on the blob *adj*. To be *riding the menstrual cycle*, to *have the painters in*, to have *fallen to the communists*.

on the bonk *adj*. Sergeant Sausage when standing to attention.

on the bus to Hebden Bridge *adj*. Descriptive of a *woman in comfortable shoes*, or *tennis fan*. From the unusually large amount of *les-*

bitious women living in the Yorkshire mill town.

on the hoy *adj. On the piss, on the razz, hoying* it down one's neck, and then back up again onto one's shoes.

on the job *adj. At it.* Busying oneself with one's partner's plumbing.

on the mop *adj.* Of a lady, to be suffering from *women's things.*

on the musical side *adj. Light on one's feet.*

on the nest *adj.* To be treating one's *bird* to a big juicy *worm.*

on the other bus *adj.* Homosexual, *bowling from the Pavilion end.*

on the pull *adj.* Fishing for *kipper, on the salmon, on the sniff.*

on the slipway *adj.* Of stools and stool movement, to have the *turtle's head. 'Get out of that fucking bathroom will you, I've got a dreadnought on the slipway.'*

on the sniff *adj. On the pull, on the tap.*

on tow *adj.* Of a woman, to be *up on blocks.* From the visible rope.

oomlaaters *n.* Very large *chumbawumbas.*

oomph! *n.* Sex appeal. *'By crikey, that Norma Major, she hasn't half got some oomph!'*

oot on the tap *adj. NE. Out on the pull,* as opposed to *on the hoy.*

OPE *abbrev.* A dazed and otherworldly sensation brought on by a visit to a mechanic, dentist, solicitor etc. Out-of-Pocket Experience.

open a packet of ham *v.* To let off a *beefy eggo.* From the practice of ham production line workers who *fart* into the packages of ham before sealing them.

open clam shots *n. Full-on oysters, close-up pink.* Artistic/medical *adult* camera angle.

open Dracula's coffin *v.* An act involving a protracted creaking noise, accompanied by an ungodly stench. To *drop a gut.*

open the hangar doors *v.* Of an experienced lady, to prepare herself for sexual intercourse. *'Wisteria was powerless to resist. His eyes burned into hers like amethysts. His muscular arms enfolded her body as she felt herself being swept away in a hurricane of passion. Gently, Renaldo laid her down on the silken ottoman in front of the roaring fire. Then, as he pulled her knickers off, she lifted her legs and opened the hangar doors.'* (from *'The lady and the South American Footballer'* by Barbara Cartland).

open your lunchbox *v.* To float an *air biscuit* reminiscent in aroma of yesterday's egg sandwiches.

opera house *n.* A large vagina with heavy pink safety curtains.

Orang Utan salad *n.* Ginger *gorilla salad. Fusewire.*

orchestras *rhym. slng.* The testicles. From orchestra stollocks = *bollocks.*

oreo *n.* An inverse *chocolate sandwich.*

organzola *n. Helmetdale.*

orgasm 1. *n.* A *fanny bomb*, a *stack blow.* 2. *v.* To *ring the bell, shoot one's load, chuck one's muck.*

Oscar *n. US. Dick*, penis.

osteopornosis *n.* medic. Degenerate condition symptomised by skeletal atrophy, progressive hypermetropia, early-onset pre-senile dementia and hairy palms.

other, a bit of the *n. Hanky panky.*

otter 1. *n.* An aquatic mammal. 2. *n.* A bald male gentleman who isn't interested in *beavers.*

otter's nose *n.* When getting *tops*

and fingers, that which is felt by the latter. *'I got a result last night. I touched the otter's nose.'* Something wet *under the bridge*.

otter off the bank, like an *sim*. Phrase used to describe a *turd* of particularly fine composition, which slips from one's *bumhole* with a certain amount of panache.

out of botty experience *n*. A *dump*.

overblaaters *n*. Pendulous *oom-laaters* which rest on a big round gut.

over the lines, colour in *v*. To spray a lady with semen after withdrawing from an orifice. To *crash the yoghurt truck* outside the delivery bay.

over the shoulder boulder holder *n*. Industrial bra, heavy lifting apparatus for *jelly water mangos*.

owner operator *n*. A *wanker*, a knight who wields his *pork sword* for pleasure, not for the benefit of fair maidens.

own goal *n*. A *fart* so obnoxious, that even he who dealt it cannot stay in its presence.

own up *v*. In a *breaking company* situation, to identify oneself as the *benefactor*.

oxygen thief *n*. A senior citizen, a *coffin dodger*.

oyster shot *n*. In the world of glamour photography, a carefully composed, lit and framed shot of a model's *clam* as she bends over, viewed from behind.

Ozzy ramble *n*. The shuffling, confused gait adopted by a man with a *horse's handbrake* and his trousers round his ankles, as he tries to manoeuvre around the sofa in order to secure a better angle to gain entrance to his good lady's *coconut husk*. From the shuffling, confused gait characteristic of shuffling, confused heavy metal pipistrelle gourmand Ozzy Osbourne.

Pp

pace car *n*. When paying a *sit down visit*, the slow, unaerodynamic leading *turd* that once out of the way, allows the fast, souped-up *botrods* behind it to put their foot down into the first bend.

packet *n*. The contents of the *kecks* visible in relief at the front of the *trolleys*. Male equivalent of the *camel's foot*. *Darcy Bussell's footrest*.

paddle the pink canoe *v*. To *frig*. Weekend recreational pursuit of the *gusset typist*.

Paddy's hankie *n*. The hand.

Paddy McGinty's goat *1. n*. Hilarious song made famous by twinkle-toothed sweater-wearing crooner Val Doonican. *2. n*. Pungent, hairy *snatch* that could eat a mayor's hat. Also *Delaney's donkey*.

padlocks *n*. *Tits* that would be better off in socks than in bras.

paedorinal *n*. In a public lavatory, the urinal which is situated alongside the shorter, small boys' version.

paedoscopes *n*. Those thick-rimmed National Health Service spectacles exclusively worn by trainspotters, scout masters and other assorted sex cases. *Paedospecs*.

paedosmile *n*. A particularly sinister grin, the type a kiddie fiddler might have.

PAFO *acron. medic*. Term used by consultants in Accident and Emergency departments to explain random cuts and bruises. Pissed And Fell Over.

pagga *n*. A free-for-all combat between anyone who wants to join in.

pagga starter *n*. A strong beer which breaks the ice at fights.

Supermarket smack.

painting the ceiling *v*. Having a go with the *naughty paintbrush* whilst in a supine position.

paint the baby's bedroom *v*. To slap a bit of *gonad gloss* around the vaginal walls.

paint the back door *v*. To drop a wet *fart, follow through*.

paint the town beige *v*. To indulge in an unambitious, lacklustre night out with one's mates.

paisley removal *n*. Pointing *Percy* directly at an area of *pebble dashing* in order to amuse oneself during a *Chinese singing lesson*. See also *piss polo*.

palace gates *n*. *Fanny lips, beef curtains*.

palma sutra *n*. The mystical art of *cranking one off* in a number of improbable positions, eg. the swan, the swooping dove, the *sticky belly flap cock*.

Palmela and her five sisters *n. prop*. The right hand.

Palmela Handerson *n*. One's dream date to go out for a cruise in the *wanking chariot*.

palmesan *n*. The result of *pulling the pope's hat off* repeatedly and excessively without pausing to perform the occasional spot of basic genital maintenance in between. Particularly rife amongst those presently seeking gainful employment. Also *dolecelatte*.

palm fruit *n*. A lady's *chestular* offerings.

palmistry *n*. A mystic art involving the flat of the hand and the *cock*. The skilled *palmist* is able to look a few minutes into the future and foresee a period of mopping up *jizz*.

palmouflage *n*. Any form of *grumbular* disguise utilized when approaching the tills at the newsagent, eg. A copy of the *'Spectator'* wrapped round *'Razzle'*, or a copy of *'Razzle'* wrapped round *'New Cunts 85'*.

palmorama *n*. A late night 'investigative' report into the American porn industry or similar, eagerly watched by single men who have a penchant for hard news. A *masturmentary, rudimentary*.

palm Sunday *n*. A relaxing *day of wrist* spent in one's own company in the absence of other weekend commitments.

palm ticklers *n*. Small, flat *lils* with protruding nipples. *Empire biscuits*.

panaconda *n*. A South American *dirt snake* of enormous length, that suffocates its victims if they get too close.

panda's eye *n*. A *ringpiece*.

pander *1*. *v*. To act as a go-between in an act of sexual intrigue. e.g, to go and buy a hamster and some parcel tape for that odd couple in the flat below. *2*. *n*. A large, bamboo-eating mammal.

panderer *n*. One who *panders*.

panhandle *n*. An erect penis, *wood, stalk*, a *bonk on*.

panhandle pipes *n*. A Peruvian sex act, whereby a woman blows across the top of several men's *cocks* of differing length side by side. Presumably in a shopping precinct.

panjammer *n*. A stool that laughs in the face of the flush. A *U-blocker*, a *plumber's bonus*, a *crowd pleaser*.

pan of burnt chips *n*. *orthodont*. Descriptive of dentition that leaves a lot to be desired. *'So in she comes with another fucking fishbone stuck in her craw. So she opens her mouth and it's like a pan of burnt*

chips in there. I know she's 102, but for Christ's sake, she should have had them out years ago.' (from *'The Memoirs of Doctor Gladstone Gamble, Balmoral GP in Residence'*).

pan pipes *n*. A simple wind instrument that plays haunting music in the *shit house*.

pan scourer *n*. A vagina covered in a coarser grade of *muff swarf. Brillo fanny*.

pan smile *n*. The crescent-shaped *piss*-bleached patch of carpet that grins yellowly around the base of the toilet. The *Queen Mum's smile*.

pantballing *n*. An involuntary, messy but exciting sport, usually played on Saturday and Sunday mornings by men who were copiously *refreshed* on dark beers and a *Ruby Murray* the previous evening.

pant hamster *n*. Natural prey of the *one-eyed trouser snake*.

pantilever *n*. *Piss handle*.

pant moustache *n*. Effect achieved when the *mapatasi* extends symmetrically beyond either side of the *shreddies*. *Thigh brows*.

pants *1*. *interj*. Exclamation of dismay. *2*. *adj & n*. Rubbish, *shit, pig's arse, bollocks. 'You're talking pants!'*

pant stripper *n*. Any fancy alcoholic drink that more or less guarantees free access to the *hairy pie*.

pantymonium *n*. A flatulent charivari. A loud volley of *farts* causing havoc in the *undercrackers*.

pap baffle *n*. The scrunched-up piece of *shit scrape* placed in the *pan* which makes the person in the next cubicle genuinely believe that your *crap* doesn't make a 'plop' when it hits the water.

paperchase *1*. *n*. The athletic pursuit of *bumwad* from cubicle to cubicle with trousers and *grundies* around one's ankles. 2. *n.* The manic sprint around the house trying to pick up all the incriminating soiled tissues and *grot mags* one has strewn about before the wife returns from her shopping expedition.

paper cut *n.* Opposite of a *wizard's sleeve*. A *fanny* tighter than an *OJ's glove*.

paper hanger's bucket *n.* A big sloppy *twat* full of wallpaper paste.

paper saver *n.* A bowel movement that leaves the paper clean straight off the tee.

Papillon's purse *euph.* The rectal orifice when used as a repository for valuables, eg. when in a prison, boarding school or whilst negotiating the 'Nothing to Declare' channel of a Turkish airport. From the film starring Steve McQueen in which the convicts stashed their cash up the pipe.

papper *v.* To *shit*. *'Oh no, I think I just pappered me trolleys. So it's over to John Kettley for the weather whilst I have a look.'*

paps *n. arch.* Olde Worlde *Tittes*.

papsack *n.* A pair of *titpants*, a *knocker hopper*. A *brassiere*.

paraffin *n. rhym. slang.* A gentleman of the road. A hobo. From paraffin lamp = *Harold Ramp*.

parallel parked *adj.* In bed together, having sex. *'Were you parallel parked with her last night?' 'Not half! I was in up to the bumper mate.'*

paralytically incorrect *n.* A consequence of heavy intoxication where one's easy-going, tolerant views are discarded in favour of a rather more robust manifesto.

parfume de plop *n.* Acrid odour which accompanies a *twin tone* and heralds the arrival in the *bomb bay* of a *Peter O'Toole*.

Parisian breasts *n.* See *lung warts*.

park and ride *1. n.* Scheme run by one's local council. *2. n.* Scheme run by one's local prostitutes. *3. n.* Hurried intercourse in the back seat of a stationary car. A *rear-end shunt*.

park the custard *v.* To vomit.

park the fudge *v.* To *shit*, pass a stool, *crimp off a length*.

park the pink bus v. To *slip* a lady a *length*. *'Time for bed. Come on, let's park the pink bus in the furry garage.' 'Okay. Then we can have a fuck.'*

park the tiger *v.* To puke, *yodel*, let out a *technicolour yawn*.

park your breakfast *v.* Light a *bum cigar, lay a cable*.

parlour *n.* Place where one is only allowed on special occasions. The *bonus tunnel*.

parp *1. onomat.* A romantic foreplay technique whereby one squeezes a breast in the same way that a clown would honk a car horn. *2. n. onomat.* A *fart*.

parson's sack *n.* The swollen state of a *scrotbag* which is as *full as a fat bird's shoe* following an enforced period of celibacy and/or masturbatory abstinence. *'Testicular pressure. The greatest internal pressure sustained in a pair of testicles is one of 65 atmospheres (995lb/sq.in) or approximately 49,400mm of mercury at sea level, in the parson's sack of the pop singer Sir Cliff Richard (GB), following a 45-year build up of seminal fluid'.* (from *'The Viz Sexist Book of Records'*, Boxtree £4.99 or 3 copies for 10p at car boot sales).

particulars *n*. Of low budget British sex comedies involving police officers, ladies' *bills*, knickers. *'Excuse me, madam, but I may need to take down your particulars. And have a look at your snatch.'*

parts of shame *n*. A God botherer's genitals.

pasata grin *n*. *Mexican lipstick, clown's smile*.

passion cosh *n*. A stout, six-inch, hand-held weapon. With all veins up the side.

passion fingers *n*. *Aus. milit*. An Australian army term for a clumsy fellow, ie. everything he touches he *fucks*.

passion flaps *n*. A more romantic alternative to *piss flaps*.

passion pit *n*. Bed, *fart sack, scratcher, wanking chariot*.

passion wagon *n*. Clapped-out van, usually a Ford Transit, with blacked-out windows and a *piss*-stained mattress and several empty beer cans in the back. Also *shaggin' wagon, spambulance*.

pass the mic *1. n*. A section from the woeful TV show *'The Hitman and Her'*, where a couple of *slappers* took it in turns to wail into a microphone. *2. v.* A scene in all decent *grumble flicks* where a couple of *slappers* take it in turns to suck the leading man's *charlie*.

pastie baby *n*. An ear-ringed neonate sucking on a *Greggs' dummy*.

pastytute *n*. A *good time girl* whose idea of a good time involves a couple of Steak Bakes and a custard slice from Greggs'. A prostitute who is a good deal heavier than her *slagboard postcard* picture might suggest.

pathfinder *n*. An *air biscuit* that lets one know in no uncertain terms that it's time for a *tom tit*.

patty *n*. A posh lady's *snatch* ie, what HM the Queen calls her *cunt*.

Paul Daniels' hankie *sim*. Descriptive of a flaccid *member* being manually encouraged into a lady's opening. From the 'hankie in the fist' trick performed by the eponymous bald magician. *Playing snooker with a piece of string, pushing marshmallows into a moneybox*.

Paula, do a *v*. To relieve oneself in a public place. From Olympic marathon live TV *shitter* and London marathon live TV *pisser* Paula Radcliffe. Also *do a Radcliffe*.

Paula, have a *v*. To interrupt an important task in order to have a 'wee'. *'Dr. Barnard, we're ready for you to put in the new heart.' 'Hang on a tick. I'm just off for a quick Paula.'*

Pauline *rhym. slang*. A *minge*. From *'Eastenders'* misery-guts Pauline Fowler = *growler*.

pavement pizza *n*. The contents of your stomach as they appear after *barfing* in the street. A *parked tiger*.

pavement skating *n*. Sliding, Torville & Dean-style, on a moist *barker's egg* whilst running for a bus.

Pavlov's log *n. medic*. Conditioned reflex action causing one's *bomb bay doors* to start opening upon seeing a toilet. From the famous experiments of Russian psychologist Professor Ernst Pavlov, who rang a bell every time his dog done a *shit*.

pay in installments *v*. To be forced

to make multiple lavatory visits to relieve the *Camillas* after a night of *Ruby Murray* and brown ales, or after eating a typical meal at a certain Scarborough hotel.

peach stone *n.* A hibernal scrotum.

peanut brittle *n. medic.* Condition of a hardened drinker whose only solid intake for some days has been items available at the bar. Symptoms include mental fragility and uncontrolled shaking. *'Harry froze as they spotted an unshaven Mr. Snape slumped at the bar of the Black Cauldron. 'We're done for now', he cried. 'No we're not,' replied Hermione. 'He's been drinking all weekend and he's completely peanut brittle.''* (from *'Harry Potter and the Wizard's Sleeve'* by JK Rowling).

Pearl & Dean necklace *n.* A frankly unlikely sexual scenario, where one *jizzes* onto one's girlfriend in the pictures, presumably whilst shouting: 'Pa-paa...pa-paa...pa-paa-paa... pa-pa-pa...paaaaow!'

pearl divers' lungs *sim.* Descriptive of the impressive ability of a man to *go down* for prolonged periods without the need to come up for fresh air.

Pearl Harbour *n. prop.* A place where one's *Jap's eye* commits atrocities.

pearl necklace *n.* Those globular consequences of having a *sausage sandwich* at the *Billy Mill roundabout* that so delight the ladies.

pebble dash *v.* To *crop spray* the toilet bowl with *clarts.*

pecker *1. n. US.* Penis. *2. n. UK.* Nose.

pecker wreckers *n.* A *bird*'s corrective orthodontical ironwork.

pecking *v.* The head-nodding

motion exhibited by one in such a *state of refreshment* that they can hardly keep awake.

pedal *rhym. slang.* To commit an act of *self-pollution.* From pedal and crank = *Jodrell Bank.*

pee *1. v.* To *piss. 2. n.* Some *piss.*

peel *1. v .* To strip, pose nude. *2. v.* When so doing, to draw back the *beef curtains. 'Crikey, have you seen Razzle? I never knew Joanne Guest was a peeler.'*

peel and polish *n.* A swiftly-administered, no frills *blow job. 'Ten quid for full sex, fifteen for anal, three quid for a quick peel and polish.'*

peeling the carrot *v.* Spanking the monkey.

peel the furry prawn *v.* To manually attend to the *pudenders* of a young lady who is disinclined to wash.

peemale *n.* A man who urinates sitting down, possibly as a means of expressing solidarity with women, but more likely through alcoholic exhaustion. One who *drives from the ladies' tee.*

peep over the garden fence *v.* To attempt to conceal an unwanted erection by flattening it upwards against the stomach and tucking the *helmet* behind the waistband of the underpants. A *Kilroy*, a *Chad.*

peg *v.* Of a lady, to do a gentleman up the *council gritter* with a *strap-on.*

PEGOOMHS *abbrev.* The sudden psychological condition which manifests itself upon completion of coitus. Post Ejaculatory Get Out Of My House Syndrome.

Pele's cock *n. medic.* An inability to attain an erection, with reference to the Brazilian goal ace's *cock drop* ads. Male sexual impotence.

pelican's beak *n.* A flappy double

chin that is unpleasant to look at, eg. that of the late Thora Hird, or Hugh Lloyd.

pelican's yawn *sim*. A *fanny* big enough to hold 50lb of fish. A *hippo's mouth*.

pelt lapper *n*. A lady in *comfortable shoes*, a *tennis fan*.

penalty pox *n*. A *clap* contracted from a bout of adulterous *futtery*.

Penfold has drowned *exclam*. A witty warning made to one's housemates that there is a mole-like substance floating in the *shit pan*. From 1970s cartoon vermin Dangermouse's annoying *turd* of a sidekick.

penguin 1. *v*. Act performed by a prostitute whereby, upon receiving payment but before providing service, she pulls the gentleman's trousers around his ankles and runs off down the alley. From the resemblance of the client's gait to that of the flightless arctic bird as he attempts to give chase, much to the amusement of onlookers. 2. *n*. The trouser-ankled, cheeks apart waddle adopted by one who has been surprised after *dropping the kids off at the pool* by a lack of *bumwad*.

penile dementia *n*. *medic*. The effect a *panhandle* has on its owner in the company of a *horn-bag*, causing him to temporarily forget about his wife and children.

penis *n*. The *Right Honourable Member for Pantchester*.

penis fly trap *n*. A precariously balanced toilet seat which stays vertical for a few moments before dropping upon unsuspecting *helmets* in its path. A *knob chopper*.

penny dreadful 1. *n*. A cheap, third-rate novel picked up when nothing else is available. 2. *n*. A cheap, third-rate woman picked up when nothing else is available.

penny farthings *n*. A comically mismatched set of breasts. Wonky *tits*.

pensioner falling downstairs *sim*. Descriptive of the noises made by a series of solid motions hitting the water in quick succession.

pensioner's banquet *n*. Free food samples in supermarkets, eg. bits of cheese, etc.

pensioner's leg *n*. A thin, pale, knobbly, varicose-veiny penis.

pensioner's tits, as low as a *sim*. Descriptive of something that is lower than one would reasonably expect. *'The ball pitched on middle and off and stayed as low as a pensioner's tits all the way to the stumps. A terrific delivery.'* (Bob Willis commentating on England v Zimbabwe, BBC Radio *'Test Match Special'*, summer 2003).

peperami wrapper *n*. The *fiveskin* or *leg warmer*.

Percy 1. *n*. UK. Penis. *'I'm just off to point Percy at the porcelain.'* 2. *n*. A small green 0-6-0 saddle tank steam train named after the late Rev. W Awdrey's small, green penis.

Percy Thrower's lawn *n*. A *muff* that has been allowed to go to seed. A hairy, unkempt *fanny*. *Terry Waite's allotment*.

period drama *n*. Moody and erratic behaviour of women at times of menstruation. A *blobstrop, tammy huff*.

period features 1. *n*. Blocked fireplaces, draughty sash windows, warped panelled doors, paint-encrusted decorative mouldings and other sundry desirable architectural bits and pieces which allow thieving estate agents to bump up the prices of houses. *2. n.* In women, short temper, sore nipples, irrational behaviour and the propensity to throw sharp objects violently across the room.

perousal *n.* The frisson of sexual arousal attained whilst flicking through a prospective purchase in *Grumbelows*.

perpetual motion *n.* A seemingly endless *shit*.

Perry Como *rhym. slang.* An easy listening *crafty butcher*.

perseverance soup *n.* The tiny tears from the *hog's eye* which precede ejaculation. The clear secretion which lubricates the glans. That which comes out of the kitchen before the main course. *Dew on the lily.*

personalities *n.* Tabloid euphemism for breasts. *Charms, assets, terrible arthritis. 'My, you've got a lovely pair of personalities.'*

Peruvian num-nums *n.* The involuntary chewing noises emitted whilst turning over in one's sleep during the early hours of the morning.

perv windows *n.* Sunglasses.

petal dick *n.* A gentleman drinker who requires the toilet before his fifth pint. A *shandy pants, shandy pandy.*

Peter O'Toole *rhym. slang.* A *Thora Hird.*

Peter two pumps *n.* An inexperienced *swordsman*. A *two push Charlie.*

petit filou *n.* A *hairy yoghurt pot* so small that the *naughty spoon* has trouble getting in. A *mouse's ear.*

pezzle *n.* How a cornish farmer probably refers to his *slag hammer.*

phalitosis *n. medic.* Post-*horatio*

breath.

phallucy *n.* Any statement made by a man about the size of his *third leg*, eg. in the readers' letters page of a *grumble mag* or a small ad in a *greet & meat* mag.

phantom farter *n.* An anonymous *benefactor.*

phantom of the opera *n.* Appearance of a *stick flick* actress after her co-star has *crashed his yoghurt truck* down the side of her face.

pharoah's tomb *1. sim.* Descriptive of a post-argument atmosphere. *2. rhym. slang.* The spare room.

philosopher's stone *n.* A *turd* that emerges after a couple of hours' intense concentration.

phlegm brûlée *n.* A particularly creamy *docker's omelette* with a hard crust. Usually hocked up during a hangover.

photo finish *n.* A session of *horizontal jogging* in which both contestants break the tape at the same time. Also *dead heat.*

phuq *n. & v.* Ingenious alternative to the word *fuck* which, whilst perfectly understandable, is able to evade the attentions of over-solicitous business e-mail censoring systems.

phwoarberries *n.* Big, ripe, juicy *tits*. With cream all over them. Breasts which, even when covered up elicit a strangulated cry of 'phwoar!' in the style of Kenneth Connor spotting Joan Sims in the shower in *'Carry On Up the Jungle'.*

piabetic *n.* A larger-boned fellow who risks falling into a coma if not kept regularly supplied with pastry-based products.

Picasso arse *n.* A lady's *chuff* in

knickers so tight that she appears to have four buttocks.

Picasso face *n.* Descriptive of a bird who is certainly no oil painting.

picture but no sound *euph.* Descriptive of the wife's mood when one rolls in from the pub as *refreshed as a newt*.

piddle *1. v.* To *pee*. *2. n.* Some *pee*.

piddle paddle *n.* An unconvincing and unathletic 'quick dip in the ocean' taken whilst at the seaside, where one ventures in only waist deep and emerges shortly thereafter with a refreshingly empty bladder. A *seawee*.

pie blight *n. Muff druff*.

pie curious *adj.* Descriptive of a person who, whilst not a full blown *Duke of Giblets*, is nevertheless not averse to a spot of sly *salad-dodging* from time to time.

pie-hider *n.* A *gunt, bilge tank, muff pelmet*. The kind of overhanging gut that allows a lady to strip from the waist down whilst still retaining her modesty.

pie-liner *n.* A femidom.

pie shifter *n.* A big-boned person who can single-handedly clear the Ginster's display in their local petrol station. *'Famous people who have died on 11th February: Pietro Cataldi, mathematician, in Bologna, Italy, 1626; Rene Descartes, mathematician, in Stockholm, Sweden, 1650; Willhelm Killing, mathematician, in Munster, Germany, 1923; Egbert van Kampen, mathematician, in Baltimore, Maryland, 1942; Vladimir Smirnov, mathematician, Leningrad, USSR, 1974; William Conrad, pie shifter, in Hollywood, California, 1994.'* (from *'Schott's Increasingly Desperate Christmas Gift Book'* 2004).

piece of piss *n.* An easy thing. *'Hey, this show jumping thing is a piece of piss'* (Christopher Reeve), *'Hey, adjusting television aerials is a piece of piss'* (Rod Hull).

pieceps *n.* Bulging stomach muscles made famous by former Everton goalkeeper Neville Southall.

pieman's wig *1. n.* An artificial hairpiece worn by a purveyor of pastry-enveloped foodstuffs. *2. n.* An untidy *cunt-rug*.

pig at a tatty, going at it like a *sim. Yorks.* To engage in an act of oral pleasure with uninhibited gusto in Yorkshire. *'Eeh, by gum, Cathy lass. Slow tha' sen down a bit', said Heathcliffe. "Appen tha's going at it like a pig at a tatty.'* (from *'Wuthering Heights'* by Charlotte Bronte).

pig at the gate *euph.* A *mole at the counter*.

pig bite *n.* A poetic term for the vagina. *'A daughter of the Gods, divinely tall / And with a pig bite like a horse's collar.'* (from *'A Dream of Fair Women'* by Alfred Lord Tennyson).

pigboard *n.* The rear wall of a metropolitan phonebox.

pigbox *n.* A Nissan Micra full of rough women, driving round a provincial town playing Destiny's Child and hunting for *cock*.

pigeon's breakfast *n.* Some sick. A *pavement pizza*.

pigeon's chest *n.* The female swimsuit *lunchbox*. The *beetle bonnet, shark's fin*.

pig fart *n.* The erotic sound a lady's intimate parts may occasionally make whilst she is in the process of getting a good *stuffing*. A *queef*.

pig's tits *rhym. slang.* The *shits*.

'After you've been to the rub a dub, climb the apples and pears to the Curry Capital, Bigg Market, Newcastle upon Tyne, for a Ruby Murray that will give you the pig's tits, or your money back.' (Advert in *'Country Life'* magazine).

pig's toe *n.* *Beetle bonnet, camel's foot.*

PIK *acronym.* Pig In Knickers. An extremely unattractive fleshy woman.

pikea *n.* Open air broken furniture showroom. Usually set up in Essex laybys after the travellers have moved on.

pikey bollards *n.* Large rocks and boulders placed along roadsides in areas where the local inhabitants already have plenty of pegs.

pikey's banquet *n.* The sort of dodgy-looking and hideously-over-priced burgers and hotdogs which are sold at fairgrounds and festivals.

pikey's bonus *n.* A *grumble flick* found inside a stolen video recorder. A *scouser's jackpot.*

pikey's pit stop *n.* A visit to a garage forecourt to refuel one's car when one has neither the means nor inclination to pay. A *splash 'n' dash.*

pikeys' wedding *n.* A *pagga,* a fierce fight. *'January 18th, 1915. This morning some of the chaps went over the top. The German guns were merciless, cutting them down like wheat stalks before the scythe. I have never witnessed such a pikeys' wedding and I'm sure it will haunt me for the rest of my days.'* (from *'The Diary of Rupert Brooke'*).

pile high club *1.* *n.* The notional society of fellows who have distin-guished themselves by *pappering their trolleys* whilst seated. *2. n.* Exclusive brotherhood of those who have earned their *brown wings.*

pile of dead fannies, smells like a *sim.* Descriptive of something which gives off a foul, fishy odour. *'Bloody hell, Dr. Von Hagens. What have you got in your garage? It smells like a pile of dead fannies.' 'It's a pile of dead fannies, mein dear chap.'*

pilgrim's pocket *n.* A particularly dry *fanny. 'Edwina was powerless to resist. John's eyes burned into hers like semi-precious lapis lazulis. His strong arms enfolded her body as she felt herself being swept away on a mistral of passion. She gasped as she felt his powerful, but gentle fingers teasing at the moist flower of her secret sanctum. 'Fuck me, your minge is sopping,' he exclaimed. 'Norma's twat's always dry as a pilgrim's pocket.''* (from *'The Junior Health Minister and The Chief Whip'*, by Barbara Cartland).

pillicock *n. arch.* A *tummy banana.* From the pig's *pizzle* used in an early form of badminton.

pillock *n.* Tame, TV sitcom-friendly insult. Possibly derived from *pillicock.*

pillow biter *n.* One who bites their pillow, often in a moment of steeply-raked horticultural delight. Also *mattress muncher.*

pillow mint *1. n.* Small, inexpensive chocolate treat left on a guest's bed in better hotels in order to create the illusion that customer satisfaction is of the slightest importance to the management. *2. n.* A hefty *feeshus* left in the *pan* with the express intention of offending the next occupant of the *shithouse*.

pills *n*. Pods, knackers, niags.

pilot light *n*. An ex-socialite now restrained by the *pink handcuffs*, ie. one who never goes out.

pinballing *v*. To make progress home from the boozer by a series of ricochets from one item of street furniture to the next. Accompanied by the ringing of bells and clunking noises.

pinch a loaf *v*. To *curl one off*.

pinch of snuff *rhym. slang*. A *crafty butcher*.

pineapple *rhym. slang*. Semen. From pineapple chunk = *spunk*.

pinhole *n*. A *Mary* that makes a *mouse's ear* look like a *hippo's mouth*.

pink *v*. Of a lady, to make a *fanny slug* on a window for the amusement and edification of passers by.

pink, the *n*. A really good eyeful of the female genitals, esp. in a *meat mag*.

pink bat's face *n*. A nocturnal, high-pitched *fanny*.

pink berets *n*. Large, flat breasts with stiff *nips*.

pink cigar n. Penis. *'Tell me Madam, do you perchance smoke the pink cigar?'* Not to be confused with *bum cigar*, except in Germany.

pink Darth Vader *n*. *Knob*. From the *'Star Wars'* character with a *bell end* helmet.

pink oboe *n*. Penis. *'Tell me Madam, do you perchance play the pink oboe?'*

pink pillows *n*. Ladies' *love cushions*, bosoms.

pink shit, have a *v*. The end of a romantic evening of *back door work*. The termination of the process of anal intercourse.

pinksmith *n*. One who is expert in *fannycraft*. A *crumpeteer*.

pink steel *n*. Even harder than *wood*.

pink ticket *n*. Imaginary *vadge* visa issued to a husband when he spends the night apart from his wife. *'Eureka! I've got my pink ticket for the conference on Tuesday.'*

pink velvet sausage wallet *n*. Short for *quim*.

pink wafer *n*. A *blurtch* which resolutely refuses to exude *fanny batter* even after being lovingly coerced for several minutes.

pint glass figure *n*. Like an hourglass figure, but with very little narrowing in the middle, eg. Vanessa Feltz, Fern Britton.

pintle *n*. Olde Worlde Chopper. *Pipe cleaner*.

pip *n*. An upper class *hat* of the kind one might imagine Penelope Keith *dropping*.

pipe *1. n. Fr.* An act of oral love. A *nosh, chewie, blow-job*. *2. n. Cock*.

pipe bomb *n*. An explosive *shit* that goes off without warning in the *pan*, causing massive collateral damage.

pipecleaner *1. n*. Furry wire used by children to make models in playschool. *2. n*. The first *piss* taken after committing an act of *self-pollution*. *3. n*. A *blood sausage*.

pipe smoker *1. n. US. Botter*. *2. n*. A person who smokes a pipe.

pirate *n*. A *breastitute* lady, ie. one with a sunken chest.

pirate of men's pants *n*. Swashbuckling term for your *jolly rogerer*, *cock*, penis.

pirate's piss *n*. The *piss* you have with one eye shut to improve tar-getting after a long night *on the pop.*

piss *1. v.* To micturate. *2. n.* Some micturition. *3. adv.* Extremely. *'That driving test was piss easy'. 'Your three-point turn was piss poor.'*

pissabled *adj.* A state of drunken infirmity whereby one is unable to walk upstairs, park one's car properly, etc. Also *shandycapped.*

piss bliss *n.* The moment just before a long-awaited *scoot*, when a gentleman keeps it in for a couple of seconds longer, primarily for a cheap thrill.

pissed *1. adj. UK. Soused, potted, refreshed. 2 adj. US.* Annoyed. *'That cotton-pickin' Osama Bin Laden has gotten me real pissed, bub.'*

pissed as a tramp *adj.* To be so inebriated as to not care where one sleeps.

pissed up *adj.* Descriptive of a fellow who is comprehensively *refreshed.*

piss flaps *1. n. Labia, beef curtains. 2. interj.* Exclamation of disappointment. *'Oh piss flaps! I never win the Lottery!'*

piss-fork *n.* A post-coital bidirectional urine flow. *Twin-jets.*

pisshead's labourer *n.* A barman.

pissing in the wind *v.* Wasting one's time, attempting the impossible.

piss it up the wall *v.* To fritter away something, eg. money, talent, urine.

piss it *v.* To do something *piss* simple, *piss* easily.

piss like an American fighter pilot *v.* When extremely *Brahms*, to micturate in a haphazard and inaccurate fashion, ie. spraying urine all over the floor, seat, shoes, John

Simpson, etc.

piss mist *n.* The fine mist that forms around a urinal trough at shin level when having a *gypsy's kiss.* Only noticeable when wearing shorts. *Wee fret.*

piss off *1. exclam.* A polite form of *fuck off. 2. v.* To annoy.

piss on your chips *v.* To put yourself at a long-term disadvantage through a foolhardy short-term action. *Fart on your Weetabix*

piss, piece of *n.* A portion of easiness. *'Hey, flying this Concorde out of Charles De Gaulle Airport is a piece of piss.'*

piss polo *1. n.* Game of skill whereby disinfectant tablets are pointlessly manoeuvred in a urinal trough by the participants' *wazz* streams. *2. n.* A very unsuccessful flavour of sweet.

piss porch *n.* The skin awning which protects a lady's *bald man in a boat* from the weather.

piss pot *1. n.* Lavatory bowl. *2. n.* Idiot, fool. *3. n.* Old-fashioned motorcyclist's helmet.

piss proud *adj.* To be the owner of a *dawn horn*, a *morning glory.*

piss rusty water *v.* To pass liquid *feeshus.*

piss sauna *n.* The all-enveloping fog of urine steam in an outside pub lavatory on a cold winter's evening.

piss up *n.* An ale soirée, a social gathering of boozing companions.

piss whip *n.* The effect created by drunkenly waving one's *pezzle* up and down whilst having a *gypsy's kiss.*

piss whistle *n.* A *bed flute*, a *pink oboe.*

piss with the lid down *v.* To do something very foolish, to make a schoolboy error. *"Mr. Paravicini's* *murderer is in this very room, and I'm afraid it is you, Brigadier Lewerthwaite!' cried Miss Marple. The room fell silent. 'After murdering him, you dressed him in his pyjamas and carefully put his cufflinks on the dressing table to give the impression that the crime had been committed after bedtime, when you were playing bridge with myself and the Bishop. However, I'm afraid you pissed with the lid down, Brigadier,' she said. 'What the deuce do you mean?' he blustered. 'Simply this,' she continued. 'You placed the cufflinks on the right hand side of the dressing table when the position of the inkwell on his Davenport clearly showed him to have been left handed.' (from 'Ten Little Black and White Minstrels', by Agatha Christie).*

pissy fit *n.* The kind of foul-tempered strop that can only be achieved when one is *blind refreshed*.

pisticuffs *n.* A comical, drunken attempt at combat.

pisto *n.* Nasally-abusive miasma prevalent in tower block lifts, multi-storey car park stairs or around gentlemen of the road. 'Ah, pisto.'

pistorectomy *n. medic.* The act of vomiting up one's own internal organs whilst life-threateningly *merry*.

pit bull *n.* A stocky, tenacious *Thora*, usually the final one of a visit, that hangs onto the *ringpiece* like grim death. An *angry monkey*, a *Harold Lloyd*.

pitch a tent *v.* To get *wood* either beneath the bed linen, or conspicuously in your trousers.

pitch inspection *n.* The checking of one's *bills* for any sign of a *bonus ball* after a risky *Exchange & Mart*.

pitch invasion *1. n.* Entertaining 1970s football match behaviour in which the crowd unexpectedly leaves the stands and makes its way onto the field of play. *2. n.* Entertaining *farty-arse* behaviour in which a quantity of *feeshus* unexpectedly leaves the *arse* and makes its way onto the *gusset* of the *trolleys*. A *follow through*.

pit clit *n. coll.* Gorgeous lycra-clad *blart* that stand around holding umbrellas on the starting grid of F1 races.

pit fillers *n.* Massive *thruppeny bits* which emigrate towards a bird's oxters when she's lying on her back.

pit prop *n.* Strategic structural member found in a *passion pit*. A *tent pole*, a *dawn horn*.

pizzle *n. medic.* A sorry-looking *penis*, like one would imagine the Pope has.

placket *n. arch.* A Medieval maiden's *cunt*.

plamff *n. Scot.* One who, apparently bored of sniffing bicycle seats, opts to cut out the middle man and sniffs the gussets of ladies' soiled *bills* instead, eg. Jonathan Ross OBE.

Planter's hum *n.* The nauseating smell of *air croutons*. From the aroma of a freshly-opened bag of dry-roasted peanuts.

plasterer's radio *sim.* Descriptive of a lucky lady who is heavily adorned with *jelly jewellery*. Frequently found on Japanese and American cyber-scud.

plastic cockney *n.* A *mockney*. A posh person who affects to be an

Eastender, eg. Ben Elton, Nigel Kennedy, Shane McGowan.

plasticine hammer, knocking a nail in with a *sim.* Descriptive of the difficulty experienced when trying to *bang* a young lady who has signally failed to provoke a sufficient level of tumescence in one's *chap.* *Playing snooker with a piece of string.*

plastic paddy *n.* A posh person who affects to be Irish, eg. Shane McGowan.

plate *1. n. Arch. Horatio. 2. n. Arch. Cumulonimbus.* A general purpose term for oral/genital shenanigans performed behind a Victorian skip. *'How much, love?' 'Twenty bob for full, ten for hand or fifteen for plate.'*

playaway *n.* Masturbatory technique of chaps not overly-endowed in the trouser department, eg. Pygmies, Jamie Theakston, the Rt. Hon. Jack Straw MP. From the song lyrics: 'One finger, one thumb, keep moving.'

play dough *n.* Disposable income.

play good cock/bad cock v. A popular method of *self-interrogation* in which alternate violent and gentle strokes are employed to get the suspect to *spill his guts.*

playing Buckaroo with Muhammad Ali, like *sim.* Descriptive of a situation where one cannot lose, eg. racing Eddie Large up Mount Snowdon, entering the 'Midday Money' competition on ITV's 'Good Morning' programme, or standing for election against John Redwood.

playing chopsticks *v.* A beginners' duet. Mutual masturbating.

playing snooker with a piece of string *sim.* Trying to *sink a pink*

with a *marshmallow cue.*

playing the accordian *v.* To alternately pull apart and squeeze together the cheeks of one's *arse* when perched on the *choddy hopper* in an effort to encourage the last bit of *shit* to drop off before polishing one's *nipsy.*

playing the bone-a-phone *v. Wanking,* pulling oneself a *hand shandy.*

playing the invisible banjo *v.* George Formby-style female masturbation technique.

playing the upside-down piano *sim.* The overture to the second movement of *hiding the sausage. Firkyfoodling.*

play statues *v.* To stop suddenly in the street with a pensive look upon one's face as one tries to determine whether one has just done a *guff* or a *poo.*

play the B-side *v.* To swap from the Missionary position to the *doggie* position. *'I got fed up with looking at her face while I was giving her one, so I flipped her over and played the B-side.'*

play the back nine v. *Irish golf.* To use one's *wood* to play into the bunker, *get the dog in the bathtub.*

play the bacon kazoo *v.* To *nosh* noisily on a *lab kebab.*

play the pink oboe *v.* To perform oral sex on a man, presumably with a thin reed sticking out of his *hog's eye.* Often used to denote homosexuality. *'I didn't know Michael Barrymore played the pink oboe.'*

play the violin *v.* To scrape your *bow* against a lady's *G-string.* To make sweet music with a lady after merely pushing the *driptray* of her *dunghampers* to one side.

play the whale *v.* To *spew.*

pleasure *v.* Tabloidese, to *suck* or *wank off.* To perform a lewd act on oneself or on someone else.

pleasure trove *n.* A dazzling collection of *niff mags* found under a hedge or on top of an older brother's wardrobe.

plinth *v.* Of males *on the job*, to manoeuvre oneself into a comfortable position for penetration.

plonker *1. n.* Penis. *2. n. Crap* put-down line from Britain's favourite tedious TV sitcom.

plop corn *n.* Thrill-seeking undigested yellow foodstuff which rides one's *log flume.*

ploughing the sand *1. v.* A seemingly never ending and unrewarding job, eg. painting the Forth Rail Bridge, watching an *'Only Fools and Horses'* Christmas Special. *2. n.* Being *on the job* whilst far too *inebriated* to *shoot one's stack.*

ploughman's *n.* The *barse, taint, notcher* etc. The area between the cheese and the pickle. *'Mr. Kneivel's motorbike hit the last bus at an approximate speed of 120mph, before careering into several fruit machines and a tuppenny waterfall. He suffered severe internal injuries including fractured ribs, two broken legs and a fractured skull. He also ripped his ploughman's wide open on the petrol tank.'* (Doctor's report, Las Vegas County General Hospital, 1978).

pluke *n.* A facial spot. A zit.

plumbago *n.* painful ache in the *Gladstones* caused by over-revving the *spunk* engines without releasing the *horse's handbrake. Lover's nuts.*

plumber's bonus *n.* A *U-blocker* of such proportions, it has to be dealt with by someone who has served an apprenticeship. A *windfall.*

plumber's lung *n.* A violent *arse bark.*

plumber's privilege *n.* The ancient right granted to plumbers, which entitles them to relieve themselves into whichever appliance they have just installed, eg. sink, bath, washing machine etc.

plumber's toolbag *n. Furry bicycle stand, mott.*

plumber's wipe *n.* The art of shoving one's hand into a lady's *driptray*, and rubbing backwards and forwards, in the same way that a plumber would wipe a recently-soldered joint.

plum duff *rhym. slang.* A homosexualist.

plumpa-lumpa *n.* A short fat *bird* with a bright orange face.

plumper *n.* A *Buffet slayer.* A lady of ample proportions.

plums *n. Knackers, balls,* testicles.

plum sauce *n.* Ejaculate.

plunker *n. US. Johnny,* a jumpsuit for a plonker. A *Trojan.*

Plymouth Argyles *rhym. slang. Piles.*

poacher's folly *1. n.* In traditional countryside parlance, the act of shooting at rabbits and thereby scaring away the big game. *2. n.* In nightclub parlance, the act of chatting up the first rough *bird* one sees in a club and thereby scaring away the decent *tussage.*

poacher's pocket *1. n.* A fashion accessory favoured by illicit hunters and shoplifting television celebrities. *2. n.* A very large *fanny.*

Pob lips *n.* The state of the *ringpiece* during an acute bout of diarrhoea. From the low budget spitting Welsh children's TV puppet of the same name.

pobolycwm *n. Welsh.* Literally 'People who like quim.'

pocket battleship 1. *n.* A compact, heavily-armed warship, such as The Graff Spee. 2. *n.* A short, yet aggressive *hard on.* A Bob Hoskins amongst erections. 3. *n.* An ugly, short *bint,* eg. that fucking nightmare off 'Wife Swap'.

pocket billiards *n.* A game for one player, two *balls,* and a *cock.*

pocket bonk-on *n.* Like pocket chess and pocket Scrabble, a genital erection that is for some reason smaller than usual, but still perfectly functional. Ideal for caravan holidays.

pocket fisherman *n.* He who plays with his *tackle* through his trouser pockets.

pocket frog *n.* A *fart, botty burp, anal announcement.*

pocket pinball *n.* A game where one's testicles are fired up into one's chest, where they ricochet from organ to organ whilst bells ring and one's eyes spin round.

pocket rocket 1. *n* A small, but powerful motorbike. 2. *n.* A small, but powerful *knob.*

podge-on *n.* A small *semi on* which presents one's *old man* in a more favourable light than it deserves. *Half a teacake.*

pod purse *n.* Where the loose change for a *money shot* is kept.

pod race *n.* To *crack one off* in a high-pressure situation where time is of the essence, eg. while the missus is out making a cup of tea.

poe *n.* The *fadge.*

poe slap *n.* A *fanny nanny.*

POETS day *acronym.* Friday. From Piss Off Early, Tomorrow's Saturday.

poffle *v.* To *shart. Gamble and lose.*

pog *n. Scratter.*

pogie *n. US.* Where American *plonkers* go dressed in their *plunkers.*

pogue mahone *exclam. Gael.* Kiss my *arse,* to be sure.

pointer sisters *n.* A slightly perkier version of the *Winslet twins.*

point Percy at the porcelain *v.* To have a *wee-wee.*

poke *v.* What *plonkers* do to *pogies.*

poke holes in a cheap door *phr.* Property of a *diamond cutter.* 'When Elizabeth was near, D'Arcy's heart raced, and he got a panhandle that could poke holes in a cheap door.' (from 'Pride and Prejudice' by Jane Austen).

pokelore *n.* Mythical yarns of exciting sexual adventures spun to mates down the pub.

poke the spider's eye *v.* To dig at one's *claypit* through one's *farting crackers.*

polestruck *adj.* A shallow lady who is erotically fascinated by firemen and their equipment.

pole vault *n.* Vagina, *stench trench,* strong room where the *spam sceptre* can be safely housed.

police horse fart *n.* A *change of heart* capable of dispersing an unruly mob.

policeman's dinner *n. US.* An *arsehole.*

policewoman's treat *n.* A bobby's *bob.*

polish a turd *met.* To fruitlessly attempt to dress up something *shite,* eg. the relaunch of the Morris Marina as the Ital, or putting a baseball cap on William Hague.

polish one's spectacles *v.* To surreptitiously *masturbate* one's penis through one's pockets, eg. when looking for change in a strip club or when sexually aroused on a tube train.

polish the lighthouse *v.* To *throttle Captain Birdseye* in the bath.

POLO *acronym. milit.* Code used on military correspondence prior to coming home from a posting abroad. Pants Off, Legs Open.

polony party *n.* A social gathering of two or more consenting adults where party games include *hide the sausage, park the salami* and *split the kipper*. And one's party bag would contain a slice of cake and a dose of the *clap*. An orgy.

Pompey pineapple *n.* The high tension raked-back hairstyle favoured by *bingo clink*-clad southern slappers.

pompom *n. Jam.* A furry thing waved by cheerleaders to entertain a crowd.

ponce 1. *n.* A *pimp.* 2. *n.* Brian Sewell soundalike. 3. *v.* To borrow something with no intention of giving it back, eg. cigarettes, garden tools, the Elgin marbles.

pong *n.* The smell of a *poot*.

pony *rhym. slang. Shit.* From pony and trap = *crap*.

poo 1. *exclam.* A word spoken with fingers on nostrils to describe an unpleasant odour. 2. *n. Shit.* 3. *v.* To do a *duty*.

pooaplegic *n. medic.* One who, having sat on the toilet for too long, has lost all feeling below the waist. A *crapple*.

Poocomknockerphilication *n. Cleveland steaming*, as performed by Ken Dodd.

poof *n.* A man who doesn't want another pint.

poo fairy *n.* Magical entity which regularly visits the female half of the population, resulting in the male half being under the handy illusion that ladies never need to *lay a cable*.

poof dust *n.* Phrase used by schoolboys to describe talcum powder in the days before there was such a thing as diversity training.

poof's pizza *n.* Quiche. Also *puff's pizza*.

poofter *n. Aus.* An Australian man who doesn't want another ten pints.

poogina *n.* A lady's back *front bottom*.

poomerang *n.* A *turd* which is able to return from the U-bend with twice the force with which it was flushed away in the first place.

poon *n. Fanny, crumpet, toosh.* 'I guess, this means my poon days are over.' (Abraham Lincoln after his inauguration in May 1776). 'Knickers off, this is poon city!' (Bill Clinton after his inauguration in June 1993).

poond *n.* A *gunt*, a *fupa*. From the Geordie 'a poond o' tripe'.

pooning *v.* The act of sniffing ladies' bicycle seats.

poontang 1. *n.* A *fanny*. 2. *n.* Some *fanny*.

poo packer *n.* A *dinner masher*, a *Marmite driller*.

poop catchers *n. Knickers, dung-hampers, bills.*

poop chute *n. The bumhole, arse.*

poo preview *n.* An *air buffet*, an *Exchange and Mart*.

poornography *n. Grumble* of a core which is somewhat less than tumescent. The sort of soft-focus marshmallow-strength *grot* broadcast on Bravo, Men & Motors, or on Channel 5 in the old days before they started doing primetime *farm-*

yard pig wanking. (From poor + nography).

poor sense of direction, have a *v.* Of a man, to be *good with colours.*

poosex *n.* A charming word for *brown love.*

poosticks *n.* Game whereby lolly sticks are inserted into *barkers' eggs* by curious children. *"What are you doing?' squeaked Piglet excitedly. 'I'm pushing a lolly stick into a dog shit,' replied Christopher Robin.'* (from *'When we Were Very, Very Young'* by AA Milne).

poot 1. *v.* To sound one's *botty bugle*, often after eating *musical vegetables.* 2. *n.* A *flies' dinner gong.*

poo tea *n.* An unrefreshing brown infusion made by allowing *logs* to brew in the pot for a long time.

poot flute *n. Trouser trumpet, singing ring, botty bugle, bumhole.*

pooter *n.* The *bum* bellows with which you *poot.* The *poot flute.*

poove *n.* A *puff,* a *ginger beer,* a *pinch of snuff.*

poovery *n. Bottery* and everything associated therewith. *Bumcraft.*

POP *acronym.* Post Orgasmic Piss. *'Thanks for the fuck, Your Majesty. I'm just nipping to the lavvy for a pop.'*

pop a knocker *v.* Of a lady, to over-react to a situation in a melodramatic fashion. *'Christ, love, it was only a chewie off your sister. There's no need to pop a knocker.'*

popazogalou *n.* A *chewie,* a *gobble,* a *blow job.* From the name of the landlord in the film 'Personal Services' who accepted payment in kind.

Popeye eating spinach *sim.* To engage in enthusiastic *cumulonimbus.* With a pipe in one's mouth.

'And the husband of Bathsheba did venture forth for Regal Super Kings that numbered two score and did leave Bathsheba alone in the tent. And David did enter the tent and did know Bathsheba. And David did kneel before Bathsheba, and lo, he did go at it like Popeye eating spinach.' (from *'The Book of Clive'* Chapter 6, vv 3-5).

pop her cork *v.* To give a lady an orgasm. Presumably by pushing her *clit* up with one's thumbs.

poppycock *n.* Nonsense, bollocks. From the Dutch pappekak = *soft shit.*

pop shot *n.* Scene in a *grumble flick* in which a male actor is required to splash his *population paste* for the camera, after being suitably prepared by the *fluffer.* See *Margold.*

pop the turkey in the oven *v.* To pluck the feathers from one's penis and put it in a vagina at gas mark six, prior to getting one's father-in-law to cut it into slices. To *fuck.*

population paste *n. Joy gloy,* semen, *spunk, Aphrodite's evostick.*

pop-up book *n.* A special type of reading matter where things magically spring into three dimensions as one leafs through the pages. *Bongo mag, art pamphlet, DIY manual.*

pop-up panic *n.* The bowel loosening fear that comes from having to hurridly close down internet *grumble* sites one has been ogling due to the impending approach of a boss, spouse or parent, only to be suddenly assaulted by a barrage of obscene pop-ups that multiply the more one tries to delete them.

pop your cherry *v.* Lose your virginity, *break your duck.*

porcelain tingle *n.* The cold shock that occurs when one's *bell end* touches the lavatory pan when sitting on the *throne*. A *harprick*.

pork *1. v. Aus.* To *fuck*. *'I couldn't pork her because she had the painters in.'* *2. n. Aus.* The *cock*.

pork 'n' stalk *n.* A lady with whom one has had a whirlwind one-night romance, who continues to bomard one with texts, phone calls and cooked pets. A *bunny boiler*.

pork and beans *adj.* A term to describe a *happy shopper*, or *Betty Both*. One who *bowls from both the Pavilion and the members' end. Half rice, half chips. 'Birthdays: David Bowie, formerly pork and beans, now just beans, singer, 56 today.' ('The Times'* Jan 8th, 2003).

pork pills *n. pharm. Cock drops, blueys.* Viagras.

pork prescription *1. n. Cock*, to be swallowed twice a day before meals. *2. n.* Doctor's authorisation for a *meat injection*.

pork scratchings *n. medic.* Irritation of the *old chap* as a result of a misguided liaison with a promiscuous lady. A *dose*. *'Excuse me, barman. But have you got pork scratchings?' 'Yes. I got them when I fucked your missus under the pier last week'.* (Bamforth's *'Seaside Chuckles'* postcard by Donald McGill, 1926).

pork stork *n. 'Dad, where do babies come from?' 'The pork stork, son.'*

pork sword *n.* Penis, *bacon bazooka, lamb cannon*.

pornbroker *n.* The man at work who can be relied upon to lend you a bit of *mucky* to see you through hard times. A *pornmeister*.

porn buddy *n.* A *cliterary executor*.

A single fellow's best friend who, in the event of his untimely death, is charged with the important task of removing and disposing of his stash of *grumble* before his grieving parents arrive to search through his effects for touching mementoes and stuff to put on eBay. If former Poet Laureate and lifelong jazz enthusiast Philip Larkin's porn buddy had managed to carry out the Hull University librarian's final wishes, it is estimated that the resulting bonfire of hardcore *art pamphlets* would have been visible from the Moon.

porn flakes *n.* The crusty bits found on the sofa/sheets the morning after a late night *scruff video* session.

porn fuzz *n.* Characteristic picture quality of an 18th generation *bongo vid*.

porn glare *n.* The cruel, frustrating shaft of light which partially obscures the spreadeagled *bird* on the double page spread of an *art pamphlet* as the victim strives for *vinegar*.

porn horn *n.* A three-quarters hard erection regularly seen being fed into the models in *scud films*. An *Indian rope prick*.

pornithologist *n.* One who enjoys looking at pictures of *birds* rather than going out and looking at them in the flesh. A *cock twitcher*.

pornithology *n.* The scientific study of two birds *at it like fucking knives*.

porn mauve *n.* Distinctive colour assumed by all male genitalia in *grumble vids*, although rarely if ever seen in real life.

porn mirage *n.* A cruel trick of the light, whereby a *tug*-hungry adolescent spots some *grumble* under a hedge, which on closer inspection turns out to be an Argos catalogue or the '*Sunday Mirror*' TV guide.

pornogamy *n*. Amongst impoverished gentlemen, the practice of remaining continuously faithful to the same dog-eared *seed catalogue* for all their sexual and emotional needs.

pornoisseur *n*. A gentleman who appreciates only the finest things in one-handed life.

porno mouth *n*. A young lady whose coital utterances closely resemble the dialogue from *grumble flicks*, eg. '*split me in two with your big cock*' etc.

porn on the fourth of July *sim*. Temporary Tom Cruise-style male lower body paralysis that occurs when attempting to stand up to turn off the video after letting off several rounds from the *mutton musket*.

pornorama *n*. A magnificent, breathtaking array of *meat mags*, arranged in a vista to provide variety and spectacle whilst having a *tug*. A *wank crescent*.

porn penguin *n*. A brisk, comical waddle across the living room in order to pause, rewind or fast forward through the plot-related bits of a *tug film*.

porn sacrifice *n*. A poorly-hidden stash of low quality *grumble* designed to put your missus off the scent of the barely-legal stuff. A *blue herring*.

porn trauma *n*. Upon reaching the *vinegar strokes* whilst watching an *art film* and finding the screen suddenly filled by a big, sweaty bloke with large sideburns, to be too late to stop, and *gwibble* to a disap-

pointing finish. See *vinegar Joe*.

pornucopia *n*. A seemingly endless supply of *jazz*, eg. the top shelf of the magazine rack at Barton Park lorry services on the A1.

porn vortex *n*. A whirling fifth dimension where time has no meaning, encountered when looking for *left-handed websites* on the internet. One could fall into a *porn vortex* and emerge ten minutes later to discover that three days have elapsed.

porridge gun *n*. Tool for distributing *population paste* quickly and efficiently.

PORT *abbv*. A politically correct term for a bird with small *tits*. Person Of Restricted Tittage, eg. Jilly Goulden.

port and starboard scran spanners *n*. *naval*. Knife and fork.

portion *n*. A large but nonspecific quantity of sex. '*I'd give her a portion, and no mistake.*' See also *one, length, a bit*.

Portuguese breakfast *n*. A hearty bowl-full to start the day. A watery, clotted *shit* that resembles the sort of thing they'd probably eat over there.

Portuguese man o' war 1. *n*. Name given to a buoyant jelly-fish, *Physalia atlantica*, characterised by the presence of one or more large air-sacs, by means of which it drifts about on the surface of the ocean. 2. *n*. Swimming shorts so inflated with *bottom gas* that they float above the surface of the pool, causing alarm to fellow swimmers.

posharean *n*. *medic*. In obstetrics, a Caesarean section performed for no other reason than to keep the mother's *twat* nice and tight.

posh wank *n*. A *mess*-free masturbatory manoeuvre undertaken whilst wearing a *jubber ray*.

postman's arse *n. medic*. Condition caused by chronic chaffing of the *bum cheeks* and thus characterised by a painful red ring around the *tea towel holder* which afflicts those whose working day involves much walking and sweating.

potato fat *n*. The starchy gloop that issues from a gentleman's *spuds*. *Spunk*.

pot brown *v*. To sink a long one into the *pocket herbert*.

potch *v. Wales*. To partake of an extra-marital affair in the valleys. *'See that Jones the song? Well he's been potching for years, isn't it, Look you, boyo, bach?'*

Pot Noodle horn *n. Brewer's droop*. A *cock like a wet noodle*.

pot pink *v*. To moor the *skin boat* in *cod cove*.

Potsdamer Platz *1. n. prop*. Area of no-man's land between dour, communist east and capitalist fun-loving west Berlin. *2. n*. The area of no-man's land between a lady's dour, communist *arse* and capitalist fun-loving *minge*. The *butfer, carse, tinter, taint, notcher, snarse, biffin bridge, Humber Bridge, niftkin's bridge* etc.

potter's wheel *1. n*. A thick, convoluted *fanny*, sagging under its own weight such that it resembles a *joskin*'s attempt to throw a clay pot on the *'Generation Game'*. *2 n*. Situation where a man carefully attempts to nurture a relationship with a lady over a period of time, only to ruin all his hard work by *copping a feel* too early. The *baker's impatience*.

potty-mouth *n. US*. Someone who shows a lack of vocabulary.

'Fucking goddamit. Fucking chicken for fucking dinner again, mom. Why the fucking fuck can't we have fucking hot dawgs?' 'My, my, Rusty, where did you hear language like that? You're turning into a real little potty mouth.'

potty slot *n*. The *bum crack*.

pouch *n*. An ageing, saggy *mott* that hangs between the legs like a sporran.

pound the pork *v*. Of *pinksmiths*, to pummel a hot *pork sword* into shape. *Pound the pudding*.

pouring Pot Noodle *adj*. To be producing an unappetizing, runny *poo*, though not quite unappetizing and runny enough to be described as Cup a Soup.

power cake *n*. A turbo-charged *cup cake* which is unleashed in front of an electric fan.

powerwank *n*. A brisk, efficient *tug* slotted into a busy work schedule. Often performed by politicians, captains of industry and de Vere Hotels bar staff on a fag break.

pox *n*. Venereal disease, specifically syphilis.

prairie dogging *v*. Of an *arse*, to have a stool poking in and out. A moving *turtle's head*.

pram face *n*. A famous woman, perhaps a pop star or TV presenter, whose face would more suitably adorn a young mother pushing a pram around a council estate, for example Jo out of S Club 7.

pram fat *n*. See *plum sauce*.

pranny *n*. Fool, *arsehole, twat*. A form of insult popular amongst The Troggs during the 1960s. Also *prannet*.

pratt *1. n*. An egg-bearing female fish. *2. n*. A *pranny, fuckwit, arsehole*.

prawn *n.* A girl with a fit body, but an ugly face. From the edible crustacean, where the body is tasty, but the head is thrown away. A *bobfoc.*

prawn crackers *n.* The crispy tissues found beneath the bed.

pre-cum *n.* Substance often referred to in the letters pages of *jazz mags* but rarely mentioned elsewhere. *Perseverance soup, dew on the lily.*

pre-emptive strike *n.* The act of emptying one's *shot pouch* a couple of hours before going into action so as to make the ensuing battle last a bit longer.

predator's face *n.* A somewhat unsettling vagina. From the film *'Predator'* starring Arnold Schwarzenegger.

preek *n. medic.* That fluid which is secreted from the *bishop's mitre* before *spoffage*, to lubricate the *gut stick. Ball glaze, tatty watter.* Contraction of *pre-cum.*

prefer one's peas minted *euph.* To be a *pastry chef.* Alluding to one who participates in the *burgling of turds.*

pregnot *adj.* Of a lady, to look like she's *up the duff* when she's in fact just fat.

premature pinch *n.* The snipping off of an unsmoked *bum cigar* when disturbed in the act, by an important telephone call for example.

prepare yesterday's lunch *v.* To go for a *shit.*

pressed ham *n.* The effect achieved by pushing one's naked *buttocks* onto the photocopier at the office Christmas party.

press the devil's doorbell *v.* To *flick the bean.*

prick 1. *n.* A penis. 2. *n.* A *twat, fuckwit,* fool. 3. *n.* A life-threatening finger injury often suffered by fairy tale princesses.

prick-stick *n.* A white DIY glue in a handy tubular dispenser used solely to stick the pages of an *art pamphlet* together.

prick tease *n.* A woman who goads one's *penis* by calling it names.

priest's hole *n.* A *minge* that's a tight squeeze. A *paper cut.*

pringle *n.* Yet another word for one who sniffs bicycle seats.

prison pussy *n.* The *anus.*

prison vision *n. medic.* A condition brought on by prolonged abstinence from female company, which causes the sufferer to lower his standards considerably, finding almost any woman attractive. *Porridge goggles, Camp X-ray specs. 'When I came out after 27 years of predominantly solitary confinement, I was suffering from terrible prison vision. Shortly after my release, I remember being entertained by Her majesty the Queen at Buckingham Palace, and getting a bit of a chirp-on when her mum bent over to pat a corgi. Truly incarceration is a terrible thing.'* (from *'The Long Walk to Freedom'*, by Nelson Mandela).

private fur *n.* A lady's *secret squirrel.*

privates 1. *n.* Inoffensive unisex term for genitalia invented by the Women's Institute in 1904. At the opposite end of the rudeness scale to *fuckstick, bollocks* and *cunt.* 2. *n.* A double entendre enabling *'Carry On'* script writers to confuse low ranking soldiers with their *meat and two veg.*

probe and drogue *n. RAF.* Repeated attempts, whilst drunk, to achieve penetration. Named after the mechanism used for in-flight refueling.

probo *n.* One who makes a very comfortable living from vagrancy. A professional *Harold Ramp* with a mobile phone and a Rolls Royce parked round the corner, of the sort only ever encountered by readers of the *'Daily Mail'*.

procrasturbation *n.* The act of repeated, and often pleasureless *self-love* brought on by the need to stave off more weighty tasks. *'For heaven's sake, Lester, stop procrasturbating and get your tax return filled in.'*

Professor Pissflaps *n. prop.* An epithet given to any bird who thinks she is more intelligent than the average bloke, eg. Carol Vorderman. *'Alright, Professor Pissflaps, you've had your say. Let someone else get a word in edgeways.'* (David Dimbleby to Germaine Greer, *'BBC Question Time'*, March 2002).

Professor Plum *1. n.* the purple-bodied player in a game of *'Cluedo'*. *2. n.* The purple-headed player in a variety of bedroom games.

promosexual *n.* One who is unnecessarily forward in promoting his homosexuality. Characterized by an unwelcome excess of exaggeratedly camp behavior. One who is forever banging on about being *good with colours.*

proud Mary *1. n.* A large Mississippi river boat. *2. n.* A lady's pronounced pubic mound. The *mons veneris, grassy knoll.*

prune juice *n.* Anal seepage.

pruning the roses *euph.* To have a chronic hangover. Once used by Brian Clough as an excuse for non-attendance at Nottingham Forest matches in the 1980s/90s.

psychedelic yodelling *n.* Vocal projection of your *biscuits* out your mouth.

pube farmer *n.* An unemployed person. A *doley.*

pube in an afro, looking for a *sim.* A crude variation on looking for a needle in a haystack. Also, *looking for a baw hair in an afro (Scot).*

pube lunch *n.* A tasty *bacon sandwich* with a token garnish of *gorilla salad*, served all day in a friendly atmosphere.

pubic library *n.* An array of *flesh books* kept on top of a wardrobe for easy reference.

pubiquity *n.* The uncanny ability of stray strands of *gorilla salad* to turn up anywhere and everywhere, eg. on a bar of soap, between one's teeth, in McDonald's burgers, McDonald's chicken nuggets, McDonald's thick shakes, etc.

pub scarecrow *n.* The inhabitant of one's boozer who has the uncanny ability to frighten away the *birds.*

pub singer *n.* A solo performer, grunting and yodelling in a cubicle whilst *laying a cable.*

pub terrier *n.* A breed of small, yappy, unpredictable, aggressive though not necessarily dangerous, man whose presence makes one feel oddly uneasy. Found in most public houses in Britain.

PUD *acronym.* Post Urinal Drip. A *wet penny in the pocket.*

pud *n.* Penis. That which was always *pulled* by Ivor Biggun (aka Doc Cox of *'That's Life'* rude vegetable fame), in his *'Wanking Song'.*

pudding burner *n.* Slatternly lady who frequents pubs on a Sunday lunchtime when she should really

be at home cooking a hearty traditional meal for her husband.

puddle jumper *n*. A *fruit feeler*.

pudendum *n*. Genital area. From
Latin *pudes* = meat pie & *dendum*
= two potatoes.

pud-whapper *n*. *US*. *Wanker*,
obnoxious person.

puff *1*. *v*. To exhale cigarette smoke.
2. *n. prop*. Magic dragon that lived
by the sea. *3*. *n*. A *eater of fancy
cakes*.

puff fluff *n*. An insufficiently malodorous *dropped hat*, which calls
the *farter's* sexual orientation into
question. A *gaseous gay, botter
burp*.

pugwash *n*. *Aus*. Cleaning of the
teeth using *tapioca toothpaste* and
a *naughty paintbrush*. A *blow job*.

puh-seh *n*. *US*. A *grumble flick
fanny*. 'Hmmmm, be-beh! I'm
gonna get ma'self a liddle piece-a
yo' puh-seh!'

puke *v*. To *throw up*.

pull *1*. *v*. To *tap*, pick up members of
the opposite sex. *'I went out on the
pull last night'*. *2*. *v*. To *wank*.
'Nowt pulled, so I went home,
watched the free ten minutes of
the Fantasy Channel and had a bit
of a pull.'

pull a pint on the piss pump *v*. To
pour oneself a 5ml *hand shandy*.

pullaby *n*. Something which, when
accompanied by a rhythmical rocking motion, soon brings on a state
of contented slumber.

pull a train *v*. To take turns at *stirring the porridge*. A *gang bang*.

pulled the ripcord *euph*. Descriptive
of a once svelte lady who has sadly
ballooned like an inflatable raft and
turned into a *bed breaker*.

pulletariat *n*. The class of society
principally engaged in *monomanu-*

al labour. The plebian social stra-
tum that lives alone and watches
sockumentaries whilst awaiting
news of gainful employment.

pullfilment *n*. The tired yet satisfied
feeling a chap has after spending an
evening perusing *seed catalogues*
or watching *socktator sports*.

pulling power *n*. The strength of
one's *fanny magnetism*.

pull off *1*. *v*. To manoeuvre a car
away from the kerb. *2*. *v*. To drag a
drunken friend away from a fight in
which he has the upper hand, usually whilst shouting *'It's not worth
it'* or *'Leave it, he's had enough.'*
3. *v*. To masturbate. *'Fucking hell!
She went downhill skiing and
pulled us both off at once.'*

pull out and pray *n*. A method of
contraception that is also a test of
faith. *Vatican roulette*.

pull the Pope's cap off *v*. To *bash
the Bishop, box the Jesuit*.

pull the turkey's neck *v*. *Choke the
chicken*. See *throttle the turkey*.

pull your pud *v*. To *wank*.

pullympics *n*. Televised ladies'
sporting events that leave a certain
type of male viewer in a somewhat
more exhausted state than the participants, eg. beach volleyball.

PUMA *acronym*. Pants Up My
Arse. A specific reference to *cleftal*
discomfort. *Hungry arse*.

pump *v*. To *fart, poot, pass wind,
shoot bunnies, drop a rose petal*.

pump action mottgun *n*. Advanced
rapid-fire development of the *mutton musket*.

pumper's lump *n*. *medic*. The condition of enhanced right forearm
muscle due to excessive *wanking*.

pumping up the tyres *v*. Involuntary
movement of the leg during the
vinegar strokes. *Elvis's leg, Elvis*

tremble.

pump up the jam *v.* To take a *cranberry dip*. To *stir the paint*.

punami *n.* In a bar, a tidal wave of binge-drinking *flange* out on a *slag night*. From *punani* + tsunami.

punani n. A lady's bits and bobs.

punani granny *n.* A significantly older woman who is none the less still worth one. A *gilf.*

punch above one's weight *1. v.* In boxing, to come out on top in a bout with a superior fighter. *2. v.* Of a gentleman, to sucesfully *woo* a young lady whom he might ordinarily consider to be out of his class, eg. Les Dennis pulling Amanda Holden, Steven Johnson pulling Charlotte Church, Shane McGowan pulling anyone at all. To *curl one in.*

punch its head in *v.* What a gentleman does to his *gentleman* when *relaxing in a gentleman's way.*

punch the clown *v.* To make *custard* shoot out the top of *Charlie Cairoli's hat*. To *wank.*

punch up the whiskers *n.* A *knee trembler* or similar romantic encounter in a train lavatory, taxi queue or Building Society doorway.

punish *v.* To put one's ladyfriend *to the sword* in an enthusiastic manner. To administer a few strokes of the *old walking stick* to a lady who wants it really.

punk cock n. A *hampton* with multifarious piercings. A *knob* bejewelled with chains, rings and pop rivets.

punks *rhym. slang.* Breasts. From punk rockers = *knockers.* *'Gonorrhoea was powerless to resist. His eyes burned into hers like topazzes. His strong arms*

enfolded her softly yielding body as she felt herself being swept away in a solar wind of passion. Before she had a chance to protest, he had whipped off her titpants and started mucking about with her punks.' (from *'The Lady and the Powdered Egg Salesman'* by Barbara Cartland).

puppies *n. Bubbies.* Affectionate euphemism for *tits.* Also *two puppies fighting in a bag.*

puppies' noses *n.* Little cold, wet nipples.

purple-headed womb broom *n.* See *purple-headed yoghurt warrior.*

purple-headed yoghurt warrior *n.* See *purple-headed womb broom.*

purple helmet *1. n. Pink Darth Vader's* headgear, *bobby's helmet, German helmet, Roman helmet, bell end. 2. n.* Any member of the former Rover Aerobatic display team.

purple pearler *n.* Extendable icing tool for decorating pink blancmanges.

purse *n.* A *fanny.*

push gas *v.* To *poot.*

push her guts in v. To have sex with a lady. *'Oh Joan Hunter Dunn / With your strong legs in shorts / Your boyish good looks / Your excelling at sports / Your long golden hair / Your ruby red lips / Let me push in your guts / Twixt the council dump skips.'* (*'Joan Hunter Dunn'* by John Betjeman).

pushing sauce *v.* The stage of coitus immediately after the *vinegar strokes,* ie. when the *yoghurt truck* has *crashed* and is in the act of shedding its *load.* Ejaculation. *'Bond and Fanny Akimbo made love on the silken sheets of the mini-sub's bed. Suddenly, the* *videophone crackled into life and the face of M appeared, seated at his familiar Whitehall desk. 'Ah, there you are 007. We've had reports that Blofeld is planning to blow up China with a big ray gun,' he said excitedly. 'I'm afraid I have my hands rather full at the moment, sir,' replied Bond, raising a quizzical eyebrow. 'Call me back in about 10 minutes after I'd pushed me sauce and zuffled me charlie.''* (from *'Tops and Goldfingers'* by Ian Fleming).

push the envelope *1. v.* In test pilot circles, to test the aeronautical capabilities of a prototype aircraft. *2. n.* In *pant shitting* circles, to *shit* one's *pants*.

push through *n.* the consequence of buying 'Economy Brand' *bumwad.* *"Would you care for another scone, Father Brown', asked Lady Chelmshurst. 'Bless you, but thank you no', replied the small priest, blinking owlishly and proffering a smelly digit towards his hostess's nose. 'I've just been to lay a cable and fear I had a push through."* (from *'Father Brown Points the Finger'* by GK Chesterton).

pussy *1. n.* Of woeful British TV sitcoms set in quiet, overstaffed department stores, a much-stroked pet cat frequently referred to by Mrs. Slocombe. *2. n.* Her *cunt.*

pussy pelmet *n.* A short mini skirt.

pussy poof *n.* A *todger dodger,* a *three wheeler,* a *friend of Valerie.*

put the red lights on *v. naval.* To have a silent *wank* in bed so as not to disturb one's wife. Also *silent running, American Beauty.*

putting from the rough *v.* Golfing equivalent of *bowling from the Pavilion end.*

putting toothpaste back in the tube *sim.* Descriptive of the difficulties encountered when attempting sexual congress whilst less than fully tumescent. *Thumbing in a slacky, playing snooker with string, pushing a marshmallow in a moneybox.*

put to the sword *v.* To make love to. *'From the Charing Cross Theatre where I saw Mr. Herbert give his Death of Icarus, to tea with the French Ambassador, and thence home to bed whereupon I put Mrs. Pepys to the sword before settling down to sleep.'* (from *'The Diary of Samuel Pepys'*).

putz *n.* A yiddish *prick.*

pygmies' cocks *n.* Erect nipples. *'Did you see Sharron Davies on Olympic Grandstand? She had jockeys like pygmies' cocks.'*

pyjama glue *n.* A handy waterbased adhesive, particularly useful for bonding and stiffening cotton fabrics. Also good for sticking together the pages of *tit catalogues,* the wife's eyelids etc.

pyroflatulate *v.* To light one's *farts.* See also *afterburner, blue streak.*

pyropastie *n.* Excrement wrapped in newspaper, then set alight on a doorstep in the hope that the occupant will stamp it out.

Pythagoras piss *n.* Ancient Greek act of trigonometrical urintiation performed such that one's forehead is propped against the lavatory wall, and one's body consequently forms the hypotenuse of a right-angled triangle.

Qq

quack *n. onomat.* A sudden sound emanating from one's *bills.*

quail *n.* A tasty young *bird* who's game for anything.

Quaker, to bury a *v.* To *lay a cable.* *'Do come in, Mr. D'Arcy. Miss Bennet has just nipped upstairs to bury a Quaker. Would you care to wait in the drawing room until she has wiped her arse?'* (from *'Pride and Prejudice',* by Jane Austen).

quakers *n. Oats.*

qualifications *n.* Breasts. *'Admittedly her CV looks a bit thin, and her interview responses were somewhat lacklustre, but she has some excellent qualifications.'* Also *first impressions.*

quality control *n.* The release of a small amount of *fart* to see how bad it is before releasing the rest. *Tasting the wine.*

quandong 1. *n. Aus.* A difficult *lay,* a hard, as opposed to an easy, woman. One who wears armour-plated *knickers.* 2. *n.* A prostitute.

quarter pounder *n.* An unacceptably thin woman.

quaynte *n. Placket.*

quaz *n.* An ugly *wanker,* a *bell end* ringer. Abbreviation of Quasimodo.

Quebec Bravos *n.* Metropolitan Police phonetic radio code. QBs = Quality Breasts, used by bored *scuffers* on Saturday night city centre duty. *'Calling all units, calling all units. Quebec Bravos in the High Street. Any units wish to assist? Over.'*

queef *n. Can.* A *Lawley kazoo,* a *hat dropped forward,* a *flap raspberry.* Also *kweef.*

queen n. See *queer.*

Queen Amidala's lipstick *n. Chod bin* seat *skidmark* named after its resemblance to the *'Phantom Menace'* character's bizarrely-applied gob make-up.

Queensway *n.* A regular mammoth rectal stock clearance where *everything must go.*

queer 1. *adj. pre-1960* Odd, peculiar. 2. *n. post-1960.* A *ginger beer.*

quiche 1. *n. Taint, notcher, barse,* whatever. 2. *n.* Puff's pizza.

quickie *n.* A swift bout of intercourse that one often fancies in the same way that one fancies a cup of tea. A hurried *one. 'Oh, it's half time. Do you fancy a quickie, love?' 'Er...go on, then. But stick the kettle on first.'*

quim *n.* Refined word for the *mapatasi* such as a gentleman might use at a hay clarse cocktail party. From the Welsh cwm = valley beneath the 13 amp fuse wire.

quimbecile *n.* A stupid fellow who is also a *cunt,* eg. Jeffrey Archer.

quimble *n.* A tremor of excitement in a bird's *snatch.* A *fanny gallop.* From quim + tremble.

quim bling *n.* Ladies' genital jewelry. *Mufflinks.*

quimby *n.* The middle person in a *threesome,* the filling in a sex sandwich. See also *lucky Pierre.*

quim chin *n. Muff mouth, cunty chops.* A bearded fellow. *'Did you see Noel Edmonds on telly last night? What a stupid fucking quim chin.'*

quiminals *n.* Prison lesbians. *Queen bees.*

quim pro quo *n. Lat.* An ancient Roman bartering system where goods and services are exchanged for *gash.*

quimle *v.* To eat *hairy pie.*

quimpotent *adj.* Descriptive of a lady who is unable to reach the required level of sexual arousal required by the gentleman.

quim strings *n.* Imaginary internal female organs, resembling *'Coronation Street'* Deirdre's neck, that tighten in stressful situations. *'Bob Cratchit raised his glass. 'To Mr. Scrooge, the founder of the feast', he said cheerily. 'Ha! Founder of the feast indeed,' screeched his wife. 'Why, I'll no sooner drink a toast to him that I would the devil himself, the mean-hearted, penny pinching, tight arsed...' 'Now, now, Sara,' interrupted Bob. 'Don't go snapping your quimstrings. It's Christmas day, and we shall drink to Mr. Scrooge.''* (from *'A Christmas Carol'* by Charles Dickens).

quimwedge *v.* To do *it* with a lady.

quince *1. n. Aus.* Mincing *queen.* *2. n.* Something owls and pussycats eat with a runcible spoon.

quoit *n. Ring, hoop, rusty sheriff's badge, balloon knot, tea towel holder.*

quornography *n.* Softcore vegetarian pornography, ie. no *meat.*

quumf *v.* To sit in waiting outside a public library and take the opportunity to sniff ladies' bicycle seats as soon as possible after their owner has dismounted and gone inside. To *pringle, snarze, moomph, garboon or snudge.*

Rr

rabbit pie *n.* The *faff*.

rabbit's chops, arse like a *sim.* Descriptive of the unsettling twitching of the *blood orange* when one is in imminent need of an *Eartha*.

rabbit's tail *n.* The split second flash of white cotton gusset caught in one's peripheral vision when a lady crosses her legs at the other side of a waiting room.

rabid dog, fanny like a *sim.* A *clown's pie, cappuccino twat*.

race snails *v.* Of a gentleman and former Conventry City manager, to drive very slowly close to the kerb in order to ask directions from a prostitute after becoming lost in a red light district.

racing dog's bollocks on a frosty morning *sim.* Descriptive of the state of one's eyes the morning after a heavy night *on the turps*, eg. hungover chef Keith Floyd.

rack *n.* Female mammarial display, collectively the *tits, funbags*. '*She's got a lovely rack on her. Very well presented. And nips like a fighter pilot's thumbs.*'

Radcliffe 1. *v.* To fail to finish a pint. 2. *n.* A car that at first sight looks like a good runner, but ends up completely *fucked* at the side of the road. **do a~** 3. *v.* To give up three quarters of the way through a pub crawl, fall in a gutter, and have a bit of a cry.

radge 1. *v.* To become furious, to lose one's *blob*. 2. *n.* A furious episode. '*This little bairn puked on us, so I took a fuckin' radge.*' (Mother Teresa of Calcutta). 3. *n. adj.* In a state of *radge*. **~y** 4. *n.* One who is predisposed to taking *radges*.

radio rental *rhym. slang. Radgy,*

hatstand, mental.

RAF *abbrev.* Rough As Fuck. Particularly ugly or unattractive.

rag and bone man *n.* One who doesn't mind getting a *barber's pole* now and again.

ragman's coat *n.* A *turkey's wattle*, a *raggy blart*, a *pound of liver*, a *club sandwich*. An untidy vagina.

ragman's trumpet *n.* A capacious *fanny. Big Daddy's sleeping bag.*

ragtop 1. *n.* A convertible motor car. 2. *n.* An uncircumcised *charlie*.

rag week 1. *n.* Seven days during which students get *pissed* and behave like *cunts* in the name of charity. 2. *n.* Time of the month when the *flags are out. Blob week.*

rainbow yawn *n. Puke*, a *technicolour laugh, pavement pizza*, a *sung rainbow*.

raindance *n.* The Native American-style rhythmical stamping moves made by the feet of one with a full bladder as he tries to get his keys in the front door following a night *on the pop*.

rainman *n.* A woman with phenomenal mental capacity, who can commit to memory every single male misdemeanor committed throughout the duration of a relationship, to be regurgitated during arguments, or for guilt trip purposes, emotional blackmail etc.

raisin *n.* The *corn dot, freckle*.

raisin bag *n.* The *nut sack, John Wayne's hairy saddlebags*.

raisin factory *euph.* An old people's home. From the fact that senior citizens are left there to dry out and wrinkle before being shipped out in a small box.

rake the cage out *v.* To *build a log cabin*, give birth to a *Richard*.

Ralph *onomat.* To vomit. Also *call*

Huey.

Rambo'd *adj.* To be so *pissed* that one believes that one can take on any amount of people in the car park and win.

ram job *n.* Vatican-approved, conventional heterosexual sex, as opposed to *blow job* or *hand job*. A *knobjob*.

rammadanny *n.* An enforced monthly *Jacky Danny* fast.

ram raiding on a scooter *adj.* Descriptive of less than attractive women. *'She was a worthy woman, yette sore ugglie, with a face lyke shede been ramme-raidynge onn a scooter.'* (from *'The Miller's Tale'* by Geoffrey Chaucer).

ram shackled *adj.* To be engaged in the act of *botting*.

RAM sleep. *n. abbrev.* The phase prior to deep sleep. Rapid Arm Movement.

randy *n.* Cowboy version of *horny*.

Rangoon ring *n. medic.* Curry-induced blistering of the *nipsy*. A *Wigan rosette, Japanese flag, Johnny Cash, Hawaiian sunrise.*

rantallion *n. 18thC.* One whose *shot pouch* is longer than the barrel of his *fouling piece*.

rascal wrapper *n. French letter, blob, rubber Johnny*.

raspberries in syrup *sim.* The consistency of *shit* after a night *on the pop*. The kind that makes you pull a face like Kenneth Williams going *'Ooh, Matron!'*

raspberry *rhym. slang.* Break wind. From raspberry tart = *fart*. *'Did you just drop a raspberry?' 'No. He who smelt it dealt it'. 'Ah! But he who denied it supplied it'. 'Yeh, but he who made the rhyme committed the crime.'*

Rasputin *n.* An unkempt vaginal or anal beard.

rat *n.* A lady's *bodily treasure*. The *fanny*. *'Excreta was powerless to resist. His eyes burned into hers like sequins. His strong arms enfolded her tender body as she felt herself being swept away in an Aurora Borealis of passion. Then he said the words her heart had ached to hear for so long. 'Giz a quick shot on your rat, love. I want to catch last orders.''* (from *'The Lady and the Disgraced Former Manchester United and Northern Ireland Footballer'*, by Barbara Cartland).

rat arsed *adj. Shit faced*.

rat catcher's bait box *n.* An unpleasant tasting *fanny*. A *nine volter*.

rat killer *n.* A foul *turd* capable of killing any pipe-dwelling rodent within a mile of the S-bend.

rat's cocks! *exclam.* Expression of extreme disappointment. Drat, confound it, curses, etc. *"My God!' the boatswain cried. 'What has happened to the ship?' 'The Pequod has been stove in by a Leviathan, a Great White Whale!' replied the helmsman, scarce able to comprehend the enormity of his own words. 'Rat's cocks,' yelled Ahab. 'That's fucking torn it!''* (from *'Moby Dick'* by Herman Melville).

rat's nose *n.* An inquisitive bit of *poo* poking out of the *nipsy* to see if the coast's clear. *'FX: DOOR OPENS, BUCKET CLANKS. Mrs. Mopp: There you go, Mr. Handley. That lavatory's as clean as a chinaman's chopsticks. Tommy Handley: Thank Christ for that, Mrs. Mopp. I've been stood out here* *three quarters of a fucking hour with the rat's nose. FX: RUNNING FOOTSTEPS, DOOR OPENS AND CLOSES, ZIP, FOGHORN, SOUND OF LARGE SHIT HITTING WATER. Orchestra: Signature tune to finish.'* (Script of *'It's That Man Again'*, broadcast on the BBC Home Service, March 1942).

rat stance *n.* Characteristic standing position adopted by a fellow who is having a spot of *hand to gland combat* in a shower. *'So there I was in the rat stance, I'd got to the jester's shoes and she walked in on the vinegar stroke. Nothing could stop me by then.'*

Ravi Shankar *rhym. slang.* A gentleman who plays a small, pink sitar.

razz *v.* To *hoy up, puke.*

Razzle *n. prop.* An unpretentious, no-nonsense *jazz mag.* In its own words *'The magazine that makes your cock go big.'*

Razzle dazzle 1. *n. Porn glare.* 2. *n.* Temporary blindness caused by a particularly nasty *growler shot* in a *self help book.*

Razzle stack *n.* The fondly-remembered, and deeply erotic tableau in the said *art pamphlet,* featuring six vertically-arranged *quims.* Now sadly banned due to the near suffocation of the lowermost participant.

Razzlet *n.* A slightly overweight, not too bright female, whose only hope of escaping her humdrum existence is to appear in *'Razzle',* or similar quality *bongo mags.*

reach around *n.* In *botting,* pouring your partner a *hand shandy* whilst *ram shackled.*

Reading Hoover *n.* Foot used to clean the carpet by grinding in the dirt until it vanishes. Named after the houseproud Berkshire town. *'Oh no, I've knocked the ashtray over.' 'No problem, love. I'll use the Reading Hoover on it.'*

reading the Financial Times *v.* Performing *cumulonimbus* on a particularly large, loose-lipped *clopper.*

reading the paper *v.* To examine one's used toilet tissue to catch up on the latest news of one's anal health. To peruse the *rusty bulletin.*

readybrek glow *n.* The fuzzy, red outline surrounding everyone on a 6th generation copy of a *stick vid. Porn fuzz.*

reality wank *n.* A *toss* over someone one could *poke* in real life, therefore making it better and more realistic. Likely subjects include one's girlfriend, the local *bike* or Sonya off *'EastEnders'.*

rear admiral *n.* A sailor who prefers to navigate the *Windward passage.*

rear gunner *n.* In aviation terms, a marksman who shoots one of his own side by firing his *lamb cannon* into their *bomb bay.*

rear tits *n.* The fleshy parts of the body that hang over the *titpant lashing straps* of ladies with *nice personalities.*

receiver of swollen goods *n.* Someone involved in a nefarious transaction with a *bum bandit.*

rectal retort *n.* A witty *fart.*

rectoplasm *n.* A message from the other side which makes everybody's hair stand on end. A *McArthur Park.*

red alert *exclam.* Discreet *sotto voce* warning exchanged between males, advising each other to tread carefully around the lady of the house/office due to her having *women's things*. Also *code red*.

red ring *n*. Inflammation of the *chocolate starfish* as a result of being *skittered*. See *Japanese flag*.

red sock, arse hanging out like a *sim. medic*. Descriptive of a full rectal prolapse. Such as one caused by a deliciously fatal plate of Curry Hell, the hottest curry in the world. Exclusively available at the Curry Capital, Bigg Market, Newcastle upon Tyne, the only restaurant to receive the coveted 5 Prolapses award in the *'Viz Good Curry Guide'*.

red tie *n*. To finish oneself off with a *sausage sandwich* after having had enough of the *cranberry dip*.

red wings *n*. Dubious honour bestowed upon one who eats *haddock pastie* during *rag week*.

refreshed *adj. Fucking mortal*.

refusal 1. *n*. In show-jumping, when a horse approaches the fence but only briefly puts its nose over the bar instead of jumping. 2. *n*. In *shitting,* when a reluctant *Sir Douglas* pokes its nose out of the *ringpiece* for a second before, despite Herculean efforts from the toiletee, returning back to the warmth and safety of the *dirt bakery*.

reggae like it used to be. *v*. To masturbate. Wearing a bowler hat.

relax in a gentleman's way *v. euph.* To *wank*. *'Scrooge pulled up his nightshirt, tucked it under his whiskery old chin and began relaxing in a gentleman's way, trying hard to conjour up a mental picture of Mrs. Cratchit in the rik. Suddenly the room was filled with an eerie light, and there before him stood the second spirit, the spirit of Christmas present.'* (from *'A Christmas Carol'*, by Charles Dickens).

release the chocolate hostage *v*. To liberate *Richard the Third* after his incarceration in one's *chamber of horrors*.

release the handbrake *v*. To *drop a gut* into your hand and then present it into your friend's face for his olfactory delectation. To offer a *cupcake*.

release the hounds *n*. To empty one's *arse*.

remould *n. Rubber, single finger Marigold glove, blob*.

retain water *v*. Of a *plumper,* to eat cake.

retch *v*. To vomit, but with more noise and less *puke*.

return fire *n*. A cold, sniping splash of *chod bin* water that darts straight up one's *wrinkled penny* while *bombing China. Splashback*.

return serve *n*. The reappearance of a *turd* you thought you had seen the last of.

reveille *n*. An early morning *brass eye* fanfare delivered with military precision, that makes your company jump out of bed.

reverse cowgirl *n*. A *cowgirl* who has been bucked through 180 degrees, a sexual position much favoured by *meat vid* cinematographers as one can see it *going in*. A *fucking bronco*.

reverse Doagan *n. NZ*. A *chocolate hostage* released into the *chod bin* whilst sitting the wrong way round, leaving a breathtaking *skidmark vista* for the next unfortunate lady patron of the toilet.

reverse elephant *n*. What happens when one has *flown right past Dresden* without managing to locate a lavatory. A large *Thora* hanging out of one's *bomber aris,* creating the illusion when viewed from the rear of a pink-eared, brown-trunked pachyderm.

reverse peach *n.* A rearward elevation of a lady's *parts of shame,* such that they resemble a ripe and juicy pink fruit.

reverse rucksack *n.* A large *abdominal holdall,* used by the *lard of the manor* for storing all the pies.

reverse thrust *n.* The act of *getting off at Edge Hill.* The *interruptus* of one's *coitus.*

RFHTFH *abbrev.* Phrase applied to eastern European women, or a fat lass in a Sheffield bun shop. Rather Fuck Her Than Fight Her.

rhino horn *n.* A well-matted tarantula among *arse spiders.* Definitely not an aphrodisiac.

rhythm mag *n. Jazz mag, scud book, art pamphlet,* one-handed reading material.

rhythm section *1. n.* In a pop group, the bass and drums. *2. n.* In a newsagent's, the shelf where they put the *jackage. 3. n.* In a *jazz mag,* the mucky pictures of bare ladies as distinct from the textual padding.

rhythm stick *n.* The late Ian Dury's *cock.* The *Sixth gear stick, joy stick, copper stick, giggle stick, blood stick.*

rib *n.* The missus, her indoors. From the children's fairy story '*Adam and Eve*'.

rib cushions *n. Dirty pillows.* Breasts.

Richard *rhym. slang.* A stool. From Richard the Third = *turd. 'I've just given birth to a ten pound Richard. Ooh, my poor ringpiece!'*

riddle of the sphincter *n.* A mysteri-

ous *fart* that make your nose fall off.

ride *v.* That which one does to a *bike.*

rider's block *n.* To irretrievably lose *wood* half way through intercourse as a result of a sudden, unexplained nasty sexual image entering the mind, eg. Jack Duckworth doing *oral* on his wife Vera while Ivy Tilsley *bobs* him with a *strap-on.*

ride the baloney pony *v. US.* To *wank.*

ride the clutch *1 v.* To teeter on the brink of the *vinegar strokes* in an effort to prolong the act of coitus. *2. v.* To maintain the hovering state between releasing the *pace car* and making *skidmarks* on one's underpants. To rein back the *turtle's head.* To *fight a rearguard action.*

ride the dirtbike *v.* To partake in a bit of *backdoor action.*

ride the great white knuckler *v.* To knock out a bit of *jizz* on one's *bone-a-phone.*

ride the porcelain bus *v.* To have the *squits.*

ride the waves *v.* To poke an amply proportioned lady. See also *moped.* '*It's not as bad as you might think, if you just slap the fat and ride the waves.*' (from '*Up at the Crack of Dawn - an Autobiography*' by Lenny Henry).

riding sidesaddle *n.* Descriptive of the *mincing* trot much favoured by men who are *good with colours.* The kind of gait adopted by Mr. Humphries when summoned by Captain Peacock.

right hand cream *n.* Hand and face moisturiser made from a special blend of *nut* oils.

rigid digit *n.* An erect penis, *bone, bonk on.*

rik, the *n*. That which a bare person is in. The *nuddy*.

Rigsby *n*. A no-handed urination of such vigorous release and force that the hands can be safely placed on the hips for its duration.

rim *1. n*. Circumference of the *anus*. *2. v*. To lick the *rim*.

rim job *n*. A *rimming*, a *trip around the world*.

rim shot *1. n*. That thing the drummer does after David Letterman has read out a joke. *2. n*. When having a *pony and trap*, the deeply regrettable experience of inadvertently directing a stream of urine under the seat, but over the rim of the *chod bin*, soaking one's *hoggers*.

ring *1. n. Hole, jacksie, anus, brown eye, chocolate starfish. 2. n*. The vagina.

ring bandit *n*. A *fruit feeler*.

ringbinder *1. n*. A notebook containing spring-loaded clamps for the purpose of holding loose sheets of paper. *2. n*. An exceptionally tenacious *Sir Douglas* which necessitates repeated wiping before the *freckle* is even vaguely free of *bum chutney*.

ring burner *n*. An exceptionally hot curry prepared for the entertainment of the waiters and kitchen staff in Indian restaurants.

ringlets *n*. A young lady's anal beard.

ring master *1. n*. The master of ceremonies at a circus. *2. n*. An expert *botter*.

ringmaster's dog *n*. A sexually experimental and enthusiastic lady who shocks even the most seasoned lover with her willingness to perform strange and exotic acts, ie. one who knows more tricks than a ringmaster's dog.

ringpiece *n*. A *Samantha Janus*.

ring pirate *n*. A *pirate of men's pants*.

ringstinct *n*. A mysterious seventh sense that tells a *farter* to wait until he is safely ensconced on the *chod bin*, thus preventing *follow through* in his *scads*.

ring stinger *n*. A *Ruby Murray* that induces *ring sting* and leaves one with an *arse* like *a Japanese flag*.

ring the bell *v. Pop the cork*, detonate the *fanny bomb*.

ring the waterboard *exclam*. A humorous announcement made following the birth of a particularly hefty *toilet baby*. *'Oi love. You'd better ring the waterboard and tell them to get the big knives out at the shit farm to chop that one up.'*

ringtone *n*. A *fart*.

ring worm *n*. A *shirt lifter's Jimmy Wonkle*.

rinky dink *1. n*. Stink, that unpleasant odour created by a *fyst, Richard the Third's BO. 2. adj*. Descriptive of the Pink Panther.

rinse the lettuce *v*. To wash the *beef curtains*, in situ as it were. Female equivalent of a *gentleman's wash*.

Rio *n*. A bald *cunt* with wavy lips, often seen in the 'Readers' Wives' pages of *bongo mags*, or on the pitch at Old Trafford.

ripped out fireplace *n*. A *butcher's dustbin*.

ripped sofa *n*. A *badly-packed kebab*.

ripped to the tits *adj*. A level of inebriation achieved using drink and drugs. Also *whipped to the tits*.

ripping up rags *sim*. Descriptive of the sound of a long drawn out *fart*.

rise from the dead *v*. To achieve a *bone on* by looking at erotic pictures of women who have since passed on, eg. Marilyn Monroe, Jayne Mansfield or Hattie Jacques, etc.

rising main *n*. In pubic plumbing, the *tatty watta* supply pipe usually fed in through the vagina. The *main cable*.

riveting stick *rhym. slang. Dick.* From the jeweller's instrument.

road apples *n*. Horse *shit*.

roadhead *n. US.* Hitch hiker's currency. An act of *horatio* performed in return for a lift.

roadkill *n*. A rather flat, dry, *hedgehog*.

roadkill ruby *n*. A curry containing meat of dubious provenance.

road thrill *n*. An *art pamphlet* which has been discarded in a layby by a trucker.

road to Grimsby *n*. The *farse, tinter, carse* etc, etc. The bit between a lady's *front* and *back bottoms*. So called because there's always a whiff of fish and it's not far from a *shit-hole*.

roast chicken *n*. Any member of a one woman/two premiership footballers configuration who gets cold feet at the last minute.

roast ghost *n*. An *air buffet* that is not suitable for vegetarians.

robbing the date locker *n*. The burgling of *turds*.

Robin Cook's beard *n*. A sparsely-vegetated ginger *minge*. A *grated carrot*, a *council twat*.

robocrap *n*. The ominous feeling in the lower bowel which leaves a fellow in no doubt that he only has 'twenty seconds to comply'.

rock candy *n*. An effeminate, yet intimidating fellow. A *muscle Mary*.

rocket polisher *n*. An over-enthusi-

astic cleaning of the *pocket rocket* leading to detonation on the launchpad. And *spunk* everywhere.

rocket socket *n*. Vagina.

rocket strap *n*. The waist band of the *undercrackers* when used to tether the *old man* discreetly upwards to allow a be-*travel-fatted* fellow to alight decorously from the bus.

Rockfords *rhym. slang. Arse grapes, Nobbies, Emmas, Michaels, farmers, ceramics, Chalfonts.* From the TV series 'The Rockford Piles'.

rock poodle *n*. A lightweight heavy metallurgist, complete with long shaggy hair and puffed-up leather jacket.

rocks 1. *n*. Masses of hard, stony matter, esp. extensive formation of such matter. 2. *n*. Big, hairy *bollocks*. 3. *n*. Those which one 'gets off' whilst *on the job*.

rod *n. Spam sceptre*.

Rod Hull's roof, as wet as *adj*. Descriptive of a sexually-excited lady, one who is *frothing like bottled Bass*. 'Septicaemia was powerless to resist. His eyes burned into hers like 18-carrot diamond-cut Moissanites™. His muscular arms enfolded her body as she felt herself being swept away on an El Niño of passion. She could wait no longer. 'Take me now, Kendo,' she panted. 'Me cunt's as wet as Rod Hull's roof.'' (from 'The Lady and the All-In Wrestler', by Barbara Cartland).

Rodney *n. prop. rhym. slang.* Convoluted term for a *shite*, named after the mediocre Australian fast bowler Rodney Hogg, whose name rhymes with *bog*. 'Where've you been, Olivia?' 'In the dunny hav-

ing a Rodney, Cliff.'

rod the drains v. To *back scuttle.*

rod walloper *n.* One who *wallops* his *rod.*

rodeo sex *n.* A bedroom game where the couple adopt the *doggy position.* The gentleman then calls out an ex-girlfriend's name and sees how long he can stay on for. Also *bronco sex.*

rogan splosh *n.* An incredibly runny *shit,* accompanied by a fusilade of splattering *farts* the morning after a roadkill ruby.

roger *v.* To *fuck.* Often in the past tense. *'I gave her a jolly good rogering.'*

roger ramjet *n.* A *botter.*

Roland Kirk *1. n. prop.* A jazz musician (1936-1977) rightly lauded for his ability to get a tune out of two or more horns simultaneously, and thus *2. euph.* A *jazz actress* rightly lauded for her ability to get a tune out of two or more *horns* simultaneously.

Rolf Harris eating a banana *sim.* Descriptive of the close-up intercourse scenes in a very blurred, 200th generation *scruff video.*

Rolfies *n.* The pseudo-Aboriginal gasps and grunts produced when trying to pass an extremely large *didgeridoo.*

rolling down the hill *euph.* Of a *custard,* to make its way under its own steam down the guts towards the *chuff.* *'I'd open a window if I was you, your Holiness. Only I had 'Chicken Tonight' and six pints of homebrew for tea yesterday, and I can feel one rolling down the hill.'*

rolling the dice *v.* Feeding the ducks, spanking the monkey.

rolling thunder *n.* An overlong *air buffet* served up whilst walking past a line of people, such as would be dropped by Her Majesty the Queen backstage at the Royal Variety Performance.

roll in the hay *n.* What everyone wanted to do with Julie Christie in *'Far From The Madding Crowd'.* And Donald Sutherland did with her in *'Don't Look Back'.*

roll mop *n.* A mature lady's rolled up *fanny* flaps.

roll out the carpet *v.* To unpick the end of a fresh *bogroll* in order to impress a visitor.

rollover week *n.* A week when the *painters are in.*

roll the crevice *v.* To attempt to wipe one's *freckle* with the coarse cardboard tube after exhausting the supply of *bumwad.*

roly-poly *adj.* Tabloid prefix for any celebrity who's half a stone overweight. For example, *'Roly-poly actor Leonardo Di Caprio...'*

romancing the bone *n.* An evening in alone with a meal, a bottle of wine and some soft music, followed by a top shelf *stick vid.*

romp *v.* To chase a woman in a corset round and round a bedroom, lifting the knees very high, accompanied by 'BOING!' noises when leaping onto the bed.

Ronson *rhym. slang.* Arse. From Ronson lighter = *shiter.*

rook's nest *n.* An exceptionally untidy *faff.* *'Cor! Look at her. I bet she's got a minge like a rook's nest - all shit and sticks.'*

room clearer *n.* Of flatulent emissions, a *fart* which registers one notch higher than *breaking company* on the sphincter scale.

Rooney ramble *n.* A gentle stroll through a red light district.

Rooney's charisma *n.* That mysterious and indefinable quality which allows a fat, potato-ugly, prematurely-balding prostitute addict to secure a top shelf bit of *cabbage* for himself.

rooster *n*. A lady's *nether-wattle*. *Half a pound of liver*.

root *v*. To make love to.

rope the pony *v*. To *gallop the lizard*.

rose-tinted testicles *n*. Those items through which one looks back fondly on all previous sexual encounters when trapped in a long-term relationship.

rotoplooker *n*. *US*. Penis, *chopper*.

rotters *n*. Unpleasant looking *lungs*. The sort of saggy *tits* with *kneeshooter nips* normally encountered during amateur style entertainment on Granada Men and Motors. *Nasty bags*.

roughage *n*. Unkempt pubic foliage. High-fibre *holefood*.

roughing up the suspect *v*. What a vice squad copper tells his superiors he's doing when he's caught *polishing* his *bobby's helmet* in the seized porn store room.

round at Freddie's *adj*. To be *nicely poised, good with colours, light on one's feet*. 'That Duncan Norvelle - he's married with three kids, you know.' 'Never. I thought he was round at Freddie's.' 'No. That's just an act.'

roundhead *n*. A *pink Darth Vader* after the surgical removal of his *Kojak's rollneck*, a *yiddled whanger*.

round up the tadpoles *v*. To *wank, bash the bishop*.

row the boat *v*. A dual *tug* boat, multiple *wanking*. Nautical variation on the *downhill skiing* position.

royal decrees *n*. *Movements* passed whilst sat on the *throne*.

Royal Marine *n*. A *fanny* with a buzz cut.

Royal premiere *n*. The act of menstruation, ie. *rolling out the red carpet*.

Roy Castle's last blow *n*. A frankly unimpressive *trouser trumpet* that sounds like it's feeling very sorry for itself.

rub-a-tug shop *n*. Brothel, bordello, house of ill repute. Massage parlour supplying a rub down and a *tug off*.

rubber beer *n*. Booze bought with a return ticket. A pint one hasn't seen the last of. *Jesus beer*.

rubber gash *n*. The sailor's favourite. A plastic *fanny* which the manufacturers claim is 'better than the real thing.' A bargain at £8.99.

rubber Johnny *n*. A *blob*, contraceptive, *a jubber ray*. Also *rubber*.

rubber kebab *n*. An item of fast food with a high coefficient of restitution which bounces back from the stomach onto the pavement or taxi driver's head.

rubiks *rhym. slang*. *Gorilla salad, fusewire*. From Rubik cubic hair = *pubic hair*.

Ruby Murray *rhym. slang*. A *cuzza*.

rudimentary *n*. A late night TV *wanking* opportunity, thinly-disguised as a factual programme, eg. behind the scenes looks at the worlds of lap-dancing, the US hardcore porn industry or *tits* and *fannies*. Also *masturmentary*. 'Are you coming up to bed?' 'In a minute, dear. I'm just watching a rudimentary. Do you know where there's any tissues?'

rug munchers *n*. *Fanny noshers*.

ruined *adj*. A very attractive woman whose sex appeal has nonetheless been almost entirely nullified by her association with an unsuitable gentleman. *'Christ, that Billie Piper's a horny chimpoid.' 'Yeah, but that ginger twat Chris Evans has been there. That's ruined her for me.'* Other examples include Catherine Zeta-Jones.

rummage *n*. An act of *self-delight* indulged in by a dirty lady.

rump gully *n*. Viewed from *biffin bridge*, the gradually sloping valley beyond *kak canyon*.

Rumple Foreskin *n*. Penis, *John Thomas, junior*.

rumpo *n. Rumpy pumpy*.

Rumpole suntan *n*. An alcoholic red face as modelled by the late *'Rumpole of the Bailey'* actor Leo McKern.

rump ranger *n. Chocolate cowboy*.

rumpy pumpy *n*. Lightweight sexual shenanigans, slightly more erotic than *how's your father*. US equivalent *hoochie-coochie*.

runs, the 1. *n*. What English cricketers get when they face fast bowlers. 2. *n*. What English cricketers don't get when they face fast bowlers.

run the taps *v*. To take a *leak* following a spot of *bumfoolery*. From the practice of letting the taps run in a house with rusty pipes, in order to let out any unpleasant brown residue which may be present in the water.

rushin' roulette *n*. A suicidally-dangerous game whereby a gentleman attempts to *knock one off* when there is a fairly good chance that his wife may walk in on him.

Rusholme roulette *n. Farting* in the full knowledge that there is a one in six chance of *shitting* one's *kex*. Named after Rusholme, the district of Manchester famed for its curry houses.

russet gusset *n. Skidmarks* or *dangleberrian* deposits on the *shreddies. Marmite stripe*, the *starting grid at Brands Hatch*.

Russian yawn *n*. A *thirty-four-and-a-halfer*, a *cannonball*. A self-service *suck-off*.

rusting copper pipe *n*. A *night watchman*. One of them stubborn *arse sausages* that sit in the *pan*, refusing to be flushed away, and giving off a Ready Brek-style brown aurora into the water.

rusty scone cutter *n*. A very unhygienic dough-cutting implement. The *arsehole*.

rusty sheriff's badge *n*. Ride south along *biffin bridge* from *John Wayne's hairy saddlebags* and there it lies, right in the middle of *kak canyon*. Just before you reach *rump gully*. The *anus*.

rusty trumpet, play the *v*. To perform *horatio* very shortly after receiving a *rear admiral's* attention.

rusty water *n*. Liquid *feeshus* which is *pissed* out of the *arse*.

rusty zip *n*. An improperly-wiped buttock cleft, where the *shite* has been spread about and then left to dry out. *Robert Smith's mouth*.

Ss

sack artist *n.* A womaniser, gigolo, *fanny rat. Crumpeteer.*

sacofricosis *n. medic.* A mental condition, the main symptom of which is the desire to cut a hole in one's pocket to facilitate *self-pollution* in public places. *'We've get your test results back, Mr. Ross OBE, and it's bad news. You've got advanced sacofricosis.' 'Oh, cwumbs!'*

saddle bags 1. *n.* Labia, *piss flaps.* 2. *n.* Scrotum.

saga lager 1. *n.* Sherry or mild, depending on gender. 2. *n.* Geriatric *piss. 'I'd visit my granny more often if it wasn't for the smell of saga lager.'*

saga louts *n.* Packs of tea-fuelled pensioners travelling by coach who lay waste to garden centres and stately home gift shops.

sailor's ale *n.* The thick, salty, tangy beverage drunk by *sea bent* mariners whilst on long voyages. *'Adrift upon a glassy sea / No wind upon our sail / We pulled the boatswain's trousers off / And drank his sailor's ale'* (from *'The Rime of the Ancient Mariner'*, by Samuel Taylor Coleridge).

sailor's shot sock, fuller than a *sim.* Descriptive of when something is filled to bursting, eg. a post-Christmas binliner, the 4.24pm Newcastle to Prudhoe train, Tom Jones's skin.

salad days *n.* Descriptive of the *lettuce-licking* past times of a woman who is now back chomping sausages like a good 'un.

salad dodger *n.* A contumelious epithet for a fat bastard. One who at a buffet sidesteps the lettuce and celery and heads straight for the pork pies. *"Contrarywise', continued*

Tweedledee, 'if it was so, it might be; and if it were so, it would be; but as it isn't, it ain't. That's logic'. 'That's not logic, that's bollocks, you salad dodger." (from *'Through The Looking Glass'* by Lewis Carroll).

salami slapper *n.* He who tolls upon his own *bell end.* A *wanker.*

Sally bumps *n. Peanuts* in the process of being *smuggled.* Prominent nipples. From the *chapel hatpegs* constantly visible through the clothing of *'Coronation Street'* character Sally Webster.

Sally Gunnell *n. prop.* A motor trade term to describe a used car, ie. not much to look at but a fucking good runner.

salmon 1. *rhym. slang.* Sexually excited. From salmon on prawn = *the horn. 'I saw Pam Anderson's video on the internet last night. It didn't half give me the salmon, I can tell you.'* 2. *rhym. slang.* HMP. Tobacco. From salmon and trout = *snout. "Ere, you don't half give me the salmon, Lord Archer. Fancy giving me a blow job for an ounce of salmon?'*

salmon canyon *n.* Piscatorial pass leading to *tuna town.*

salmon handcuffs *n. Pink handcuffs.* Invisible restraints that keep a gentleman from seeing any of his friends. The metaphorical restraints with which a *pussy-whipped* gentlemen is shackled. *"This is quite rum do, Jeeves', I exclaimed. 'I've met Piggy for cocktails every Friday for ten years. Where the pip can he be?' 'If I may be so bold,' intoned Jeeves in that way of his, 'he has recently taken up with a soubrette from a London show, and I fear* *she has slapped the salmon hand-cuffs on the poor cunt."* (from *'What the Fuck, Jeeves?'* by PG Wodehouse).

salmon's head *n.* A hatless *one-eyed zipper fish* as viewed from underneath.

saloon doors *n.* A pair of well-used, swinging *fanny flaps* that one's *cock* swaggers into, only to be thrown out of three minutes later. Wild West style *beef curtains.*

salsa dip *n.* A splash about in the *crimson waves.*

salt *n.* 1960s Mod term for a *bird*

salt and pepper *n.* Horrible little *tits* where the nipple area is larger and more protruding than the rest of the breast, giving them the appearance of the silver-capped condiment shakers found in cafes.

Samantha *rhym slang.* A *ringpiece.* From Samantha Janus.

Sam Plank *rhym. slang. Stoke-on-Trent.* An act of *self abuse* named after the popular Radio Stoke disc jockey. *'Did you manage to pull last night?' 'No. I went home for a Pot Noodle and a Sam Plank.'*

Samurai *n.* A fearsome, ceremonial *pork sword.*

sand hole *n.* Of crowded beaches, the hole caused by sunbathing on one's stomach in order to conceal a *Jake.*

S and M *n. Rub-a-tug shop* parlance for sado-masochism. *Mr. Whippy.*

Sandy Lyles *rhym. slang.* Haemorrhoids.

Sangatte, do a *v.* Of married men, to make a *bid for the tunnel* in the middle of the night, almost certainly to be turned back by the wife.

Santa stuck up the chimney *exclam.* Tampon removal problems, often as a consequence of drunken intercourse.

santorum *n.* Amongst people who are *nicely poised,* the frothy mix of lubricant and faecal matter that is sometimes the by product of their saucy carryings-on. Amusingly named after the anti-gay US senator Rick Santorum.

sarson's nose *adj.* The condition of the *old fella,* post *vinegar strokes,* after leaving a *salty dressing* on the *pink lettuce salad.*

satiscraptory *adj.* Decriptive of something of a poor, but adequate standard, eg. BBC local radio, McDonald's food.

sat-nav *1. n.* An in-car electronic device which allows reps to find their way to cheap hotels and massage parlours whilst avoiding areas of traffic congestion. *2. n.* An in-head device which allows *bladdered* gentlemen to find their way home on a Saturday night whilst they are unconscious with the drink.

sauce *1. n.* Booze, usually in large quantities. *'That Keith Chegwin didn't half hit the sauce, you know.' 2. v.* To seduce. *3. n.* Cheek. *'He asked to borrow me motor, and then said could I bring it round and make sure the tank was full. What a fucking sauce!'*

sausage and doughnut situation *n.* Heterosexual intercourse. *'I did NOT engage in a sausage and doughnut situation with that woman. Miss Lewinsky. She merely sucked me off a bit and then I dropped my yop on her frock.'* (President Bill Clinton giving evidence to Senator Kenneth Starr).

sausage fat *n. Jitler.*

sausage grappler *n.* A *salami slap-*

per.

sausage jockey *n.* Passive male homosexual, anyone who sits on a sausage and bounces up and down. A *sausage rider.*

sausage kennel *n.* A male homosexual's *bottom.*

sausage pizza *n.* Closest thing to a *sausage sandwich* that *Miss Lincolnshire* is able to provide. A *diddy ride* on a lady with *stits.*

sausage pot *n.* A lady's privates.

sausage sandwich *n.* A juicy *salami frotted* between two pink *baps*, the end result of which is a *pearl necklace. Dutch.*

sausage supper *n.* Female equivalent of a *fish supper.*

sausage wallet *n.* A wallet for putting sausages in. A *fanny.*

SBD *abbrev.* Of *farts* and *farting*, Silent But Deadly. A subtle release of fatally-pungent *botty gas.*

SBJ *abbrev. medic.* Doctor's notes terminology for a senior citizen. Still Breathing, Just. A *coffin dodger*, a *low flying angel*, *estate agent's dream.*

SBV *abbrev.* Of *farts* and *farting*, Silent But Violent. *Minging fizzle* from the *fart fissure.*

scads *n. Kicksies, dunghampers, thunderbags.*

scallywagon *n.* Boxy white van with blacked-out square windows, the preferred mode of transport for guests of her majesty.

scare the cat *n.* To produce a startlingly loud *Exchange & Mart.*

scarlet emperor *n.* A red, rather bruised, male reproductive organ after an extended session of *self-help.*

scat n. Form of *shite*-fixated *grumble* particularly popular amongst our saucy Germanic cousins.

scatman *1. n.* A jazz singer who improvises nonsense 'Bill and Ben' style lyrics, eg. Sammy Davis Jnr. *2. n.* A teutonic *poo-game enthusiast.*

schizophrenic face *n.* Of a lady, to have stunningly beautiful eyes, but a nose like Ricky Tomlinson's.

schlong *n. Yiddish.* A large *putz.* A *schlonger.* A *kosher dill.*

schlong shed *n.* Condom, *stopcock, stiffy stocking.*

schmeckie *n.* Opposite of a *schlong.*

scholar's bonus *n.* A rare, but cherished glimpse of a short-skirted young lady's intimate nethergarments as she pedals past in a cycle-heavy city such as Oxford or Cambridge.

schoolboy error *n. Shooting one's load* far too early whilst *on the job.* Premature ejaculation.

school dinner *1. n.* A foul, brown mess, served in a large white bowl, the smell of which makes you heave. *2. n.* A toilet full of *shit.*

school run *1. n.* The act of dropping one's kids off at the school at the same time every morning. *2. n.* The act of *dropping one's kids off at the pool* at the same time every morning.

scissor bone *n.* The rectal guillotine which chops one's *logs* into manageable lengths. The *cigar cutter.*

scissor sack *n. medic.* A non-fatal genital injury in men caused by sitting down awkwardly in overly tight trousers. A *gentleman's discomfort.*

scissors, paper, stone *1. n.* A traditional playground game. *2. n.* The hand motion used by German porn stars in *fisting* movies; First two fingers, then four, then the full monty.

scissorwork *n.* Hot *quim*-to-*quim*

lezbo action.

scleg *n.* The sweat-prone yet sensitive area of skin between a fellow's *haggis* and his leg. Not to be confused with the *barse*. From *scrotbag* + leg. Also *bluck leg*.

scobie *n.* The low-level urinal at the end of the row, used by children, midgets and Dwight York. From Scobie Breasley, the diminutive jockey of the 1960s and 70s.

scooberty *n.* That period of adolescence when the male voice oscillates wildly and unpredictably between *basso profundo* and *soprano*, and thus resembles that of a popular, cheaply-animated caretaker-hunting cartoon Great Dane.

scoobysnack *n.* *Oral sex* involving a dog and a very tall sandwich.

scooter *n.* *Arse*. From the Dutch schoeter = *shitter*.

scoots *n. medic.* An affliction characterised by morbid frequency and fluidity of faecal evacuations. The *Brads*.

score from a set piece *v.* To *pull* a *bird* who is a friend of a friend, or one on a blind date, etc.

score from open play *v.* To *pull* a *bird* one has never met before by simply bumping into her in a pub, club, chippie, funeral parlour, etc. and chatting her up.

scotch egg 1. *n.* Party foodstuff of absolute last resort. 2. *n.* A *turd* which has rolled out of the trouser leg of a *Harold Ramp* who hails from north of the border.

scotchguard shite *n.* A *Brad* which, no matter how messy it feels on exit, leaves one's *brown eye* miraculously unsullied. Named after the 3M product sold to countless paranoid housewives by surly soft furnishing salesmen.

Scotch pancake *n.* A pool of *spew*. A *pavement pizza*.

Scottish bedwarmer *n.* A *fart*, anal announcement.

Scottish breakfast *n.* Two paracetamol.

Scottish play 1. *euph.* Shakespearean drama ('*Macbeth*' or '*Hamlet*' or something), the title of which cannot be spoken by superstitious *chickenshit* actors in case ill fortune befalls them. 2. *n.* Anal sex with an otherwise respectable partner.

scouse *v.* To misappropriate opportunistically. '*I say, what a poor show. I left my dressing room unlocked for five minutes and when I came back my gold and diamond cigarette holder had been scoused.*' (Terry-Thomas, Liverpool Magistrates Court, 1960).

Scouser's cashpoint *n.* A fruit machine.

Scouser's digit *n. medic.* Affliction, particularly common in the north west of England, preventing the sufferer from keeping his fingers out of the till.

Scouser's key *n.* A crowbar, hammer, half a brick or anything used to open someone else's back door.

Scouser's laptop *n.* A pizza.

Scouser's library *n.* A job centre.

Scouse slippers *n.* Prison-issue white training shoes.

Scouse tax *n.* A cheeky charge levied out of one's pockets by lovably light-fingered Liverpudlians when shopping on Merseyside.

scran *n.* That bit of a fellow's anatomy which falls between his *hairy swingers* and his clackervalve. The *barse, tintis, notcher, stinker's bridge*. The *perineum*.

scranus *n.* The fucking *barse* again.

Scrapheap Challenge *1. n. prop.* Channel 4 programme where teams compete to construct contraptions from scrap metal. *2. n.* The prospect of having to perform *cumulonimbus* on a *bird* who is *up on blocks*. So called because of the general messyness, metallic taste and all-perrading odour of dirty blood.

scratch *v. Liverpud.* Of a scouse fellow, to sign on.

scratcher *n.* Bed, *fart sack.*

scratter *n. Halifax.* A person of limited finances and breeding, eg. 8 Ace. Also *ronker.*

screamer *n.* A raving *poofter.*

screaming monkey *n.* A bit of female genitalia. Probably the bit which looks the most like a screaming monkey.

scree *n. coll.* Shale-like nuggets of *shit.* Approximately the size of a marrowfat pea.

scree *n. Shit.*

screw *v.* To have sex piggy-style, rotating clockwise due to a corkscrew-shaped *cock.*

screwnicorn *n.* A mythical and somewhat magical sex act whereby a lesbian puts a *strap-on dildo* on her forehead and goes at her partner like a bull at a gate.

scrincter *n.* The bit between the scrotum and the sphincter. The *tintis.*

scrobbing *n. onomat.* The sound made by a dog when licking its own genitalia.

scrogg *1. v.* To partake in in an act of penetrative sexual intercourse up a lady. To *fuck. 2. n.* An act of penetrative sexual intercourse partaken up a lady. A *fuck.*

scrote *n. Knacker, bollock brain.* A versatile testicular term of abuse.

scrotum pole *n.* Old Red Indian erection at the foot of which lie *John Wayne's hairy saddlebags,* and around which *Madam Palm and her five sisters* do ritual dances to precipitate *spunkfall.*

scrotum ticklers *n.* The huge comedy moustaches favoured by the acutely-abserved homosexualists who populate the cartoons illustrating Richard Littlejohn's columns in *'The Sun'.*

scrub *n.* An exfoliant facial treatment bestowed upon the *nosher* of a *stubbly bush.*

scrubber *n. Slapper,* vulgar woman, *dollymop.*

scrubbing the cook *n. milit.US. Bashing the bishop.*

scruburb *n.* A less than desirable area to live.

scruff *n.* Pornography, *muck, grumble. "Look what I've got', said William breathlessly , as he emptied the contents of his jumper at the Outlaws' feet. 'It's a load of scruff. Jumble found it under a hedge."* (from *'William's Milk Race'* by Richmal Crompton).

scrumping *1. n. US.* Having sex. *2. n. UK.* Stealing apples.

scruncher *n.* Opposite of a *folder.*

scrunchies *1. n.* Of *slappettes,* the colourful elasticated hairbands captured by rival teenage *slappers* in battle. *2. n.* Excess batter in a chip shop. *Scraps.*

scrunger *n.* Another name for one of those bicycle seat sniffers found lurking around the bicycle racks of convents and women's drop-in centres.

scrunion *n. Aus. medic.* The wrinkly scrotal remnant immediately preceding the perineum.

From scrotum + onion.

scrunt *n. coll. Blart, flange, gusset.* A group of attractive women. *'Suddenly, at the age of 25, the Prince was cast as the world's most eligible bachelor. On a Royal tour of New Zealand in 1973, he found himself having to batter off top-end scrunt with a shitty stick.'* (from *'HRH The Prince of Wales'* by Jim Bob Dimbleby).

scrut *n.* Hardcore *grumble* that would satisfy the curiosity of even the most ardent amateur gynaecologist. *Close up pink.*

scruttock *n.* The area of skin 'twixt *scrot* and *bot.* The *barse.*

scuffer *n.* A *cozzer,* a *rozzer,* a *tithead,* a *filth.*

scuff it 1. *v.* In football, to lose concentration at the critical moment, leading to a disappointing shot. 2. *v.* in *fucking,* to lose concentration at the critical moment, leading to a disappointing *shot.*

scumbag *n.* The ultimate term of abuse known to British tabloid journalists.

scumble 1. *n.* A *shit,* heavily-dated paint effect inflicted on the participants of TV room makeover programmes. 2. *n.* A language spoken exclusively by *Harold Ramps.* From Scottish + mumble.

scumper *n.* Someone who lays sheets of bog roll on the seat of a public toilet so as his *arse* does not touch the same place as someone else's *arse* has touched. The late *'Carry On'* star Kenneth Williams was known to *scump.*

scum shovel *n.* Any form of public transport used extensively by the underprivileged, eg. the no.11 Torry to Northfield bus in Aberdeen.

scumwad *n. US.* The ultimate term of abuse known to American tabloid journalists.

scuns *n. Scads.*

scutter *n. Slut, shag bag.*

scuttle *v.* To *sink the pink,* or *brown,* in a hurried fashion from behind.

scuttler *n.* A fellow who, for whatever reason, will not *piss* alongside another at a urinal, but instead scuttles off into a cubicle, usually locking the door too.

sea bent *adj.* Descriptive of a matelot whose sexual tastes have been re-oriented due to a prolonged period of enforced maritime abstinence. Of otherwise heterosexual sailors, to have a *ride on the other ferry* whilst at sea. *'Kiss me Hardy, I'm feeling distinctly sea bent.'*

sea biscuit 1. *n.* Famous racehourse. 2. *n.* A *Richard the Third* washed up on a beach.

seagulling *v.* The mischievous act of *bespangling* a passer by from a height, eg. a tree, a roof or a Status Quo hotel room balcony. Could lead to *Graham Norton's hair.*

seagulls' wellies *n.* Maritime used *blobs. 'How was your swim, Captain Webb?' 'Awful. I was only in the water ten minutes and I swallowed a turd and three seagulls' wellies. I'm going to write to the council.'*

seal of Hades *n.* The boundary between our world and the *devil's kitchen.* The *ringpiece.*

sea monster *n. Swamp donkey, hipocrocapig.*

seaside shithouse, fuller than a *sim.* Descriptive of something that is replete to bursting point. *'Take that bin bag out will you, Your*

Highness. It's fuller than a seaside shithouse.'

season cliff hanger *1. n. US.* In TV drama series, a final show which ends just at the exciting part, encouraging viewers to watch the next series. *2. n.* A large *shit* which cuts off at the exciting part causing one to wait for what feels like an eternity to get the ending.

secaturds *n. medic.* The muscles surrounding the *nipsy.*

second post *n.* A supplementary delivery of *anal parcels* which takes one by surprise half way through the morning.

second sitting *n.* An immediate, unavoidable return visit to the *shitter* after wiping and washing.

secret smile *n.* A *cunt.*

sediment *n.* The *totty crud* that remains unsyphoned at chucking out time in a night club.

see a friend to the coast *euph. Drop the kids off at the pool.*

seed *n.* That which is scattered in a *ladygarden.*

seed catalogue *n.* A *flesh mag.*

seeing to *n.* Sexual servicing, a 'jolly good' one of which is often said to have been given to a woman by a man.

see you next Tuesday *acronym.* Ingeniously offensive parting pleasantry allowing you the satisfaction of calling someone a *cunt* to their face without them knowing it.

self-catering *n.* See *self discipline.*

self-cleaning oven *1. n.* In the world of kitchen appliances, a cooker which does not in any sense whatsoever clean itself. *2. n.* The *cludge* of a female *ejaculatrix.*

self discipline *n.* Character-building regime engendered in the armed forces and public schools. *Masturbation.*

self help manual *n.* An item of literature that aids relaxation. An *art pamphlet*, a *flesh mag*, a *bachelor's newsletter.*

selling Buicks *v. US.* Vomiting. From the similarity of the sounds made by a chunderer to the cries of the Buick street vendors of Detroit, 'Buick! Buick!'

semen *n. Aphrodite's Araldite, joy Gloy, gunk, spunk, goo.*

semenal *adj.* A highbrow, intellectual way of referring to something as being *wank.*

semen-olina *n. Spunk* of an especially lumpy nature.

semi *1. n.* A *lazy lob on*, a *dobber*, a half erect penis. *2. n.* A house joined to one other house.

semi-demi-on *n.* A *quarter-on, half a lob on.* The first stirrings of *dobberdom.*

semi-on *n.* A partially-tumescent generative organ. *Half a teacake.*

send a sausage to the seaside *euph. Sink a few U boats.*

senorita beater *n.* Any Spanish lager, such as San Miguel etc.

separate-us apparatus *n.* A *condom, stiffy stocking.* 'Did you remember to bring the separate-us apparatus?' 'Oh, Rat's cocks! I didn't. Perhaps we'd better just play the bagpipes tonight.'

serpent socket *n.* That hole into which the *one-eyed trouser snake* is plugged.

serpent's tongue *n.* A forked *piss* caused by a *jazz egg* blocking the *hog's eye.* Twin jets. 'Jesus! You've pissed on the floor again.' 'Sorry, love, only I had the serpent's tongue this morning.'

serving it up *v.* Of a gentlemen, to

be *having it off* with, or *slipping a length* to, a lady. *'Throughout the early eighties, Prince Charles was plagued by persistent rumours that Major James Hewitt was serving it up to Princess Diana.'* (from *'Charles the Biography'* by Little Jimmy Dimbleby).

Seth Armstrong in a SARS mask *sim.* An erotically alluring description of a vaginally hirsute lady wearing thong underpants.

setting the video *v.* Sexual position, in which the lady is on her knees and elbows, with her *arse* in the air, tutting exasperatedly.

seven pint stunner *n.* A *bird* whose inner beauty only struggles to the surface after one has quaffed the best part of a gallon of *Nelson Mandela.*

seven/ten split *1. n.* In ten-pin bowling, a *pair of skittles* so far apart that hitting them both with a single shot is almost impossible. *2. n.* A really wide *fanny.*

seventy-one-er *n.* A *sixty-niner,* but with two fingers up the lady's *bonus tunnel.*

sex *1. n. It, the other, dirties. 2. v.* To pump someone full of semen. *'Babe, I'm gonna sex you up'* (*'Sex You Up'* song lyric, George Michael). *3. n.* A lady's *mingepiece. 'I want your sex' ('I Want Your Sex'* song lyric, George Michael).

sex act *n.* Versatile, vague tabloid term used to describe and denigrate specifically non-specific acts or *shenanigans.* Usually prefixed 'vile', 'lewd' or 'sordid.'

sexcrement *n. medic.* The foul mix of bodily fluids that is passed through the *nipsy* after several sessions of *backdoor love. Santorum.*

sexile *n.* A forlorn, lonely fellow in a bar, constantly checking his watch and desperately trying to make a half last all evening because his flatmate is *getting his end away.*

sex wee *1. n.* An ejaculation of *spongle. 2. n.* The *spongle* that is ejaculated. Coined on Channel 4's *'Bo Selecta!'* by Avid Merrion.

Shabba *n.* Plural *J. Arthurs.*

shackled *adj.* The condition of a man searching the house for *arse paper* with his trousers and underpants round his ankles.

shaft *1. v.* To *shag, screw. 2. n.* The penis. *3. n. pro.* A black private dick that's a sex machine to all the chicks in town.

shafterburn *n.* Painful friction-induced scorching of the *skinclad tube* caused by excessively *relaxing in a gentleman's way.*

shag *1. v.* To copulate, to *fuck.* A once shocking term, now lame enough to be used by 'right on' vicars. *2. n.* A sexual encounter, a *screw. 3. n. US.* 1950s dance craze. *4. n.* Type of sea bird. *5. n.* Tobacco. *6. n.* Something to do with carpets.

shag bag *n.* Loose woman, *a bike.*

shag dust *n. Fuck powder.* Make-up.

shag factory *n.* Joint which is heaving with *blit, knickerville, blart city.*

shaggability *n.* Measurement of how *shaggable* a person is on an arbitrary, non-scientific scale.

shaggable *adj.* Having a high degree of *shaggability.*

shagged out *adj.* Exhausted, *jiggered, buggered, zonked, fucked.*

shaggin' wagon *n.* A *passion wagon,* a *fuck truck,* a *spambulance.*

shagging a bike *sim.* To describe sex

with an extremely thin woman. *'These supermodels, nice faces, some of 'em, but get 'em in the fart sack and it'd be like shagging a bike.'*

shagging a waterbed *sim.* To describe sex with an extremely fat woman. *Riding the waves.*

shag monster *n.* A not necessarily ugly woman who has a voracious appetite for something to do with carpets. A *nymphomentalist.*

shagnasty *n.* A *shag monster* who is also extremely ugly.

shag slab *n.* The *altar of lurve,* bed, *passion pit, cock block, fart sack, scratcher.*

shag tags *n.* Love bites, *hickies, suckers.* Bruises from a physical game of *tonsil hockey.*

shake a tit *v.* To defecate spooneristically.

shake hands with the French *v.* To push one's finger through the *bumwad* when wiping the *freckle.* To *breach the hull, push through.* From the similarity to the moment when the two bore drills met in the Channel Tunnel and the English bloke forced his hand through the thin divide to shake the hand of his Gallic counterpart. *'Did you wash your hands before kneading that dough, Nigella?' 'Erm, no, Charles. But it's okay, it's not as if I've shaken hands with the French today.'*

shake hands with the wife's best friend *v.* To perform an act of *self-pollution.*

shake hands with the Wookie *v.* Of those men blessed with eight-foot-long hairy *cocks* that make growling noises, to *wank.*

shake the bishop's hand *v.* To have a *piss,* as opposed to sticking your

hand through a hole in the lavatory wall *and wanking* him off.

shake the lettuce *v.* Of females, to *pe,* and specifically, to give the *beef curtains* a quick tumble dry afterwards.

shake the snake *v.* Male equivalent of *shake the lettuce,* the object being to dislodge any *forget-me-nots* before returning the *schlong* to the *shreddies.*

shaking hands with the unemployed *n. Wanking.*

shaking like a shitting dog *sim.* A bad attack of the DTs after a night on the *sauce.*

shaking like an flatpack wardrobe *sim.* Descriptive of the female equivalent of *vinegar strokes.*

shampoo the rug *v.* To lose one's *population paste* on a *mapatasi.* Perhaps when *getting off at Edge Hill.*

Shamu *n.* An overly-acrobatic *dreadnought* that splashes the spectating testicles. From the performing whale of the same name.

shandy andy *n.* A *jizzmop.*

shandydextrous *adj.* To be blessed with the ability to give one's *monkey* an equally vicious *spanking* with either hand.

shandy sunbed *n.* A bench in a park or a precinct.

shandy tan *n.* The ruddy-red complexion sported by tramps after spending too long asleep on the *shandy sunbed.*

shark *v.* To go on the *pull,* using aggressive, sly or cunning tactics.

shark's fin *n.* The profile of a neighbour's *beetle bonnet* viewed through a tight bikini bottom whilst sunbathing on the beach.

shark's mouth *n.* A somewhat unsettling term for a gentleman's urinal.

sharks sniffing, have the *euph.* Of a lady, to be afflicted with monthly uncleanliness. *"My darling, at last we are alone,' murmured Heathcliff, as he took Cathy in his arms. 'I cannot wait a moment longer. I must have you now.' 'Sorry, love, I've got the sharks sniffing,' she replied."* (from *'Wuthering Heights'* by Tracey Bronte).

shart *v.* To pass wind with an unexpected non-gaseous component. To *follow through.*

shat on from a height *v.* To be badly exploited, humiliated, let down.

shatin underwear *n.* The amusingly soiled *undercrackers* found up back alleys, in shop doorways and stuffed through building society letterboxes on Sunday mornings.

shatkins *n.* Rapid, astonishingly-effective diet based on the somewhat controversial theory that the most effective way to lose weight is to acquire a bacterial stomach infection by the intake of meat only, especially 2am burger bar fayre. *'Good grief, you've lost weight since yesterday.' 'Yes, six stones. I've been on the shatkins diet.'*

shat trick *n.* The professional goal of the salaried worker, ie. three *Mr. Browns* in one working day.

shave a horse *v.* To have a *piss, take a leak.*

shaven haven *n.* A bald *monkey's forehead.*

shed *n.* Large, promiscuous woman. Somewhere to stick one's *tools.*

shedded *adj.* Trousered, cattled.

sheep dog trials *rhym. slang.* Carpet tiles.

sheep's heart on a Vim tin *sim.*

Scot. Descriptive of a *hard on* to be proud of.

sheep sitting *adj. On the blob,* dropping clots.

sheezer *n.* A woman who exhibits a disproportionate number of male traits in her everyday behaviour, eg. drinking, watching football, excessive masturbation.

Sheffield hammer *n.* A rolled-up newspaper, used to hammer nails into bits of wood, and which can be unrolled before the *scuffers* arrive.

Sherman *rhym. slang.* A *tug.* From Sherman tank = *wank.*

Shetland rabbit, hung like a *sim.* To have a *cock* like that of Bobby Davro. Also *hung like a Chinese mouse.*

she-tox *n.* A period when a married gentleman's spouse is away, during which he cleanses his system of her wholesome influences. A welcome relapse into bachelorhood ways of drinking, *wanking* and curry-eating himself daft.

shift *v.* To *shag, screw.*

shift, put in a *v.* To have sexual intercourse with a partner when one can't really be *arsed. 'What's up, George? Why the long face?' 'Oh, it's me and the missus's 34th wedding anniversary. She'll be expecting me to go home and put in a shift tonight.'*

shims *n.* Ladyboys.

Shipman, to do a *v.* From Harold Shipman. To inject a lady much older than oneself. *Granny banging.*

shirt fly *n.* A 'yes man'. One who is always up the gaffer's *arse.* A *fartsucker,* a *brown noser,* a *Penfold.*

shirtful *n.* A well-stocked *rack. 'My, what a shirtful. You've got the job.'*

shirt lifter *n.* One who gently lifts the tails of another man's shirt before sticking his *cock* up his *brown eye*. An *uphill gardener*, a *brown hatter*.

shirt potatoes *n.* Tits, melons, top bollocks.

shirt raiser *n.* A mighty zephyr from the *brass eye*. An enormous *fart*.

shit *1. v.* To *shit*, defecate, *sink the Bismarck, build a log cabin, crimp one off, light a bum cigar. 2. n.* Crap, excrement, stools, assorted faecal matter. *3. n.* Git, sod, get, a *shitty* person, usually 'little'. *4. adj.* Crap, useless. *'Shit weather for this time of year, eh, vicar?' 5. exclam.* Oh dear.

shit a brick *1. interj.* Exclamation of surprise. *2. v.* To be scared, to *papper* one's *trollies*.

shitboy *n. Northumb.* Term of abuse for one engaged in menial employment. *'How, Shitboy! Big Mac and chips!'*

shitcloud *n.* A common meteorological phenomenon involving a silent movement of wind and a strong smell of bad eggs.

shit diamonds *v.* The end result when one is desperate for a *number two*, but is nevertheless denied access to the *chod bin*, so that one's *feeshus* get packed tightly into the *bomb-bay*. *'Hurry up in there, your Holiness. I'm shitting diamonds out here.'*

shite *See shit.*

shite alight *n.* A doorstep incendiary *Thora* used as an offensive-smelling weapon against one's neighbour's slippers.

shit-eating grin *n.* Exaggerated, smug, self-satisfed smile as worn by the likes of Noel Edmonds.

shite house *n.* Outside lavatory,

shiter *n. Arse, kak cannon.* That which *shites*.

shit-faced *n. Arseholed*, intoxicated, *para-fuckin-lytic*.

shit house *n. 1.* A *crapper. 2. n.* A domicile of poor quality.

shit house shin pad *n. nav.* A concealed *grumble mag* wrapped around a sailor's leg under his sock as he makes his way to the HMS Ark Royal *crappers* for a *wank*.

shitingale *n.* One who breaks into song whilst *dropping a length of dirty spine*, usually in order to shield his audience from the slightly less tuneful sounds being produced by his *turtle guillotine*.

shit kiss *n.* A small, star-shaped brown mark left on the chin of a none-too-fussy *cumulonimbulist*.

shit limpet *n.* A lady who is hopelessly devoted to her loutish *cunt* of a boyfriend, despite regular beatings and his constant infidelity.

shit locker *n. Arse, bomb bay, chamber of horrors.*

shitmus test *n.* Like a litmus test, only instead of indicator paper in a laboratory there's *arse paper* in a lavatory, and instead of an acid/base there's an *anus* that might have let *something slip* whilst *stepping on a duck*. *'Crikey, I think there was something in that. I'd better go and take a shitmus test.'*

shit on your own doorstep *euph.* Foul the nest. eg. *shag* one's mother-in-law whilst totally *pissed. Piss on your chips.*

shit pump *n.* The television. *'I'm off to bed, love. Don't forget to turn the shit pump off when you come up.'*

shits, the *n.* Of *smallroom dancing*, those up-tempo *trots* which include the *Tijuana cha-cha*, the *sour apple quickstep* and the *Aztec two-step*.

shit scrape *n. Arse wipe.*

shit-smuggler's rucksack *sim.* The *ne plus ultra* of halitosis. *'Fuck me, what have you been eating, Your Majesty?' 'I don't know what you mean, Lord St. John.' 'Your breath smells like a shit-smuggler's rucksack, ma'am.'*

shitsophrenia *n. medic.* The condition where the sufferer alternates between having wild *squirts* and normal bowel movements.

shit splitter *n.* A g-string worn so tight on the lady's *heave-ho* as to fillet the *brown trout* in the unlikely event that she *follows through* on a *cheese cracker.*

shit stabber *n.* A homosexual *pork swordsman.*

shitstopper *n.* An unexpectedly large household bill, derived from the practice of reading the mail whilst on the toilet.. *'And now we move onto the case of Mr. Jack Trubshaw of St Neots, who last winter received a right shitstopper from British Gas, even though his central heating is oil-fired.'* (Nicky Campbell, *'Watchdog'*, BBC TV).

shitter *1. n.* Anus, *kakpipe, council gritter. 2. n.* A sit down lavatory, the pan.

shitterati *n. coll.* Collective term for the heroic figures of the age who turn up on programmes such as *'I'm a Celebrity, Get me Out of Here', 'Britain's Worst Celebrity Drivers'*, etc. The kind of people who would happily fuck a pig if it were to get their face on TV, eg. Bubble off *'Big Brother'*, the coughing major off *'Who Wants to be a Millionaire'*, The Hamiltons,

Jeremy Spake etc.

shitter chatter *n.* Long-winded anal babble emitted when a *shit* is expected.

shitter's ridge *n.* The *scranus* etc.

shit tickets *n. Bumwad, arsewipes, turd tokens, brown shield stamps.* Bathroom tissue.

shitting through a sponge *n.* A novel toilet ability gained after a night eating delicious curries at the Curry Capital.

shit trigger *n.* The first cigarette of the day, which has the effect of pulling the pin out of the *chod grenade. 'I Love Phillip Morris king size. It's not just because they're clean and fresh tasting. It's not just because their mellow taste gives me mouth and throat comfort and freedom from cigarette cough. And it's not just because they have a great shit trigger action and give me all day smoking enjoyment. I love them because they're the mildest high tar cigarette on the market.'* ('I Love Philip Morris' advertisement featuring Lucille Ball, 1953).

shitty shitty gang bang *n.* A particularly messy *arsefest.*

shitty stick *n.* A stick, covered in *shit*, used by men with powerful cars to stave off advancing *scrunt.*

shitwreck *n.* The broken-up remnants of a scuttled *dreadnought*, lying in deep water by the S-bend.

shit your pants *v.* To *drop a brick, cake your kecks, papper your trolleys.*

shniffle-piffler *n.* Somebody else who sniffs lady's bicycle seats.

shoelace view *n.* A gentleman's surreptitious glimpse of a bird's gusset gained whilst pretending to tie his shoelace.

shooting boots on, to get one's 1. *v.* Football commentator's phrase, to describe the actions of a player who has excelled in the 'kicking the ball at the goal' part of the game. 'Rooney's certainly got his shooting boots on for Manchester United today, Gary.' 2. *v.* Phrase describing the bizarre contortions a gentleman's feet go through in the moments leading up to a *pop shot*. *'Rooney's certainly got his shooting boots on up that raddled old prostitute today, Gary.'*

shooting bunnies *n.* Polite euphemism for *farting*. Passing wind, *blowing off.* Also *kill the Easter bunny.*

shooting times *n. Self help literature, DIY mags.* Bongular magazines.

shoot in your boot *euph.* To be so sexually excited as to ejaculate into the top of one's footwear.

shoot your load/bolt/wad/stack *v.* To ejaculate, *lose your mess, discharge the mutton musket.*

shopkeeper *n.* A sudden, movement of *stoolage* into the *bombbay*, that occurs completely unexpectedly. Named after the fez-wearing fancy dress shopkeeper in *'Mr. Benn'*, who would habitually appear in a similar unnerving manner.

shopping *n.* The underpant aftermath of *follow through.* 'Did I detect a twin tone there, your Honour?' 'I'm afraid so. Court adjourned for fifteen minutes whilst I check my trolleys for shopping.'

shot at the title *n.* A do-or-die chance to have a go on a bird's *snatch.*

shot from the starter's gun *euph.* A *cock* up the *arse.* See *jockey's starting position.*

shotgun fart *n.* A sudden ballistic *poot* which peppers pellets of *crapnel* into the toilet bowl or underpants.

shoulder boulders *n.* Big breasts, *gazungas.*

show off *v.* Of a woman, to exhibit the hystrionic symptoms of premenstrual tension.

shpaddiel *n.* The long-winded comedy anecdotes told by David Baddiel which result in a death-like silence.

shramp *v.* To enjoy the incredibly common hobby of sniffing ladies' recently-vacated bicycle seats. To *quumf, snudge, snurgle, snuftify.*

shreddies *n. Undercrackers, kecks, trolleys.*

shrek *n.* A large, shaven-headed man with bad teeth and protruding ears found on low-brow, daytime moron-bating programmes such as *'Trisha'.*

shrimp *v.* To suck someone's toes for perverted sexual gratification.

shrink-wrapped gammon *n.* A lady who wears clothing several sizes too small for her *lovely personality.*

shtup *v. Yiddish.* To have sex, *fuck, bang.*

shunt *v.* To *shtup.*

Siamese quims *n. Scissor sisters. Lezzas* who are constantly *bumping fur.*

side winders *n. Spaniel's ears* which appear to be gravitating towards the oxters. *Pit fillers.*

sideburns *n.* The marks left on multi-storey car park walls by women who could really do with power steering.

sidepipe *n.* A semi-erect *cock* visible down one leg of a tight pair of trousers, as sported by *rock poo-*

dles and gentlemen in tightly-packed London Underground carriages.

sidesaddle *1. n.* A demure horse-riding style preferred by ladies so as not to snap their *virgin strings* before their wedding night. *2. n.* Non-conventional *porcelain pony*-riding style favoured by the more capaciously-buttocked defecator.

Signora Romero *n.* An apparently beautiful woman who, on closer inspection, is sporting a moustache under her makeup. From the natty facial hair visible in close-ups of Cesar Romero's Joker in the 1960s 'Batman' TV series.

sign the visitor's book *v.* To leave a note of appreciation at the bottom of another's *skidpan*. *Sign the guest book.*

Sigourney Weaver *rhym. slang.* Beaver.

silencer *n.* A *pap-baffle.*

silent movie, watch a *1. v.* To enjoy the slapstick, dialogue-free antics of Buster Keaton, Harold Lloyd, Fatty Arbuckle and friends. *2. v.* To anxiously thrash one's genitals within an inch of their lives whilst watching a *grumble vid* with the sound muted so as not to disturb the wife asleep upstairs.

silicone strap *n.* The strap of a shoulder or handbag which pulls tightly in between the *baps,* enhancing their size and profile without the need for costly cosmetic surgery. A *tit splitter.*

silicone valley *n.* The cleavage 'twixt adjoining *bazongers.* The *Bristol Channel.*

silly string *1. n.* A light-hearted novelty *shit* that squirts out of one's *aeros-hole* in a rapid and erratic manner. Breaks the ice at parties.

Occasionally incorporating small solid lumps, when it is known as a *bicycle chain. 2. n.* Sticky substance light-heartedly sprayed in the face of an actress in a slapstick *art film.* Kept in a cannister that requires vigorous shaking.

Simon Cowells *rhym. slang.* Bowels, ie. things that can be irritable and are usually full of *shit.*

sing a rainbow *v.* To *shout soup.*

sing at St. Pauls *v.* To perform *cumulonimbus* on a woman with a *bucket fanny.*

Singer *n.* Sexual athlete, he or she who goes *at it* like a sewing machine.

singing into the mic *sim. Horatio* performed in the style of a *slag night* karaoke star.

singlie rosettes *n.* The discarded *jizzmops* that adorn the floors of unattached men's rooms. *Poppadoms, wanker's crisps.*

sing sweet violets *v.* Airy version of *building a log cabin,* to *take a dump.*

sink a few U boats *v.* To drop a few *depth charges.*

sink plunger *n.* A *tug* administered by an inexperienced woman where she appears to be attempting to snap your *banjo* and pull your *five-skin* over your *clockweights;* the action she would use when unblocking a sink. Opposite of a *squid wank.*

sink the Bismarck *v.* To pass one *fucking* enormous stool, deposit a *U blocker.*

sink the sausage *v.* To get one's *leg over.*

siphon the python *v.* To take a *Chinese singing lesson, see a man about a dog.* To go for a *piss.*

Sir Anthony *rhym. slang.* A proper

charlie. From Sir Anthony Blunt = *cunt*.

Sir Cliff's neck *n*. The bit of taut, elongated *scrotum* just above the bit that's got your *knackers* in.

Sir Douglas *rhym. slang. Shit*. From Sir Douglas Hurd ~*turd*.

SISO *acronym*. A gentleman who suffers from premature ejaculation. A *two-push Charlie*. From Straight In Straight Out.

sitting on an elephant *adj*. To be highly *burbulent*, to have *brewed a massive one up*. *"Would you kindly evacuate to the drawing room, my dear, and take the girls with you' Mr. Bennet whispered. 'I indulged myself in partaking of rather a surfeit of cook's magnificent sprouts this lunchtime, and I fear I am now sitting on an elephant."* (from 'Pride And Prejudice' by Jane Austen).

sitting on the stove *euph*. Of a lady, to have been *scuttled* from behind so hard and so often that she develops twin circular red glowing patches at the back and top of her thighs, as if she has been resting her *arse* on the two front rings of the cooker hob.

six-back *n*. The not-overly-attractive rolls of lard on the backs of fat grannies. *Back tits*.

six nowt *n*. Descriptive of something performed with gusto and enthusiasm.

six-pack grip *n*. See *tenpin*.

six point niner *n*. (6.9) A *sixty-niner* which is interrupted by a period.

sixteen valve *n*. A stunner, a corking *bird*.

sixth gear *n*. *Wanking*, especially in a parked car. See *stick shifter*.

sixtitty-nine *n*. A sort of splendid

lesbian version of *looping-the-loop* which somehow involves four knockers.

sixty grit *1. n*. The coarsest grade of sandpaper available. *2. n*. The coarsest grade of woman available. *'Up betimes, and much perturbed to find a veritable piece of sixty grit alongside me in the fart sack. Resolved never again to mix the port and the stout.'* (from 'The Diary of Samuel Pepys').

sixty-eight *n*. Oral sex undertaken on the understanding that the favour will be returned. *"Ere, give us a sixty-eight and I'll owe you one.'*

sixty-nine *n*. *Soixante-neuf, loop the loop*. A *sixty-niner*.

size ten *euph*. How girls of sizes fourteen to eighteen describe themselves prior to going on a blind date.

skeet *1. v. US*. To shoot clay pigeons. *2. v*. To *shoot your load*. To come off at the *Billy Mill roundabout*.

skeeze *v. US*. To *shag, schtup*.

skelpit erse *sim. Scot*. Descriptive of a face that looks like a *smacked arse*.

skid marks *n*. Severe *russet gusset, pebble dashing* of the *undercrackers*, the *turtle's brylcreem*.

skidmata *n*. The miraculous brown wounds which manifest themselves on the fingertips of one who is a martyr to thin *bumwad*. Also *taxi driver's tan*.

skiing position *n*. *Wanking* two men off at the same time while wearing only a helmet, goggles and thick mittens.

skin boat n. Penis. *'I think I'll sail the old skin boat to tuna town.'*

skin chimney *n*. A flue that requires

regular sweeping with a *womb broom*.

skin-clad tube *n*. A *live sausage*, a *girlometer*.

skin flick *n*. A tame *fuck feature*, blue movie, *mamba matinee*.

skin flute *n*. A *fleshy flugelhorn*, *bed flute*, *pink oboe*.

skin grafts *n*. Somewhat unimpressive *tits*.

skinternet *n*. Ceefax, teletext. From skint + internet.

skipper *n*. A lady's *clematis*, a *love button*, a *wail switch*. See *a man in a boat*.

Skippy *n*. A promiscuous male who jumps about from *bush* to *bush*. A *fanny hopper*.

skirt *n*. *coll*. Fanny, blart, toosh, talent. *'I've got a pink ticket tonight. Let's get down the bar and pick up a bit of skirt.'*

skirt lifter *n*. The female equivalent of a *shirt lifter*. A *carpet muncher*, a *lezza*.

skit *v*. To *shit* diarrhoea.

skittered *adj*. Afflicted with the *skitters*.

skitters, the *n*. The *shits*, the *squirts*, the *Earthas*.

skittling *n*. *Dining at the Y* during *rag week*. From the popular fruit-flavoured confectionery catch-phrase, ie. *'Taste the rainbow'*.

skittuin *n*. The product of the *skitters*, especially in dogs, *canine paint stripper*, puddles of brown acidic gunge on the carpet.

skull buggery *n*. Pugwashing, sala-mi-sucking. Also *skull-fucking*.

skyagra *n*. A quick flick through the satellite TV channels before bed-time, made by a middle-aged gentleman in search of something to boost his flagging sex-drive.

slabberdash *v*. In fighting or romance, to slap one's opponent or lover upon the side of the face with a semi-erect penis. To *chap*.

slack mabbut *n*. A *hippo's mouth*, a *beef wellington*.

sladger *n*. A west country term for a lady's *minge*. A *Cornish fanny*.

slag 1. *n*. A woman of little virtue, *slapper*. **2.** *n*. Waste material from a mine. **3.** *n* Term of abuse (pro-nounced *slaaaaaag*) applied liber-ally to male criminals in 'The Sweeney.' **~off 4.** *v*. To deprecate verbally.

slagazine *n*. Ladies' periodical that does not make too many intellectu-al demands on its readership, eg. *'Take a Break'*, *'Chat'*, *'Hello'*, *'OK'*, *'Spare Rib'* etc.

slagbait *n*. Aftershave.

slag bat *n*. A crude term for the *blood stick*.

slaggle *n*. *coll*. Collective noun for a group of young ladies who are gen-erous with their affections. From slag + gaggle.

slag hammer *n*. A *tool* a gentleman uses for *banging fannies* rather than nails.

slag heap *n*. A run-down pub or nightclub in any northern town.

slag night *n*. High-spirited female binge drinking excursion in a town centre. A *hen night*. Also *slag do*.

slag stamp *n*. A tattoo applied to the small of a *salad dodger's* back in the mistaken belief that it will dis-tract attention from her enormous *arse*.

slag wellies *n*. Knee-high boots.

slam dumping *n*. A light-hearted jape whereby the prankster *shits* in the cistern rather than the bowl. *Top decking*.

slam hound *n*. US. Slapper, slut.

slam in the lamb *v*. Bayonet

manoeuvre involving the *mutton musket*.

slam on the brakes *v*. To stop wiping one's *arse* for some reason, eg. the house burning down, with the full knowledge that the process is incomplete, resulting in *skid marks* or *russet gusset*.

slam spunk *v*. To have sex.

slap and tickle *n*. A sex act, a bit like *rumpy pumpy*, whereby a man wearing a dress shirt and sock suspenders chases an excited lady round a bed before catching her, playfully slapping her *buttocks*, tickling her ribs and *fucking* her. A *romp*.

slap and trickle *n*. A perfunctory, routine act of *self abuse* that elicits only a half-hearted return on one's *wristy investment*, possibly as a result of the four *wanks* one has had in the previous couple of hours. A low budget *money shot*.

slaphead *n*. A *chrome dome*, a *baaldie*.

slaphood *n*. A *slapper's* prime of life.

slapper n. *Slag*, dirty woman. She who has been around a bit. From the Yiddish 'schlepper' meaning 'I don't fancy yours much.'

slapperazzi *n*. *coll*. The humorous youths who use their mobile telephones to make amusing films of their friends committing acts of grievous bodily harm on innocent bystanders. *Happy slappers*.

slapper trapper *n*. A man who, lacking the wherewithal to trap a *fox*, settles for hunting *swamp hogs*.

slappertite *n*. A hunger for loose women. *'Do you fancy a fuck, Bill?' 'No thanks, Hillary. I don't want to ruin my slappertite.'*

slappette *n*. A betracksuited, *hick-ied*, bubblegum-chewing, *scrunchie*-wearing fledgling *slapper*.

slapster *n*. A *slaphead*.

slapstick *n*. A light-hearted, comical *wank*.

slap the monkey *v. Bash the bishop*. Also *spank the monkey*. To do a *Mary Chipperfield*.

slash *n*. A *piss, wee wee*.

slash and burn 1. *n*. Third world deforestation technique. 2. *n*. A painful symptom of the *pox* and the *clap*.

slash palace *n*. Public lavatory.

slash point *n*. Sheltered area in a town centre which affords privacy for the purpose of depositing urine. *'Hang on lads, I've just got to nip to the slash point before I flood me Calvins.'*

slate layer's nailbag *sim*. Descriptive of very saggy or battered *labia*.

slats 1. *n*. Ribs. *'I'm gonna rattle her slats with me womb broom.'* 2. *Aus. Beef curtains. 'I'm gonna part her slats with me womb broom.'*

sledge *n*. A bloke who is constantly *pulled* by *dogs*.

sledging 1. *n*. Unsporting cricket match repartee designed to put batsmen off their stroke. 2. *n. Aus.* Consenting impolite *rumpy pumpy*. Acts of intercourse during which one or both parties abuse each other with colourful profanities. Foul-mouthed pillow talk. *'August 6th. To the BBC for a recording of 'Call My Bluff' with Frank (Muir), Ian (Ogilvy), Angharad (Rhys), Hannah (Gordon) and Joyce (Grenfell). Joyce afterwards invited me to take tea in her room at the Savoy. One thing led to another and we ended up sledging into the early hours. Gracious, what a potty-mouth she can be.'* (from

'Fiddling in the Foliage', the memoirs of Arthur Marshall).

sleep in a tent v. To have a large penis. 'Fancy coming back to my place? You'll not be disappointed. I sleep in a tent.'

sleeping beast n. Flaccid cock, marshmallowed main pipe. A dead budgie.

sleeping fruit bat n. A vagina with flaps so big and leathery, it appears that the lady has a member of the genus Pteropus napping between her legs. A resting pterodactyl.

sleeping policeman 1. n. A hump in the road, designed to slow down traffic and remove exhaust pipes from sports cars. 2. n. An officer of Her Majesty's Constabulary in his pyjamas with his eyes shut. 3. n. An angry penis, tucked up behind the belt in order to conceal it from family or friends.

slice n. A portion of hairy pie. A vagina.

slice of cheesecake n. A portion of horatio. 'Belgravia was powerless to resist. His eyes burned into hers like caborundums. His strong arms enfolded her tender body as she felt herself being swept away in an Aurora Australis of passion. Eagerly she fell to her knees, pulled down his scuds and helped herself to a slice of cheesecake.' (from 'The Lady and the Darts Player', by Barbara Cartland).

Slimbridge, dawn chorus at sim. The cacophonous symphony of hooting, quacking, honking and whistling which emanates form a lavatory cubicle occupied by a person paying in installments for a particularly virulent and delicious slap-up feed from the Curry Capital, formerly the Rupali Restaurant, Bigg Market, Newcastle upon Tyne. From the aural similarity to the early morning sounds heard at the late Sir Peter Scott's famous duck zoo.

slime v. Aus. To ejaculate, chuck one's muck. 'Have you slimed yet Rolf?' To reach Lake Wendouree.

slip a length v. To fuck, from the male viewpoint. 'I'd slip her a length any day of the week.'

slip her a crippler v. A few notches up from slip her a length, to shag someone so hard they can't walk.

slippery as a butcher's cock sim. Untrustworthy, sly. From the well known fact that all butchers take carnal advantage of the meat in the back room before selling it.

slit n. Blit, fanny, vertical bacon sandwich.

slob's oven sim. Descriptive of an overused and undercleaned fanny. With black, carbonized chips lying round the bottom of it. One that would benefit from a good scrubbing with Mr. Muscle and a wire brush.

sloom n. medic. The lubricating secretion of the lady's Bartholin's glands. Blip, moip, chin varnish.

slop dodger n. A prudish or frigid lady who for some reason objects to getting her face bespunkled by a gentleman.

slop on n. A state of female sexual arousal. A wide on.

sloppy seconds n. To stir the porridge. To stick one's naughty paintbrush into a billposter's bucket.

slot n. Slit.

slot garnish n. A frilly bit of nothing which looks nice, but is quickly pushed to one side so one can tuck into the meaty main course. Any ladies' *farting crackers* bought from the Ann Summers shop.

slot machine *n*. A battery-powered neck massager, shaped like a big nobbly *cock*. A vibrator.

slow puncture *euph*. One of those days when one seems to be constantly losing gas. *'I don't know what was in my delicious curry from the Curry Capital Restaurant, Bigg Market, Newcastle upon Tyne last night, but I seem to have a slow puncture today.'*

slut *n*. Slapper, slag, bike.

slybrarianship *n*. In gentlemen, the discreet stewardship of their *grumble* stash.

smackanory *n*. The heart-rending tale of woe with which heroin addicts routinely regale passers by in the hope of relieving them of their small change.

Smackdonalds *n*. Residence in a less than salubrious neighbourhood where money is deposited in one window and pharmaceuticals dispensed at another.

smacket *n*. A drug addict's multi-pocketed coat worn when skulking round shops.

smack generator *n*. An electrical goods retailer used by thieves to convert stolen goods into cash for heroin.

smack oneself about *v*. To *relax in a gentleman's way*. To masturbate.

smackpool illuminations *n*. Extremely premature and gaudy Christmas lights found adorning houses in the country's less salubrious locales.

smacksuit *n*. A set of market-bought athletic clothes of the sort favoured by youngsters on Britain's more vibrant estates.

smack tokens *n*. Items of second-hand electronic equipment, eg. car radios, laptop computers, videos with the plugs cut off.

smear test *1. n. medic*. Medical procedure which detects precancerous cells in the cervix. *2. n*. Toilet procedure to determine if one has got all the *shit* off one's *nick*.

smear test pizzas *n*. Budget supermarket pizza on which the toppings have been kept to a minimum for reasons of economy.

smedgie *n. Can*. An hilarious practical joke whereby a lady's *bills* are vigorously yanked up her *clopper*. From *smeesh* + *wedgie*.

smeesh *1. n. Can*. Female reproductive *farmyard area*. The *snapper*. *2. n. Can*. A collective noun for ladies. *Blart, tussage, cabbage*. *3. n. pej. Can*. A doltish fellow. A *fuckwit*.

smeg *1. n. Knob cheese*. *2. n. prop*. Amusingly-named Swedish manufacturer of white goods. *3. n*. A substitute for *fuck* overused in *'Red Dwarf'*.

smeg cup *n*. The cupped hand traditionally used by *wankers* as a receptacle to catch their *muck* when *relaxing in a gentleman's way* in a standing position. A *wanker's chalice*.

smegma dome *n*. A baby *bell end*, with a waxy, red skin. The *lid*.

smegma *n*. See *smeg*.

smeg peg *n*. An unwashed penis, with a gamey aroma redolent of cheese, *spunk* and stale *blip*.

smellmet *n*. A smelly *helmet*. From smelly + *helmet*.

smellody *n*. A *fart* of a musical timbre.

smig *n. W. Yorks*. A person of *shit* quality from Huddersfield.

Smint shuffle *n*. The practice

whereby a gentlemen allows a small breath-freshening mint to dissolve under his *fiveskin* in order to make his *herman gelmet* cool and tingly in preparation for a subsequent *wank*. The technique can also be used by the more considerate *noshee* prior to receiving a *nosh* to mask the aroma of *hedam* and thus make the experience slightly less vile for his *noshatrix*.

Smithfield porter's cap *n*. A *clopper* deprived of its necessary monthly launder.

SMOG *acronym*. Suck Me Off Gob. A lady's mouth which appears capable of drawing a golfball through 200 yards of garden hose, eg. Angelina Jolie, Sophie Marceau or any Brazilian bird one cares to mention.

smoke *n*. A *chewie*, a *nosh*. A *blow job*. *'Excuse me, Miss Taylforth, this is a no-smoking taxi.'*

smoke out the mole *v*. To induce a reluctant *feeshus* by means of lighting up a cigarette.

smoke the bald man *v*. To light up a *salami cigarette*.

smoke the white owl *v*. To commit an act of *horatio*.

smoking bangers *sim*. Descriptive of a woman with a lovely personality, ie. a *bird* who looks as though she's been lighting up fireworks.

smoo *n*. *Aus*. A *minge*, a *sportsman's gap*.

smuggling a brownie *v*. To have the *turtle's head*. *'He seemed quite anxious to get away. I suspect he was smuggling a brownie.'*

smurfing *v*. *Blue surfing*. Trawling the information superhighway on the lookout for pictures of *tits* and *fannies*.

smush piece *n*. The *faff*. A lady's *front bottom*, a *clopper*.

smut *n*. Mild *jazz*. *Porn lite*, as seen on Channel 5.

snag your jeans on a nail *v*. To emit a high-pitched, rasping *ringtone*.

snail's doorstep *n*. A *clapping fish* that is as *wet as an otter's pocket*.

snail trail *n*. *Smoo juice* in a lassie's well-worn *scuns*.

snake *v*. To *fuck, poke, bang, futter*.

snake charmer *n*. A girl who has an uplifting effect on your *pant python*. *'Phoar! She's a bit of a snake charmer. I'm pitching a trouser tent right here and now.'*

snakeskin *1*. *n*. The clothing sloughed off in one piece and found at the bottom of the bed after a night on the *piss*. *2*. *n*. The dried, flaky layer that tends to form overnight on the stomach of an unhygienic male who nods off after commiting an act of *self-pollution*.

snake spit *n*. The clear fluid that precedes the *jizz bolt*. *Pre cum*.

snap and tickle *n*. Of a particularly lengthsome *Eartha*, the phenomenon of it touching the bottom of the *chod bin* before snapping off at the *clackervalve*, and then striking the back of the *chicken skin handbag* as it falls.

snapdragon *n*. A normally agreeable female who under certain circumstances, ie. when *up on blocks* or full of *tart fuel*, becomes a vicious, fire-breathing monster.

snapped candles *sim*. Descriptive of one's legs after a night *on the piss*.

snapper *1*. *n*. North-east colloquialism for a thin fellow. *2*. *n*. *milit*. Royal Naval slang for one who is *nicely poised*. *3*. *n*. A lady's *bodily treasure*.

snap the key off in the lock *v*. To suffer an unsatisfying *shit*. *'Good* dump, dear?' 'Sadly not, my petal. I'm afraid I've snapped the key off in the lock. I'll have this pine cone in all night now.'

snart *n*. To sneeze and *fart* at exactly the same moment, resulting in *nose jizz* on the face or *rabbit tods* in the *bills*. Or both.

snatch *n*. *Quim*, vagina, *liver sock*.

snatch 22 *n*. A woman whom, paradoxically, one requires so much beer to *poke*, that one can't *get it up*.

snatch fence *n*. An invisible, *cock*-proof barricade erected down the centre of a matrimonial bed following a domestic argument. A *gash barrier*.

snatchlings *n*. Up-and-coming talent.

snatchment area *n*. The geographical radius from which a drinking establishment draws its female clientele.

snatchmo *n*. A *fanny* with lips strong enough to play *'Basin Street Blues'* on an E-flat trumpet.

snatch mouse *n*. A tampon. A *cotton mouse*, a *Prince Charlie*, a *chuftie plug*.

snatch patch *n*. A feminine hygiene product. A *fanny nanny*.

snatchphrase *n*. A particularly successful chat up line.

snatch quack *n*. *medic*. One who has the sexy, enviable job of examining malfunctioning *minges*. A *box doc*. A gynaecologist.

snatch rats *n*. Ladies' sanitary products. Tampaxes, *jam rags*, etc.

snatch worms *n*. Tiny pieces of tightly-rolled bog paper that lurk in the labial folds, normally only discovered during expert *cumulonimbus* which dislodges them from their hidey-holes.

sneaky Hitler *n*. The surreptitious slipping of one's index finger under one's nose in order to savour the aroma of one's ladyfriend's *blip*.

snedge 1. *n*. Snow. **2**. *n*. *Jism*.

snedger *n*. *Snufty, snurglar, snudger, quumfer*. Another name for a sniffer of ladies' bicycle seats.

sniffers' row *n*. In a strip club, the seats that are closest to the stage.

sniggerette *n*. A *tab* containing a quantity of *happy baccy*. A *spliff*.

sniping *n*. Accidentally shooting a jet of *slash* through the gap between the rim of the *chod bin* and the underside of the seat and onto your *kex* whilst sat down having a *tom tit*. A *Wee-Harvey Oswald*.

snipper reflex *n*. *medic*. The counter-productive and inexplicable urge to cut a *cable* before it is fully *laid*, usually resulting in an *arse like a Marmite pot*.

snippit valve *n*. The *anal sphincter*. The *nipsy*.

snitches *n*. *Two aspirins on an ironing board, stits, fried eggs*.

snob sick *n*. Vomit with plenty of canapés and Chardonnay in it outside a wine bar.

snobtoss *n*. An act of *self-pollution* committed whilst watching a sophisticated, subtitled movie on FilmFour.

snog *v*. To *swap spit, tongue wrestle, play tonsil hockey*.

snogging water *n*. A male grooming lotion that smells like *Joan Collins' knickers*. After shave.

snoodling *n*. An unlikely-sounding sexual practice reputedly favoured by gents who are *good with colours*, whereby one of them pulls his *fiveskin* over the *herman gelmet* of his chum. Also *docking*, a *clash of heads.*

snookered behind the red *adj.* Unable to *sink the pink* due to the time of month. The only pot on is a *difficult brown*.

Snoopies *n.* *Spaniel's ears, Ghandi's flip-flops.*

snoregasm *n.* A wet dream.

snorkeller's lunch *n.* A fish dish which is a particular favourite amongst *muff divers.*

snorkelling *n.* The holding of a gentleman's *nollies* in a lady's mouth whilst she applies a repetitive stroke to his *favourite member.*

snorker *n. Sausage,* both eating and hiding varieties.

snot *n.* The perineum of the lady. Because it's not etc. etc.

snoutcasts *n.* Those poor workplace unfortunates who are forced to huddle in doorways to enjoy their cigarettes. *Fag lepers.*

snout pout *n.* That haughty uptilt of the nose favoured by *pedigree ratters* with ideas somewhat above their stations, eg. Posh Spice, Candice off *'Coronation Street'.*

snowball *v.* To blow *salami cigarette* smoke back into the tobacconist's mouth... sort of thing.

snowdropper *n.* Underwear fetishist who steals to sniff, usually from washing lines. A *knicker bandit.*

snudge *v.* To sniff a lady's bicycle seat after she leaves it chained to the railings. *Quumfing.*

snuffling for truffles *sim.* Descriptive of a loud and somewhat messy performance of *cumulonimbus.* From the act's resemblance to the phenomenon of a large, wet-nosed beast rooting through the topsoil looking for a pungent, yet valuable actinomycete. Though presumably without a large mob of excitable French peasants watching.

snufty *n.* One who *snudges.*

snurge *v.* To *snuft, snudge, shramp, quumf, scrunge, pringle, snerge, snedge, snaffle, snarze, snerk, snerdle, shnuffle-piffle, nurf, moomph, barumph, garboon, poon, snarf, snurdle* or *snurge.* To sniff the recently-vacated bicycle seats of young ladies, a hobby that seems to be named more often than it is performed.

snurglar *n. Quumfer, snudger,* bicycle *snufty.*

snurgle *v.* To *snuft,* to *quumf.*

soap dropper *n.* One who is *good with colours.* One who is *light on his feet.* From the prison shower etiquette where, like a Georgian lady dropping her handkerchief in the park to attract the attention of a suitor, a big, hairy *nick-bent* psychopath with an erection drops the soap in the showers to woo a prospective companion. A *botter.*

so solid poo *n.* An extremely troublesome *dump* which feels like passing a handgun wrapped in a sock.

soap-on-a-roper *n.* One who prefers not to bend down in communal showers.

soapy tit wank *n.* A *sausage sandwich* served in the bath or shower.

sob stopper *n.* A small present of little value which is acquired on the way home by a thoughtful man who has drunk too much and stayed out too late, in the hope of stopping his missus turning the fucking waterworks on. Examples include cheap chocolates bought from all night garages and bunches of flowers stolen from cemeteries.

social hand grenade *n.* A married man who comes out *on the pop* so infrequently that when he does he is a major liability to those around him.

sockbreaker *n*. A *wank* of such vim and vigour that the weft of the sock is eroded.

sock jock *n*. One who likes to ride the *baloney pony* harnessed with a trusty item of hosiery.

sock method *n*. To *roll the dice* into a sock in the absence of anything else to *roll the dice* into. See *crunchie*.

sock sucker *n*. A prudish woman who insists on one donning a *dunky* before *noshing* on one's *slag hammer*. A *French puritan*.

socktator sport *n*. Any game played by scantily-clad and copiously-perspiring young ladies which is broadcast to a rhythmically appreciative male audience. Who are *pulling themselves off* into a sock. Also *pullympics*.

socktits *n*. Very long, saggy, pendulous breasts. *Spaniel's ears*.

sockumentary *n*. A *masturmentary, rudimentary, palmorama*. A TV programme best enjoyed whilst wearing an odd number of socks.

sod *n*. A loose piece of turf in an *uphill garden*.

soggy moggy *n*. A romantic epithet to describe the *back to front* of a lady who has reached a sufficient state of arousal so that it will *go in* without too much fuss.

soixante-neuf *n*. Top-to-tail *horatiocumulonimbus*. French for *sixty-nine*. *Loop the loop*.

solicitor's tie *n*. *Fr*. A *pearl necklace*. Costing £160 an hour.

someone's tinkered with Herbie *exclam*. A witty riposte one delivers when one *backfires* unexpectedly. From the lines delivered in

'The Love Bug' after the baddy has sabotaged the eponymous VW beetle, causing its engine to cough and splutter.

sonic bog lock *n*. The random assortment of whistles, coughs, hums and throat clearings that are made by the patron of a public *crapper* cubicle with no lock on the door.

sooker *n*. *Scots*. A *tit*.

Sooty and Sweep's frying pan *n*. Capacious women's genitalia.

Soprendos *n*. A series of gentle *farts* which precede a *Thora*. From the catchphrase of Victoria Wood's obese magical faux-Spaniard ex-husband, 'Piff, paff, poof'.

soreskin *n*. A sore *foreskin*.

soup but no croutons *adj. medic*. Descriptive of a low *springle count, spoogeless spaff*. To be *firing blanks*.

soup cooler *n*. A lipless *fart* that has the characteristics of a gourmet gently and silently blowing across a bowl of lobster bisque in a posh restaurant.

sour apple quickstep *n*. Another diarrhoea dance. The *Tijuana cha-cha*. *'Your wife is taking rather a long time in the powder room'. 'Yes, I'm afraid she's dancing the sour apple quickstep tonight.'*

sour mash *n*. A particularly soft morning *shit*, usually sponsored by Jack Daniels or Jim Beam.

southern sideburns *n*. *Thighbrows*.

southmouth *n*. The *snatch, fadge, fanny*.

Southport 1. *n*. The *arsehole*. *'Fancy a trip to Southport tonight, love?' 'Yeah, alright then.'* 2. *n*. Lancashire town at the mouth of the Ribble Estuary. *'Fancy a trip to Southport tonight, love?' 'Eurgh!*

Certainly not. Don't be disgusting.'

SOW *1. acronym.* Sexy Older Woman. A lady one wouldn't ask to leave the bed, despite her advanced years, eg. Honor Blackman, Nanette Newman, Geri Halliwell. *2. n.* One notch up from 'cow' on the female insult scale.

spacers *n.* A pair of breasts which, though large in size, exhibit no cleavage due to their distance apart. *East-westers.*

space shuttle *n.* A *shit* that has a tendency to break up on entry into the *bog bowl.*

SPAD *acronym.* Signal Passed At Danger. To drive your *Interclitty 125* at full pelt into the *tunnel,* despite seeing the red warning signs at the entrance. To stick your *cock* into *Billy Connolly's beard.*

spaddel *n. Spooge, spoff, spaff, spangle, gunk, jitler.*

spadework *n.* The hard graft that must be undertaken before planting one's *seed* in the *ladygarden. Frigmerole.* Foreplay.

spadger *n. Aus.* Vagina.

spaff *v.* To *spoff* or *spod. 'No, no, no, Gunter! Be professional, spaff on the chest, not in the pussy.'* (from an unidentified *grumble flick,* circa 1980).

spam alley *n.* The target zone for *spam javelin* throwers.

spambidextrous *adj.* The ability to *beat one's truncheon meat* with either *wanking spanner.*

spambulance *n. Shaggin' wagon.*

spam butterfly *n.* A finger-assisted *close-up pink* shot in a *bongo mag.* A *peel.*

spam castanets *n.* Percussive *scallops.*

spam danglers *n.* The sloppy, pro-truding inner flaps of a lady's *hooter.* Generously-portioned *bacon strips.*

spam fritters *n.* Labia. *Dangly ham,* especially when served in *batter.*

spam javelin *n.* An 8-foot long *cock* with a sharpened end.

spam monkey *n.* A monkey that is partial to indulging itself with *luncheon meat.*

spamogram *n.* Stylised pictographic representation, or hieroglyph, of a disembodied set of male genitalia, usually seen scrawled on toilet walls, bus shelters, religious text-books and the backs of photo-graphs of washing machines post-ed to disc jockey Mike Read. A *pud.*

spamouflage *n.* Copies of *'Time', 'The Economist', 'London Review of Books'* etc. picked off the lower shelves of newsagents in an effort to give the impression that one's copy of *'Hot 'n' Horny'* was mere-ly an ironic afterthought. *Palmouflage.*

spam purse *n.* A particularly unsightly *snapper,* usually found in the nether regions of women with *lovely personalities.*

spam sceptre *n.* The ceremonial rod that sits atop the *crown jewels.*

spandrels *n. Men overboard, crou-tons, tiger nuts.* General vaginal detritus.

spangle *1. n.* A sticky, unpleasant mouthful that is most often spat out. *2. n.* Spunk.

spangle bangle *n.* A hair band kept close to her bed by a keen *fellatrix,* in order to keep her hair out of her eyes as she performs *horatio.*

spaniel's ears *n.* Sagging, flat *thruppenny bits. Snoopies, Fred Bassets.*

Spanish archer *n.* The push, the 'El

Bow.' *'She caught me in bed with her sister and her mum, and she gave me the old Spanish archer. Tchoh! Women, eh?'*

Spanish cravat *n.* A *pearl necklace*. Also *Dutch cravat, Chinese bow tie.*

Spanish plumbers *n.* Ill-tailored trousers, from their tendency to pinch the base of the urethra and thus 'always leave it dripping'.

spank banks *n.* A mental reference library of erotic imagery, which can be consulted when *spanking the monkey*. Also *mammary banks.*

spankerchief *n.* A tissue, or square of fabric for mopping up post-*monkey-spanking banana yoghurt.*

spanking *n.* A form of corporal punishment still practised in *rub-a-tug shops.* See *Mr. Whippy. Fladge and padge.*

spankrupt *adj.* Descriptive of a gentleman who, upon *advancing the manly meat*, finds himself bereft of masturbatory inspiration.

spank the monkey *v.* To *bash the bishop, burp the worm.*

spank the plank *1. v.* To play the electrical guitar in a 'pop' beat combo. *2. v.* To *toss* oneself off.

spanky hanky *n. Jit gel rag, wank sock.* Anything used for clearing up *gunk* after a *tug.* A *spankerchief.*

spanner *1. n.* Not the sharpest tool in the shed, a right *fuckwit. 2. n.* Top *stoat*, one who 'tightens one's nuts'.

spare *n.* In a *meat market*, that *flap* which is not yet sold.

spare elbow skin *n. John Wayne's hairy saddlebags, chicken skin handbag.* The scrotal sac.

spare room offence *n.* Any minor misdemeanor that upsets a wife or

girlfriend, eg. coming home drunk, forgetting her birthday, *fucking* her sister etc.

sparrowfart *n.* Early morning.

sparrowfuck *n.* A rapid act of *congress* between a man and a woman, reminiscent of the 1-second *spunk up* of the common house sparrow, *Spuggius domesticus.*

spasm chasm *n. Spam alley.*

spastard *n.* A politically incorrect term for one who exhibits the qualities of both a spastic and a *bastard.*

spatchelor *n.* A single fellow who results to *floor-scraping* tactics in order to pick up the crusty bits of what's left off the dance floor at chucking out time.

spat out toffee, face like a *sim.* Descriptive of a lady with a physiognomy reminiscent of a *stripper's clit.*

spawning *v.* The saucy act of masturbating in a public swimming pool.

speaking clock *n.* A fellow afflicted with premature *spoffage.* A *two-push Charlie.* From the fact that he never gets past the third *stroke.*

speak up caller, you're through *exclam.* Humorous phrase uttered after someone has *dropped a gut.* Also *a bit more choke and she would have started.*

speak Welsh *v. Shout soup, blow chunks, yoff.*

spear the bearded clam *v.* A trick involving a *spam javelin* and a hairy bivalve.

spear the blow hole *v.* To have sex with a *BWR.*

speed dating *n.* The act of looking out of a train or bus window into the bedroom windows of passing houses in the hope of seeing a nice pair of *milkers*.

speedophile *n*. A suspicious-looking man in a swimming pool who does a lot of watching but very little swimming.

spend a pound in pennies *v*. To play the *tuppenny waterfall*, to *shit the jackpot*. To suffer a *fall of old shoes from one's loft*.

spend one's money before one gets to the shop *euph*. Of an over-eager gentleman, to *spongle* his *spaff* before the *glebe end* has entered the *faff*. To suffer the enjoyable, time-saving affliction of premature ejaculation.

spend tuppence in ha'pennies and farthings *v*. To pass loose stools, have diarrhoea. To release a *flock of pigeons*.

spent fuel rod 1. *n*. A bar of depleted uranium following its removal from the nuclear reactor. 2. *n*. A sadly-depleted and flaccid *gigglestick* following its removal from the *clopper*.

sperm *n*. *medic*. Doc-speak for *spunk, gism*.

sperm burper *n*. A sensible lady who isn't afraid to guzzle *spadge*.

sperm curdler 1. *n*. A Victorian kitchen utensil made from copper. 2. *n*. A satanically *fugly woman*, eg. Anne Widdecombe, Cathy Staff, Tracey Emin.

sperm noodle *n*. An airing cupboard-dried sleeping bag which has been recently used by a sexually-overactive male who has inadvertantly impregnated it with a quantity of *dream topping*. Best avoided by ovulating, damp females.

sperm wail *n*. A low grunting noise emitted at the moment of *spouting*. An ejaculatory ejaculation. See *spuphemism*.

sperm worm *n*. The penis.

spew 1. *v*. To vomit, *park a tiger*, be sick. 2. *n*. The sick itself. '*Mum. This fucking soup tastes like tramp's spew.*'

sphinny *n*. The *nipsy*. '*I think we should stop, Dave. Me sphinny isn't what it used to be.*'

Spice island *n*. *Stinkhole Bay, Dilberry Creek*. A foul-smelling archipelago favoured by sailors on their *trips around the world*. The *arsehole*.

spiddle *n*. A term for the *piss* a lady takes after intercourse. A mixture of *spunk* and *widdle*.

Spiderman wank *n*. Of a gentleman, an act of *self-pollution* undertaken whilst wearing a pair of lady's *bills* on the head, such that the *gusset* is directly over the nose, leaving eyeholes in the place normally filled by legs. A *musk mask*.

Spiderman, do a *v*. To *spunk up* into one's hand, then attempt to remove it by *flicking ropes* against the wall.

spiders' legs *n*. Of *muffs*, rogue pubic hairs which protrude beyond the knicker line, a *pant moustache*.

spill one's beans on the worktop *v*. To *ice* a lady's *buns*. To *lob ropes*.

spin cycle *n*. The final, frenzied stages of a *gentleman's act of relaxation*, when the floor starts to vibrate and nearby crockery starts to rattle and fall off shelves etc. A *wanker's vinegar strokes*.

spinner 1. *n*. Member of semi-religious, polo-neck wearing folk band without whom no variety programme in the 1970s was complete. 2. *n*. A petite lady who can be spun on one's *cock* like the propellor on a beany hat. A *throwabout*, a *cock puppet*.

spinning plates *n*. An old-fashioned novelty act in which the performer attempts to keep both of a lady volunteer's nipples erect at the same time.

spirit level arse *n*. A little bubble of *fart* that lodges between the *arse cheeks* and acts as an indicator of one's inclination.

spirit levelled *adj*. To be in the ultimate state of *refreshment*. To be as *refreshed as a fucking newt*.

spiss *n*. The mixture of sperm and urine produced during a post-coital wee-wee. *'That was a truly beautiful lovemaking experience, darling. Now keep toot for the scuffers while I have a spiss in Bradford & Bingley's doorway.'*

spit *v*. What fussy women do instead of *swallowing*.

spit a nut *n*. To *gamble and lose*. To *follow through*, to *shoot the breeze*.

spit her rag out *v*. Of a lady during *cricket week*, to uncontrollably eject her *jammy dodger* onto the floor whilst undergoing a spontaneous and unnecessary bout of *showing off*. Also *pop a knocker*.

spit roast *n*. Someone simultaneously skewered at both ends by *pork swords*. A *sausage jockey* who plays a *pink oboe* whilst still in the saddle. A *corn on the cob*.

spla water *n*. Semen, *gunk*.

splashback 1. *n*. An area of tiles behind a sink. 2. *n*. Unfortunate tidal effect of a *depth charge* or *belly flopper* within the pan, resulting in splashing of the *arse* and *barse*.

splash diet *n*. A weight loss programe that involves the shedding of pounds of unsightly excrement.

A *dump*. *'I can't do these jeans up again. I'd best just go on a splash diet. See you in ten minutes.'*

splashdown *n*. *milit*. Official Parachute Regiment terminology for a *wetting of one's bed* after a mammoth drinking session.

splash me boots *v*. To have a *piss*, take a *leak*.

splat *n*. *medic*. *Bollock batter, fetch*.

splay *v*. *US*. To *schtup, snake, skeeze*. Specifically, to draw back the *beef curtains* and enter.

splice *v*. British version of *splay*.

splinge *n*. A particularly lubricious *kipper mitten*. A *bag of slugs*.

split a kipper *v*. To *part the whiskers*, to *have it off*.

splitarse *n*. An offensive, sexist term for a bird. *'Birthdays: TV and film actor Tom Selleck, 57. Olympic Gold medalist diver Greg Louganis, 43. Splitarse boffin Germaine Greer, 64.'* (from *'The Times'*, Jan 29th 2003).

split bag of mince *n*. A *gutted rabbit*, a *butcher's dustbin*.

splitter cable 1. *n*. An adaptor from Maplins for plugging two television sets into a single chipped satellite decoder. 2. *n*. A *Thora Hird* which is so humungous that it rents one's *Jap's flag* in twain.

split the beard *v*. To *part the whiskers*, again. After 20 minutes or so. And a fag.

split the winnings *euph*. To halt the *laying of a cable* halfway through. *'And after four days without movement Job took up his toilet and great was his relief. But even as he released his burden there came a voice and it was the Lord. And the Lord spake in a loud voice saying Come unto Me Job. And Job replied saying Oh God, what is it this* time, for I have only just sat down. And great was the wrath of the Lord. And He commanded Job to split the winnings and come now unto Him. And great was Job's discomfort.' (from 'The Book of Job' Ch.6).

splod 1. *n. Sprag, spoff.* 2. *v.* To *sprag, spoff.*

splodge *v.* To masturbate semen over a glossy magazine.

splosh 1. *n.* Money. 2. *n.* Britain's leading periodical for those interested in genito-spaghetti pursuits.

spluff 1. *v.* To *spunk up.* 'She took her bra off and I spluffed my pants.' 2. *n. Spunk.* 'Nice tits, Thora. By the way, is there anywhere I can put these pants? They're full off spluff.'

splurry *n. Fizzy gravy.* Diarrhoea.

splutterbeans *n.* The *Eartha Kitts.*

spock *v.* To make a 'V' with one's fingers and boldy go where no man has gone before, ie. two up the *twat* and two up the *arse.*

spocks *n.* Socks that have been used as a ejaculation receptacle or post-masturbation clean up device. From *spodge, spadge, spoodge, spaff, spangle, spingle, spongle,* etc. + socks.

spod *n.* See *spooge.*

spof *n. Spod.*

spoilers 1. *n.* Aerodynamic wing modifications that allow Citroen Saxos to grip the road when driving up and down in Burger King car parks. 2. *n Buttocks, mudflaps.*

spoilsports bra *n.* An item of intimate apparel used by women who unaccountably wish to suppress the natural movement of their *bangers.*

spondle *n. Spooge, spluff, spangle, jitler, knob toffee.*

sponge 1. *n.* Of homosexual relationships, the submissive partner, the *noshee* as opposed to the *nosher.* Usually the thin one. See also stone. 2. *n. prop.* A silent character played by Colin Bean in 'Dad's Army'.

spooch *n. Spooge, spodge, spadge, splang* etc. *Jism.*

spooge *n. US. Spof.*

spooge scrooge *n. Blob,* condom, *rubber policeman.*

spooge stick *n. Gut stick, fuck rod.* The penis.

spoot *n. Scot.* A word for *spunk.* Usage limited to Campbeltown on the Mull of Kintyre.

sporran catalogue *n.* A *grot mag.* Specialising in ladies with snapshut, shaggy grey *snatches.*

sports bag *n.* A handy *cottaging* accessory in which one partner stands to conceal his feet and avoid detection by lavatory attendants looking under the door.

sports model *n.* A woman who has had her *tubes* tied providing worryfree sexual fun for caddish gentlemen.

spouse 1. *n.* One's marital partner. 2. *n.* Her *fanny.*

sprag 1. *n. Spoff, splod.* 2. *v.* To *spoff, splod.*

spreader *n.* A variation on a *moonie,* whereby the buttocks are manually pulled apart to reveal the *freckle.*

spreadsheet *n.* Shiny, crinkly toilet paper found in public lavatories which only succeeds in smearing the *shit* around one's *arse* like a plasterer's float.

sprew *n. Spongle, jitler, spragg. Spunk.*

spring clean *n.* A gentleman's first morning visit to the *crapper* after a night on the *lash,* where he has a *dump* and a *slash*, blows his nose, picks the sleep from his eyes and generally begins the miraculous process of coming back to life.

spring onion roots *n.* An elderly *tart's* unruly *gorilla salad*. The *welcome mat* of a lady of advanced years.

sprogdrop *n. medic.* Pregnancy. A state of *up-the-duffness*, to be expecting a *lawn monkey*.

sprouts *n.* Children.

spud, to *v.* To deliberately mess up a job interview in order not to jeopardize one's benefits. Named after the character in *'Trainspotting'*.

spuds deep *adj. Up to the maker's nameplate*.

spuffing dust *adj.* A term used to describe the plight of a gentleman who is experiencing a marked lack of ejaculate, following a 6-hour *wanking* marathon.

spuncle *n.* A sperm donor. From *spondle* + uncle.

spunctual *adj.* Of a gentleman *grumble thespian*. To be able to *spoff* on cue or to a pre-arranged schedule.

spuncture *n.* An incidence of latex failure at a critical moment whilst using a *jubber ray*. A leak in a *beef Wellington*, a bursted *blob*.

spunk 1. *n.* Semen, *seed.* 2. *n.* Spirit, pluck. 3. *n. Aus.* Good looking man, dish, hunk. 4. *n.* Tinder made from fungus. 5. *v.* To ejizzulate, to *spooge*, esp. ~*up*.

spunk-curdling *adj.* Descriptive of a woman who can induce an instantaneous *derection* at a hundred paces. *'Deaths; Andrea Dworkin, spunk-curdling American feminist writer, 58.'*

spunk-drunk *adj.* Delirious nature

brought on by over-consumption of *root beer*.

spunk dustbin *n.* A *spooge bucket, box of assorted creams.* An exceptionally accommodating young lady.

spunk gurning *n.* The delightful faces a *grumble flick* actress pulls as she excitedly anticipates the *tipping* of the romantic lead's *cement* onto her face.

spunk juggler *n.* An *onanist.*

spunkled *adj.* Besprinkled with *spunk*.

spunkling *adj.* Sparkling or glistening as a result of being *spunkled,* eg. Gillian Taylforth's chin.

spunk mail *n.* The lifelong postal monsoon of unsolicited pornographic brochures and catalogues received as a result of foolishly buying a Linzie-Dawn McKenzie video from the back of the *'Sunday Mirror'* twelve years ago.

spunk rat *n.* A good looking bloke, as described by females.

spunk run *n. RN.* On her majesty's warships, the 2-inch gap down the side of a sailor's bunk where he stows *pop-up books,* soiled *grundies* and tissues on which he has *blown his nose.*

spunk shuffle *n.* The walk adopted by one's girlfriend to stop the *congregation* leaving the *cathedral* before she reaches the *bog.*

spunky wrench *n.* A *wanking spanner.* A gentleman's hand.

spuphemism *n.* A humorous *sperm wail.* A jolly shout upon *spoffage,* eg. *'There she blows!' 'Timberrrrr!'* and *'Yabba Dabba Dooooo!'*

Spurt Reynolds *n.* Pet name for the tearful *bald man* sitting on the *hairy beanbags.*

spurt your curd v. To spread your *spunk*, to *spunkle* others with your pluck and spirit.

squack *onomat.* The sound of a male ejaculation.

squaddie's delight n. A woman in the armed forces who is not *on the bus to Hebden Bridge*. A heterosexual Army, Navy or Air Force lady.

squaddie's mattress n. *milit.* Army version of the naval *matelot's mattress*. A lady who *spreads* for soldiers, especially round the back of Cheeks nightclub, Aldershot.

squashed spuggy/spoggy/sparrow n. An elderly lady's vagina. *Granny's oysters.*

squat 'n' squirt n. A manoeuvre often performed up dark alleys by ladies returning from the pub, and filmed by CCTV operators. A *splash 'n' dash*.

squatter n. An annoying little *turd* that takes up residence in one's *arse* and refuses to leave, unless threatened by Bermondsey Dave.

squeak the breeze v. US. To *fart, talk German, pass wind.*

squeaky toy n. A *fart* which sounds, and indeed occasionally smells, not unlike the popular shrill noise-producing dog amuser.

squeeze the cheese v. Dairy equivalent of *sausage stretching*, to *wank.*

squeeze the fig v. When needing a *tom tit* in a public place, to keep one's *nipsy* firmly clenched to prevent the *turtle's head* poking out.

squeeze the lemon v. Of women, to urinate. Possibly onto a pancake.

squench 1. n. A moist *fart* which feels like one has *gambled and lost*. 2. n. A character in Dickens's 'The Old Curiosity Shop' who suffered a *fall of soot* during Little Nell's funeral.

squidge n. A vagina with a *wide on*.

squid legs n. The thin, rubbery tentacles found floating on the water after a bathtime *dolphin waxing* session.

squid marks n. Fishy *skids* in a lady's *fairy hammock*.

squid wank n. The kind of *wank* received from a lady inexperienced in the provision of *wanks*. Derived from the distinctive cuttlefish-like movement of the hand.

squirrel covers n. A lady's *dunghampers*.

squirter's alley n. *medic.* The vagina.

squirting like a badly laid paving slab *sim. medic. Shitting* through the *eye of a needle, pissing rusty water* out of one's *arse*.

squirts n. *medic.* In proctology, a series of fiery eruptions from the *chamber of horrors* resulting in a pyroclastic flow from the *farting fissure*. A condition also known as the *skitters*, the *Earthas*.

squirty dirt n. *Medic.* Faeces of an extremely low viscosity. *'Come to the Curry Capital, Bigg Market, Newcastle upon Tyne - for a curry you won't forget in a hurry.'*

squishpot n. US. The area right below the *devil's doorbell*.

squits n. *medic.* Dangerous wet *farts*, constantly bordering on the *follow through*. Junior *squirts*.

STA *abbrev. Grumble* industry code denoting the job prospects of a starlet with less than conventional good looks. Straight To Anal.

St. Bernard's chin *sim.* Descriptive of a *muff* that has had lots of *ropes lobbed* at it. A heavily *bespunkled mingepiece*. Also *bloodhound's* *jowls.*

St. George *v.* To lance one's old dragon from behind. To take part in a *dog's marriage.*

St. Ivel *n.* An imperial measurement of beer, equal to 2 ½ quarts or ⁵⁄₈ of a gallon. Five pints. *'Mr. Barratt appeared unsteady on his feet as he got out of the car. I asked him if he had been drinking and he replied 'Not really. I've only had a St. Ivel.''* (from the traffic officer's charge sheet after the arrest of Michael 'Shakin' Stevens' Barratt, Dec 31st 2001).

stabbin' cabin *n.* A secondary residence kept for the sole purpose of quick extra-marital encounters, eg.a discreet flat in Belgravia, a small cottage in the Cotswolds, or a 12-foot caravan on the cliffs at Scarborough.

stabbing the cat *n. Wanking.* From the motion of knifing an invisible feline on one's lap. Similar to *feeding the ducks,* but with the emphasis on the downward stroke.

stack blow *n.* A gentleman's *organism.*

stacked *adj.* Overstocked *rack* in the *snork* department. *'I fell in love with my wife at first sight. She is particularly well stacked.'*

stagecoach *n.* A cramped, filthy ride which leaves you in need of a wash. Also *riding shotgun.*

stalagshites *n.* Naturally-occurring, upward-pointing turdiferous deposits which form in porcelain basins.

stalk *n.* Erection, *stiffy.* A *third leg, middle stump. 'Excuse me, if I look like a tripod. I just can't seem to get rid of this stalk. Anyway, let's carry on. Ashes to ashes, dust to dust.'*

stalk fever *n.* Condition affecting men on *big cock day.*

stall shy *adj. medic.* The psychological condition that renders certain gentlemen unable to micturate in public lavatories unless there is vacant stall between them and the next micturater. *Stage fright.*

stamp on the toothpaste *v.* To ejaculate in an over-excitable manner.

standby on *n. Half a teacake.* A penis in a state of *semi-tumescence.*

stand on *n.* A *bone on,* a *stalk.*

standing on the fireman's hose *sim.* At the conclusion of the evening's fourth or fifth bout of *Jesuit boxing,* a complete failure to release *jaff.* An *air horn.*

standing ovation *n.* Mark of respect given to a *digestive transit* which is so impressive that one has to get up to have a good look at it.

stand lunch *v.* To provide an *air buffet* which stops anyone in the room feeling hungry any more.

stanky *n.* The glaze that is left on the *shaft* of the *choad* after a bout of *kipper splitting.* May be *zuffled* on curtains or wiped on a *stankychief.*

starboard bow *n. RN.* The *arse.*

starch pill *n.* A Viagra tablet, a *bluey.*

starfish trooper *n.* An *arsetronaut.*

starfucked *adj.* The loss of credibility suffered by a product as a result of its endorsement by a *shit* celebrity. Walkers crisps (Gary Lineker), Benecol margerine (Carol Vorderman) and Homebase DIY (Neil Morrissey) have all been *starfucked.*

starter button *n.* The *clematis,* the *wail switch.* The *clit.*

starter leads *n.* Suspenders.

starting line at Brands Hatch *sim.* Descriptive of severely *be-skid-marked undercrackers*. Guaranteed to cause embarrassment the first time they are handed to one's newly-wedded bride for washing.

start the horn mower *v.* To perform the particularly vicious upstroke often demonstrated by the inexperienced female *masturbatrix*.

Star Wars door *sim.* In *back door work,* descriptive of the manner in which the *deathstar* closes after the *pink Darth Vader* is removed.

stauner *n. Scot.* A dour, granite-hard *bone on*. An *Old man of Hoy*.

steak drapes *n. Gammon goalposts, beef curtains*.

steakwich *n.* The external genitalia of a lady of a certain age which resembles the traditional British pub snack.

stealth bomber *n.* A subtle *leg lifter*. A mystery *benefactor*, phantom raspberry blower. An anonymous *donor*.

stealth moose *n.* An *LRF*.

steg *n.* A woman resembling a ferocious, spiny, squat, prehistoric dinosaur. Abbrev. of stegosaurus.

stellanoia *n.* The state of aggressive paranoia which one attains shortly after imbibing one's tenth pint of *wifebeater*.

stellaporter *n.* A futuristic form of instantaneous transportation which warps the time/space continuum, leaving one outside the front door mere moments after leaving the pub. Often with a trouser leg full of *piss* and a half-eaten kebab.

stellarisation *n.* Process by which a man is rendered unable to father children. *'Sorry love, I can't do it. I've been stellarised, see.'*

stellavision *n.* Premium strength beer goggles.

stemmer *n.* A *chewie* in which the dirty lady is able to swallow the whole shebang. A *deep throat*.

stench trench *n. Fanny*.

Stephen Hawking's treadmill *sim.* Descriptive of something or someone of little use, eg. 'personal transport revolution' the Sinclair C5, 'comedian' Richard Blackwood.

step on a duck *v.* To create a quack, fart. *'Pardon me, Ladies and Gentlemen. Do not adjust your wireless set, Mrs. Simpson just stepped on a duck.'* (from The Abdication Broadcast of Edward VIII, 1937).

step on a frog *v.* To *step on a duck*.

Steptoe's face *n.* A saggy non-too-fussy set of *flackets*. ie. they will take in any old *rag* or *bone*.

Steve *n.* A Scottish male homosexualist, eg. Jimmy Somerville. From Steve McQueen.

Stevie Wonders, the *n. medic.* The involuntary wobbling of the head that one exhibits when desperately trying to stay awake, eg. a student in a Friday afternoon lecture or a lorry driver on the M6. From the erratic head movements of the Motown star. *'The trial of the Millennium Dome Jewel Robbers was held up today after Judge Michael Coombe was spotted having a severe attack of the Stevie Wonders during the defence council's summing up.'* (Nicholas Witchell, *'BBC News'*, November 2003).

stick at 15 *v.* From the pontoon playing gambit, to settle for a low quality score; thus to go for the first half decent *bird* who shows interest in a night club.

sticklebrick *n.* A particularly difficult and uncomfortable *tod*. A *pine cone*.

stickman *n*. A *fanny hopper*, a *skippy*.

stick shifter *n*. *Wanker*.

sticky belly flap cock *n*. Post *curd*-spurting condition enjoyed by *monkey spankers*.

sticky toffee pudding *n*. A thick, dense *Thora* that sticks to everything it touches, particularly one's *arse cress*.

sticky wicket *n*. A well used *crease* with all the bounce *fucked* out of it. A *box of assorted creams*.

stiff drink *n*. A warming tot of *vitamin S* quaffed by females and *puddle jumpers*. A *drink on a stick*.

stiff lock *n*. A *piss-proud spooge stick*.

stiffy *n*. A *stalk*.

stiffy stocking *n*. *Rascal wrapper, cheesepipe clingfilm, Spurt Reynolds' sickbag*.

stig *n*. One who is a little bit *council*. One who is *common as shite*. *'Birthdays: JK Galbraith, economist, 95. Arthur Schlessinger, historian, 86. Mario Puzo, author, 83. Sarah Ferguson, Royal stig, 44.'* (*'The Times'*,Oct 15th 2003).

still fighting *adj*. Of a curry or spicy meal, to display the same aggression on the way out as it did when it went in. *'Are you all right in there, love?' 'No. It's that chilli I had last night. It's still fighting.'*

stilton *n*. A long, thin, cheesy erection.

stilton muffle *n*. A pungent and unwashed *fish mitten*. A particularly stenchsome *trench*.

Sting wank *n*. A post-pub act of *self- pollution* which, as a result of the amount of alcohol one has consumed, becomes a turgid marathon

lasting many hours. From the former Police frontman's notoriously fruitless attempts to *go off* up his missus.

stink 1. *n*. The distinctive odour of well-matured *knob cheese*, eggy *air biscuits*, a *stilton muffle* etc. 2. *v*. To emit such a smell, to *ming*. 3. *n*. A fuss. 4. *n*. Aus. A scrap, fight, *pagga*.

stink sponge *n*. A chair or bus seat which someone has just *dropped a gut* into.

stinky finger *n*. Having ate the *captain's pie* without a knife and fork. *Stinky pinky*.

stinky Mervin *n*. The *Finsbury bridge, biffin bridge, barse, carse, taint, notcher*, etc.

stir the tanks *v*. To have a *wank* without ejaculating. From the routine procedure on the ill-fated Apollo 13 which inadvertently led to an explosion. See *almosturbate*.

Stirling *rhym. slang*. A *wank*. From Stirling Moss = *toss*.

stirring the porridge *n*. Having *sloppy seconds*, dipping into a *billposter's bucket*.

stits *n*. Small *tits*.

stoat *n*. In the world of pant nature, the natural prey of the *one-eyed trouser snake*.

stobart *n*. An articulated *turd* that jack-knifes in the pan.

Stockport overcoat *n*. A thick coating of glitter spray which, when combined with a boob tube and miniskirt, keeps the young ladies of the Cheshire town snug and toasty on the bitterest of winter evenings. A *Bigg Market duffle coat*.

Stoke chamois leather *n*. An orbital sander, used to remove grafitti from the boarded up windows which are commonplace in the popular Potteries shithole.

stonads *n*. Testicles which have fossilized due to under-use. *'A lifelong celibate, Sir Isaac got the idea for his popular Newton's Cradle executive toy when his stonads banged together as he was sitting down under an apple tree to invent gravity.'* (from *'Connections'* by James Burke).

stone *n*. Of *gay* men and women, the opposite to a *sponge*, the dominant partner. And usually no oil painting neither.

stone cold stunner *1. n*. A wrestling move, actually a variation on the ace cutter, made popular by redneck grapple fave 'Stone Cold' Steve Austin. *2. n*. An actress in a vintage black and white movie who manages to give one the *horn* despite the fact that she is almost certainly dead.

stoner's grocer *n*. An all-night petrol station selling family-sized chocolate bars and biscuits to narcotics enthusiasts at unsociable hours.

stones *n. arch*. Olde Worlde *balls. Bollocks, knackers.*

stonker *n*. Erection, *hard on, stiffy*.

store defective *n*. A retail store *fuckard*.

stout trout *n*. The impressively charcoal-hued *Eartha* that transpires following an 18-hour sampling of dark ales and burgundy pie.

straightening your hat *v*. Raking one's kex out the crack of one's *arse*.

strain your greens *v*. To have a *piss*.

strange *n*. Any woman whom one has not had *carnival knowledge* of. An antidote to a *groundhog lay. 'I know she's minging com-*

pared to the girlfriend, but you can't beat a bit of strange, can you?'

stranger, the *n*. The act of sitting on one's hand until it falls asleep before a bout of *bishop rage*, giving the feeling of a *hand job* from someone else.

strangle Kojak *v*. To *make the bald man cry*, to *peel the carrot*.

stranks *n*. The delightful 'fridge magnet bunch of grapes'-style *shit* clusters one finds plastered to the porcelain in public convenience *chod bins*.

strapadictomy *n*. Routine operation to strap on a *dildo*.

strawberry Sunday *n*. Of a gentleman, the point when he is so desperate for a *scuttle* that he no longer cares that *rag week* is not yet over.

stray steaks *n*. Outsized flappage. *Beef curtains* of Brobdingnabian proportions.

streaker *1. n*. One who removes their clothes and runs about at sporting events whilst the BBC pretend they are not there. *2. n*. A *Richard the Third*, slightly smaller than a *U-blocker* and with a slightly pasty consistency, which leaves behind a brown streak as it scuds around the *pan* on being flushed away. A *brown arrow*.

Stretch Armstrong *n*. One gifted with the ability to eat *gorilla salad* whilst simultaneously *finding Radio Luxembourg*. Also *Superman*.

stretched quimosine *n*. An extremely elongated *fanny* that has taken plenty of people for a ride.

strike a damp match *1. v*. To stimulate oneself against an unwitting stranger in a crowd, eg. on a tube train, in a queue to see the Pope lying in state. To *frotter*. 2. *v.* To attempt to have a *wank* with a *soft on*.

strike oil *v.* When doing a *duty* on the lavatory, to eject a *feeshus* with such force that its impact causes a vertical spout of water which hits one squarely in the *jotter*.

strike up the colliery band *euph.* To produce a protracted *trouser cough* of a particularly musical timbre.

strike while the iron's hot *v.* To have an opportunistic *Barclays* as a result of spotting something completely *wankworthy* when out and about, eg. in the bus station toilets after spotting a cracker on the number 38, or in a department store toilet after encountering a really sexy mannequin in the lingerie department.

string *n.* *Wood*, tumescence. *'Quick, everybody, Gunter's got string. Fluffer off set, please and roll camera.'*

stringbean *n.* A long, thin, probably green, penis.

string of pearls *n.* A series of tiny *botty burps* released in quick succession whilst walking. *Air croutons*.

stripper's clit, face like a *adj.* Of a woman, to have a *charming personality*.

stripy laugh *n.* A *parked tiger*, a *Welsh monologue*.

stroke mag *n.* An item of top shelf literature, *art pamphlet*, *gentleman's interest magazine*.

stroke of midnight *n.* A free *one off the wrist*, courtesy of the Adult Channel. A *discount wank*.

stroker 1. *n.* A *wanker*, ie. one who masturbates, eg. Jonathan Ross. 2. *n.* A *wanker*, ie. one who is a *twat*, eg. Jim Davidson.

stroker's cough *n.* The retching gag reflex of a lucky lady who has bitten off more than she can chew.

stroke the dog through the letterbox *euph.* To slide one's hand down the front of a lady's knickers.

strop 1. *n.* A sort of leather thing that old fashioned barbers use to sharpen their razors. 2. *n.* A lady's, usually period-propelled temper tantrum. A *wobbly*, a *wendy*. 3. *n.* That which a gentleman does to *relax* whilst reading a magazine or watching Granada Men & Motors.

struggle nugget *n.* A troublesome *duty* that only comes out after putting up a fight.

strum *v.* A relaxed *tug*.

strumpet *n. arch.* Olde Worlde Prostitute.

strumping *v.* Predatory behaviour by a *bird*, female equivalent of *sharking*.

strum the hairy harp *v.* Of a *dirty lady*, to essay a few arpeggios on her *invisible banjo*. To *shuffle the Kit-Kat*, to gus*set type*.

student garden *n.* An uncared-for *fritter*. A scrubby area of *cunt turf*. With a fridge in it.

student knob *n. medic.* A *cock* that has been *wanked* black and blue.

stuffing a marshmallow in a piggy bank *v.* Of those unfortunate situations involving *brewer's droop*, to attempt to force one's *loose sausage meat* into the *slot*.

stunt cock *n.* In a *bongo vid*, when the leading thespian is unable to sustain *wood* or provide a *money shot*; cue the *stunt cock*, a fat ugly cameraman with a *concrete donkey* on a *hair trigger*.

stuntman's tyre *sim.* Descriptive of the state of the *council gritter* after spicy food, ie. like a tyre that has been doused in petrol and set on fire ready for a daredevil to jump through.

succubus *n.* A phantom night-time *cocksucker* once thought to be responsible for *nocturnal emissions*.

suckers *n. Shag tags.*

suck face *v. US.* To kiss. *'Git a goddamn move on an' finish your mother fuckin' popcorn, you sonofabitch. I wanna suck some face.'*

suckhole *n.* In radio studios, one who laughs at everything Chris Moyles says. A *brown noser, toady, arselick, sycophant, fart catcher.*

suckhole's dilemma *n.* Of a shirt fly, to be in a situation where they don't know whose *arse* to lick first, eg. a salesman in a room full of purchasing managers, or Ben Elton in a palace full of Royals.

sucking a tramp's cock, like *sim.* Descriptive of the consumption of something which is unpleasant, or which leaves a foul taste in the mouth, eg. Netto budget fishcakes.

suck off *v.* To perform *horatio*, to do a *chewie*, give some *head.*

sugar-free spongle *n.* The ejaculate of a vasectomised male. *Australian gravy.*

sugared almond *n. Clematis.*

sugar walls *n.* Sheena Easton's *slice* sides.

suitcase handle, gusset like a *sim.* Descriptive of the petrified state of a dirty bird's crusty 3-week-old knickers.

summoning Moira *n.* The desperate act of frantically conjuring up a mental picture of cadaverous newsreader Moira Stewart in order to suppress a potentially embarrassing *diamond cutter* just before

getting off the bus.

sump *n. medic.* The part between the *front* and *back bottoms* on a lady. The *manifold,* the *rocker box,* the *fire break,* the *kerb.* The *tinter.*

sunnies *n. Aus Tits, baps.*

supermarket smack *n.* Special Brew.

surfboard 1. *n.* A flat-chested female, *Miss Lincolnshire.* 2. *n. Aus.* A piece of equipment used by women to *catch the waves* when the *red flag is flying.* A *fanny nanny* for a heavy *aunt Flo.*

surfing the crimson wave *n. Riding the menstrual cycle.*

surf 'n' turf 1. *n.* The act of orally probing a lady's *rusty sheriff's badge* during an act of *cumulonimbus.* 2. *n.* An 1980s-style meal served at a Berni Inn, consisting of a fish and steak combo that tasted like one was orally probing a lady's *rusty sheriff's badge* during an act of *cumulonimbus.*

surprise, sur-fucking-prise! *exclam.* Remark made at a depressingly predictable event, eg. England losing on penalties.

survivor *n.* A buoyant *stool* which resists all attempts to *send it to the beach.*

SWAB *acronym.* Young ladies who respond to a gentleman's attempts at wooing with monosyllabic disinterest. Single Word Answer Bitches.

Swaffham *v.* Of a lady, to practise the gentle art of cramming both a gentleman friend's *clockweights* in her mouth at the same time. Named after the town in Norfolk, where all the womenfolk, without exception, are experts in the practice.

swagman's hat *n. medic.* Condition of the *anus* when infested with numerous *tagnuts*. *'Holmes surveyed the lavatory cubical before announcing, 'The game is afoot, Watson, and our quarry has a bandy-legged gait'. 'How the devil do you know that, man?' I exclaimed. 'Elementary. The Izal toilet paper means he will almost certainly have a ringpiece like a swagman's hat.''* (from *'The Red-Ringed League'* by Sir Arthur Conan Doyle).

swallow *v.* What proper women do.

swallow the bear *v.* To perform *cumulonimbus* on a lady with a right old *biffer* on her.

swallow the oysters *exclam.* A phrase of friendly encouragement to a lady who is being a little too fussy about eating all her *porridge* up.

swamp *v. milit.* To *piss*, urinate.

swamp donkey *n.* Female not overly endowed with physical beauty. A *tug boat, boiler, sea monster, steg.*

swank 1. *v.* To walk into a room like one was walking onto a yacht. 2. *n.* A secretive *five knuckle shuffle* utilizing minimal wrist action which is enjoyed whilst lying next to one's sleeping partner. Normally practised following the rejection of drunken sexual advances. An *American beauty.*

swap spit *v.* To *suck face.*

sweatermeat *n.* Phrase used to alert friends to the presence of a nice pair of *tits.* Usually accompanied by clockface directional information. *'Sweatermeat at 3 o'clock.'*

sweater puppets *n. Fondleberries.* Particularly animated breasts that keep a fellow entertained.

sweats *rhym. slang.* An affectionate term for people of Caledonian extraction. From sweaty socks = jocks.

sweaty Morph *n.* A *mudchild,* a turd.

swedge *n.* That piece of folded bogroll which a sweating *pie shifter* wedges in his *potty slot* in order to stop his *farting clappers* rubbing together. A *manpon, botcap, toffee rizla.* *'Substantial Andrex swedge worn by Bad Manners frontman Buster Bloodvessel (Douglas Trendle) whilst performing 'Just a Feeling' in a deep-sea diver's suit on 'Top of the Pops', c. May 1981. Complete with certificate of authenticity. Estimate £3000 - £4000.'* (extract from Christie's Rock Memorabilia Auction Catalogue, August 2004).

Swedish *n. Greek.*

Sweeney *exclam.* A humorous utterance shouted out in the style of DI Jack Regan by a man when *kicking a lady's back doors in.*

sweep's brush *n.* A *Judith.*

sweep the yard *v.* To loudly scratch one's pubic area making a sound like sweeping paving slabs with a hard-bristled broom.

sweetbreads *n.* The testicular component of the *family jewels.* The *clockweights,* the *plums,* the *knackers.*

sweetcorn itch *n.* An itchy ringpiece due to insufficient wiping. *IRS.*

sweet FA *acronym.* Sweet Fanny Adams, *fuck all,* absolutely nothing. Nowt.

sweet tits *n.* Affectionate male term of endearment for females. *'Goodnight, goodnight! Parting is such sweet sorrow / That I shall say goodnight until it be morrow, sweet tits.'* (from *'Romeo and*

Juliet' by William Shakespeare).

swift *n*. A bit like a *swallow,* only faster. So fast, in fact, that there isn't the option to spit.

swill out the trough *v*. Female equivalent of *cleaning inside the farmer's hat.*

swim against the tide *v*. To take a *dip* whilst the *red flag* is flying.

swing both ways *v*. To be a *switch hitter.*

swingers 1. *n*. Sinister, grim-looking couples who have uninhibited sex in suburban houses with other sinister, grim-looking couples. **2.** *n*. *Clockweights, knackers, pods, gourds.*

swirly *n*. Bullies' lavatory game whereby the victim's head is pushed into the *crapper* and the flush pulled. *'I say you chaps, look out! Campbell and Milburn are in the bogs and they've just given Robin Cook a swirly.'*

Swiss *adj*. Completely useless. *'Did you see Henman play at Wimbledon? He was completely fucking swiss.'*

Swiss finger *n*. An erect *todger* with a pink iced topping, upon withdrawal from a lady on the eve of a week's *visit from the painters,* or in the 24 hours following their departure. From the similarity to the doughy confection of the same name to be found in the window of all Ainsley's branches.

Swiss kiss *n*. A *post-horatio spangle*-flavoured snog.

Swiss movement *n*. A *chod* dropped in the *pan* with almost nazi-like precision by a person with disciplined and regular bowel habits.

switchcraft *n*. The magical ability of a woman to make incredible amounts of cash disappear into thin air whilst out shopping.

switch hitter *n*. US. Person who *bats with both hands*, a bisexual, *Happy Shopper*. One who approaches the *oyster* and *snail buffet* with a broad plate.

swive *v*. 17thC. Fuck. *'A horse, a horse. My kingdom for a swiving horse.'*

swope *n*. The hairstyle affected by balding men whereby strands of hair on one side of the head are grown long and swept over the dome, giving the impression of a full head of hair, eg. Robert Robinson, Bobby Charlton, Desmond Morris.

sword swallower *n*. A circus *fellatrix.*

syrup *n*. Hairpiece. From syrup of fig = *Irish jig.* *"Q: 'Just look at this, 007.' Bond: 'What is it, Q? Looks like an ordinary syrup to me.' Q: 'Yes, but one tug on the chinstrap and it turns into a miniature helicopter.' Bond: 'Hmm! Hair raising!"' (From 'Never Say Never Again', 1983).*

Tt

tabby afro *n*. A collection of different-coloured *pubes* found blocking the plug hole of the bath in a shared flat.

tackle *n*. The *family jewels* and the *spam sceptre*. The *fruitbowl*.

tacklebags *n*. Underpants.

tackleshack *n*. *Tacklebags*.

taco tickler *n*. A *gusset typist*.

tadger *n*. *Todger*.

tadpole net *n*. *Blob, rubber Johnny, cheesepipe clingfilm*.

tadpole yoghurt *n*. *Gentleman's relish*, dressing for a *sausage sandwich*.

tagnuts *n*. *Toffee strings, winnets, clinkers, dangleberries, bead curtains*.

tail 1. *n*. arch. Penis. 2. *n*. Fluff, *totty, skirt, talent*. 3. *n*. Bum.

tail ender *n*. Small dollop of *do* that one must wait for after the main stool has been expelled, the finial on a *log cabin* roof. *Geetle*.

tail gunner *n*. A *rear admiral. Arse bandit at 6 o'clock*.

tailpipe *n*. US. *Ass-hole*.

tail shot *n*. The release of *tail wind*.

tail wind *n*. *Botty gas. Air biscuits* tending to push one forwards.

taint *n*. *Niftkin's bridge*. Because *"tain't your arse and 'tain't your fanny.'*

take a packed lunch *v*. To take one's girlfriend on holiday to avoid all the *fucking about* and loss of drinking time that goes with finding a suitable female at one's destination. *'I went to Ibiza last year and wasted the first day and a half sorting myself out with some tart to bang. I'm going to Agya Napa this year, and I'm taking a packed lunch.'*

take an air dump *v*. To *fart, blow off*.

take Captain Picard to warp speed *v*. To masturbate. To *strangle Kojak, pull Paul Daniels' head off*.

take one in the company's time *v*. Whilst at work, to hold in a *number two* until one's unpaid break is over, thus ensuring that one gets paid the full hourly rate for having a *shit*.

take the cat to the vet *euph*. To knock off work early.

take the crust off *v*. Nautical term describing the precautionary pre-disembarkation *wank* taken by trawlermen before they are reunited with their ladyfriends.

take the edge off *v*. To *relax in a gentleman's way* in order to prolong a putative *scuttle* with one's partner. To *put a wank in the bank. 'Got a big night with the missus planned. I'd better go and take the edge off first.'*

take the goalie off the pitch *v*. To withdraw contraception in a positive effort to conceive a *turf chimp*.

talent *n*. coll. *Crumpet, bush*, attractive females.

talent scout *n*. A designated member of a group who looks round the pub door to check that the *blart* inside is worth pushing one's way to the bar for.

talk German *v*. To *fart, blow off*, puff on an imaginary *bum cigar*.

talk on the great white telephone *v*. To be sick in the lavatory. *Drive the porcelain bus*.

talk to the boss *exclam*. A married man's response to his wife's request for some of his hard-earned cash to fritter away on luxuries. An instruction to perform an act of *horatio. 'It's no good, love. I'm going to have to go shopping. We're right out of baby food and the twins need new shoes.' 'It's not up* *to me, you'd better talk to the boss.'*

talk to the judge *n.* To *suck a copper's truncheon* by way of avoiding a speeding ticket. *'I know I was doing 50 in a 30 zone, officer, but is there any way we can work this out? Perhaps if I spoke to the judge behind that skip?'*

tallywhacker *n. 18thC.* Penis, *old man.*

tammy dodger *n.* A gentleman forced to go to the pub, chippy, video shop, church, round the world balloon attempt etc, to avoid his *blob-stropping* missus.

tammy huff *n.* A monthly feminine mood swing. A *blob strop.*

tampon *1. n.* A small, highly-sophisticated implant which enables women to play tennis. *2. n.* An injury-prone footballer, from the fact that he is 'one week in, three weeks out', eg. Darren Anderton, who didn't play for Spurs and England, and currently doesn't play for Birmingham.

tam rag *n.* Variation of *jam rag.*

tamtrum *n.* A monthly exhibition of petulance. From Latin tampus = fanny rags & trum = hissy fit. A *blobstrop,* a *tammy huff.*

Tamworth *n.* Perjorative term for a ginger person, named after them pigs which have ginger bristles and funny-looking eyes.

tandoori whisper *n.* Silent, yet exquisitely rancid, burst of *wind* following an Indian meal.

tango butter *n. Fanny slobber.*

tank *v.* To *scuttle, roger.*

tank driver's hat *n.* A particularly hairy *fanny* with flaps that fasten under your chin. A *biffer.*

tanked up *1. adj.* Usefully drunk, sufficient to fight or drive a car

very fast. *2. adj. milit.* To be sufficiently equipped with tanks.

tank slapper *1. n.* An exciting incident that happens to a motorcyclist prior to a thrilling ride in an ambulance. *2. n.* An ugly biker's moll.

tanorexia *n. medic.* Psychological disorder common in footballers' wives types who, despite daily *cancer shop* sessions, still believe they are pasty when in fact they have the skin tone of an Oompaloompa.

tantric shit *n.* An extremely prolonged visit to the porcelain *chod bin,* where one sits for four hours, *humming.*

tap off *v.* To successfully *tap up.*

tap up *1. v.* Of football managers, to make an illegal approach to a player who is signed to another team. *2. v.* Of Football Association officials, to chat up and attempt to instigate a sexual liaison with a typist in a lift at FA headquarters.

tapioca tash *n.* Facial ornamentation, popular amongst *stick vid* starlets.

tapioca toothpaste *n.* Dental gel for a *trouser leg trombonist.*

tapping on the high hat *v.* Rhythmic, percussive masturbation.

tapping the ash *n.* Refers to the vigorous shaking and pulling apart of the buttocks in an attempt to force out the troublesome *turd* that ends a *shitting* session, but refuses to drop into the *pan,* akin to tapping the end of a cigarette in order for the ash to drop. *'Are you going to be long in the crapper, Archbishop?' 'Shouldn't be long now, Your Majesty, I'm just tapping the ash.'*

TAPS *acronym. medic.* Technical term used by doctors on medical notes, Thick As Pig Shit.

Tara's tits *euph.* Nothing. Fuck all. From the notorious It-Girl Tara Palmer Tomkinson's distinct lack of *bikini filler*. *'We have spent three months searching the secret bunkers and military bases of Iraq in search of chemical warheads and weapons of mass destruction, but thus far I must report to the Security Council that we have found Tara's tits.'* (Dr. Hans Blix's report, 27th Jan 2003).

Tarantino hangover *n.* The kind of hangover whereby one's memory behaves in the style of *'Pulp Fiction'*; one's recollections of the night before appear in a seemingly random order and one has to wait until one has seen all of them to finally understand what happened.

tar baby *1. n.* A sticky, black trap that nearly proved the undoing of Brer Rabbit in the *'Uncle Remus'* stories. *2. n.* A sticky, black *crap* that proves the undoing of anyone who has spent a night quaffing Guinness.

Tarbucks *n.* A set of *tits* so impressive that the viewer involuntarily shouts 'ho-ho!' in the manner of the cheeky, gap-toothed scouser comedian and golf enthusiast Jimmy.

Tardis fanny *n.* A deceptively spacious *snatch*. A disappointing *cathedral* when one was expecting a *priest's hole*.

tarmac round the garage *sim.* Descriptive of a slightly grubby *path to the back door*, making *rear entry* an unpleasant prospect.

tarrantless *adj.* To possess even less talent than Chris Tarrant, eg. Steve Penk, Eamonn Holmes, that arsehole mate of Robbie Williams's

who used to do *'You've Been Framed'*.

tart *n.* *Slapper, dolly bird.*

tart farmer *n.* A *pimp.*

tart fuel *n.* Any alcoholic drink consumed by young women which gets them going. *'She's very light on tart fuel. She'll go all the way to Cockfosters on three bottles of Hooch.'*

tart ink *n.* That which is used to draw a more attractive face onto a plain woman. Make-up.

tart's window box, a *n.* What one smells like when one has too much aftershave on.

tart-throb *n.* A low grade hunk who is unaccountably alluring to ladies from the lower echelons, eg. Peter Andre, Robson Green.

Tarzan cord *n.* The narrow lace which attaches *Kojak's roll-neck* to the *bobby's helmet*. The *guy rope*, the *banjo.*

tash *n.* See *Hitler tash.*

tassel *n.* Innocent schoolboy term for the penis. *Winkle, willie, winkie-woo, slag hammer.*

taste the rainbow *v.* To have a little taste of everything from the 'All You Can Eat' *pant buffet.*

'taters *n. Nads, balls, bollocks.* The testicles. Contraction of potatoes. *'We Englishmen are conscious of our status / Which is why the beastly foreigners all hate us / But it's always seemed to me / that it's simply jealousy / Cos they're envious of the size of English 'taters.'* (From *'The Stately Genitals of England'* by Noel Coward).

ta tas *n. Noinkers, jubblies, cajooblies, jugs, bubbies, charms, baby's dinners, fun cushions, paps, bojangles, thrupennies, assets mambas, dirty pillows,* *chebs, charlies, diddies, doos, puppies, Bristols, airbags, Gert Stonkers, kahunas, shirt potatoes, boobs, melons, oomlaaters, nellies, choozies, chubblies, chumbawumbas, blimps, sweater fruit, knockers, churns, whammers, yoinkahs, begonias, mumbas, pink pillows, top bollocks, neddies, chichis, cab man's rests, baps, funbags, bumpies, zeps, bazongers, headlamps, whammies, norks, bangers, tits, dumplings, hogans.* Breasts.

tatties *n.* Testicles, *spuds.*

tatty watta. *n. Nat. Am.* Red Indian word for *spud juice,* semen. Literally *'potato water.'*

taxi *v.* To *come* late. Or never at all.

taxi driver's minute *n.* Any period of time which is longer than half an hour.

taxi driver's tan *1. n.* An area of sunburn on the right index finger caused by hooking it on the top of the cab whilst driving along. *2. n.* A similar effect caused by *breaching the hull.* A *filter tip.*

taxi for Brown *exclam.* A witty riposte to an anal retort, such as what Dorothy Parker or Oscar Wilde might have said after they *dropped their guts.*

taxi tiger *n.* A desperate last-chance lunger on the way home.

Taylforth *1. n.* A disastrous *blowjob* in a car. *2. n. medic.* A severe attack of pancreatitis which can only be relieved by being *sucked off* in a layby.

Taz *1. n. prop.* A hairy cartoon beast that dribbles, found in the Antipodes. *2. n.* A hairy *grotter* that dribbles, found in ladies' *dunghampers.*

TBS *abbrev.* Toxic Bott Syndrome. Severe noxious emissions or *brew-*er's farts. *Burning bad powder.*

TCM *abbrev. medic.* Turd Cutting Muscle, *crimper,* anal sphincter. The *nipsy, secaturds.*

TCS *abbrev.* Traction Control System. When *farting* following a bellyfull of *dizzyade* and/or curry, the precise control of the *nipsy* required to allow one to squeak one out without producing any wheelspin, thus preventing *laying rubber* in the undies.

teabagging *v.* To make a strong brew with *Fussell's Milk* and two lumps. A last resort sexual practice whereby the man lowers his *pods* into the lady's mouth.

tea chicken *n.* Game played by severely hungover flatmates, whereby they sit immobile waiting for the first one to bottle it and offer to put the kettle on.

teaching William a lesson *n. Punishing Percy, pulling the Pope's cap off. "What's all this banging and groaning?' bellowed Mr. Wilkins as he burst into the dorm. 'Please, Sir,' piped-up Venables. 'It was Darbishire teaching Jennings a lesson."* (from *'Jennings and the Mysterious Body Hairs'* by Anthony Buckeridge).

tea cosy *n.* A place to hide one's *spout* whilst thinking about the true object of one's affections. *'Deaths: Lady Diana Spencer, shopping enthusiast, landmines campaigner and Prince's tea cosy, 36.'*

tea fairy *n.* term used to describe a rather poor drinker. *'Come on, George, you big tea fairy. One drink won't hurt you.'*

tea pot *n.* A male from the Larry Grayson school of posturing.

teapot shuffle *n.* Descriptive of the

pose adopted by internet-fuelled *self-polluters* ie. *pulling themselves off* with the left hand, whilst the right arm is extended to faciltate control of the mouse.

teapot sucker *n*. A *bottom shelf drinker*, a teetotaller.

tear in a coalman's jacket *sim*. A large, raggy *blart*.

tear off a piece *v. US*. To have sex. *Tear one off.*

tearful wank *n*. A light-hearted taunt directed at a newly heartbroken male colleague. It involves sticking the bottom lip out, and doing a masturbating gesture with one hand and a 'boo hoo' gesture with the other.

tea strainer *n*. A bowel movement that is forceably withheld during teabreak so that one can have a *tom tit* on the company's time. *Time and a turd.*

tea towel holder *n*. Anus, *ringpiece, freckle*. From the 1950s plastic 'finger poke' style kitchen accessory.

technicolour yawn *n*. A *yoff*.

Tecwens *n. medic*. An attack of pathetic fake coughing that one effects at work the day before one throws a sickie. From the *'Who Wants to be a Millionaire'* coughing arsehole Tecwen Whittock. *'The lads are playing Locomotiv Moscow tomorrow, live on Sky, only the kick off's at two in the afternoon. Cough! Cough! Ooh, dear. I can feel a touch of the Tecwens coming on.'*

ted *n*. The *Teddington*.

Teddington *rhym. slang*. The Penis. From Teddington Lock = *corn on the cob*.

teddy's leg *n*. State of stool expulsion somewhere beyond the *turtle's head*, but prior to *touching*

sock. Point midway through *smoking a bum cigar. Bungle's finger.*

tee off *v*. To *wank* and/or *fart*. Not necessarily at the same time.

Tees duck *n*. Sky rat, *shitehawk*. A seagull.

teeter meter *n*. Calibration scale assessing the attractiveness of women based on how far from sober one would have to be to *slip them a length*. eg. Kylie Minogue would be 0 on the teeter meter, whereas Gail Tilsley off *'Coronation Street'* would be 15 pints of Stella with whisky chasers.

teggat *n*. A short-necked *turtle's head* which is unable to *touch cloth*, and retreats back into the *bomb bay*.

temazepalm *n. medic*. Hand-induced insomnia relief.

ten minutes' peace and quiet *n*. An offensive term used by sexist men to describe getting a *chewie* off their *bit of fluff*. *'Mr. Campbell-Bannerman: Yes, Mrs. Pankhurst, I agree that the introduction of universal suffrage is a worthy political objective, and I shall endeavour to include it in the King's speech at the beginning of the next parliamentary session...but only if you give me ten minutes peace and quiet. Mrs. Pankhurst: Glub! Glub!'.* (Cartoon in *'Punch'* by Bernard Partridge, 1905).

Tennants poetry *n*. A moving sonnet of threats and expletives, usually *scumbled* by a dishevelled Scotsman while leaning forwards.

tennis fan *n*. A woman who takes the *other bus* to Wimbledon. A *lady golfer*.

tenpin *v*. To place digits simultaneously in the *tea towel holder* and the *fish mitten*. From the grip used in ten pin bowling. To *spock*.

ten pint princess *n*. A *donner*.

Tenpole Tudor *n*. A *slapper*, ie. one who has had the *swords* of a thousand men.

ten-to-two shuffle *n*. A perfunctory dance that *pissed up* gentlemen engage in with the *floor sweepings* at the end of a long and unspectacular evening *on the pull*. *'Any luck last night?' 'No. Ended up doing the ten-to-two shuffle with some dental receptionist. Gave me a bit of duck sausage and got the last bus home.'*

tent pole *n*. *Stiffy*, erect penis, especially in bed. A *trouser tent, morning glory, wake up with Jake up.*

tequila sunrise *n*. The awe-inspiring visual effect produced when a man's bright yellow urine flows into the *pan* where the previous (female) occupant has *blobbed*.

Terry Funk *1*. *n*. *prop*. A popular Discotheque personality in the Midlands, circa 1970. *2*. *rhym. slang*. Marijuana cigarettes, from Terry Funk = skunk. *3*. *rhym. slang*. Spooge, from Terry Funk = spunk. *'Waiter. There's some Terry Funk in my soup'*. *'Yes, Mr. Winner. That's because the chef, the entire kitchen and serving staff, and indeed the rest of the customers have masturbated into it.'*

Terry Waite's allotment *sim*. Descriptive of a badly-overgrown *ladygarden*. *'Marriette was powerless to resist. His eyes burned into hers like emeralds. His muscular arms enfolded her body as she felt herself being swept away in a monsoon of passion. 'Bloody hell! You've got a twat like Terry Waite's allotment!' he cried, as he* pulled out the waistband of her bloomers and peered inside.' (from 'The Peasant Girl and the First World War Soldier' by Barbara Cartland).

tescosexual *n*. A man whose incidence of sexual activity peaks during his wife's trips to the shops.

test card wank *n*. A *tug* one has, not because one is feeling particularly *fruity*, but simply because there is nothing else to do. A *loose end away*.

test ride *n*. In the executive world, the act of taking the *office bike* out for a *fuck* before deciding whether or not to dump one's missus for her.

textbook dog *n*. The recognition of an absolutely perfect *doggy-style* position seen in everyday situations, eg. a secretary crawling on the floor to find a contact lens.

thatch hatch *n*. Vagina, *hairy pie*.

thatched cottage *n*. *arch*. A delightfully picturesque half-timbered *cunt* with roses round the *pissflaps*.

that one's got a skin on it *exclam*. Humorous riposte following the release of a *fart* that has been *stewing* a little too long in the *back boiler*. From the similarity to a milky coffee that has been left too long in the cup.

Thelonius *rhym. slang*. Semen. Named after the jazz pianist Thelonius Spunk.

the other *n*. *It*, the old *how's your father*.

there we are then *exclam. acronym*. A covert way of calling another person a *twat*.

thesbian *n*. A *grumble flick* actress who does *girl on girl* professionally, but is not a *tennis fan* in real life.

the third place *n. Splaystation 2.* The *arse*.

thick as a ghurka's foreskin *sim.* Descriptive of someone who is as *thick as a Welshman's cock*.

thick repeater *n.* A large bore semi-automatic, single barrel *mutton musket*.

thick spunk *n.* Extremely fertile, high motility *spaff. Jitler* that requires factor 40 contraception. *'I've got eight brothers and six sisters thanks to Pop's thick spunk. Gee whiz, his sperm count is so high, I'll bet mom has to chew before swallowing.'* (Little Jimmy Osmond interviewed in *'Look In'*, 1972).

thigh ticklers *n. Bugger's grips, face fannies, sideboards. 'Ooh, Dr. Rhodes Boyson. What a magnificent set of thigh ticklers.' 'Thank-you, Your Majesty.'*

thighbrows *n.* A profusion of bikini overspill. *Loose baccy.*

think of the money shot *n.* In *bongo videography*, the less than enthusiastic expression on the lead actress's face as Ron Jeremy, Bill Margold or Ben Dover, or possibly all three, empty their *pods* into it.

third leg 1. *n.* Cricketing position between mid-off and gully. 2. *n.* The *middle stump*.

thirty-four-and-a-halfer *n.* A gentleman blessed with the miraculous ability to perform *horatio* upon himself.

Thora bird *n.* A *nana Kournikova.*

Thora Hird 1. *n. prop.* Pelican-throated actress of stairlift testimonial fame, no longer alive at time of going to press. 2. *rhym. slang.* A *turd.*

Thorntons, little bit of *sim.* Euphemism used when attempting to talk the wife into a bit of *back-door action.* From the famous gift toffee manufacturer's advertising slogan, ie. *'Skilled in the ways of the chocolatier'. 'Roll over, love. I fancy a little bit of Thorntons tonight.'*

thousand island dressing *n.* The sauce which coats one's *naughty spoon* after mixing the *gorilla salad* when *cranberry dip* is on the menu.

thrap *v.* To masturbate furiously, to give it *six nowt* on the *Right Honourable Member for Pantchester.* Also *thrape.*

three card trick *rhym slang. Prick. 'She got her jazz bands round me three card trick and started giving it six nowt.'*

three coiler *n.* A canine *turd*, the curled and crimped result of not having walked the dog, usually found on a carpet.

three dick gob *n.* A capacious mouth. *'The next record is 'You're So Vain' by Carly Simon, the lady with the three dick gob. And it's for Terry, who is seven today. Lots of love from mummy, daddy, nana and granpa Johnson and nana Robins.'* (Ed 'Stewpot' Stewart, *'Radio 1 Junior Choice'*, 1974).

three-fag omelette *n.* For a non-smoker, the satisfying yet unfamiliar pattie of phlegm coughed up the morning after having drunk enough to *ponce* a few fags off a mate at about ten past eleven.

three for a bob *rhym. slang.* The penis.

three-legged race *n.* When *fuck-struck*, to stumble up the stairs with a *bone on.*

three mile island *n.* An extremely noxious rectal meltdown with a half-life of about ten minutes. A *Smellafield*.

three piece suite *n.* That which has to be plumped up and rearranged on a regular basis to ensure seated comfort. The *Meat and two veg, wedding tackle*. The male *undercarriage*.

three wheeler *rhym. slang. Dyke, lesbian*. From three wheeled trike.

throb on *n.* A *wide on*.

throne *n.* The Queen's *crapper*.

throne room *n.* The Queen's *shit house*.

throng *adj.* Descriptive of a fashionably skimpy item of intimate apparel being worn by someone who really should have known better, eg. women with nice personalities, oldies or Jade Goody. From thong + wrong. *'Did you see what Bob's bird was wearing when she bent over?' 'Aye Joe, that's just throng, that.'*

throttle pit *n. Aus.* The *dunny*. Toilet.

throttle the turkey *v.* To masturbate in Norfolk.

through a hedge backwards *exclam.* Phrase to indicate the sexual attractiveness of a lady. *'Phoar! I could fuck her through a hedge backwards.'*

througher *n.* A 24-hour drinking session. A *Leo Sayer*.

throw *v.* To *barf, hoy, chuck*.

throwabout *n.* A petite woman who can be easily and casually 'thrown about' from one position to another during sex. A *laptop*.

throwing a Woodbine up Northumberland Street *sim. NE.* Unsatisfying sex with a *bucket-fannied* individual. *'Why man, it was like hoyin' a Woodbine up Northumberland Street'*. Also

throwing a sausage up Briggate (Leeds), chucking a fag down Parliament Street (Nottingham) Alluding to the *last hot dog in the tin, wall of death*.

throw one's cap into the hangar *v. milit.* To have sex with a lady endowed with a *poacher's pocket*. From the naval act of throwing a rating's hat into the bowels of a through-deck cruiser. Also *throwing a kitbag in a dry dock*.

throw out the garbage *v.* To flush out one's *spooge pipe*.

throw your bollocks at the clock *exclam.* An exclamation of total exasperation. *'We've been talking about the future of power sharing in Northern Ireland for five weeks now, and they still won't sit in the same bloody room. It's enough to make you want to throw your bollocks at the clock.'* (Senator George Mitchell, Report on the Northern Ireland Peace Process).

thrupenny bits 1. *rhym. slang. Tits.* 2. *rhym. slang.* The *shits.*

thruster *n. medic.* A muscle, somewhere in the neck or jaw, the tensing of which forces out stubborn *shits* and *farts.*

thumb a ride on the rocket *adj.* To *take Captain Picard to warp speed.*

thumb bumming *v. Touching last night's tea.*

thumbing in a slacky *v.* The first act of an optimistic bout of lovemaking for which the gentleman's spirit is willing, but his flesh is weak. *Pushing a marshmallow into a moneybox.*

thumbrise *n.* The time of day at which a gentleman in a loving relationship is allowed out the house by his other half for a drink with his mates.

thumbset *n*. The time by which he has to be back in the house with his *pink handcuffs* on.

thumper *n*. A big, pounding erection, a *stalk*, a *stiffy*.

thumpology *n*. The resolution of disputes by recourse to physical argument. *Closing time counselling*.

thunder bags *n*. Underpants, *trolleys*.

thunderbirds *n*. Women of ample proportions. *Barge arses*.

thunder box *n. arch*. Lavatory, *shitter*. Also *thunder bowl*.

thunderbox shuffle *1. n*. A song by Skiffle king Lonnie Donnegan that reached no. 3 in 1960. *2. n*. The *arse* dance performed whilst sitting on the *chod bin* trying to dislodge the *pit bull*.

thundercrack *n*. The kind of *fart* that requires one to check one's *kex* for *bullets*.

thunder mug *n*. Chamber pot, *piss pot*.

thunderslash *n*. A splendidly loud urination delivered *con gusto* directly into the water of the pot. A *dad's piss*, a *round of applause*, a *standing ovation*.

ticket to tottieville *euph*. See *token for the cockwash*.

tickle Fat Ed *v*. Of a fellow, to *pleasure himself* in a leisurely, almost lackadaisical manner. As one would do on a chaise-longue in a gazebo, or in a blazer and straw boater whilst drifting in a punt.

ticklers *n*. Corrugated condoms, amusing *French letters*

tickle tackle *n*. *Anteater's nose, cock collar*. The *fiveskin*.

tickle the baby *v*. To engage in a spot of sexual intercourse with a pregnant ladyfriend. *'What was the milkman doing upstairs?' 'Nothing love. He was just tickling the baby.'*

tickle the pickle *v*. See *jerkin' the gherkin*.

tickle your pip *v*. To be aroused sexually by Leslie Philips or Terry-Thomas..

tickling the scampi *v*. A means of getting *fish fingers*. Feminine *monkey spanking*.

tied by the brown rope *adj*. To be confined to the *chod bin* by an intractable *Brad*.

tiffin *n*. An afternoon *fuck* off Sid James in a pith helmet.

tiffter *n*. An unwanted erection, *Jake*.

tiger's back *n*. The decorative striped effect left in the *pan* after a particularly sticky *Meatloaf's daughter* has *gone to the beach*.

tightie *n. Scot. medic*. The feeling of discomfort experienced when attempting to peel back the *fiveskin* due to it being stuck to the *helmet* with *cheese*. Possibly something to do with the humid atmosphere found inside a kilt.

Tijuana bible *n*. A *jazz mag*.

Tijuana cha-cha *n*. The *trots*. See *sour apple quickstep, Mexican screamers*.

tile hanger's nailbags *sim*. Sagging, lumpy *charlies*. *'She had tits like a tile hanger's nailbags'*.

time and a turd *n*. The art of having a *tom tit* at work whilst being paid overtime by an unwitting employer.

Tim Henman *n*. A *penis* which promises great things but fails to achieve anything even vaguely resembling hardness, ie. it doesn't even get to the *semi* stage.

Timmy twostroke *n*. A gentleman

blessed with the enviable ability to *blow his stack* after a couple of *cock stabs*. A *two-push Charlie*.

tincture *n*. An alcoholic drink taken for medicinal purposes, perhaps at breakfast time or during an early morning walk back from Boozebuster.

tinker's curse *n*. An involuntary and highly ill-timed erection that takes the gloss off social occasions. *'Do you, Charles Philip Arthur George, take Diana Frances...oops, sorry about that. I've got the tinker's curse.'* (Dr. Robert Runcie, the Marriage of Prince Charles and Lady Di, 1981).

tin of Vim with an apple on top *sim*. A fictitious penis measurement.

tinter 1. *n*. High class *totty*, top class *talent*. *'That Mick Hucknall's a jammy get. A face like his and he still gets all the top tinter.'* 2. *n*. A lady's *barse*, because *"tin't 'er arse and 'tin't 'er fanny.'* The *taint*.

tipping the teapot *n*. Situation which occurs when, owing to a fully or semi-erectivated state, a fellow is unable to aim his *tassel* at the toilet bowl for a *slash* and must therefore bend his whole body to attain the required angle of incidence.

tipping the velvet *n*. Of TV companies, the practice of promising *full-nutted* viewers explicit *lesbo cumulonimbus* in order to boost ratings.

tipple *n*. The very tip of the nipple.

tip-toe tottie *n*. The various *wank pamphlets* adorning the top shelves of *Grumbelows*, which would thwart shorter men such as Ronnie Corbett, diddy David Hamilton and wee Jimmy Krankie.

tip your concrete *v*. A sophisticated term for ejaculation when *cough your filthy yoghurt* seems inappropriate.

tisnae *n*. A scotch lassie's perineum. The *McSnarse*.

tisn'ts *n*. Very small, practically non-existent breasts. *Knockers* that barely merit the description *tits*.

tissent *n*. The *taint, tinter, tintis*.

Titanic *n*. A lass who *goes down* first time out. An *Ikea bulb*.

tit fairies *n*. Mythical visitors who magically transform the wife's *fried eggs* into *TNTs* during and after *sprogdrop*.

tit for twat *n*. The act of fondling a woman's breast in the vain hope of getting her sufficiently aroused to permit one to have a shot on her *clopper*.

titilate *v*. To excite with bosoms.

tit kitten *n*. A diminutive lady who makes up for her small stature by having superior *leisure facilities*. A *midget gem*.

tit leech 1. *n*. A baby. *'Births: Fforbes Hhamilton. 23rd November, at The Portland Hospital. To the Hon. Hector and Julia (nee Ffyffe-Lewethwaite-Ffyffe), a 6lb 4oz tit leech, Tarquin Hector Sebastapol, brother for Semolina. Deo Gracias.'* ('The Times', Dec 2nd 2001). 2. *n*. A bloke who enjoys sucking on his wife's *jugs*.

tit man *n*. He who prefers *Bristols* to *arses* or *gams*.

titnotised *adj*. To be involuntarily mesmerised by a smashing pair of *churns*.

tit pants *n*. A bra.

tit pizzas *n*. Big, round, mottled, crusty aereolae.

tits 1. *n.* Breasts, *knockers.* *'What a pair of tits.'* 2. *n.* Foolish or derisory people. *'What a bunch of tits.'* 3. *n.* Nerves. *'Christ, that Justin Lee Collins gets on my tits.'*

tits on a fish *n.* Descriptive of a supremely useless thing. *'Did you see (insert name of striker currently having a run of bad form) play on Saturday? He was as much use as tits on a fish.'*

tits out for the lads, get your *exclam.* A compliment proffered by a large group of aggresively drunken men to any female above the age of puberty.

tit scrap *n.* The fighting motion of the breasts of a very fat council estate woman who chooses not to wear *tit pants* as she walks to Netto, BoozeBuster or bingo.

tit splitter *n.* A lady's fashion bag worn diagonally across the torso such that it bisects the *headlamps.*

tit tap *n. medic.* A nipple. *'Camera three. Forget about the crazy paving, zoom in on her tip taps, quick.'* (Director's instruction, *'Ground Force'*, BBC TV).

tittoo *n.* A small piece of body art found in the breastular region. A *tit* tattoo.

titty fuck *n.* A *sausage sandwich*, a *diddy ride.*

tit up *v.* To get one's *tops* off a *bird.* *'The Man Who Titted Up the Lord Mayor's Mother During the Loyal Toast'.* (Cartoon in *'Punch'* by HM Bateman, 1926).

tit wank *n.* A *soapy tit wank*, without the soap.

titwicks *n. medic.* Ladies' nipples. *'When it comes to feeding baby, breast really is best. Mother's milk contains the perfect balance of nutrients that your child needs,* and although the titwicks may be painful for the first few days, feeding quickly becomes a relaxing and bonding time for both.'

TNTs *abbrev.* Two Nifty Tits.

toad in the hole *n.* An ugly bloke accompanied by an absolute stunner, eg. Rod Stewart.

toast a bum crumpet *v.* To *fart.* *'Houston, we have a problem. We're down to our last two hours of oxygen and Fred has just toasted one hell of a bum crumpet.'* (Mission Control TX log. Transmission from Jim Lovell, Commander, Apollo 13).

toasted cheese sandwich, like a *sim.* Phrase used to describe a woman's *kitten purse* that hasn't seen any saucy action for an inordinately long time, if at all. *'Right then. Would you shag Ann Widdecombe for a grand?' 'I don't think it'd be possible. It would be like trying to pull apart a toasted cheese sandwich.'*

toaster *n.* A crumb-filled vagina with two slots and a spring mechanism that you have to fish your *cock* out of with a wooden spoon.

toast to the Queen *n.* A *fart* that scores highly in all three categories; volume, longevity and stench. Often followed by a round of applause.

Toblerone tunnel *n.* The gap, triangular in cross section, between the tops of a slender woman's thighs and her *skin gusset*, into which the popular confection would slide neatly.

tockley *n. Aus.* The *gut stick.* *'Ooyah! I've caught me tockley in me zip.'*

toddlers *n.* Collar bone decorations of the sort worn by Tara Palmer-

Tomkinson. *Dutch Alps, stits.*

todger *n.* Penis. Also *tadger, tockley, tool.*

todger dodger *n.* One who leaps out of the way of an on-coming *male genital.* A lesbian.

toffee apple *n.* The glans of the *gut stick* after it's been dipped in something hot and sticky.

toffee Rizla *n.* An absorbent pad of toilet paper worn in the *arse cleft* of a *double sucker* to absorb moisture and guard against *buttering* of the *cheeks.* A *manpon.*

toffee strings *n.* See *bead curtains.*

toggle and two *euph. Nav.* A Jack Tar's *meat and two veg.*

toilet duck *n.* An untimely and probably unwanted erection which manifests whilst one is sitting on the *pot.* Named after the well known brand of *chod bin* cleaner which boasts of 'reaching under the rim'.

toilet snails *n.* Cryptozoological molluscs that slither around the *bog pan* in student houses, leaving *skidmarks* that no-one claims responsibility for.

toilet suicide *n.* A loud explosion followed by a low groan from a lavatory cubicle.

token for the cockwash *n.* A romantic gift bestowed upon a lady by a man, (eg. flowers, chocolates, bottle of wine) in the hope that it will get him *a bit. 'I'm just nipping down the off licence to get a token for the cockwash.'*

Tokyo optician *sim.* A light-hearted term of abuse for a *slapper,* ie. one who has seen her fair share of *Japs' eyes.*

Tom 1. *n.* Prostitute. 2. *v.* To carry out prostitution. *'Are you tomming it?'* 3. *rhym. slang.* Tomfoolery =

jewellery.

tomato boat has docked *euph.* Phrase used when *Arsenal are playing at home.*

tomb raider *n.* A gentleman whose preference in ladies lies at the more mature end of the scale. A *granny fucker.*

Tom Hank *rhym. slang.* A *Jonathan Ross.*

Tommy Cooper, to do a *v.* To die on the big stage in mid-performance. To lose *wood,* just like that. *'Sorry, love, we'll have to stop. I've done a Tommy Cooper.'*

Tommy's out *n.* A light-hearted party game where one of the guests secretly lays a cable in the house and shouts 'Tommy's Out', whereupon everyone else tries to find it. *'To Aldeborough for the weekend, guest of Benjamin (Britten). What a hoot. Simply everyone was there including Larry (Olivier), Ivor (Novello), Terrence (Rattigan) and Alfie (Bass). Charades in the orangery, then after supper we played a game of Tommy's Out which ended at three in the morning when Kit (Hassall) found a dead otter in the piano stool, courtesy of Johnny (Gielgud).'* (From *'The Diary of Noel Coward').*

toms *rhym. slang.* The *splatters.* From *tom tits = squits. 'Please excuse Peaches Honeyblossom from games today as she's got the toms something rotten. Yours sincerley, Sir. B. Geldof (dad)'*

Tom Thumb's arsehole, a fanny like *sim.* The kind of *twat* one would imagine Emily Bishop off *'Coronation Street'* to have. A *mouse's ear.*

tongue and groove 1. *n.* Basic carpentry technique. 2. *n.* Basic *car-*

pet-munchery technique.

tongue fu *n*. An over-zealous act of *cumulonimbus* which leaves the victim feeling like her *gammon flaps* have just gone five rounds with Jackie Chan.

tongue job *n*. A lick, as opposed to a *blow job*.

tongue punchbag *n*. A *bald man in a boat*, a *clematis*.

tongue shui *n*. See *tongue wrestling*.

tongue wrestling *n*. *Tonsil hockey*.

tonk *v*. To *fuck, poke*.

tonsil hockey *n*. Kissing, *spit swapping*.

Tony Martin *n*. The act of *giving it* to someone from behind with both barrels. A *back scuttle*.

tookus *n*. *Totty, scrunt*.

tool *n*. Penis, *manhood*. All the *DIY* enthusiast needs, along with his *wanking spanners*, to get the job done.

toosh *n*. *Totty, blart*.

toot *v*. A child and vicar-friendly term for a *fart*.

toot meat *n*. Penis. From the fictional musical sweet of a similar name. *Bed flute, meat flute, pink oboe*.

toot toot *1. n*. Risqué BBC parlance for vagina. *2. onomat*. The noise made by a *blow job*.

tooth coming through, have a *euph*. To be suffering from *IRS*. To have a *wire spider*, a *sweetcorn itch*. To have a very itchy *arse*.

toothless gibbon *n*. A *clapping fish*.

toothless sea lion *sim*. A smelly and unkempt *minge*. '*I don't think I'll see her again, Cilla. She had a fanny like a toothless sea lion*.'

top banana *exclam*. Give that man a coconut, whacko-the-diddle-oh. Jolly good.

top bollocks *n*. Breasts, *jubblies*.

top bum *n*. A woman's bosom.

top deck *v*. Of a house guest, to defecate in one's host's cistern, rather than, more conventionally, in the toilet, for comic effect. "*I say, Jeeves, he was a bit of a rum cove, what? Did you see him pass the port from left to right?*' '*Indeed I did, Sir,*' *replied the sage retainer. 'I took the liberty of top decking the servants' bathroom before leaving*." (from '*Heil Hitler, Jeeves!*' by PG Wodehouse).

top dog *n*. An unattractive woman in a workplace whom one fancies simply because all the others are even worse. The least unattractive of a set of unattractive ladies. Default blart.

top dressing *n*. A term used in the catering industry for an *air crouton* dropped next to a table by a disgruntled waiter.

top hat *n*. The implausible achievement of a lady with three blokes up her *wizard's sleeve*. After a dish of the same name in the restaurant on the Stenna Ferry, consisting of three pork sausages in mashed potato sitting in a Yorkshire pudding.

topless hand shandy *1. n*. A lemonade and beer drink, pulled from a pump by a barmaid naked from the waist up. *2. n*. A milky drink pulled from a *love pump* by a masseuse naked from the waist up. *Topless relief*.

topless relief *n*. The cheapest item on the menu in a *toss parlour*.

toploader *n*. A shared marijuana joint, in which the roller has generously overfilled his half in order to get himself more *monged* than the sharee.

top of a coconut *n*. Descriptive of a

Hitler tash which has been neglected.

tops and fingers *adj.* Scale on which sexual achievement is measured by teenage males. *'Get far last night?' 'Not bad. I got my tops and two fingers.'*

top stealth *n.* The art of entering a shop, grabbing your desired *bongo mag,* paying and leaving with such cunning that no-one bats an eyelid.

toss 1. *v.* To *wank,* usually *'oneself off.'* 2. *v.* To flip pancakes through 180° during cooking.

tossed salad *n.* US. Anal sex between male prisoners. *'More tossed salad, Lord Archer?' 'No thanks, Mr. Big, I'm completely stuffed.'*

Tosser del Mar 1. *n.* prop. Principal town on the Spanish Costa Brava. 2. *n.* A discreet underwater *wank* at a topless beach, rendered undetectable by the laws of refraction and Mediterranean murk.

tosser's twitch *n.* Nervous affliction suffered by *wankers* during periods of abstinence.

tossing the caber *v.* Having *one off the wrist* with a 16-foot-long, splintery *cock.*

toss parlour *n.* A *rub-a-tug shop.*

tosspitality *n.* The thoughtful facilities provided for hotel guests who wish to *relax in a gentlemanly manner,* eg. *grumble* channels on the telly, box of tissues on the bedside table etc.

toss pot 1. *n.* a jar for keeping *toss* in. 2. *n.* A person held in low esteem, a *fuckwit.*

tosstalgia *v.* The act of *smacking oneself about* whilst fondly remembering a former ladyfriend.

Tottle *n.* A bath-time *air biscuit.* From the joke with the punchline

'But, sir. I distinctly heard you say, 'What about a water bottle, Tottle?''

totty *n. coll.* Girls, *fanny.* *'Hey, this car's a fanny magnet . Since I bought it I've been beating off the totty with a shitty stick.'* Singular if prefixed 'a nice bit of~.'

touch *v.* To *fondle,* usually 'up'.

touching cloth *adj.* That stooling stage immediately after *turtle's head* when the *Sir Douglas* establishes contact with the *trollies.* *'Is there a bog round here mate? I'm touching cloth.'*

touching socks *adj.* The stage by which time it is too late to look for a toilet, but time to look for a trouser shop.

touch last night's tea *v.* To insert a digit into the *ringpiece* of a lady with loose morals.

touch on *n.* The first stirrings of a *panhandle,* caused by something like the swimwear pages of the Grattan catalogue, or the problem pages of a tabloid newspaper. A *twitch on.*

touching ball 1. *n.* In snooker, a situation where one ball is touching another, allowing the participant to shoot in any direction without a penalty. 2. *n.* In pornography, exactly the same. *Newton's cradle.*

tourist's touchpool 1. *n.* In a marine wildlife complex, the much-visited but rarely-cleaned crab-infested section which smells of fish and where members of the public can dip their hands in. 2. *n.* A dirty bird's *clout.*

towbar *n.* A bulbous *turtle's head.* With a 1-volt output.

towel hook *n.* A *hard on* that's strong enough to support the weight of a damp bath towel.

tow oneself round the cabin *v. naut.* To indulge in a bout of vigorous *self abuse.*

Toxteth airshow *n.* A low-level aeronautical spectacular performed by police helicopters chasing *twockers,* drug traffickers and other sundry ne'er-do-wells. A *Moss Side airshow.*

TPTs *abbrev. Tara Palmer Tomkinsons.* See *braille tits.*

tracer fire *n.* Type of food that passes through the alimentary canal entirely unscathed (eg. sweetcorn), and shows up the next day in the toilet.

tractor pull 1. *n.* A sophisticated entertainment enjoyed by inbred redneck Americans whereby a large block of concrete is dragged along some mud by a piece of souped-up farm machinery. 2. *n.* A romantic Italian lovemaking technique whereby the gentleman sticks his *charlie* up his bird's *shitter* whilst he has his *pods* stuffed up her *clopper.*

tradesmen's entrance *n.* The *back passage.*

trade spit *v.* To osculate.

traff *v.* To *fart, let off.*

traffic calming measure *n.* A *turd* in the road that could take your exhaust off.

train horn *n.* A lady's party trick in which she *drops a gut,* and *drops her hat forwards* in quick succession, creating a two-toned blast. Also known as a *Robson and Jerome.*

trampagne *n.* A homeless person's celebratory beverage, laid down for special occasions, eg. White Lightning, Red Label Thunderbird, Mr. Muscle Drain Foamer. *'Break out the trampagne, boys. I've* found an Embassy with 10 left on it.'

trampari *n.* A turpentine substitute aperitif taken as an appetiser before a bin-rifling buffet.

tramp duty *n.* A guilt-based tax levied on one who passes a *Harry Ramp* on a regular basis.

tramp eating a kebab *sim.* An enthusiastic performance of *cumulonimbus.* The male equivalent of a *dog eating hot chips.*

tramp grill *n.* Any city centre area where *Harry Ramps* gather in the summer to soak up the sun.

trampon *n.* A tampon that hasn't been changed long after it should.

tramp's aftershave *n.* The manly and sexy aroma which wafts out of a pub at eight o'clock in the morning, and drives the bag ladies wild.

tramp sauce *n.* The rancid, sticky substance painted over the tongue and on the corners of the mouth by elves whilst one is asleep following a night *on the piss.*

tramp's breakfast *n.* A *docker's omelette.* A pavement *greb.*

tramp stamp *n.* Any tattoo on a slatternly *bird's* body, usually around the base of the spine or on the left *qualification.* A *tittoo.*

tramp's delight *n.* Low cost cider.

tramp's housewarming *n.* The act of *pissing* oneself.

tramp's hat *n.* A large, shapeless, sweaty and discoloured *clopper.* With knitted pubes.

tramp's jackpot *n.* A perfectly-intact discarded cigarette.

tramp's mate *n.* Someone who looks like they probably stink, eg. Jim Royle, Jocky Wilson.

tramp's tan *n.* The healthy, ruddy complexion achieved by spending a lot of time in the fresh air. Drinking metal polish.

tramp's tiara *n*. A bobble hat.

tramps' treacle *n*. Special Brew.

tramps' truffles *n*. Discarded chips.

trampton *n*. An area frequented by those of no fixed abode where they consume copious amounts of *trampagne* and watch the world go by, generously sharing their profanities with members of the public.

trampy tea *n*. Unsavoury beverage made by someone who, despite having filthy, scabby fingers, insists on squeezing the teabag against the spoon with their thumb. Into your fucking tea.

tramp Vegas *n*. telephone booths, vending machines and parking meters that are regularly checked for rejected coins by *gentlemen of the road*.

tranny 1. *n*. An old fashioned radio. 2. *n*. Transvestite, transparency or transit van. eg. A fetish photographer might say *'Shit. I left that tranny of the tranny in the back of the tranny.'*

transformer *n*. One who, on coming out, transforms instantaneously into a being that lives up to every homosexual stereotype, eg. purchasing tight T-shirts, adopting a mincing gait, drinking G&T and constantly going on about Jayne Macdonald.

Transit of Venus 1. *n*. Small spot crossing the face of the Sun behind thick clouds once every 150 years. 2. *n*. A mobile boudoir, ie. A van containing a heavily stained mattress and the smell of *spunk*. A *shagging wagon*, a *fuck truck*, a *lust bus*.

trap *n*. A toilet cubicle in a line of toilet cubicles.

trapped in the Himalayas *adj*. To be

mid *tit wank*.

trap pirouette *n*. The light-footed on-a-sixpence-style 180 degrees twirl performed when a fellow walks into an empty lavatory cubicle only to find that it has been the subject of a *dirty protest,* been *pebbledashed* with *arse-gravy* or is full of *bangers and mash*.

travel fat *n*. Unwanted *stalk* which sprouts on public transport. A *stiffy* generated by sitting on a seat located directly over the axles of a corporation omnibus. Also *travel fat, traveller's marrow, diesel dick, routemaster, Varney teacake..*

travel iron 1. *n*. A small, hard thing that puts creases in one's trousers on holiday. 2. *n*. A small, hard thing that puts creases in one's trousers on a bus.

Travelling Wilberries 1. *n*. Short-lived pensioner supergroup. 2. *n*. Time-served *clagnuts*.

trawlerman's wellie, fanny like a sim. Descriptive of a commodious *snapper*. With the eye-stinging smell of dead kipper.

trawler's bilge *n*. Festering *moip,* stagnant *blip*.

treacle 1. *n*. Term of affection used solely by Pete Beale in *'EastEnders'*. 2. *rhym. slang*. An *air biscuit*. From treacle tart ~ *fart*.

treading water *v*. Light *strumming* on the banjo in order to keep one's interest up during the dull plot bits in a *grumble flick*. To maintain a *satiscraptory* level of *wood*. *'You're under arrest, Mr. Herman.' 'But officer, I wasn't wanking, I was just treading water.'*

tread on a frog *v*. A wetter sounding version of *step on a duck*.

treasure trail *n*. The female equivalent of the *crab ladder*. The hairy line of fluff that joins the navel to what's buried down below.

tree log *n*. A *chocolate shark* whose snout is in the water before its tail leaves one's *arse*, a *Cuban bum cigar*, a *bridger*.

tree monkey *n*. A *hand on heart*.

tremble trigger *n*. The male *G-spot*, lurking up the *chocolate starfish*. Just behind the *doughnut*.

trick *n*. Customer in a *rub-a-tug shop*, a *Hilman Hunter*, a *gonk*.

trick or treat *n*. A *tree monkey* that could easily *drop a log*. A *possible follow through*.

triggernobetry *n*. The ability to produce instant ejaculation in a man by prodding his prostrate gland with the finger, practised by pros, nurses and Countess of Wessexes.

trilogy *n*. Also known as *brown Star Wars*. A *turd* of such epic proportions it has to be released in three instalments. The first can stand on its own as a complete adventure. The second links to the first, but has a dark, inconclusive feel generating an air of foreboding and leaving itself wide open for an unknown ending. The final chapter has drama, excitement and moments where you think all is lost. A grand battle is waged where good overcomes evil and peace is restored in your gut.

trim *n*. Tidy *bush, talent, totty*.

tripe hound *n*. A *fugly dog*.

triple crown 1. *n*. The Holy Grail of Rugby Union players; to win matches against the other three home nations. 2. *n*. The Holy Grail of Rugby Union players; to *shout soup, piss* and *shit* oneself in the back of a taxi.

triple jump 1. *n*. A soft playground sport as practised by grinning God-botherer Jonathan Edwards. 2. *n*. To *have* all three available *holes* in one session.

Trisha fodder *n*. *coll*. Those Burberry-clad inhabitants of *nillionaires' row* whose personal tragedies and woes are meat and drink to the producers of plebeian Channel 5 daytime talk shows.

Trisha porn *n*. Cheaply-produced *grumble vids* where thick, single mothers get 'seduced' and *fucked* by the likes of Ben Dover and Marcus Allen.

Trisha trash *n*. The kind of human vermin that appear on mid-morning riff-raff debates. British *trailer trash*.

trogg *n*. A simpleton, or *fuckwit*. See also *pranny*.

Trojan *n*. *US*. An American brand of war-like, Greek *French letters*.

Trojan arse *n*. A toilet bowl invasion that takes one by surprise in the middle of the night and sends one back to bed in a state of sleepy bemusement. A somnambulodefecation.

trolley dash *n*. Of a punter, to chase a prostitute who has stolen his trousers down a back alley, wearing his underpants, shoes and socks.

trolley dolly 1. *n*. An air hostess. 2. *n*. A *ladyboy*.

trolleys 1. *n*. *Kecks* 2. *n*. *Underkecks*.

trollop *n*. See *trull*.

trollop snack *n*. *Helmet cheese, foreskinzola*.

tromboning *v*. A thoroughly impractical sex act in which a woman or *Colwyn* man *rims* a fellow's *brass eye* whilst simultaneously reaching round the front to give it some elbow on his *horn*, the action being akin to playing a trombone. A

George Jism.

troop the colour *v.* To leave a *skidmark* down the right or left hand side of the pan as a result of sitting side-saddle on the *crapper,* like the Queen on parade.

trots, the *n.* Frequent rapid foot movement required to convey a diarrhoea sufferer to the lavatory. See also *Tijuana cha-cha, sour apple quickstep, Turkish two-step.*

trouser arouser *n.* A fit lass, good looking *bird.*

trouser bandit *n.* Slightly more polite version of *turd burglar.*

trouser browser *n.* In a lap-dancing establishment, public park or cinema specialising in continental 'art' films, a gentleman engrossed in an increasingly agitated search for loose change in his pockets.

trouser chuff *n. Trouser cough.*

trouser cough *n.* A clearing of the nether throat.

trouser department *1. n.* Section of a department store dealing with men's legwear. *2. n.* Area of the body in which middle-aged men experience problems.

trousered *1. adj.* To be wearing trousers. *2. adj. Wasted, arseholed, wankered, shit faced.*

trouser folder *n.* A person who, one would imagine, would have to carefully fold their clothes after taking them off before they could indulge in sexual intercourse, eg. Sven Goran Ericsson, Simon Cowell, Bruce Forsyth.

trouser jazz *n.* A session of different- sounding blasts on the *bum trumpet* released in quick succession.

trouser leg trombonist *n.* Popular female musician who plays in the same ensemble as the *skin flautist* and *pink oboe* virtuoso.

trouser Mauser *n.* A small rapid firing *porridge gun.* A *pump action mottgun, mutton musket.*

trouser rain *n.* A small downpour in the *keg* region leading to a few damp patches in the south. A *wet penny in the pocket.*

trouser rake *n.* A stiffer version of the *trouser snake.* Often pops up and hits women in the face when stood on.

trouser rouser *n.* A *brass eye*-opener. A *Bronx cheer.*

trouser snake *n.* See *one-eyed trouser snake.*

trouser tent *n.* Embarrassing portable erection made from canvas or other trouser material, with a zip up one side, supported by a rigid *wood shaft.* If occurring whilst seated this can easily be concealed with one's bowler hat.

trouser tits *n.* A large pair of prominent *testicles. Man marbles. 'I tell you what, Colin. My trouser tits battered her chin.'*

trouser trout *n.* Something one tickles in one's *trolleys* before taking it out and banging its head against a rock.

trouser trumpet *1. n.* Solo on the *botty bugle. 2. n.* The *anus.*

trouser truncheon *n.* The stiff *pole* a copper takes out in the back of his van on a Saturday night.

trout *v.* To *pull. 'I was out trouting last night. Ended up with a right old five-to-twoer. Had to chew me own arm off this morning.'*

trout jelly *n.* Artificial sexual lubricant. *I can't believe it's not batter, Grandma's little helper, granny batter.*

trucker's mate *n.* Someone who looks like he could be a sex case, eg. Roy off *'Coronation Street'*.

trucker's Tizer *n.* Brownish-yellow liquid, thought by many to be the urine of long-distance lorry drivers, often spotted in plastic bottles reposing on the hard shoulders of motorways, disguised as pop.

truffle hunting *v.* To take a *trip around the world*. To *rim*.

truffleshuffle *n.* The characteristic gait of one who has *split the winnings*.

trull *n. 19*th*C.* A prostitute, a *hooer*. With fat *tits* but not many teeth, as stabbed up by Jack the Ripper.

trump *v.* To *fart* or *pass wind* in a chair-shaking way.

trumpeter's lips *n.* The involuntary pursing of the *tea towel holder* at moments of extreme fear. *'Any man who tells you he is not afraid to go into battle is either a fool or a liar. It is the fear that makes him fight. I personally had the trumpeter's lips throughout the North African campaign.'* (from *'The Memoirs of Field Marshal Montgomery'*).

truncheon *n.* A solid, one piece *turd* which, if grasped, firmly could be used to stun a miscreant.

truncheon voucher *n.* A *ticket to the policeman's ball*. A constabulary bribe.

trunk *n.* A large *knob* which squirts water over Johnny Morris.

trying to get the last pickled onion from the jar *euph.* Deep *gusset typing*.

try on the comedy beard *v.* To perform *cumulonimbus*.

tubby chaser *n.* A man who thinks *thunderbirds* are go, eg. Lenny Henry. Also a woman who prefers her *beefcake* to be a *salad dodger*, eg. Mrs. Pavarotti.

TUBER *acronym. medic.* Doctor's shorthand written on the notes of good looking female patients. Totally Unnecessary Breast Examination Required.

tubesteak *n. Beef bayonet on the bone.*

TUBFUF *acronym.* Thumb Up Bum, Finger Up Fanny. All business.

tug *v.* To *pull*, as in a *pud*. A light-hearted *wank*. *'Dinner's ready, Sidney!' 'Down in a minute, dear. I'm just having a little tug.'*

tug boat *n.* A woman of plain appearance and compact, muscular build. A *swamp donkey*.

tuggernaut *n.* A lorry driver *wanking* in his cab at Barton Park Services on the A1.

tug of love *n.* A masturbation.

tug of phwoar *n.* A spontaneous and urgent *one off the wrist* brought on by a particularly *horny* sight, eg. an attractive *bird*, the bra adverts on Underground escalators.

tugpusher *n.* Of schools, workplaces and police stations, the individual who has taken on the responsibility for distributing hardcore *art pamphlets* amongst his colleagues. A *pornbroker*, a *grumblemonger*.

tug pamphlet *n.* A *jazz magazine*.

tugwax *n. Spongle, spadge, jitler.*

tumblepube *n.* A fur ball of *clock springs* and other discarded pubic foliage which wafts around when the *bog* door opens.

tummy banana *n.* A *gut stick*.

tummy Tetris *n.* The strange, yet not unpleasant, sensation whereby one's unborn *change of hearts* slot together satisfyingly in one's alimentary canal, before disappearing with an amusing noise.

tummy truncheon *n. Sixth gear*

stick, porridge gun, penis.

tump *n. Welsh.* The *beetle bonnet,* the *monkey's forehead.*

tumwiper *n.* Any unfashionable item of clothing received as a gift from a well-meaning relative or friend that is immediately relegated to the function of wiping *spoof* off one's stomach after *self help.*

tuna taco *n.* A hot dish, not requiring cutlery, served when *dining at the Y.* If eaten with a side order of *cranberry dip,* it could lead to *Mexican lipstick.*

tuna town *n.* The female genitalia, *Billingsgate box.*

tup 1. *v.* To have sex, *fuck.* 2. *v.* Of sheep-to-sheep shagging, red hot horny ram on ewe action.

tuppence licker *n.* A *lesbo, bean flicker.*

tuppenny all-off 1. *n.* A cheap, no-nonsense haircut popular amongst national servicemen in the 1960s. 2. *n.* A no-nonsense *fannicure.* A *Brazilian.*

tuppie *n. Scot.* A Dundonian term for a lady's *fluffit.* *'There's nae a kitten, moose or puppy / Ha'f sae soft as ma wife's tuppie.'* (from *'The Song O' the Dundee Growler'* by Robbie Burns).

turbo shit *n.* The high-speed *dump* required to fool a lady into thinking you had only gone for a *gypsy's kiss.* A *greyhound's egg.*

turbot for tea *exclam.* Announcement that the *fish supper* is served. *'Never mind that tug, Sidney. It's turbot for tea.'*

turd *n.* A cylindrical unit of *shit,* longer than a *tod.* A link of *feeshus.*

turd burglar *n.* Stealthy thief who forces entry into the rear of a person's premises via the inside of the *chocolate drainpipe.*

turd clippers *n. US.* Buttocks.

turd degree burns *n. medic.* Post-curry *shitting* injuries. *'A man was taken to hospital last night after being found unconscious on the pavement outside a curry restaurant in Newcastle upon Tyne. He was suffering from shock, alcohol poisoning and had turd degree burns covering 90% of his anus. A spokesman for the restaurant said 'Come to the Curry Capital, formerly the Rupali Restaurant, Bigg Market, Newcastle upon Tyne.''* ('BBC News 24', 1st Jan).

turd eagle *n. Aus.* A large *blowfly.* A *dunny budgie.*

turder *n.* The begetter of a *feeshus.*

turd fairies *n.* Mythological creatures that are thought to be the cause of the mysterious *ghost shit* phenomenon, those stools of which there are no trace when one turns round to admire them in the *pan.*

turdis *n.* One of them detached, modern, portable, space-agealooking public conveniences. A *turd tardis.*

turdsearch *n.* A desperate hunt for reading material one embarks upon when *Mr. Brown is at the window.*

turdulence *n.* The area of dirty air affected by a particularly foulsome *trouser trumpet,* usually dispensed by a man walking in front of one in a tightly-packed shopping establishment, eg. the make-up section at John Lewis.

turf out 1. *n.* An anal spring clean. A well needed *tom tit.* 2. *v.* To excrete.

Turin shroud 1. *n.* Famous medieval sheet with a face painted on it. 2. *n.* A piece of lavatory tissue draped tastefully over a floating *log* that will not flush away.

turistas *n.* *Turkish two-step.*

turk *v.* To take someone or something up the *council*. *'Sit down please, Lord Archer.' 'If it's all the same with you, Governor, I'd rather stand. I've just been turked in the showers by Jonathan King.'*

turkey *n.* The *cracker* you think you've pulled whilst drunk at the office Christmas party who turns out to be a rough old *bird* who only gets *stuffed* once a year.

turkey moss *n.* Serious *fluff* on a bird's *bodily treasure*. *Gorilla salad.*

turkey-neck *n.* That which is *throttled* in Norfolk.

turkey twizzler *1. n.* Unappetizing helix of nondescript brown matter of mysterious and sinister provenance, served to schoolchildren in lieu of real food. *2. n.* A thin, spiralling *turd* which retains its corkscrew shape even after it has been dropped into the *pan*.

turkey's wattle *n.* A *ragman's coat*, a *club sandwich*.

Turkish *1. n.* Heterosexual *back door work*, whilst wearing curly slippers. *Irish. 2. rhym. slang.* An excrement. From Turkish delight = shite. *'What's the matter, Eric?' 'Jocky Wilson done a Turkish in me shoe. Again.'*

Turkish bath *n.* A *Glasgow shower.*

Turkish dagger *n.* A curved *Thora.* With a jewel-encrusted handle that one wouldn't fancy holding in one's teeth.

Turkish revenge *n.* A *stab* up the *arse.*

Turkish rinse *n.* A quickfire bathing technique popular amongst *soap-dodgers*, consisting of a rudimenta-ry scrub of one's armpits, gusset and *giggle stick.*

Turkish shower *n.* A *Glasgow shower.*

Turkish slippers *n.* The *jester's shoes.*

Turkish two-step *n.* *Smallroom dance* not dissimilar to the *sour apple quick step, Tijuana cha-cha,* or *Aztec twostep.*

turned-out trouser pocket, arsehole like a *sim.* A dropped *clacker valve*, resulting from either an excess of *Turkish*, or a red hot Indian.

turn Japanese *v.* Of *wanking*, to *apploach the Birry Mill Loundabrout.*

turn your bike round *v.* To go to the lavatory. *'Excuse me, I'm just going to turn my bike round. Have you got any arse paper?'*

turpsichord *n.* A public house pianoforte, as played by rubber-fingered drunks.

turps nudger *n.* A *top shelf drinker*. *'Have you seen that bloke who reads the news on Tyne Tees? Jesus, what a fucking turps nudger.'*

turquoise *n.* A lady who allows the *dog in the bathtub*. One who doesn't object to being *turked* up the *bonus tunnel.*

turtle *1. n.* A passive sexual partner. *'Get her on her back and she's fucked.' 2. n. coll.* Blit, fanny, fluff, talent. Birds. *3. n.* One of the least sexy *bum games* a flatulent couple can play in the bedroom, the winner being the last one to poke their head out from under the duvet.

turtleberries *n.* Winnets, dangleberries, Payne's Poppets.

turtle bungee *n.* The dangerous

sport of releasing and retracting *turds* by clever use of the sphincter muscles just before they *touch cloth*. *Prairie dogging, gophering.*

turtle guillotine *n.* The *nipsy*.

turtle power *n.* The unstoppable superhero-like strength exhibited by a determined *chod* as it tries to overcome the tightly-clenched *nipsy*.

turtle recall *v.* The brief retraction of the *turtle's head* whilst en route to the *thunderbox*.

turtle's breath *n.* The very final warning *fart* before the turtle pokes its head out to *autograph the gusset*.

turtle's den *n.* The *bomb bay*.

turtle's head *n.* The initial protrusion of a stool though the *tea towel holder*, the point at which contracts are exchanged for the building of a *log cabin*. *Touching cloth.*

tush *n.* US. *Bum* (but not a tramp), *ass* (but not a donkey).

tussage *n.* *Talent*, female *buffage*.

TV *1. abbrev.* A television. *2. abbrev.* A tranny.

twanger *n.* Whanger.

twangers *n. onomat.* Generic term for ladies' undercrackers, but more specifically those worn by dirty *scutters*. Named after the sound the gusset makes as it leaves the crotch when pulled hastily down from either side. *'And Lady Diana Spencer looks resplendent as she walks down the aisle, keeping up the age old traditions. She's wearing an old 18th century tiara, a magnificent new wedding dress, a diamond necklace borrowed from her friend the Duchess of Argyll, and a pair of blue twangers.'* (Sir Alastair Burnett, Royal Wedding commentary, ITN, 1981).

twang the wire *v.* To pluck out a *jazz rhythm* on the *one-stringed banjo*.

twankunt *n.* Descriptive of someone who is not just a *twat*, but also a *wanker* and a *cunt* to boot. *'Birthdays: Lord Archer - author, politician and twankunt, 62 today.'* (*'The Times'*, April 15th 2002).

twat *1. n.* A *minge*. *2. n.* Stupid person. *3. v.* To hit, beat up.

twatalogue *n.* A magazine of *pornotholgical* interest. An *art pamphlet.*

twat burglar *n.* A man, presumably wearing a mask and stripy jersey, who steals another bloke's missus.

twaterpillar *n.* Female version of the *willipede*. A *cloppular crab.*

twatful *1. n.* A good *seeing to* in the sexual sense. *'Just 8 pints tonight, lads. Got to get home to give the rib a twatful.'* *2. n.* An imperial measure of *spangle*, equal to 2 *nutsworths* or $\frac{1}{16}$ of an *Almond*. *'Sister Amoeba was powerless to resist. His eyes burned into hers like a sort of stone. His papal arms enfolded her body as she felt herself being swept away in some sort of weather system of passion. Then he lifted his cassock and gave her a twatful.'* (From *'The Mother Superior and the Holy Father'*, by Barbara Cartland).

twat mag *n.* *Bongo literature.*

twatmates *n.* Gentlemen who have both had a portion of the same *haddock pastie*, eg. Bryan Ferry & Mick Jagger, Michael Jackson & Nicholas Cage, and Sir Donald Campbell & Claude Greengrass off *'Heartbeat'*. *Custard cousins.*

twat nappy *n.* See *clot mop*.

twat nav *n.* Motoring terminology; the wife with a road atlas.

twat pamphlet 1. *n.* A *grumble book* or *flesh mag* purchased by people who fancy a *wank*, eg. *'Razzle'*, *'Knave'*, *'Splosh'* etc. 2. *n.* An aspirational lifestyle magazine read by *wankers*, eg. *'Dazed & Confused'*, *'Wonderland™'*, *'Wallpaper'*.

twatplates *n.* Car registration plates where the numbers have been respaced or mutilated in order to make them spell out something that they don't from a distance, eg. those on a Fiat Punto where the owner has placed a black screw at the bottom of the two 1s in P11 NTO.

twat rats *n. Cunt mice* for ladies with a heavier flow of *fanny jam*. Industrial strength *tammys*.

twat rattler *n.* A *plastic cock,* a vibrator.

twatriot *n.* Someone who waves a Union Jack and shouts 'Come on Tim', between every point whilst Tim 'Spoilt Bastard' Henman gets thrashed at Wimbledon again. Also found wearing a plastic Union Jack hat singing *'Land of Hope and Glory'* at the Last Night of the Proms.

twat seats *n.* The back two rows on the upper tier of a double-decker bus or an EasyJet flight from Newcastle to Alicante, reserved for cap-headed *scratters* who wish to cycle through their ringtones, engage in foul-mouthed shouted debates and/or light-hearted vandalism and otherwise *act the twat.*

twatslapping *n.* The untraceable slapping noise generated *below the stairs* when a man and a lady are doing *thingy.* A *Blair's ovation.*

twatters *n.* Smashing *churns.* The sort that Nell Gwynn would have sported.

twattoo *n.* A badly-conceived, situated, designed and/or executed piece of body art, eg. the word 'Brooklyn' written above someone's *arsecrack* in Ye Olde English capital letters.

twatwrapper *n.* A multi-pocketed garment of the sort worn by the sex cases who stand at the end of railway platforms spotting trains. An anorak.

tweedle 1. *n. rhym. slang.* Male ejaculate, *jitler* or *Thelonius.* From Tweedledum = *cum.* 2. *n. rhym. slang.* Urine, *wazz* or *piss.* From Tweedledee = *wee.*

28th of Mayhem *n.* The day marking the start of *rag week.*

twice off the same hard 1. *n.* Of a gentleman, the once-in-a-lifetime phenomenon of achieving two orgasms from the same erectivation with no intervening *floppery.* 2. *euph.* Any once-in-a-lifetime phenomenon. *'And what is there to look forward to in the night sky next year? Well of course, the big story is the return of Halley's Comet which is only visible every 76 years. So it's a real twice off the same hard for most astronomers.'* (Patrick Moore, *'The Sky at Night'*, 1985).

twig & giggle berries *n.* The *fruitbowl,* the *meat and two veg.*

twinkie 1. *n. US. Turd, chocolate log.* 2. *n.* An apprentice *mudhole plumber.*

twin peaks 1. *n. prop.* An experimental television series of the early 1990s created by David Lynch. 2. *n.* Smashing *tits* like Audrey's in the series.

twin tone *n.* A *fart* which suddenly and ominously drops in pitch, indicating something other than *marsh* *gas* may have been expelled. A *follow through*.

twin tub *n*. Back then frontal penetration.

twirly *n*. An affectionate term used by omnibus drivers to describe senior citizens who attempt to use their free passes before 9.00am. ie, they are 'too early' and have to be thrown off the bus.

twist *1. rhym. slang. US*. Girl. From twist and twirl. *2. n.* Of *carpet munching* relationships, the *carpet*, as opposed to the *muncher*. A passive *lesbo*. *3. v.* From the pontoon playing gambit, to risk losing a scoring hand in the hope of getting a better one; thus to turn down the advances of a half decent lady in the hope that one will *cop off* with something better.

twister *n. US*. Pervert, a *nonce*.

twitching Buddah *n*. A short, fat, excitable erection.

twitter *n*. A lady's perineum, that area of the anatomy between the *twat* and the *shitter*. The *chin rest, duffy's bridge, biffin bridge, tinter*.

Twix lips *n*. A *front bottom* version of *hungry arse. Knicker sausages*.

two am grab bag *n*. In a night club, the ropey assortment of frankly second-rate *tussage* which is all that is left to choose from at chucking out time. The *floor sweepings, bin rake*, sediment.

two aspirins on an ironing board *sim*. Descriptive of the bosoms of the slimmer-figured lady. Flat *stits, fried eggs, lung warts*.

two bagger *n*. Someone so ugly that two bags are required in order to go *quim wedging* with them; one over their head and one over yours, just in case theirs falls off.

two bob billionaire *n*. A young man in an £80 shirt who still lives with his mum and dad.

twoc *v*. Take Without Owner's Consent. To borrow someone's car, not in order to steal it, but to merely drive it through Dixon's window and set it on fire. Also *twock*.

two can Van Damme *n*. In the pub, the jumped-up little *shit* that starts acting like the hardest man on the planet after a couple of drinks.

twocker *n*. A cheeky rapscallion who *twocks*. A loveable rogue, a lively urchin.

two pot screamer *n. Aus*. Someone who cannot hold their beer. A more reserved British equivalent would be the *halfpint Harry*.

two puppies fighting in a bag *n*. Large, mobile and unrestrained breasts.

two ring circus *n*. The greatest show on earth. *Over the shoulder boulder holder*, a bra.

two up *n*. A *twos up*, a *threesome* with two gentlemen and a lady.

two wombles looking over a balcony *sim*. Descriptive of *NGT*s.

twunt *n*. Useful, satisfying yet inoffensive combination of two very rude words which can safely be spoken in the primmest and properest company.

Tyne Bridge *adj*. Descriptive of the position adopted by a dog trying to lay a particularly tenacious *egg*.

Uu

UB40 winks *n.* A mid-afternoon nap taken after a hard morning at the telly face.

U-bend straightener *n.* A mighty powerful *shit*.

U-blocker *n.* A titanic *dreadnought* so big it causes a *jobbie* jam in the foul drainage system. The Moby Dick of *brown trouts*.

udders *n.* Breasts with absolutely no erotic qualities whatsoever.

udderpants *n.* A bra.

udder scudder *n.* A *sausage sandwich*.

UDI *abbrev.* Unidentified Drinking Injury. Mysterious bodily damage sustained during a *bender* and of which the victim has no recollection.

ugly bus *n.* A vehicle that mysteriously turns up after one has had 8 pints on a Friday night and takes all the ugly women home, leaving the pub full of beautiful ladies.

ugly duckling *n.* A long-protracted *Exchange & Mart* launched midwalk, where the benefactor 'walks with a quack and a waddle and a quack'.

ugly lights *n.* A revealing lighting apparatus which is switched on in pubs at chucking out time.

ugly taxi *n.* A vehicle which mysteriously delivers an unattractive *bird* into one's *fart sack* on a Saturday morning.

Ulrikas *n.* A pair of *kahoomas* that look smashing in clothing, but pitifully saggy when released on a beach.

unblock the sink *sim.* To have a vigorous and impatient *wank*, presumably with both hands.

Uncle Albert's beard *n. Jelly jewellery*.

Uncle Doug *rhym. slang. Self abuse.* From Uncle Doug = *tug*.

Uncle Fester *n.* A *goolie*-ish *bald headed man* from the *old Adam* family, who occasionally rises up and puts the willies up your missus.

undefuckable *adj. Bust*, damaged beyond repair. *'Oh, and there goes Barricello's engine on the warm up lap. He'll head straight for the pit lane, but that looks pretty undefuckable. It's certainly the end to his Portuguese Grand Prix, Martin.'* (Murray Walker as Frentzen's front left wheel came off on the final lap, Belgian Grand Prix 1999).

underbeard *n.* A *minge*.

undercarriage *n.* Genitals, usually male. *Wedding tackle, pudendas*.

underchunders *n. Trolleys*.

undercoat *n.* A soft drink ordered to accompany the first pint of a long session which prepares the stomach's surface for the later layers of alcoholic emulsion.

undercrackers *n. Underchunders*.

underdaks *n. Undercrackers*.

underkecks *n. Underdaks*.

undertaker's privileges *n.* Acts of carnality performed by a *corpse packager* on his recently-deceased clients. *'Wanted. Hard-working young man to train as Mortuary Attendant in a busy London hospital. Must have 4 GCSEs at grade C or above. 35 hours per week, occasional weekends. Starting salary £10,000 plus clothing allowance & undertaker's privileges.'*

under thunder *n.* Violent rectal belching of the *arse's* natural *kak gases* which erupt from the *fart fissure*.

unit 1. *n.* The genitals, usually male. 2. *n. Bird*, an individual piece of talent.

unleash the dobermans *v.* After a night on the Guinness, to let loose with a particularly savage and uncontrollable outburst of *black and tan* from the *back gate*.

unload *v.* To drop a *depth charge* or launch an *air biscuit*.

unmentionables *n.* Roman Catholic word allows mother-in-laws to mention genitals or underwear.

unmown crease 1. *n.* An unprepared cricket pitch. 2. *n.* A particularly hirsute clopper. *Terry Waite's allotment, a biffer, Judith* etc.

untidy sock drawer *n.* A *ripped sofa, badly-packed kebab, ragman's coat*.

unwrap the meat *v.* To *let the twins out*. Of a lady, to get her *tits out for the lads*.

up and over like a pan of milk *euph.* Descriptive of a gentleman who is so good at sex that he can ejaculate before he's even got his pants off.

up and twichin' *adj.* The point at which the gentleman is ready to engage in the courses of love.

upchuck *v.* To *chuck up*.

upgrade *v.* To go to the *chod bin* for a *number one*, but decide to take the opportunity to have a *number two* whilst one is there.

upgrade a fart *v.* To go for a *shit*. '*I would love to stand here chatting all day, Your Majesty, but I really must go and upgrade a fart.*'

uphill gardener *n.* He who sows his *seed* on the *brown allotment*, pusher of a *pork wheelbarrow* up the *lavender* path. A male homosexual.

up on blocks *adj.* Of a woman. A monthly *MOTT* failure due to a recurring leak under the *beetle bonnet*.

up periscope *n.* Bathtime game for up to one person. *Polishing the lighthouse*.

upstairs *n.* The *rack, top bollocks.* '*What's she got upstairs?*' '*Stacked mate! Looks like a dead heat in a Zeppelin race.*'

up the Beeston ginnel, one *n.* The act of *making love* up the *wrong 'un*, from the name of a narrow, malodorous passage in the environs of the notorious Leeds shit hole. '*Tamoshanta was powerless to resist. His eyes burnt into hers like agates. His muscular arms enfolded her body as she felt herself being swept away on a dustpan of passion. 'I'm sorry, Your Grace, but you'll have to give me one up the Beeston ginnel this morning as I am up on blocks at present.*' (from '*The Milkmaid and the Bishop*' by Barbara Cartland).

up the duff *adj. medic. Up the pasture.*

up the Jimmy Savile, to take a lady *v.* To indulge in a session of *back door work*. So called because of the warbling 'eeurgh!-eeurgh!-eeurgh! now then! now then!' noises made by the lucky recipient.

up the pasture *adj. medic. Up the poke.*

up the poke *adj.medic. Up the stick.*

up the stick *adj. medic. In the club.*

up to the apricots *adj. Up to the back wheels.*

up to the back wheels *adj. Up to the buffers.*

up to the buffers *adj. Up to the bumper.*

up to the bumper *adj. Up to the cannon wheels.*

up to the cannon wheels *adj. Up to the eggs.*

up to the eggs *adj. Up to the maker's nameplate.*

up to the maker's nameplate *adv.* An engineering term for being *conkers deep.* Also *up to the boilermaker's nameplate.*

up to your nuts in guts *adj. Aus.* To throw oneself fully into *backdoor* intercourse.

up to your pots *adj.* Amazingly enough, not to be *up to the apricots, wheels, buffers, bumper, cannon wheels, eggs or maker's name plate,* but to be *ripped to the tits* on drink. *Pissed.*

up, in, out and off *phr.* Plot synopsis essential to all *grumble flicks.*

Urals, the *n.* Vague and tenuous British film comedy euphemism for the testicles. See also *the Balkans.*

Uranus *1. n.* A large planet with brown rings around it. And a big smelly *shit* coming out a hairy hole in the middle of it. *2. n. Urarse.*

urban cockerel *n.* A loud, rasping *fart* emitted from under the duvet around sunrise, with enough volume to wake everyone in the street. A *dawn chorus.*

uri *rhym. slang.* Premium Belgian lager. From cutlery-fucking man of mystery Uri Geller = Stella. Also *Nelson Mandela.*

urineapple chunks *n.* The fruit-like yellow cubes that nestle around the plughole of a *shark's mouth.*

urine shroud *n.* A cotton or nylon artefact, clearly showing the miraculous crusty image of a *bearded clam.* ie, a pair of discarded *scads* found sunny side up on a lady's bedroom floor.

UTBNB *abbrev.* Up The Bum, No Babies. A reliable, yet malodorous contraceptive device. Opposite of an IUD.

Vv

vadge *n.* A *fadge*. A *fanny*.

vag *acronym.* The Volkswagen Audi Group.

vaggie *n.* An uncomfortable front-tuck for a lady. A vaginal *wedgie*, a *smedgie*.

vagilant *adj.* On the sharp-eyed look out for *cunker*.

vagimix *n.* Noisy electrical appliance which makes life easier for housewives. Usually has three speeds and is perfect for whipping up a light and frothy *batter*.

vagina decliner *n.* The male equivalent of a *todger dodger*. A *beaver leaver*, a *pie-shy guy*.

vaginosaur *n.* A rather mature actress in a *meat flick*.

vagitarian *n.* He who only eats *hairy pie, fur burgers,* and *vertical bacon sandwiches.* Plus the occasional *fish supper.* An inveterate *diner at the Y.*

vagitation *n.* Agitation of the vagina. *Bean flicking,* female masturbation.

Valentine's day porridge *n. Semen-o-lina, spaff, spangle, snedge, gunk, liquid pearls.*

vampire *n.* A *bird* who forces her fat *arse* into tight jeans and who obviously can't see herself in the mirror.

vandal grease *1. n.* Substance used to deter Liverpudlians from climbing onto the tops of public buildings. *2. n.* Substance used by *botters* to lubricate their bottoms so that they can be *botted* by other *botters.*

vanilla *n. US.* A term used by sadomasochists to refer to normal, respectable people, eg. doctors, lawyers, etc. who do not share their perversion. Also *civilian* (UK).

vanilla strip *n.* The *tinter,* the *carse,* the *taint.* A lady's perineum, named after the vanilla strip which, in a tub of Neapolitan ice cream, is found precisely between the pink and the brown.

varnish the cane *v.* To give the old *walking stick* a one-handed waxing.

Vatican roulette *n. Pull out and pray.* A method of contraception practised by *left-footers* with very large families.

V-bone steak *n.* A sumptuous, meaty meal, eaten off a *hairy plate.*

vein strainer *n.* A *hog's-eye*-popping *diamond cutter* of potentially life-threatening proportions, which could quite easily place intolerable demands on one's circulatory system. *Pink steel* that looks like it's in danger of going off like that bloke's head in 'Scanners'.

veiny bang stick *n.* Penis, the *gut stick,* the *giggle stick.*

velcro arse *n. medic.* Descriptive of the condition of the *bum cheeks* after a long, hot day.

velcro triangle *n. Minge, mott, mapatasi.*

Velma, to give her a *v.* The act of deliberately or accidentally shooting *jitler* into one's *bird's* eyes, reproducing the disorientating effects suffered by Velma from 'Scooby Doo', each time she lost her glasses. *Spunkblind. St. Valentine's Day mascara.*

venetian bind *n.* An awkward situation in which a gentleman finds himself when there isn't a curtain available to wipe his *cock* on.

verminillionaire *n.* A lottery winner who doesn't deserve it, has a criminal record as long as your arm and spends all the money on helicopters and Ferraris.

versnatche *n*. A designer *cunt*.

vertical bacon sandwich *n*. That which is clearly visible in *hamburger shots*. Also *vertical smile, vertical taco*.

vertical eyebrow *n*. A *fanny* that has been trimmed to within a quarter of an inch of its life. A *Pires's chin*.

vesser *n*. A silent *fart*.

vesta vespa *n*. The two-stroke engine-like noise one's *anus* makes the morning after eating a box of the foul, dried curry substitute. Accompanied by a puff of blue smoke.

vicar's calling card *n*. Sticking the *organ* up the *reredos*. A *sting in the tail*. *Bumming*.

vicar's piss *n*. Any particularly weak beer.

Victorian photographer *n*. A gentleman *cunning linguist* who performs under the skirts of a lady.

video cripple *n*. One who can normally walk perfectly well, but loses this ability when returning a video to the shop and has to park right outside, even if it's a double yellow line or is restricting traffic. Similar to a *cashpoint cripple*.

Vin Diesel 1. *n. prop*. Gravel-voiced bald actor who always wears sunglasses. 2. *n*. Happy Shopper wine costing less than £2, and which leaves one gravel-voiced, bald and wearing sunglasses.

vidiot *n*. A translucent, spotty youth who spends most of his time cooped up in his bedroom kidding himself he's in the magical land of Zelda and not Basingstoke.

Viennetta *n*. A rich and satisfying multi-layered toilet pudding, consisting of several alternating layers of *turd* and *bumwad*. *Bangers and mash*.

vinegar Joe *n*. The *stick vid* actor responsible for causing the *porn trauma*.

vinegar string *n*. The *banjo*.

vinegar strokes n. Of males *on the job*, the final climactic stages of intercourse or masturbation. From the similar facial expression associated with sipping vinegar. *'Would you believe it? The phone rang just as I was getting onto the vinegar strokes. I nearly ran into the car in front.'*

vinegar tits *n*. The sort of miserable, sour-faced woman that looks, one might unfairly judge, like her *lils* would deliver neat Sarson's into the mouth of any unfortunate suckling infant, eg. Estelle Morris MP.

viper's tongue *sim*. A figure of speech, or trope, illustrative of the bifurcated stream of *piss* which issues from a *jap's eye* partially occluded by post-coital *sponglement*, fossilised *smegma* or a piece of sweetcorn. *Twin jets*.

virgin oil *n*. The facial grease secreted by *scoobescent* teenagers.

virgin poo *n*. The first *turd* laid at work after the cleaning lady has scrubbed the rim.

visit from aunt Flo *euph*. Having *the painters in*. *Sheep sitting*.

vitamin P *n*. The luminescent lime green *wazz* produced after one has consumed high dose multivitamins.

vitamin S *n*. A naturally-occurring substance which men insist is very good for women when taken orally in 5ml doses. Often added to McDonald's burgers by disgruntled staff.

vixen *n*. Wily *bird*, a young temptress, a foxy *chick*. eg. Stevie Nicks in about 1978.

vogue *1*. *n*. A briefly fashionable pose-striking dance made popular by Madonna. *2*. *v*. To strike an artistic pose prior to *dropping one's guts* in order to amuse friends or charm young ladies into bed.

Volvo, drop a *v*. To do a *poo* that keeps its headlamps on during daylight hours and has very poor aerodynamics, but would score 5 stars in the Euro/NCAP crash tests.

vommunition *n*. Anything eaten to line the stomach before a drinking session.

voodoo butter *n*. The raw material of *squid marks*.

vote for Tony Blair *v*. To rush enthusiastically into the cubicle expecting big things, only to get a pathetic little *fart*. To be constipated.

VPL abbrev. Visible Panty Line.

Vulcan bomb doors *sim*. *RAF*. Huge, gaping *pissflaps*, making the *fanny* resemble the underside of the eponymous delta-winged bomber.

vurp *n*. A burp which brings up a small but foul-tasting quantity of stomach contents which is small enough to be gulped straight back down again. A *broat*.

Ww

wab *n*. Penis.

wad *1. n*. The large sum of money which Harry 'Loadsamoney' Enfield waved around. *2. n*. That featured in a *money shot*. A small package of *hot fish yoghurt* flying out the end of a *mutton musket*. A *jizzbolt*.

wad chomper *n*. A lady who is anxious to please. One who enjoys a portion of *blurt* and sees no reason to spit it out.

wade in *1. v*. To move in for the kill immediately prior to pulling a *bird*. *2. v*. To walk towards the centre of a *pagga*, with one's arms above one's head in order to join the fun.

Wagon Wheel *1. n*. A sickly, cream-filled confection. *2. n*. A large *cock*. From the 1980s advertising slogan for *1*. '*You've got to grin to get it in.*'

wail switch *n*. An excitable lady's *clematis*.

waist height delight *n*. A fun-size lady, ideal for vertical *horatio* or enthusiastic *cowboy*. A *laptop*, a *throwabout*.

wait for the wings, to *v*. To eagerly anticipate the demise of an elderly loved one to fund the purchase of luxury items in their memory. '*I've got this smashing VW Golf VR6 with 17-inch low-pros. But my granny is ill and I'm just waiting for the wings and I'm going to get the 8 by 18-inch Wolfrace Spirit alloys*'.

waiting for the red cheque to clear *euph*. Of a married man, to endure the monthly 4 to 5 day period of sexual limbo which occurs whilst *Aunt Flo is visiting* his wife's *below stairs areas*.

wake up with Jake up *v*. To have a *dawn horn, morning glory*.

walk in the country *n*. The taking of a gentle stroll with the index and middle fingers through, in and around a woman's *ladygarden*.

walking condom *n*. Descriptive of a breed of Scouse male who is up to no good in a baggy tracksuit with a hood.

walking on the Moon *1. n*. The feeling one experiences after depositing a particularly weighty *Thora*, similar to that encountered by astronauts in one-sixth gravity. *2. n*. Autobiographical song written by Sting out of the Police after he'd just done a really big *shit*.

walking stick *1. n*. Long piece of nobbly wood grasped by senior citizens on buses. *2. n*. That old object upon which a fellow gives it *six nowt* whilst *relaxing in a gentleman's way*.

walking tripod *sim*. A well-endowed male, *donkey-rigged* individual. When admiring *buffage* a sexist lady might offensively remark '*Look at the third leg on that. He's a walking fucking tripod.*'

walking wounded *n. milit*. Women who go out on the pull despite the fact that they are *bleeding from a shotgun wound*. '*I wouldn't bother buying her a drink, Geordie. She's walking wounded.*' '*So? She's got a mooth, hasn't she?*'

walkman shit *n*. Pairs of dead AA or AAA batteries found on bus seats and in other public places.

walk the plank *1. rhym. slang*. To masturbate. Whilst a jeering monocular unidexter jabs a cutlass in your *arse*. *2. v*. To avoid *splashback* at a urinal when doing a high-pressure *gypsy's kiss* by standing three or four feet back, and walking slowly towards the *shark's mouth* as the flow recedes.

Wallace *rhym. slang.* To vomit. From Wallace & Gromit. *'He's Wallaced all over my new carpet.'*

wall of death 1. *n. Attack of the helicopters.* 2. *n. Last hot dog in the tin.*

wallop *n. Cookin'.* Any beer bought by a hearty *twat* with a beard who calls the barman Landlord or Squire.

walnut 1. *n.* The leaky washer in an old man's *waterworks.* The prostate gland. 2. *n.* The little bits of *Eartha* that 'walnut' come off. *Tagnuts, dangleberries.*

walnut manoeuvre *n.* The legendary method by which good looking nurses are trained to poke one's prostate in order to obtain an instant *Thelonius* sample.

walnut whip *rhym. slang.* A minor operation which removes the *cream*, but leaves the *nuts* intact. The *snip.*

wand waver *n. Flasher*, sexual exhibitionist.

wang *n. Whanger.*

wangst *n.* Post-masturbatory anguish. A *wank hangover.*

wanic *n.* The state of perturbation that occurs when a wife or girlfriend returns home unexpectedly as one is reaching the *vinegar strokes* in front of one's favourite *scud mags.* A *wank panic.* A *jazz funk.*

wank 1. *n.* A bout of *self help.* *'If you have a wank every day you'll go blind.'* 2. *n.* Rubbish. esp. a pile of~. *'Don't talk wank.'* 3. *v.* To masturbate. *'My brother wanks all the time and he's got perfect eyesight.'*

wankarium *n.* A box room contain-

ing a chair, a computer and a sock drawer.

wankathon *n.* A single man's right arm excercise endurance test. Days of frenzied *self abuse* heralded by the arrival of a large brown envelope with a Dutch postmark. Often ends with a dehydrated and disorientated *self-harmer* being wrapped in a large sheet of tin foil.

wank clamp *n.* A hand.

wank crank *n. medic.* Elbow.

wanker 1. *n.* One who practises a secret vice. 2. *n.* A fellow road user, a motorist at whom one waves.

wankerchief *n.* A *spanky hanky*, a *jizz sock*, a *toss rag.*

wankered *adj.* Very drunk, *arseholed, shit-faced.*

wanker's badge *n.* A moustache. From the fact that most people sporting moustaches tend also to be wankers, eg. Steve Wright, Des Lynam, Anne Robinson. *'Short back and sides, is it sir? Not too much off the top and tapering at the neck? And would you like me to trim the wanker's badge?'*

wanker's block *n.* A complete absence of imagination or inspiration when trying to stimulate feelings in the *trouser department.* Often occurs when one has the *horn* but is too *pissed* to think of anything rude.

wanker's cocoa *n.* A late night *tug* that induces a restful night's sleep.

wanker's colic *n. medic.* Of seasoned factory/warehouse workers, a humorous diagnosis of the cause of hiccups or burps in their younger colleagues.

wanker's crisps *n.* Brittle, ready-salted tissues found under any healthy gentleman's bed.

wanker's genie *n.* The irresistible force that resides inside one's *magic lamp* and summons one to release it on a regular basis.

wanker's hankie *sim.* Descriptive of something very brittle. *'Come along to the Curry Capital, formerly the Rupali Restaurant, Bigg Market, Newcastle on Tyne, where the food is hot, the beer is cold and the popadoms are as brittle as a wanker's hankie.'* (Press release from Abdul Latif, Lord of Harpole).

wanker's rickets *n.* The wobbling movements of the legs caused by orgasmic weakening of the knees.

wanker's tache *n. medic.* The vertical line of hair between the navel and the top of the *pubes.* Develops as a consequence of masturbation, along with spots, hairy palms, shortsightedness, insanity and stunted growth.

wanker's tan *n.* Ghostly pallor effected by young men who spend far too much time alone in their rooms with the curtains shut. *'I've just got Grand Theft Auto San Andreas for Christmas, so I'll be spending the next few months working on my wanker's tan.'*

wankety blank *n.* The state of mental blockage during attempted masturbation when one's *mammary banks* are in the red. *Wanker's block.*

wank handle *n. medic.* In sex, a male erection of the penile shaft and glans.

wank hangover *n.* Post *self abuse* self-loathing. *Wangst.*

wanking chariot *n.* A single bed.

wanking ears *n.* Descriptive of the bat-like, heightened sensitivity of hearing achieved by a fellow indulging in a bit of *self discipline,* allowing him to detect the faint sound of his wife's, girlfriend's, parents' key entering the lock two floors below. *'September 2nd, 1666, Morning. Up betimes, and finding the house deserted, was minded to settle down with a hose for a brief strum over the corsetry pages of Mr. Grattan's estimable catalogue. However, Mrs. Pepys return'd unexpectly, and, had it not been for my wanking ears, would surely have discovered me in a most compromising situation. Afternoon. London burned down.'* (from *'The Diary of Samuel Pepys'*).

wanking jacket *n.* Dressing gown.

wanking Jap, grin like a *sim.* To smile broadly in the style of a *spamurai warrior.* To *turn Japanese.*

wanking parlour *n.* Brothel, house of ill repute, any club popular with *gonks.* A *toss parlour.*

wanking spanners *n. Cunt scratchers.*

wanking studs *n. medic.* Warts on the hands or fingers.

wankish *adj.* Slightly useless. *Mouse, Swiss. 'That Eamonn Holmes is a bit wankish, isn't he.'*

wank it dry *v.* To ossessively persevere with something long after there is any benefit to be gained, eg. ITV's scheduling of *'You've Been Framed'* every day, Mohammed Al Fayed going on about his conspiracy theory, *'Viz Comic'* coming out every 5 weeks. *'Christ, not Norman Collier doing his broken microphone routine again. He wanked that dry thirty years ago on the Wheeltappers' and Shunters' Social Club.'*

wankle 1. *n.* A type of rotary engine. 2. *n. medic.* The wrist.

wank-me-downs *n*. Heirloom *bongo mags* inherited from an elder brother or friend. Also *one-hand-me-downs*.

wank or bank *n*. The quandary faced by a gentleman who must decide whether to *knock himself about a bit* or conserve his fluids until his ladyfriend's next visit when he can *make a deposit*.

wank pie *n*. Something third rate, eg. any programme with Jimmy Carr in it.

wankquiliser *n*. A self-administered, stress-relieving bedtime *knockout yop*. A *knuckle nightcap, pullaby*.

wank robber *n*. Onanistically speaking, a parent who, returning home unexpectedly early, robs their teenage son of his *money shot*.

wankrupt *adj*. Descriptive of one who has *spent his wad*.

wank séance *n*. Whilst *pulling one's pud*, the eerie feeling that one is being watched disapprovingly by dead relatives. Also *Doris Strokes*.

wanksmith *n*. An enthusiastic or workmanlike *onanist*.

wank sock *n*. Sock tied to a bedpost designed to indicate when wind conditions are suitable for *monkey spanking*.

wank stain *n*. *Bum scrape, piss flap, dip shit, toss pot*. General purpose insult.

wankstop *n*. medic. The flange that prevents the *wanking spanner* disengaging from the end of the *shaft* when revving your *single cylinder engine*. The *brim* of the *herman gelmet*. The sulcus.

wank tanks *n*. *Balls, nads, knackers*.

wankticipation *n*. Feeling of hollow, mounting excitement experienced by a man sitting in front of his computer with his trousers round his ankles and his *giggle stick* in his hand, whilst he waits for his *cyber scud* to download.

wankton *n*. A unicellular life-form that inhabits the shallow waters of the bath after a session of *dolphin waxing*. *Dutch jellyfish*.

wank window *n*. An opportune moment during which a crafty gentleman can enjoy a swift bout of *relaxation*. '*A woman tells her husband she is just popping to the shops to get a pint of milk and a loaf of bread. The shops are 4 miles away and her husand knows that his wife's car travels at an average speed of 22 mph. He also knows that his wife will spend ten minutes selecting each of the items from the shelves of the supermarket and a further twelfth of her total journey time queuing at the till. For how long is the man's wank window open?*' (Associated Examining Board GCE Applied Mathematics paper, Summer 1986).

wank xerox *1.n*. One who *knocks one out* repeatedly throughout the day, only to find the quality diminishes as his *toner* runs out. *2. n*. Masturbating over and over again to the same *jazz mag. Groundhog wanking*.

wanky *adj*. Self-indulgent, pretentious, eg. '*Newsnight Late Review*'.

wannocks *n*. The area of no-man's land between the *nuts* or the *fadge*, and the *ringpiece*. The *biffin bridge, notcher, barse, taint, tintis*.

wanquility *n*. The all too brief post-toss period of serenity experienced immediately before the loathing, self-hatred and shame sets in.

wanxious *adj.* Anxious for a *wank.*

wap-waps *n. medic.* A lady's mammary glands.

warm Norman *n.* A *hotplate, Cleveland steamer.*

warm up the choirboys' breakfast *n.* Of a vicar, to *relax in a gentleman's way.*

war paint *n.* Of *birds* getting ready to go out at night, their make-up.

warren *n.* Generic term for one not blessed with attractive features. From *'Warren ugly bastard.'*

warthog whammies *n.* Fantastic *tits* on an ugly woman. *Hefferlumps.*

wartime searchlights *n.* Descriptive of the amusingly dis-collimated vision of one who is in an advanced *state of refreshment,* whose eyes appear to be independently raking the heavens for incoming Heinkel bombers.

washing machine doors *n.* Export strength *beer goggles.*

Washington refill *n.* The type of night-time urination carried out in a rush in order to return to the warmth of one's bed as soon as possible. From the speedy nature of petrol station customers in Washington DC and surrounding districts during their recent sniper shenanigans.

wash the cosh *v.* To polish the *love truncheon.*

waste *n.* An attractive feature on an otherwise unattractive individual. *'Jesus. Have you seen the chebs on that Kerry Catona, your grace?' 'I know, Archbishop. What a fucking waste.'*

water babies 1. *n.* Aquatic fairies featured in the Victorian novel by Charles Kingsley. 2. *n.* Floating clumps of semi-congealed *merry monk* in the bath, toilet, *'Sunday Times'* restaurant critic's drinking glass etc.

watering can wazz *n.* The uncontrollable multi-directional *gypsy's kiss* taken after a bout of *horizontal jogging* or a *five knuckle shuffle.*

water puppies *n.* Term used by swimming pool lifeguards to draw each other's attention to a large pair of *milky swingers* bobbing playfully up and down whilst their owner does the backstroke.

water sports *n. Recreational Chinese singing.* To express romantic feelings for another by *pissing* onto their face, etc.

waving a sausage in the Albert Hall *n.* Sticking one's *cock* in a *fanny* that can seat 5000 people and the London Symphony Orchestra.

wax one's slats *v.* Of a woman, to *play the invisible banjo* until her *blip tap* begins to drip.

wax the bonnet *v.* To *spoff* over a *bird's* bodywork, then lean over and polish it in until the desired shine is achieved.

wax the dolphin *v.* To *polish the lighthouse.*

wazoo *n. Jacksie, anus.*

wazz *v.* Variously to *piss,* to *puke,* to *wank.*

wazzed *adj. Pissed* on, *puked* on and *wanked* off.

wazzock *n.* One who is *pissing, puking* and *wanking* all at the same time.

wear a Twyfords collar *v.* To *drive the porcelain bus,* to *shout soup,* to *yoff.*

Wearside vines *n.* Exposed outcrop of *annabels* which looks for all the world like an attractive bunch of

Gamay grapes, glistening on a sun-kissed slope.

wear the beard 1. *v.* To perform *cunning linguistics* on a woman. *To impersonate Stalin.* 2. *v.* Of *bean flickologists*, to be the *stone*. '*You can tell which one of them two wears the beard.*'

webbed tits *n.* Breasts of elderly Hollywood actresses with a highly stressed membrane between, caused by the sheer weight of implants.

wedding milk *n.* *Spingle, spangle, spint, spongle, spadge, spedge, spidge, spodge, spudge,* etc. *Spunk.*

wedding tackle *n.* The male genitalia. Also *wedding furniture.*

wedge *v.* To pull another's *bills* up the crack of their *arse.*

wedgie *n.* Wedged *bills.*

wee heid rules the big heid *phr.* *Scot.* Descriptive of the moment when a gentleman, usually wearing *beer goggles,* decides that sexual intercourse with the woman he has just met is the correct course of action.

wee hole surgery *n.* Do-it-yourself medical experiments carried out by bored bachelors, involving the insertion of foreign objects into the urethra.

weenie *n.* US. Penis. Also *wienie, wiener.*

weenie waggler *n.* A *wand waver.*

weenis *n.* A minuscule *veiny bang stick,* such as those sported by jockeys, Arctic explorers and current Foreign Secretaries.

weft *n.* Of a lady's *pubes,* to all lie in one direction after she has been wearing particularly tight briefs. *Twat nap.*

weggy *adj.* Of a flatulent emission, to be wet and eggy. From wet + eggy.

weigh anchor *v.* To drop an immensely large *turd,* being careful not to break the porcelain.

welder's bench *sim.* An ugly woman, *a face like a~.* Also *blind cobbler's thumb, burglar's dog, box of frogs, sack of chisels, bag of spanners.*

well fair state *n.* The state of drunkenness only achievable for many on Giro day.

welly top *sim.* A term used to describe the larger *Mary.* A *yawning donkey.* '*She had a fanny like a welly top.*'

welly tubbies *n.* Small, fat lasses squeezed into *slag wellies* out *on the lash.* So-called due to their similarity to the children's TV characters, in both their appearance and limited vocabulary.

Welsh *n.* Masturbation while listening to a male voice choir.

Welsh letter *n.* Same as a *French letter,* but with a leak.

Welshman's cock *sim.* Descriptive of someone who is short and thick, eg. Dennis Wise.

Welsh mist *n.* A particularly dense and clammy *fart* which hovers around ankle level and chills the bones.

Welsh shot *n.* The knocking back of the contents of a *smeg cup.* A *Dutch oyster.*

Wendy *n.* An uncomfortable front tuck for a lady. A vaginal *wedgie,* a *vaggie.*

werecow *n.* A nice, pleasant woman who mysteriously transforms into a right *fucking cow* once a month.

western grip *n.* Manner of *wanking* in which the *cock* is held as a rodeo rider holds onto his steer, ie. with the fingers of one hand on top, the thumb underneath and the other hand waving a hat behind his head.

wet as an otter's pocket *sim.* Descriptive of the moistness of an object, eg. a face flannel, a raincoat, a *frothing gash*.

wet cress, eat *v.* During an act of man-on-lady, or indeed lady-on-lady, oral-type sex, to munch on a bit of exceptionally moist *gorilla salad*.

wet Hurst *n.* A *Wolstenholme*. The final bit of *piss* which waits until the *cock* is safely back in the trousers before dribbling out causing a *wet penny in the pocket*. From the commentary describing Geoff Hurst's final goal in the 1966 World Cup final. *'They think it's all over... it is now'.*

wetmare *n.* A dream that is both wet and a nightmare, eg. where the person who strips off is one's mum.

wet one 1. *n.* A pre-moistened cleaning tissue. 2. n. An untrustworthy *fart*, possibly a *twin tone* that would require the use of *1*. A pre-moistened *Bakewell tart*.

wet penny in your pocket *n.* A circular *piss*-stain on the trouser frontage, caused by insufficient shaking of the *wang*.

wet season *n.* That time of the month when the *crimson tide* comes in.

wet the baby's head *v.* To have intercourse with a woman who has a *bun in the oven*. *'And so it was that Mary and Joseph came to an inn in Bethlehem. And Mary was heavy with child and the innkeeper spake unto them saying, Behold, there is no room at the inn. And Joseph replied unto him saying, Yea, we have travelled from Nazareth, and my wife is heavy with child, and I have great need to wet the baby's head. And he gave unto the innkeeper a wink. And lo the wink was cheeky.'* (from *'St. Matthew'*, Ch.2, vv 14-16).

whacknicolour *n.* The luridly alluring garishly-hued inks with which *seed catalogues* are printed.

whacksmith *n.* A workmanlike masturbator who seems intent on beating his *pork sword* into a *ploughshare*. *'Birthdays: Tom Wolfe, journalist and author, 70, Jonathan Ross, TV & radio presenter, film reviewer, interviewer, whacksmith, 44.'* (from 'The Times', March 2nd 2003).

whalesong *n.* A melodic, though slightly eerie sequence of whines, squeaks, clicks and whistles that emanate from a toilet cubicle.

whaletail 1. *n.* A laughable aerodynamic feature favoured by the smaller-penissed car driver. 2. *n.* The unsightly effect produced when a lady in ill-fitting jeans's thong rides up her arse.

whammers *n. Bazoomas, Gert Stonkers,* big tits.

whanger *n.* An extremely large *wang*.

wheek *v. Scot.* To remove *jobbies* from an aeroplane toilet.

wheelie bint *n.* A woman so ugly that she only gets taken out once a week. In the dark. By dustmen.

whidgey *n. Front bottom.*

whiff of lavender *n.* Of a marriage, the suspicion of a *beardsome* bride. *'I don't know about Edward. There's a whiff of lavender about that marriage.'*

whip round , to have a *v.* To *relax in a gentleman's way*.

whirling pits n. Attack of the *helicopters*.

whisker biscuit n. A *fur burger*.

whisker pot n. *Fanny, minge, whidgey*.

whistle down the Y-fronts v. *Fart*, pass wind.

whistling gorilla n. An inviting and voluptuous *toothless gibbon*.

whistling in the dark n. *Muff diving*, eating *hairy pie*.

white arrow angels n. Van-driving messengers who bring catalogue goods to those ill-equipped to afford them.

white knuckle ride n. A solo thrill which makes your eyes bulge and lasts about three minutes. *One off the wrist*.

white mouse n. Tampon. A *cotton mouse, fanny mouse, chuftie plug*.

white-out! *exclam*. When two large, pale breasts are exposed.

white pointers n. Extremely impressive *tits* found inhabiting a wet T-shirt.

whitewash the hall v. To *spoff* up a lady's *cunt*. A far more fulfilling job than *painting the ceiling*.

whitewater wristing v. Rapid paddling of the *skinboat*. To *pull your pud*, masturbate.

white wee-wee n. Planet Skaro Dalek term for semen.

Whitney dressed as Britney n. Descriptive of a lady who's done a few miles, and is attempting to turn the clock back. *Mutton dressed as lamb*.

whoof v. To *fart*.

whoof whoof! *1. exclam*. Term of approval directed at passing *talent*. *'Whoof whoof! Give that dog a bone.'* *2. exclam*. Term of disapproval aimed at passing women who haven't made the effort to look attractive.

whoops a gaysy n. Of a gentleman, slipping over in an effeminate manner whilst emitting an unexpectedly girly whimper.

whoopsy n. A *piss*, usually in Frank Spencer's beret.

whore d'oeuvres n. The unnecessary appetizers before the main course at a massage parlour, ie. the massage.

whore from Fife n. *derrog*. A term of abuse that incorporates the two insults of being a whore and of coming from Fife. *'Hey, you've just taken my last fag, you whore from Fife.'*

whore frost n. A *good time girl's* sudden change of attitude once the *dirty deed* is done.

whoregasm n. The unconvincing appreciative noises made by a *lady of the night* to persuade her customer that he is getting his money's worth, despite sensory evidence to the contrary.

whore's bath n. An act of personal hygiene practised by ladies of the lower orders; a brief, yet fulsome handwash of the *undercarriage* often performed at a sink. *Rinsing the lettuce*.

whore's brass n. The shiny Lizzy Duke *tack* found decorating women in southern pubs. *Bingo clink*.

whoreshoes n. Fashionable pink stilettos. *Fuck me shoes*.

whorism n. The horizon-broadening practice of travelling the world to experience different and exotic cultures via the medium of going with *pros*.

why, are you hungry? *exclam*. Humorous riposte to someone who asks if one has *farted*.

whybrows *n.* The bizarre tonsorial result of a lady armed with a pair of tweezers and an eyebrow pencil, eg. Theresa Gorman.

wick *1. n.* Penis. See *dip your wick.* *2. n.* Nerves, *tit ends. 'I wish that Mark Kermode would fuck off. He really gets on my fucking wick.'*

wicked pisser *n. US.* Good egg or a good show, top notch person or experience. As in *'Thank you very much for your kindness and generosity. You really have been the most wicked pissers.'*

wicker basket *n.* A matted and tangled *bush* in which the previous night's *clacker lacquer* has been allowed to dry out.

widdle *1. n.* Childish term for a *wee wee. 2. v.* To do some *wee wee.*

wide on *n.* Female equivalent of a *hard on.*

widow wanky *n.* The first despondent, but necessary *act of self violation* indulged in after the wife or girlfriend has left for good.

widow's memories *n.* Penis-shaped sausages, cucumbers etc. Indeed, anything vaguely cylindrical in a supermarket which is fingered nostalgically by old ladies.

widower's tears *n.* The involuntary dribble of *spunk* from the end of a long-disused *cock.*

widower's tickle *n.* The short burst of pleasure a man experiences when he flushes whilst in a sitting position and his *three piece suite* is caught in the spray. A thrill of almost Netto cheapness.

wife beater *n.* An unnecessarily strong lager. *Wreck the hoose juice.*

wifectomy *n.* An extremely painful divorce. One invariably experiences an *OPE* during the operation.

wifetamer *n.* An impressive *weapon* that affords one the respect of one's spouse, like a whip and chair would on a lion in a circus. A *cuntbuster.*

wife's radar *n.* A lady's bat-like ability to detect the merest rustle of a *jazz mag* from a hundred yards.

Wigan rosette *n.* The state of the *freckle* after a particularly fierce *Ruby Murray.* A *Johnny Cash.*

Wilkinson, to do a *v.* To perform a defecation in a hovering, squatting position over a *pissy*-seated pub *bog.* From the pose's similarity to the hand clasped, sticky-out-*arsed* stance struck by rugby star Jonny before he makes a kick and goes off injured.

willets *n.* A type of *jugs.*

willie *n.* A ten-foot penis that has to be cut with a rake. *John Thomas, Percy the pork swordsman,* he who gives *Gert Stonkers* a *pearl necklace.* The *tassel,* the *Peter,* the *charlie.*

willie and the hand jive *n.* Rhythmic, throbbing cork-popping combo who perform the *Bologna bop* among other dances.

willie welly *n. French letter, French safe, English overcoat.*

willie woofter *rhym. slang. Fruit feeler.*

willipedes *n.* genital arthropods. *Mechanical dandruff.*

willnots *n. Tagnuts, dangleberries.* Toffee entwined in the *kak canyon* undergrowth which simply 'will not' come off.

Wimbornes *rhym. slang.* Haemorrhoids. From the Dorset village of Wimborne St. Garsegrapes.

wimp wiper *n.* In an office or workplace environment, one who takes his/her own toilet tissue in rather than use the rough industrial type.

wind farm *n. milit.* A barracks full of vigorously *farting* squaddies.

wind jammer *n.* A *botternist*.

window cleaner's pocket *n.* A large, sad, damp, dishevelled *fadge*.

window shopping *v.* Of a lady, to go out on the town and give gentlemen the impression that she is interested when she has no intention of opening her *purse*.

windy pops *n. Bunny-shooting bullets, chuffs, anal announcements*.

wingspan *n.* A measure of manual spreadability of *meat mag* models posing for *spam butterfly* shots. *'Have you seen Irene from Walsall in Readers' Wives? What a fugly cow.' 'Yeah, but look at the wingspan she's achieved.'*

wink the Jap's eye *v.* An emergency cutting-short of an act of micturition. To curtail a *slash*.

winking at Calvin *n.* When preparing to *hack off a lump*, the uncomfortable feeling of the *anus* twitching whilst still undoing the belt. The *point of no return*.

winking walnut *n. Brown eye, chocolate starfish*.

winkle picking *v. medic.* Anal sex with one afflicted with piles.

winky *1. n.* A tiny *cock*. *2. adj.* Having a tendency to wink a lot.

winkybag *1. n.* A tiny scrotum. *2. n.* An ugly old woman with a tendency to wink a lot.

winner *n.* Unit in which *spunk* is traditionally measured in the catering industry. *'Boil 1 small tablespoon of sago in very little water till clear. Dissolve a teaspoonful of meat or vegetable extract in a cup of boiling water. Strain the cooked sago into the made broth. Season to taste, and lastly, if a red-faced cunt is coming to dine, stir in a winner of gentleman's spendings.'* (from *'Household Management'* by Mrs. Beeton).

Winner corner *n.* Secluded quarter of a restaurant kitchen, where staff members may retire in order to discreetly prepare *perseverance soup* for their less popular customers.

winnered *adj. Wanked dry.* Term used to describe the *clockweights* of kitchen staff following a sudden rush on *chef's special sauce*.

winner's sauce *n.* That, which in the food industry, is added to the recipe wherever food critic Michael Winner eats. Spunk.

winnet *n. Kling on, dag, dangleberry, willnot, brown room hanger on.* Also *winnit*.

winnet picker *n.* Someone of arguably lower social standing than a *jizz mopper*.

winnie *n.* A lesbian, she who licks the *honey pot*.

Winslet twins *n.* A nice proper pair of cosy breasts as sported by *'Titanic'* actress Kate.

wintercourse *n.* Frosty sex, the kind had with a lady who doesn't approve of that kind of carry on. One would imagine Margo and Jerry out of *'The Good Life'* and the Queen and Prince Philip engage in *wintercourse*.

win the chocolate lottery *v.* To receive a particularly large *milkman's bonus*.

wipe your feet *v.* To vigorously *beskid* a lavatory *pan*. *"I is the only nice and jumbly giant in Giant Country! I is the Big Friendly Giant!' 'I don't care who you are,' replied Sophie. 'I'm not using that crapper. It looks like you've wiped your feet in there,* *you mucky old cunt."* (from *'The BFFG'* by Roald Dahl).

wire spider *n.* The hairs around the *chocolate starfish* that come to life when you are in a meeting or in the checkout queue at Asda.

Wirral peninsula 1. *n.* The area of land which falls between Chester and Liverpool. 2. *n.* Them bits of skin that separate *cunts* and *arse-holes.* The *taint, notcher, carse, snarse, biffin bridge, Humber Bridge, tinter* etc.

witch doctor's rattle *n.* Descriptive of a woman with a nice personality. A *monk's pin-up.*

witch's cave *n.* A *wizard's sleeve, clown's pocket, wall of death.* An enormous *fadge.'Soldier, soldier, would you marry me / For you are so strong and brave / Oh no, sweet maid, I cannot marry you / With your twat like a witch's cave"* (Traditional folk song).

witch's lips *n.* The cold kiss of a porcelain toilet bowl on one's *bell end* occasionally felt whilst *dropping off the shopping.*

witch's trick *n.* The phenomenon of a *back beauty, backstabber* or *golden deceiver* who appears stunning from behind, only to reveal herself as looking like Grotbags off *'Emu's World'* from the front.

with one's cock out, do something *v.* To perform a task or action badly. *'My right honorable friend would have us believe that he can increase government spending in the health service whilst at the same time delivering tax cuts across the board. Well I'm afraid he must have written this budget with his cock out, because I can tell him that the figures simply do not add up.'* (Rt. Hon. Michael

Howard MP, *'Hansard'*).

witten *n.* See *winnet.*

wizard's sleeve *n.* A *clown's pocket.* A particularly capacious *sausage wallet. 'I can't feel a bloody thing, Mother Teresa. You must have a fanny like a wizard's sleeve.'*

wizards' hats *n. Dunces' hats.*

WOAT *acronym.* A light-hearted term for a woman at a football, rugby or cricket match. Waste Of A Ticket.

wobbly boots *adj.* Uncontrollable alcoholic footwear. *Seven pint boots.*

wobbly landing *n.* Trying, when drunk, to manoeuvre your under-inflated *zipper Zeppelin* safely through your wife's *hangar doores.*

wolfbagging *v.* To have sex with a wolf inside a large bag.

wolf bait *n.* An unusually meaty, pungent *fart,* similar to the smell of opening a tin of Butcher's Tripe Mix.

wolf bite *n.* A really painful *arse-hole,* eg. after a curry. *'Would you care to ride with us to Wenlock Edge, Captain Tremaine?' she asked. The Captain winced. 'I regret I must decline your kind offer, Mrs. Dugdale,' he replied. 'I lately partook of a monstrous vin-daloo with the Lord of Harpole, and I still have a wolf bite upon my postillion.'* (from *'Middle-march'*, by George Eliot)

woman in comfortable shoes *n.* A *tennis fan,* a *lady golfer.*

women's things *n. medic. Flangina.*

wombies *n. Tits,* breasts, *baps.*

womfer *n.* The female equivalent of a *barse. Chinrest* used to avoid cramp at a *hairy pie* tasting.

womit *n.* Dribbly sick.

wonderwank *n.* An act of *self abuse*

carried out without the use of visual stimulation. Named after the pop singer Stevie Wonder.

Wonder woman *n*. A lady with a *lovely personality*. A *boot* that only a blind man could fancy.

wongle *v*. To rive one's *passion cosh* up and down one's wife's *arse* in an attempt to wake her up for a *poke*.

wonk *n*. A desperate and ultimately unsatisfying act of *self help* with multiple interruptions. *'Bless me Father for I have sinned.' 'Do you mind coming back in about ten minutes, my son? I'm half way through a wonk in here.'*

wood *n*. Erectivity of the penicular appendation.

woodpecker *n*. A woman who performs rapid, hands-free *horatio*. From the movement of the *bird's* head as she hammers your *trunk*.

woody *n*. An erectivation.

wookie hole *1. n.* Uninspiring tourist attraction consisting of a hole in the ground and a gift shop. *2. n.* A particularly hairy *Mary Hinge*. A *biffer*, a *Judith*.

wool *n. coll. US*. Fluff, blart, fanny, totty.

woolly wardrobe *n*. A bulky, cavernous receptacle in the bedroom where gentlemen stuff their *roll neck sweaters*.

work a split shift *v*. Of a lovable, lucky, cheeky chappie, to have two *ladyfriends* on the go at the same time.

working from home *euph*. Spending the day *relaxing in a gentleman's way*.

world of leather *n*. The *parts* of an aged lady. *Granny's oysters*.

worm's belt, tighter than a *sim*. Descriptive of a particularly unaccommodating *snatch*, a *butler's cuff, mouse's ear, mole's eye*. *'DUCHESS OF BERWICK: My dear Lord Plymdale. I really do not understand why you associate with Mrs. Erlynne. She is such a tiresome conversationalist. LORD PLYMDALE: Conversation is, I find, a somewhat over-rated virtue, your ladyship. Besides which, Mrs. Erlynne kindly vouchsafed me tops and fingers in Lord Darlington's gazebo last night and believe you me, her twat's tighter than a worm's belt.'* (from *'Lady Windermere's Fanny'* by Oscar Wilde).

worth a squirt *adj*. Sexually desirable.

wring the rattlesnake *v. Siphon the python*. To *piss, strain the greens*.

wrinkled penny *n. US*. The *ringpiece, balloon knot, tea towel holder, nipsy*.

wrist flick *n*. A *grumble vid*, a *stick film*.

wristicuffs *n*. A bout of *knocking oneself about a bit. Boxing the Jesuit*.

write the letter 'M' *v*. To inscribe the thirteenth letter of the alphabet in *arse* sweat on the toilet seat whilst having a *Queensway*.

wu-wu *1. n.* Childish name for a *fufu*. *2. n.* The noise a train makes.

wuffle nuts *n*. The fruits of the *dangleberry* tree.

Wurzel *1. n. prop*. A member of the English rock supergroup of the 1970s. *2. n.* An embarrassingly small penis. An *acorn*, a *Jack Straw*.

Xx

X-piles *n*. Mysterious, unidentified throbbing objects from your *anus*.

X-ray specs *n*. Spectacles available only by mail order from the back of pubescent boys' comics which enable the wearer to see through a woman's clothing. 50¢. Also used to detect fractures in hospital Accident & Emergency departments.

XX *adj*. Special video certificate awarded to pornographic films of poor sound and picture quality.

XXX *adj*. Special video certificate awarded to pornographic films of exceptionally poor sound and picture quality.

xylophone *1. n*. Like a piano, but you twat it with little sticks. *2. v.* To move along a line of naked women who are all bending down, and spank their bottoms - which are of varying sizes - with one's penis. To play a tune on women's buttocks. From the Greek xylo = wood & phonnicus = to be hit tunefully by a fat astronomer at a Royal Variety Performance.

Yy

yabba dabbas *n*. In stone age cartoon intercourse, the climactic stages of coitus which immediately precede the *doooooooos! The vinegar strokes*.

yachting *n*. The stirring sight of a dog in full sail, tacking its way across the living room carpet attempting to remove the *barnacles* from its *keel*.

yaffle the yoghurt cannon *v*. To suck on a *cock*, voraciously.

yak *1. n*. Big hairy animal of untidy appearance. *2. n*. A big hairy *fanny* of untidy appearance. A feminist's *beaver*, a *minge* with a *pant moustache*.

yambag *n*. The wrinkled retainer in which the *gourds* are kept.

yang *n. US*. A *wang*.

yank *1. n*. An inhabitant of the northern states of America. *2. n*. A 'one-man-band'-type device with which an American sex case attaches his penis to his ankle in order to *pull himself off* whilst walking about. $4.99.

yank off *v*. To *relax* vigorously *in a gentleman's way*.

yank the plank v. To *tug* one's *wood*.

yarbles *n*. Testicles.

yard *1. n. arch*. Olde Worlde Penis. *2. n*. The *ladygarden*.

yardbrush *n*. A bristly *fanny* one could sweep out the garage with.

yard high club *n*. The exclusive group of sexual adventurers who have made love in the lavatory of a static caravan.

yard on *n*. An extra large *hard on* achieved when particularly aroused, although probably still smaller than 3 feet.

Yarmouth clam *n*. Similar to a *Viennese oyster,* only performed by a malodorous woman from the Norfolk seaside town.

Yasser *abbrev. US*. Erection. From 'Yasser Crack-a-fat'. A lame pun on the name of the late tea-towel-tit-fered Palestinian Ringo Starr lookalike.

yawnography *n*. Dull, uninspiring *grumble* of the sort shown on Channel 5, where they don't let you see it *going in*.

Y-bone steak *n*. Female opposite of a *tube steak*. The *beef curtains*.

Y-box *n*. Much more fun than an X-box, and only costs the price of a bunch of flowers from the 24-hour garage.

yeti's welly *n*. A voluminous *fadge*, a *donkey's yawn*.

yinyang *1. n. US*. Arse, bum. *2. n. Fuckwit*, dupe.

yitney *n*. One who is *yitten*.

yitten *adj*. To be scared of something very tame.

yobble *v*. To *shit* somewhere other than a toilet, usually for the amusement of others. eg. onto a cow from a tree.

yodel in the canyon/valley *v*. To *growl* at a very *capacious badger* whilst wearing a small hat with a shaving brush stuck in it.

yodel *v*. To vomit, to *sing a rainbow*.

yoinkahs *n*. A pair of *twin peaks* that cause a volcanic eruption in your *underkrakatoas*.

Yoko *1*. A bird who accompanies her boyfriend everywhere, eg. down the pub with mates, work, the fucking lot.

yongles *n. US. Clockweights*, testicles.

yoni *n*. Ancient Hindu Female genitals, *fanny*.

yonks! *exclam*. Popular speech balloon reaction to finding a tenner on a cartoon pavement.

york *onomat.* To vomit, *call Huey*.

Yorkie bar *n.* A *puddle jumper, botter* or *gaylord*. From the popular chocolate confection advertising slogan. 'It's not for girls'.

Yorkshire flamingo *n.* A tired-looking, malnourished, pink-faced *bird* who, due to the sorry state of her shabby surroundings (eg. the Frontier Club, Batley), appears exotic and alluring to the untrained eye.

you milk? *interrog.* A phrase used by far-eastern prostitutes to ascertain whether or not their client has *dropped his yop*.

yo-yo knickers *n.* *Bike,* loose woman, woman whose knickers go up and down faster than Richard Branson's hot air balloons.

yummy mummy 1. *n.* A middle-aged woman worthy of a good *seeing to*, eg. Helen Mirren. 2. *n.* A young mother with a fantastic *arse* pushing a buggy. 3. *n.* On a cannibal menu, a delicious, well-cooked mother.

Zz

Zebedee *n*. A tea-time erection that pops up unexpectedly, signalling that it is time for bed.

Zeps *abbrev. Zeppelins.* Large, hydrogen-filled, flammable breasts, *Hindenburgs. Blimplants.*

zerotica *n. Wanking* material of the lowest imaginable potency, eg. a thermal underwear catalogue or a picture of a nuns' hockey team.

zig-a-zig ahhhh! *onomat. arch.* To have a bloody good *wank* watching a Spice Girls video.

Zinzanbrook *rhym. slang. NZ.* To *fuck.*

zipperfish *n*. Penis, or *trouser trout.*

zipper sniffer *n*. Keen penis enthusiast of either gender.

zipper Zeppelin *n*.Shiny, cigar-shaped craft which occasionally explodes at its moorings.

zip snip *n*. An unintentional circumcision and/or vasectomy operation performed using the flies of one's trousers. Usually carried out under about ten pints of general anaesthetic.

zit *n*. A *pluke.*

Zoes *n. Balls,* testicles. From the former Radio 1 presenter Zoe Bollocks.

zonked *adj. Pissed, wankered, wazzed. Trousered.*

zoob *n*. Penis.

zook *n*. A prostitute, a *ho'.*

Zorba *1. rhym. slang.* To have a *piss.* From Zorba the Greek= leak. *2. v.* To have sex in the *Greek* style. *'Sorry I can't sit down. I've been zorba-ed.'*

Zorro mask *n*. A Saturday morning disguise worn by the wife of a big drinker. *Nature's make-up.*

zounds *n. arch.* God's wounds. 17th century swear word banned by Act of Parliament in 1651, but okay now if used in moderation. Also *g*dzooks.*

zucchini *n. US. Cock.*

zuffle v. To wipe one's *charlie* clean on the curtains after having a *bang,* usually in a posh *bird's* house.

zuffle coat *n*. The topmost coat of the pile on the bed at a party. Used by a male party guest to clean the *sloom* off his *three card trick* after a furtive *poke.*

ZZ bottom *n*. An exceptionally long haired *muff,* from the resemblance to the unsightly, unkempt beards sported by the rock band ZZ Top. But not the drummer.

ZZ tops and fingers *n*. The act of fondling one's missus while she's asleep.

zylophone *n*. Incorrect spelling of *xylophone.*

Acknowledgments

Roger Mellie OBE would like to thank the following people, without whom this book would not have been possible: Caroline Addy, Stuart Brown, Alex Collier, Chris Donald, Simon Donald, Wayne Gamble, Stevie Glover, Greg Hughes, the ghost of Samuel Johnson, Abdul Latif (Lord of Harpole) and all the foul-mouthed readers and visitors to *www.viz.co.uk* who sent in contributions. And an especially big thanks to Will Watt for spotting what he believed to be a typing error, but which turned out not to be, on page 195.